THE HEART OF BOSWELL:
Six Journals in One Volume

THE HEART OF

BOSWELL

SIX JOURNALS
IN ONE VOLUME

James Boswell

Edited by

MARK HARRIS

MC GRAW-HILL BOOK COMPANY

New York   St. Louis   San Francisco
Hamburg   Mexico   Toronto

1 2 3 4 5 6 7 8 9 D O D O 8 7 6 5 4 3 2 1

LIBRARY OF CONGRESS CATALOGING IN PUBLICATION DATA

Boswell, James, 1740–1795.
The Heart of Boswell
"A distillation of the first six volumes of The Yale editions of the private papers of James Boswell"—Pref.
Includes index.
Contents: London journal—London to Holland—Boswell on the grand tour, Germany and Switzerland—[etc.]
1. Boswell, James, 1740–1795—Diaries. 2. Authors, Scottish—18th century—Biography. I. Harris, Mark, 1922–   II. Yale editions of the private papers of James Boswell.   III. Title.
PR3325.A822   1981   828'.603 [B]   81–1568
ISBN 0–07–026775–8   AACR 2

Book design by Christine Aulicino.

Contents

Preface
vii

PART I
LONDON JOURNAL
15 November 1762–30 May 1763
1

PART II
LONDON TO HOLLAND
17 May 1763–18 June 1764
67

PART III
BOSWELL ON THE GRAND TOUR
18 June 1764–16 December 1764
117

PART IV
CORSICA BOSWELL
24 December 1764–13 February 1766
161

PART V
BOSWELL IN SEARCH OF A WIFE
28 April 1766–25 November 1769
217

PART VI
BOSWELL FOR THE DEFENCE
14 March 1772–21 September 1774
309

Index
393

THIS VOLUME IS A DISTILLATION of the first six volumes of The Yale Editions of the Private Papers of James Boswell, which are in turn derived from discoveries and purchases of Boswell's papers at intervals between the year of his death, 1795, and the middle years of the present century.

Successive discoveries of new Boswell writings, often under dramatic circumstances, and sometimes in the shadow of dispute, suggest the persistence of Boswell himself, whose pursuit of his objectives is often the spine of the action of his journal.

Boswell's journal not only survives but flourishes, providing him with existence unfolding far beyond his grave. Trepidation about his death, and questions of afterlife, occupy many pages of his writing, many hours of his reflection, and a position central in his conversation and his dreams. "Yesterday you awaked in great disorder, thinking that you was dying, and exclaiming, 'There's no more of it! 'Tis all over.' " So he addressed himself on Sunday, March 25, 1764, when he was a student of the law in Holland. Less than three weeks later a dream of death merged itself with another of Boswell's preoccupations—execution. "Yesterday you awaked shocked, having dreamt you was condemned to be hanged."

If Boswell preserved his life so completely by committing it to paper, he may have been oddly ambivalent about the fate of the paper itself. He could neither destroy it, nor, on the other hand, take extraordinary steps to preserve it. He entrusted it to his executors, who reliably protected Boswell's heirs by permitting them the choice of allowing the papers to become exposed to the eyes of the world. The papers were transported with their owners from place to place, or became scattered, not to be recovered until, beginning in 1927, they were traced to their repositories in Ireland and Scotland. The persistence of several scholars and the generosity of Col. Ralph H. Isham in purchasing papers which had lain in neglect nearly a century and a half united Boswell's journal at last, at Yale University. Some of the papers, I understand, "reached America as late as the summer of 1950," and others—"a considerable number of scraps and tatters," according to the interesting account from which I am quoting—as recently as the summer of 1961.

At Yale, for more than forty years, the work has gone forward of deciphering, verifying, and organizing for publication thousands of pages forming the journal. The first of the volumes of the Yale series was published in 1950, subsequent volumes have appeared, and others are yet to come. When the journal is entirely published, it will have carried Boswell from his youth, entering London shortly after his twenty-second birthday, to the year of his death thirty-two years later.

It also will have provided readers with the pleasures of comedy and tragedy, producing—for me at least—substantial enlightenment. My own "discovery" of Boswell occurred in Japan in 1958, when I was looking for something to read in the otherwise limited library of the Department of English at the University of Hiroshima. There I found a Japanese edition of the *Life of Johnson,* a book I had been bored by (that is, a book to which I had brought too little experience) as an undergraduate at college. This thin little Japanese edition was but a fragment of the *Life,* and I thought I would try it. Its effect upon me was not alone to make me now seek the whole book but also to arouse my curiosity about its author. It was at this time that I heard from a Japanese professor that Boswell's journal was in the process of publication.

Once begun upon Boswell's journal I never ceased, seizing each new volume as it came from the publisher, catching up with those volumes that had passed me by. Boswell carried me to another place, to an enlightenment mingled with self-awareness, to accounts resembling my own past and prophesying my own future. The place he took me turned out to be my own, the world. Life among Scotsmen and Englishmen struck me suddenly as very like life among Japanese and Americans quite apart from small questions of oceans and centuries.

I was attracted also, after the first shocks of recognition, by the skillful way in which the editors perceived Boswell's life as dramatic segments rather than as an undifferentiated chronology; how they supplied background information and footnotes at precisely the length and exactly the moment I seemed to require them. From the place to which I was taken I could never return. The volumes of journal have so far enriched me that to be entrusted now with my own related editorial task is a reward I cannot quite believe.

This volume, however, is in an extremely limited way my own. The text of course is Boswell's, clarified by several scholars; my brief introductions to the six principal divisions of this book depend wholly upon the basis of knowledge and information established by other men and women. In a distillate much is inevitably lost. My principle of abridgement has been to pursue the straightest possible narrative, following Boswell to the completion of those tasks he had more or less assigned to himself: to meet Mr. Johnson, to complete his study of the law, to meet M. Rousseau, to meet M. Voltaire, to tour Europe, to rescue Corsica, to pacify his father, to become a published author, to find a wife, to defend John Reid at law. Along the way I have also followed him upon certain adventures doubtfully related to the major objectives of his life, those sidewise excursions which may sometimes have been the cause of his heirs' discouragement from passing Boswell's journals freely to the world. Boswell was not writing for history but for himself, an inventory or accounting of his own life for his own purpose.

This volume remains finally but a fragment of Boswell, as the Japanese *Life of Johnson* was but a fragment of itself. By the same token, a fragment may lead to the whole. For any reader this volume may be the beginning of a transforming journey, as my happenstance in Hiroshima was for me. To have made the journey once more, as the means of shaping this volume, has been a singular experience for me.

Nobody, I suspect, can become engaged with Boswell in our age without feeling the particular presence of Professor Frederick A. Pottle, of Yale, whose leadership has enforced the high quality of all that has been so meticulously done. I am especially grateful to Dr. Irma S. Lustig, of Yale, for her creative perception of my plausible connection to this work; to Mr. Thomas H. Quinn, editor, for his continuous support; and to Professor Marshall Waingrow, Claremont Graduate School, for his having so kindly received my inquiries over the years.

Mark Harris

BOSWELL'S
LONDON JOURNAL

MEETING MR. JOHNSON

15 November 1762—30 May 1763

INTRODUCTION

THE FIRST THING the whole world knows about James Boswell is that he was the biographer of Samuel Johnson. Between the moment of the publication of the *Life of Johnson* in 1791 and the revelations of the astounding findings of Boswell's papers in our own time, that fact was almost all we *did* know. Boswell was an attachment to Johnson.

Our best psychological guess might have told us more: that one man prancing along behind another taking down everything the great man said (such was our inherited image of Boswell) must have been less than the picture. If the prancing man made, as it turned out, an immortal book of his jottings and note-taking, he must have been of solider stuff than prancing implies, for a great book cannot rise wholly unannounced from a characterless man.

Why did Mr. Johnson permit Mr. Boswell to follow him around like that, eavesdropping on his life? Something in Boswell must have recommended itself to Johnson, who was not in every situation a man of indiscriminate patience. Think of their intimacy! In 1773, ten years after the beginning of their acquaintance, the two men traveled together for nearly three months through the Hebrides. During many of those days they had no companionship but each other, and accommodations so primitive as to have forced intimacy upon them had they not already accepted it.

Consider merely the mechanical difficulties of Boswell's undertaking. To have recorded the thought, wit, rhythm, and logic of Johnson's conversation with such felicity and probable accuracy was itself an achievement no man could match without bringing to the work a complex life and mind of his own.

There was a Boswell before that James Boswell whose name at a certain moment became merely inseparable from Johnson's. He was born in Scotland in 1740. His father is known to us, ironically enough, principally through the pages of this journal he so actively disapproved —"your strange journals," he called it upon one occasion. Lord Auchinleck, whose title he earned as a jurist, not by lineage, cared nothing for fame. "He is content to do his duty," Boswell said of his father. "He does not seek to be known beyond his own circle." Lord

3

Auchinleck disapproved not only of his son's journal but on the whole of the son himself. He comes to us, through Boswell's eyes at least, as a cold man, however steady or well intentioned; a supremely practical, material man who viewed as pointless and dangerous his son's periodic flights to the literary community of London. His letters to his son, which we may read here and elsewhere, elegantly spell out values whose desirability he has never questioned. Boswell's seeking out Johnson and other compatible men may have been beyond a literary quest a search for paternal warmth he had never known.

Of his mother, Boswell tells us little. Through Lord Auchinleck's letters she appears mainly as an obedient presence. "Your mother is in her ordinary, so is Johnny. Both remember you with affection." Since she was powerless to affect Boswell's course of life, he engaged little enough in any crucial analysis of her character. My own first image of their relationship may do it an injustice: upon hearing of his mother's death, Boswell traveled home from Paris in the company of Rousseau's lifetime companion, Thérèse Le Vasseur, to whom he made love, as we say, thirteen times in eleven days.

In Part I, which immediately follows, we encounter a fellow just turned twenty-two, a well-educated young man, not yet employed and without clear prospects of becoming so. Eventually he may inherit a good estate in Scotland, but that reward may first require a lifetime of obedience to his father. Meanwhile the son receives from his father a modest allowance at the father's discretion. The son is filled with schemes. He appears confident that the life for him is the Foot Guards—"the only scene of real life that I ever liked"—but his strategy for obtaining an appointment to the Guards is ineffective, and the reader may realize before Boswell does that Lady Northumberland, who promised to intervene in his behalf, no longer intends to do so.

Boswell is beautifully innocent. His father wishes that he would study law. "I told him that I could not study law, and being of a profession where you do no good is to a man of spirit very disagreeable." Twelve years later the "man of spirit" confronted his implacable father in a capital case at the law, their persons complete: one would be all his life spokesman for the defense, and the other man judge.

In London, Boswell is distracted, caught up in a variety of pursuits not clearly relevant to a secure future, not likely to please his father, and often weakening or disabling to himself. His passions produce terrors. Unfortunate sexual affiliations produce disease. His obsessive attendance at public executions produces nightmare and depression. He seeks the company of illustrious men, one of whom is Samuel Johnson.

"Though then but two-and-twenty," Boswell wrote afterward in the *Life*, "I had for several years read his works with delight and instruction, and had the highest reverence for their author, which had grown up in my fancy into a kind of mysterious veneration, by figuring to myself a state of solemn elevated abstraction, in which I supposed him to live in the immense metropolis of London."

Several occasions had promised meetings which did not occur. But at seven o'clock on the evening of May 16, 1763, in the bookshop of one Tom Davies, Boswell met Johnson at last, apparently without plan. Johnson instantly razzed Boswell for being a Scotsman. "This stroke stunned me a good deal," Boswell recorded. But not to speechlessness. Quickly, on another issue, Boswell challenged Johnson in a manner which was to characterize his method of evoking deeply felt responses from that great man, who did not, as it happened, live always in a state of solemn elevated abstraction. Johnson had complained to Davies of Garrick's not giving him tickets to the theater. "Eager to take any opening to get into conversation with him, I ventured to say, 'O, Sir, I cannot think Mr. Garrick would grudge such a trifle to you.' 'Sir, (said he, with a stern look,) I have known David Garrick longer than you have done: and I know no right you have to talk to me on the subject.' "

In this inauspicious way a friendship began between two men thirty-one years apart, which was to continue mainly unimpaired from that moment forward. The young man would become his elder's biographer and, in the process, take for himself mentor, counselor, source, and confidant, aspects of an ideal father he had not known.

I have therefore determined to keep a daily journal in which I shall set down my various sentiments and my various conduct, which will be not only useful but very agreeable. It will give me a habit of application and improve me in expression; and knowing that I am to record my transactions will make me more careful to do well. Or if I should go wrong, it will assist me in resolutions of doing better. I shall here put down my thoughts on different subjects at different times, the whims that may seize me and the sallies of my luxuriant imagination. I shall mark the anecdotes and the stories that I hear, the instructive or amusing conversations that I am present at, and the various adventures that I may have.

In this way I shall preserve many things that would otherwise be lost in oblivion. I shall find daily employment for myself, which will save me from indolence and help to keep off the spleen, and I shall lay up a store of entertainment for my after life. Very often we have more pleasure in reflecting on agreeable scenes that we have been in than we had from the scenes themselves. I shall regularly record the business or rather the pleasure of every day. I shall not study much correctness, lest the labour of it should make me lay it aside altogether. I hope it will be of use to my worthy friend Johnston, and that while he laments my personal absence, this journal may in some measure supply that defect and make him happy.

MONDAY 15 NOVEMBER. Elated with the thoughts of my journey to London, I got up. I called upon my friend Johnston, but found he was not come from the country, which vexed me a little, as I wished to bid him cordially adieu. However, I excused him to myself, and as Cairnie told me that people never took leave in France, I made the thing sit pretty easy. I had a long serious conversation with my father and mother. They were very kind to me. I felt parental affection was very strong towards me; and I felt a very warm filial regard for them. The scene of being a son setting out from home for the wide world and the idea of being my own master, pleased me much. I parted with my brother Davy, leaving him my best advices to be diligent at his business as a banker and to make rich and be happy.

At ten I got into my chaise, and away I went.

TUESDAY 16 NOVEMBER. We had a safe day, and got at night to Durham.

WEDNESDAY 17 NOVEMBER. We had a very good day of it, and got at night to Doncaster.

THURSDAY 18 NOVEMBER. We got at night to Biggleswade.

FRIDAY 19 NOVEMBER. When we came upon Highgate hill and had a view of London, I was all life and joy. I repeated Cato's soliloquy on the immortality of the soul, and my soul bounded forth to a certain prospect of happy futurity. I sung all manner of songs, and began to make one about an amorous meeting with a pretty girl, the burthen of which was as follows:

> She gave me *this,* I gave her *that;*
> And tell me, had she not tit for tat?

I gave three huzzas, and we went briskly in.

I immediately went to my friend Douglas's, surgeon in Pall Mall, a kind-hearted, plain, sensible man, where I was cordially received. His wife is a good-humoured woman, and is that sort of character which is often met with in England: very lively without much wit. Her fault is speaking too much, which often tires people. He was my great adviser as to everything; and in the mean time insisted that I should have a bed in his house till I got a lodging to my mind.

SUNDAY 21 NOVEMBER. I got up well and enjoyed my good situation. I had a handsome dining-room and bed-chamber, just in Pall Mall, the finest part of the town; I was in pursuit of my commission, which I was vastly fond of; and I had money enough to live like a gentleman.

I went to Douglas's and drank tea.

Since I came up, I have begun to acquire a composed genteel character very different from a rattling uncultivated one which for some time past I have been fond of. I have discovered that we may be in some degree whatever character we choose. Besides, practice forms a man to anything. I was now happy to find myself cool, easy, and serene.

THURSDAY 25 NOVEMBER. I had been in a bad situation during the night for I dreamt that Johnston did not care for me. That he came to see me set off on a long journey, and that he seemed dissipated and tired, and left me before I got away. I lay abed very gloomy. I thought London did me no good. I rather disliked it; and I thought of going back to Edinburgh immediately. In short, I was most miserable.

I got up and breakfasted. I got a card from Lord Eglinton asking me to the House of Lords. I accordingly went and heard the King make his speech. It was a very noble thing. I here beheld the King of Great Britain on his throne with the crown on his head addressing both the Lords and the Commons. His Majesty spoke better than any man I ever heard: with dignity, delicacy, and ease. I admired him. I wished much to be acquainted with him.

I went to Love's and drank tea. I had now been some time in town without female sport. I determined to have nothing to do with whores, as my health was of great consequence to me. I went to a girl with whom I had an intrigue at Edinburgh, but my affection cooling, I had left her. I knew she was come up. I waited on her and tried to obtain my former favours, but in vain. She would by no means listen. I was really unhappy for want of women. I thought it hard to be in such a place without them. I picked up a girl in the Strand; went into a court with intention to enjoy her in armour. But she had none. I toyed with her. She wondered at my size, and said if I ever took a girl's maidenhead, I would make her squeak. I gave her a shilling, and had command enough of myself to go without touching her. I afterwards trembled at the danger I had escaped. I resolved to wait cheerfully till I got some safe girl or was liked by some woman of fashion.

FRIDAY 26 NOVEMBER. I waited on Lord Adam Gordon, who was very polite. I liked to see a Colonel of the Guards in his elegant house. I was much difficulted about lodgings. A variety I am sure I saw, I dare say fifty. I was amused in this way. At last I fixed in Downing Street, Westminster. I took a lodging up two pair of stairs with the use of a handsome parlour all the forenoon, for which I agreed to pay forty guineas a year, but I took it for a fortnight first, by way of a trial. I also made bargain that I should dine with the family whenever I pleased, at a shilling a time. My landlord was Mr. Terrie, chamber-keeper to the Office for Trade and Plantations. He was originally from the Shire of Moray. He had a wife but no children. The street was a genteel street, within a few steps of the Parade; near the House of Commons, and very healthful. I went to Mr. Cochrane, my banker, and received £25, my allowance every six weeks.

SATURDAY 27 NOVEMBER. Lord Eglinton and I talked a little privately. He imagined me much in the style that I was three years ago: raw, curious, volatile, credulous. He little knew the experience I had got and the notions and the composure that I had obtained by reflection. "My Lord," said I, "I am now a little wiser." "Not so much as you think," said he. "For, as a boy who has just learned the alphabet when he begins to make out words thinks himself a great master of reading, so the little advance you have made in prudence appears very great, as it is so much before what you was formerly." I owned that there was some justice in what he said.

SUNDAY 28 NOVEMBER. I breakfasted with Mr. Douglas. I went to St. James's Church and heard service and a good sermon on "By what means shall a young man learn to order his ways," in which the advantages of early piety were well displayed. What a curious, inconsistent thing is the mind of man! In the midst of divine service I was laying plans for having women, and yet I had the most sincere feelings of religion. I imagine that my want of belief is the occasion of this, so that I can have all the feelings. I would try to make out a little consistency this way. I have a warm heart and a vivacious fancy. I am therefore given to love, and also to piety or gratitude to God, and to the most brilliant and showy method of public worship.

At six I went to Mr. Sheridan's Court and was splendidly dressed. I was introduced to Mrs. Sheridan, a woman of very homely looks, but very sensible and very clever, as appears from her *Memoirs of Miss Sidney Bidulph*. I let myself appear by degrees, and I found that I was agreeable to her, which flattered me a good deal.

I asked for Mr. Samuel Johnson. Sheridan said he now could not bear him, because he had taken a pension of three hundred a year from the Court, by the particular interest of Lord Bute, and yet he still railed against the royal family and the Scots minister. I said I imagined he put it upon this: that the pension was not a *favour* but a reward *due* to his merit, and therefore he would show still the same principles of opposition freely and openly. "No, Sir," said he. "Johnson took it as a favour; waited on Lord Bute, said he could not find an English word to express what he felt, and was therefore obliged to have recourse to the French: 'I am *pénétré* with his Majesty's goodness.' This being the case, his business was to be silent; or, if called upon to give his opinion, to say, 'Gentlemen, my sentiments are just the same that they were. But an obligation forbids me to say much.' " It hurt me to find Sheridan abusing a man for whom I have heard him profess the greatest regard. He added, "The bearish manners of Johnson were insupportable without the idea of his having a good heart. But since he has been made the object of royal favour, his character has been sifted and is bad." I drank tea and coffee and was very well. I came home and went to bed.

MONDAY 29 NOVEMBER. Then dined Lady Frances Erskine's. Both her sons were there, and Mr. Grant, son to Sir Ludovic. We were very genteel and very dull. We just said the same things that everybody in town were saying.

TUESDAY 30 NOVEMBER. I dined with Mr. Sheridan. He was quite enthusiastic about oratory. He said Garrick had no real feeling; that his talents for mimicry enabled him to put on the appearance of feeling, and that the nicety of his art might please the fancy and make us cry, "That's fine." But as it was art, it could never touch the heart. Mr. Sheridan's distinction was just, but does not apply to Garrick, because he often has touched the heart and drawn tears from multitudes.

I thought my present lodgings too dear, and therefore looked about and found a place in Crown Street, Westminster, an obscure street but pretty lodgings at only £22 a year. Much did I ruminate with regard to lodgings. Sometimes I considered that a fine lodging denoted a man of great fashion, but then I thought that few people would see it and therefore the expense would be hid, whereas my business was to make as much show as I could with my small allowance. I thought that an elegant place to come home to was very agreeable and would inspire me with ideas of my own dignity; but then I thought it would be hard if I had not a proportionable show in other things, and that it was better to come gradually to a fine place than from a fine to a worse. I therefore resolved to take the Crown Street place, and told my present landlord that I intended to leave him. He told me that he was very sorry, and that he would allow me to make my own terms rather than quit his house; for he was in such circumstances that he was not obliged to let lodgings for bread, and that as I was extremely agreeable to the family, he begged I would stay, and he would let me have my three rooms for £30. I thanked him for his good opinion of me, but told him that economy at present was my object, although I was very happy in his house; and that I could not ask him to let me have three rooms in a genteel street as cheap as two in an obscure one. He paused a while and then told me that I should have them at the same price. He only begged that I would not mention it, as he certainly let them below value. I therefore struck a bargain and settled myself for a year.

I do think this a very strong proof of my being agreeable.

WEDNESDAY 1 DECEMBER. On Tuesday I wanted to have a silver-hilted sword, but upon examining my pockets as I walked up the Strand, I found that I had left the most of my guineas at home and had not enough to pay for it with me. I determined to make a trial of the civility of my fellow-creatures, and what effect my external appearance and address would have. I accordingly went to the shop of Mr. Jefferys, sword-cutter to his Majesty, looked at a number of his swords, and at last picked out a very handsome one at five guineas. "Mr. Jefferys," said I, "I have not money here to pay for it. Will you trust me?" "Upon my word, Sir," said he, "you must excuse me. It is a thing we never do to a stranger." I bowed genteelly and said, "Indeed, Sir, I believe it is not right." However, I stood and looked at him, and he looked at me. "Come, Sir," cried he, "I will trust you." "Sir," said I, "if you had not trusted me, I should not have bought it from you." He asked my name and place of abode, which I told him. I then chose a belt, put the sword on, told him I would call and pay it tomorrow, and walked off. I called this day and paid him. "Mr. Jefferys," said I, "there is your money. You paid me a very great compliment. I am much obliged to you. But pray don't do such a thing again. It is dangerous." "Sir," said he, "we know our men. I would have trusted you with the value of a hundred pounds." This I think was a good adventure and much to my honour.

This afternoon I was surprised with the arrival of Lady Betty Macfarlane, Lady Anne Erskine, Captain Erskine, and Miss Dempster, who were come to the Red Lion Inn at Charing Cross. It seems Lady Betty had written to the Laird that if he would not come down, she would come up; and upon his giving her an indolent answer, like a woman of spirit, she put her resolution in practice. I immediately went to them.

To tell the plain truth, I was vexed at their coming. For to see just the plain *hamely* Fife family hurt my grand ideas of London.

THURSDAY 2 DECEMBER. At nine o'clock I waited upon the Duke. He received me with the greatest politeness. He is a man of the greatest humanity and gentleness of manners, has good plain sense, and is very cheerful notwithstanding of the severe shocks that he has met with. He told me that he found it very difficult to get me a commission, but that he would try.

FRIDAY 3 DECEMBER. I began now to be much at home in my lodgings and to get into a regular method. I resolved to want a servant for my first year and in every respect to be frugal, that I might learn the value of money, see what I could afford to do with my allowance, and rather live within than exceed my income. I am really surprised at the coolness and moderation with which I am proceeding.

At nine I went to Lord Eglinton's but returned to Gould's at ten, as he insisted upon it, having invited Sir Alexander Gilmour of the First Regiment to meet me; but he did not come. We had a nice light bit of supper and were very happy. The Colonel talked of battles and dreadful wounds, which made us shudder. Really, these things are not to be talked of, for in cool blood they shock one prodigiously.

SATURDAY 4 DECEMBER. At night, Erskine and I strolled through the streets and St. James's Park. We were accosted there by several ladies of the town. Erskine was very humorous and said some very wild things to them. There was one in a red cloak of a good buxom person and comely face whom I marked as a future piece, in case of exigency.

SUNDAY 5 DECEMBER. I then went to Dempster's, where I met with the Kellie family. I let myself out in humorous rhodomontade rather too much. We were very hearty. We disputed much whether London or Edinburgh was the most agreeable place to a Scotch gentleman of small fortune. Lady Betty said that it must be very cutting to find so many people higher than one's self and to see so many splendid equipages, none of which belong to one. "Lady Betty," said I, "you have the pleasure of admiring them. But your taste is too gross—you want to have the solid equipages themselves, to embrace and carry in your arms the thick tarry wheels."

In reality, a person of small fortune who has only the common views of life and would just be as well as anybody else, cannot like London. But a person of imagination and feeling, such as the Spectator finely describes, can have the most lively enjoyment from the sight of external objects without regard to property at all.

Dempster, talking of *Irene,* a tragedy written by Mr. Samuel Johnson, said it was as frigid as the regions of Nova Zembla; that now and then you felt a little heat like what is produced by touching ice.

MONDAY 6 DECEMBER. I waited on General Douglas, who told me that the Duke told him that he thought it would not be in his power to get me a commission. This was a discouraging piece of information. I left him in bad humour, cursed a state of waiting for anything from great men, and in short despaired a good deal of getting it.

At one I went to the Duke's, and being in a kind of despair, I talked freely and boldly to him. He was gently informing me that the thing was very difficult. To show him that this did not affect me, "My Lord," said I, "it is as difficult as can be imagined, yet I should think your Grace's interest might do it." (I should have mentioned that I wrote a letter to him, some days ago, very fully.) "My Lord," said I now, and looked him in the face, "a state of suspense and hanging on is a most disagreeable thing. I have heard people talk of it, and I have read in the poets of it, but now I feel it. I have got an independent spirit, and I can assure your Grace that if I had not a good opinion of you as a man, upon my soul, I would not ask such a thing of you. It just comes to this; if your Grace is so generous as to make a push for me (which indeed I can scarcely ask), I believe the thing may do." I could see that the good old man was pleased with my spirit. He told me that he would do what he could with Lord Ligonier.

I drank tea at Macfarlane's. There was a most disagreeable set of women there. It was just one of the worst Edinburgh tea-drinking afternoons. Erskine and I sat out by ourselves and laughed immoderately just like two schoolboys. He went with me to Dempster's, where we sat a good while.

TUESDAY 7 DECEMBER. In the evening I went to Northumberland House, to the rout, which was indeed magnificent.

As I was standing in pleasing reverie in the gallery musing on the splendid scene around me and joining with that the ancient ideas of the family of Percy, my Lady came up to me with the greatest complacency and kindness: "Mr. Boswell, I am very happy to see you. How do you do? I hope you are come to settle among us. I was very sorry that I was not at home when you called. I gave positive orders that you should be admitted whenever you called." This put me into the finest humour. I thanked her sincerely. I chatted easily. She then carried me to my Lord, who was very glad to see me and very civil to me. This is indeed a noble family in every respect. They live in a most princely manner, perfectly suitable to their high rank. Yet they are easy and affable. They keep up the true figure of old English nobility.

I felt a little awkward this night, as I scarcely knew anybody in the room. I told my Lady so. She said that would go off by degrees. I could observe people looking at me with envy, as a man of some distinction and a favourite of my Lady's. Bravo! thought I. I am sure I deserve to be a favourite. It was curious to find how little consequence each individual was in such a crowd. I could imagine how an officer in a great army may be killed without being observed. I came home quiet, laid by my clothes, and went coolly to bed. There's conduct for you.

WEDNESDAY 8 DECEMBER. I sat in writing till one. I then strolled through the streets. I was somewhat dull and thought myself a poor sort of a being. At night I went to Convent Garden and saw *Love in a Village*, a new comic opera, for the first night. I liked it much. I saw it from the gallery, but I was first in the pit. Just before the overture began to be played, two Highland officers came in. The mob in the upper gallery roared out, "No Scots! No Scots! Out with them!," hissed and pelted them with apples. My heart warmed to my countrymen, my Scotch blood boiled with indignation. I jumped up on the benches, roared out, "Damn you, you rascals!," hissed and was in the greatest rage. I am very sure at that time I should have been the most distinguished of heroes. I hated the English; I wished from my soul that the Union was broke and that we might give them another battle of Bannockburn. I went close to the officers and asked them of what regiment they were of. They told me Lord John Murray's, and that they were just come from the Havana. "And this," said they, "is the thanks that we get—to be hissed when we come home. If it was French, what could they do worse?" "But," said one, "if I had a *grup o yin or twa o the tamd rascals I sud let them ken what they're about.*" The rudeness of the English vulgar is terrible. This indeed is the liberty which they have: the liberty of bullying and being abusive with their blackguard tongues. They soon gave over. I then went to the gallery and was really well entertained with the opera.

THURSDAY 9 DECEMBER. I called on Erskine and related to him the history of the opera. I was in an immoderate flow of spirits and raged away. We then sauntered through the streets. He gave me a very sensible advice against repeating what people said, which may do much harm. I have an unlucky custom of doing so. I acknowledged my error and promised to be on my guard.

FRIDAY 10 DECEMBER. I went to Northumberland House in the forenoon. The porter told me there was nobody at home; but looking at me, "Sir," said he, "is your name Boswell?" Upon my answering, "Yes," "My Lady is at home, Sir," said he. Upon which I was shown up to her Ladyship, with whom I sat about twenty minutes in the most easy, agreeable way. She told me that she had a private party every Friday for particular friends, and that she would always be glad to see me there when I had nothing else to do. I exulted, and thanked her, and said that I could not think how I deserved all this, but that I hoped we should be better acquainted, and that I should run about the house like a tame spaniel. An old gentleman then came in. I sat a little longer and then withdrew, full of joy at being reckoned a particular friend of the heir of the great Percy and a woman of the first consequence in London. She mentioned my commission, and kindly desired me not to be impatient, and I would get it. If the Duke does not do it for me, she will be my next resource. But it is better to have but one patron at a time and stick close to him.

SATURDAY 11 DECEMBER. The truth is with regard to me, about the age of seventeen I had a very severe illness. I became very melancholy. I imagined that I was never to get rid of it. I gave myself up as devoted to misery. I entertained a most gloomy and odd way of thinking. I was much hurt at being good for nothing in life. The particular events of my romantic life since then, my friends well know. My lively fancy always remained. Many a struggle was in my mind between melancholy and mirth. I grew better and freer of my disorder. But I could not bear the law. Indeed, I had been so long accustomed to consider myself as out of the world that I could not think of engaging in real life. At last the Guards pleased me. I was opposed in this scheme. This made me fonder of it. I also was an enthusiast with regard to being in London. The charms of poetry also enchanted me. I became acquainted with Captain Erskine, which kept this turn alive. To get away from home, where I lived as a boy, was my great object. It was irksome beyond measure to be a young laird in the house of a father much different from me, of a mind perfectly sound, and who thought that if I was not a man of business, I was good for nothing.

With these notions I am pushing to get into the Guards, where to distinguish myself as a good officer and to get promotion will be my favourite objects. If that does not succeed, I am at least living happily, I am seeing the world, studying men and manners, and fitting myself for a pleasing, quiet life in old age, by laying up agreeable ideas to feast upon in recollection. Thus shall I perhaps enjoy a serene felicity at the delightful Auchinleck, the ancient seat of a long line of worthy ancestors. Here will I end my days in calm devotion. If I shall be cut off before that time, I am satisfied. God is good; He will take care of me. O happy situation of mind which I now have! All things look well. I hope I shall be very happy. Let my mind be never so much distempered, I have devotion towards God and benevolence towards mankind. I have an honest mind and a warm friendship. Upon my soul, not a bad specimen of a man.

SUNDAY 12 DECEMBER. My landlord is a jolly, civil man. His wife a quiet, well-behaved woman, and his sister a neat-handed, clever girl. They do everything to serve me. Mr. Terrie is in a public office, so that he supplies me with paper and all materials for writing in great abundance, for nothing. Mrs. Terrie gets all things that I want bought for me, and Miss sews the laced ruffles on my shirts, and does anything of that kind. They have always a good plain dinner. I have the art to be easy and chatty and yet maintain a proper distance. In short, I live very comfortably. I order any little alterations that I wish. For instance, there was no communication between my dining-room and bedchamber. I ordered a door to be struck out, which was instantly done. I ordered some large breakfast cups and a carpet to my bedchamber and a bureau to my dining-room. It is inconceivable with what attention and spirit I manage all my concerns. I sat in all this evening calm and indulgent. I had a fire in both my rooms above-stairs. I drank tea by myself for a long time. I had my feet washed with milk-warm water, I had my bed warmed, and went to sleep soft and contented.

MONDAY 13 DECEMBER. I waited upon the Duke, whom I found rather in better humour about my commission, as Mr. Townshend had resigned, who was his great opposer. "My Lord," said I, "commissions are certainly got by interest, and I know nobody who has better interest than your Grace." He told me he had not seen Lord Ligonier, although he had called on him twice; but he promised to see him, and also to make application soon to the new Secretary at War, which, he agreed with me, might do good. I told his Grace that I would not relinquish the pursuit but wait for my commission if it should be two years. My youthful impatience was a little unsatisfied with the calm, diffident speech of the Duke, which, however, is in truth infinitely better than talking much and making me believe much more than is true.

This forenoon Mr. Sheridan was with me. I told him that I had great difficulty to get to London. "And how could it be otherwise," said he, "when you pushed the plan most opposite to your father's inclinations?" This immediately led us to talk fully on his scheme of the Temple, which I told him my father disapproved of, as my going to London at all was the thing that he could not think of. I told him that I could not study law, and being of a profession where you do no good is to a man of spirit very disagreeable. That I was determined to be in London. That I wanted to be something; and that the Guards was the only scene of real life that I ever liked.

TUESDAY 14 DECEMBER. It is very curious to think that I have now been in London several weeks without ever enjoying the delightful sex, although I am surrounded with numbers of free-hearted ladies of all kinds: from the splendid Madam at fifty guineas a night, down to the civil nymph with white-thread stockings who tramps along the Strand and will resign her engaging person to your honour for a pint of wine and a shilling. Manifold are the reasons for this my present wonderful continence. I am upon a plan of economy, and therefore cannot be at the expense of first-rate dames. I have suffered severely from the loathsome distemper, and therefore shudder at the thoughts of running any risk of having it again. Besides, the surgeons' fees in this city come very high. But the greatest reason of all is that fortune, or rather benignant Venus, has smiled upon me and favoured me so far that I have had the most delicious intrigues with women of beauty, sentiment, and spirit, perfectly suited to my romantic genius.

I am therefore walking about with a healthful stout body and a cheerful mind, in search of a woman worthy of my love, and who thinks me worthy of hers, without any interested views, which is the only sure way to find out if a woman really loves a man. If I should be a single man for the whole winter, I will be satisfied. I have had as much elegant pleasure as I could have expected would come to my share in many years.

However, I hope to be more successful. In this view, I had now called several times for a handsome actress of Covent Garden Theatre, whom I was a little acquainted with, and whom I shall distinguish in this my journal by the name of LOUISA. This lady had been indisposed and saw no company, but today I was admitted. She was in a pleasing undress and looked very pretty. She received me with great politeness. We chatted on the common topics. We were not easy—there was a constraint upon us—we did not sit right on our chairs, and we were unwilling to look at one another. I talked to her on the advantage of having an agreeable acquaintance, and hoped I might see her now and then. She desired me to call in whenever I came that way, without ceremony. "And pray," said she, "when shall I have the pleasure of your company at tea?" I fixed Thursday, and left her, very satisfied with my first visit.

WEDNESDAY 15 DECEMBER. I then went to the Cockpit, which is a circular room in the middle of which the cocks fight. It is seated round with rows gradually rising. The pit and the seats are all covered with mat. The cocks, nicely cut and dressed and armed with silver heels, are set down and fight with amazing bitterness and resolution. Some of them were quickly dispatched. One pair fought three quarters of an hour. The uproar and noise of betting is prodigious. A great deal of money made a very quick circulation from hand to hand. There was a number of professed gamblers there. An old cunning dog whose face I had seen at Newmarket sat by me a while. I told him I knew nothing of the matter. "Sir," said he, "you have as good a chance as anybody." He thought I would be a good subject for him. I was young-like. But he found himself balked. I was shocked to see the distraction and anxiety of the betters. I was sorry for the poor cocks. I looked around to see if any of the spectators pitied them when mangled and torn in a most cruel manner, but I could not observe the smallest relenting sign in any countenance. I was therefore not ill pleased to see them endure mental torment. Thus did I complete my true English day, and came home pretty much fatigued and pretty much confounded at the strange turn of this people.

THURSDAY 16 DECEMBER. In the afternoon I went to Louisa's. A little black young fellow, her brother, came in. I could have wished him at the Bay of Honduras. However, I found him a good quiet obliging being who gave us no disturbance. She talked on a man's liking a woman's company, and of the injustice people treated them with in suspecting anything bad. This was a fine artful pretty speech. We talked of French manners, and how they studied to make one another happy. "The English," said I, "accuse them of being false because they misunderstand them. When a Frenchman makes warm professions of regard, he does it only to please you for the time. It is words of course. There is no more of it. But the English, who are cold and phlegmatic in their address, take all these fine speeches in earnest, and are confounded to find them otherwise, and exclaim against the perfidious Gaul most unjustly. For when Frenchmen put a thing home seriously and vow fidelity, they have the strictest honour. O they are the people who enjoy time; so lively, pleasant, and gay. You never hear of madness or self-murder among them. Heat of fancy evaporates in fine brisk clear vapour with them, but amongst the English often falls heavy upon the brain."

We chatted pretty easily. We talked of love as a thing that could not be controlled by reason, as a fine passion. I could not clearly discern how she meant to behave to me. She told me that a gentleman had come to her and offered her £50, but that her brother knocked at the door and the man run out of the house without saying a word. I said I wished he had left his money. We joked much about the £50. I said I expected some night to be surprised with such an offer from some decent elderly gentlewoman. I made just a comic parody to her story. I sat till past eight. She said she hoped it would not be long before she had the pleasure of seeing me again.

This night I made no visible progress in my amour, but I in reality was doing a great deal. I was getting well acquainted with her. I was appearing an agreeable companion to her; I was informing her by my looks of my passion for her.

FRIDAY 17 DECEMBER. I engaged in this amour just with a view of convenient pleasure but the god of pleasing anguish now seriously seized my breast. I felt the fine delirium of love. I waited on Louisa at one, found her alone, told her that her goodness in hoping to see me *soon* had brought me back: that it appeared long to me since I saw her. I was a little bashful. However, I took a good heart and talked with ease and dignity. "I hope, Madam, you are at present a single woman." "Yes, Sir." "And your affections are not engaged?" "They are not, Sir." "But this is leading me into a strange confession. I assure you, Madam, my affections are engaged." "Are they, Sir?" "Yes, Madam, they are engaged to you." (She looked soft and beautiful.) "I hope we shall be better acquainted and like one another better." "Come, Sir, let us talk no more of that now." "No, Madam, I will not. It is like giving the book in the preface." "Just so, Sir, telling in the preface what should be in the middle of the book." (I think such conversations are best written in the dialogue way.) "Madam, I was very happy to find you. From the first time that I saw you, I admired you." "O, Sir." "I did, indeed. What I like beyond everything is an agreeable female companion, where I can be at home and have tea and genteel conversation. I was quite happy to be here." "Sir, you are welcome here as often as you please. Every evening, if you please." "Madam I am infinitely obliged to you."

This is just what I wanted. I left her, in good spirits, and dined at

Sheridan's. "Well," said he, "are you going into the Guards?" "Yes, Sir," said I; "the Temple scheme would not have done. It would only have been putting off time. I would not have applied. You cannot get a man to undergo the drudgery of the law who only want to pass his life agreeably, and who thinks that my Lord Chancellor's four and twenty hours are not a bit happier than mine. Don't you think, Sir," said I, "that I am in the right to pursue the plan I like?" He replied, "I won't speak to you on the subject. But I shall always be glad to see you."

We talked of Johnson. He told me a story of him. "I was dining," said Johnson, "with the Mayor of Windsor, who gave me a very hearty dinner; but, not satisfied with feeding my body, he would also feed my understanding. So, after he had spoke a great deal of clumsy nonsense, he told me that at the last Sessions he had transported three people to the Plantations. I was so provoked with the fellow's dullness and impertinence that I exclaimed. 'I wish to God, Sir, I was the fourth.'" Nothing could more strongly express his dissatisfaction.

Mrs. Sheridan told me that he was very sober, but would sit up the whole night. He left them once at two in the morning and begged to be excused for going away so soon, as he had another visit to make. I like to mark every anecdote of men of so much genius and literature.

I found out Sheridan's great cause of quarrel with him was that when Johnson heard of his getting a pension, "What!" said he, "has *he* got a pension? Then it is time for me to give up mine." "Now," said he, "here was the greatest ingratitude. For it was I and Wedderburn that first set the thing a-going." This I believe was true.

SATURDAY 18 DECEMBER. I then went to Louisa's. I was really in love. I felt a warmth at my heart which glowed in my face. I attempted to be like Digges, and considered the similarity of our genius and pleasures. I acquired confidence by considering my present character in this light: a young fellow of spirit and fashion, heir to a good fortune, enjoying the pleasures of London, and now making his addresses in order to have an intrigue with that delicious subject of gallantry, an actress.

I talked on love very freely. "Madam," said I, "I can never think of having a connection with women that I don't love." "That, Sir," said she, "is only having a satisfaction in common with the brutes. But when there is a union of minds, that is indeed estimable. But don't think Sir, that I am a Platonist. I am not indeed." (This hint gave me courage.) "To be sure, Madam, when there is such a connection as you mention, it is the finest thing in the world. I beg you may just show me civility according as you find me deserve it." "Such a connection, Sir, requires time to establish it." (I thought it honest and proper to let her know that she must not depend on me for giving her much money.) "Madam," said I, "don't think too highly of me. Nor give me the respect which men of great fortune get by custom. I am here upon a very moderate allowance. I am upon honour to make it serve me, and I am obliged to live with great economy." She received this very well.

At night I went to Mr. Thomas Davies's shop and sat a while. I told him that I wanted much to see Johnson. "Sir," said he, "if you'll dine with me on Christmas day, you shall see him. He and some more men of letters are to be with me." I very readily accepted this invitation.

SUNDAY 19 DECEMBER. I drank tea with *Louisa*. Her brother was there. I was very chatty and gay with looking at so fine a woman and thinking what delight I should have with her. She had a meeting with Mr. Stede, an old gentleman late Prompter and now in the Cabinet Council of Covent Garden Theatre. So I was obliged to leave her at seven.

MONDAY 20 DECEMBER. I went to Louisa's after breakfast. "Indeed," said I, "it was hard upon me to leave you so soon yesterday. I am quite happy in your company." "Sir," said she, "you are very obliging. But," said she, "I am in bad humour this morning. There was a person who professed the greatest friendship for me; I now applied for their assistance, but was shifted. It was such a trifle that I am sure they could have granted it. So I have been railing against my fellow-creatures." "Nay, dear Madam, don't abuse them all on account of an individual. But pray what was this favour? Might I know?" (She blushed.) "Why, Sir, there is a person has sent to me for a trifling debt. I sent back word that it was not convenient for me to let them have it just now, but in six weeks I should pay it."

I was a little confounded and embarrassed here. I dreaded bringing myself into a scrape. I did not know what she might call a trifling sum. I half-resolved to say no more. However, I thought that she might now be trying my generosity and regard for her, and truly this was the real test. I thought I would see if it was in my power to assist her.

"Pray, Madam, what was the sum?" "Only two guineas, Sir." Amazed and pleased, I pulled out my purse. "Madam," said I, "if I can do you any service, you may command me. Two guineas is at present all that I have, but a trifle more. There they are for you. I told you that I had very little, but yet I hope to live. Let us just be honest with one another. Tell me when you are in any little distress, and I will tell you what I can do." She took the guineas. "Sir, I am infinitely obliged to you. As soon as it is in my power, I shall return them. Indeed I could not have expected this from you." Her gratitude warmed my heart. "Madam! though I have little, yet as far as ten guineas, you may apply to me. I would live upon nothing to serve one that I regarded."

I did not well know what to think of this scene. Sometimes I thought it artifice, and that I was taken in. And then again, I viewed it just as a circumstance that might very easily happen. Her mentioning returning the money looked well. My naming the sum of ten guineas was rash; however, I considered that it cost me as much to be cured of what I contracted from a whore, and that ten guineas was but a moderate expense for women during the winter.

I had all along treated her with a distant politeness. On Saturday I just kissed her hand. She now sung to me. I got up in raptures and kissed her with great warmth. She received this very genteelly. I had a delicacy in presuming too far, lest it should look like demanding goods for my money. I resumed the subject of love and gallantry. She said, "I pay no regard to the opinion in the world so far as contradicts my own sentiments." "No, Madam, we are not to mind the arbitrary rules imposed by the multitude." "Yet, Sir, there is a decency to be kept with the public. And I must do so, whose bread depends upon them." "Certainly, Madam. But when may I wait upon you? Tomorrow evening?" "Sir, I am obliged to be all day with a lady who is not well." "Then next day, Madam." "What? to drink a dish of tea, Sir?" "No, no, not to drink a dish of tea." (Here I looked sheepish.) "What time may I wait upon you?" "Whenever you please, Sir." I kissed her again, and went away highly pleased with the thoughts of the affair being settled.

I went and sat a while with Captain Webster. He told me that the fatigues of a German campaign are almost incredible. That he was fourteen nights running without being under cover, and often had scarcely any victuals. He said he never once repented his being a soldier, although he cursed the sad fatigues. "Men," said he, "are in that way rendered desperate; and I have wished for an action, either to get out of the world altogether or to get a little rest after it."

WEDNESDAY 22 DECEMBER. I stood and chatted a while with the sentries before Buckingham House. One of them, an old fellow, said he was in all the last war. "At the battle of Dettingen," said he, "I saw our cannon make a lane through the French army as broad as that" (pointing to the Mall), "which was filled up in as short time as I'm telling you it." They asked me for a pint of beer, which I gave them. I talked on the sad mischief of war and on the frequency of poverty. "Why, Sir," said he, "God made all right at first when he made mankind. ("I believe," said the other, "he made but few of them:") But, Sir, if God was to make the world today, it would be crooked again tomorrow. But the time will come when we shall all be rich enough. To be sure, salvation is promised to those that die in the field." I have great pleasure in conversing with the lower part of mankind, who have very curious ideas.

This forenoon I went to Louisa's in full expectation of consummate bliss. I was in a strange flutter of feeling. I was ravished at the prospect of joy, and yet I had such an anxiety upon me that I was afraid that my powers would be enervated. I almost wished to be free of this assignation. I entered her apartment in a sort of confusion. She was elegantly dressed in the morning fashion, and looked delightfully well. I felt the tormenting anxiety of serious love. I sat down and I talked with the distance of a new acquaintance and not with the ease and ardour of a lover, or rather a gallant. I talked of her lodgings being neat, opened the door of her bedchamber, looked into it. Then sat down by her in a most melancholy plight. I would have given a good deal to be out of the room.

We talked of religion. Said she, "People who deny that, show a want of sense." "For my own part, Madam, I look upon the adoration of the Supreme Being as one of the greatest enjoyments we have. I would not choose to get rid of my religious notions. I have read books that staggered me. But I was glad to find myself regain my former opinions." "Nay, Sir, what do you think of the Scriptures having stood the test of ages?" "Are you a Roman Catholic, Madam?" "No, Sir. Though I like some parts of their religion, in particular, confession; not that I think the priest can remit sins, but because the notion that we are to confess to a decent clergyman may make us cautious what we do." "Madam," said I, "I would ask you to do nothing that you should be sorry to confess. Indeed I have a great deal of principle in matters of gallantry, and never yet led any woman to do what might afterwards make her uneasy. If she thinks it wrong, I never insist." She asked me some questions about my intrigues, which I nicely eluded.

I then sat near her and began to talk softly, but finding myself quite dejected with love, I really cried out and told her that I was miserable; and as I was stupid, would go away. I rose, but saluting her with warmth, my powers were excited, I felt myself vigorous. I sat down again. I beseeched her, "You know, Madam, you said you was not a Platonist. I beg it of you to be so kind. You said you are above the finesse of your sex." (Be sure always to make a woman better than her sex.) "I adore you." "Nay, dear Sir" (I pressing her to me and kissing her now and then), "pray be quiet. Such a thing requires time to consider of." "Madam, I own this would be necessary for any man but me. But you must take my character from myself. I am very good-tempered, very honest, and have little money. I should have some reward for my particular honesty." "But, Sir, give me time to recollect myself." "Well then, Madam, when shall I see you?" "On Friday, Sir." "A thousand thanks." I left her and came home and took my bread and cheese with great contentment, and then went and chatted a while with Webster.

I had not been at Lord Eglinton's for ten days. Last night I received a card from him: "Lord Eglinton presents his compliments to Mr. Boswell, and returns him a great many thanks for being so good as call on him so often. He is sorry he happened to be always out when Mr. Boswell called."

This he intended as a sharp reproof. However, as Lord Northumberland had called for me, I thought Lord Eglinton might do so, as I was quite independent of him. The card was not written with his own hand, which I was not pleased at. I am the easiest fellow in the world to those who behave well to me. But if a man has treated me with the least slight, I will keep him to every punctilio. I sent him for answer: "Mr. Boswell presents his compliments to Lord Eglinton; hopes he will excuse his writing this card with his own hand; he has not a secretary. Mr. Boswell has paid his respects to Lord Eglinton several times. He lodges at Mr. Terrie's in Downing Street."

This had a proper effect, for today he called when I was abroad, which satisfied me much.

FRIDAY 24 DECEMBER. I waited on Louisa. Says she, "I have been very unhappy since you was here. I have been thinking of what I said to you. I find that such a connection would make me miserable." "I hope, Madam, I am not disagreeable to you." "No, Sir, you are not. If it was the first duke in England I spoke to, I should just say the same thing." "But pray, Madam, what is your objection?" "Really, Sir, I have many disagreeable apprehensions. It may be known. Circumstances might be very troublesome. I beg it of you, Sir, consider of it. Your own good sense will agree with me. Instead of visiting me as you do now, you would find a discontented, unhappy creature." I was quite confused. I did not know what to say. At last I agreed to think of it and see her on Sunday. I came home and dined in dejection. Yet I mustered up vivacity, and away I went in full dress to Northumberland House. There was spirit, to lay out a couple of shillings and be a man of fashion in my situation. There was true economy.

SATURDAY 25 DECEMBER. The night before I did not rest well. I was really violently in love with Louisa. I thought she did not care for me. I thought that if I did not gain her affections, I would appear despicable to myself. This day I was in a better frame, being Christmas day, which has always inspired me with most agreeable feelings. I went to St. Paul's Church and in that magnificent temple fervently adored the God of goodness and mercy, and heard a sermon by the Bishop of Oxford on the publishing of glad tidings of great joy.

I then sat a while at Coutts's, and then at Macfarlane's, and then went to Davies's. Johnson was gone to Oxford. I was introduced to Mr. Dodsley, a good, jolly, decent, conversable man, and Mr. Goldsmith, a curious, odd, pedantic fellow with some genius. It was quite a literary dinner. I had seen no warm victuals for four days, and therefore played a very bold knife and fork. It is inconceivable how hearty I eat and how comfortable I felt myself after it. We talked entirely in the way of Geniuses.

We talked of poetry.

DODSLEY. "We have poems in a different way. There is nothing of the kind in the last age superior to *The Spleen.*" BOSWELL. "And what do you think of Gray's odes? Are not they noble?" GOLDSMITH. "Ah, the rumbling thunder! I remember a friend of mine was very fond of Gray. 'Yes,' said I, 'he is very fine indeed; as thus—

> Mark the white and mark the red,
> Mark the blue and mark the green;
> Mark the colours ere they fade,
> Darting thro' the welkin sheen.'

'O, yes,' said he, 'great, great!' 'True, Sir,' said I, 'but I have made the lines this moment. '" BOSWELL. "What do you think of Johnson?" GOLDSMITH. "He has exceeding great merit. His *Rambler* is a noble work." BOSWELL. "His *Idler* too is very pretty. It is a lighter performance; and he has thrown off the classical fetters very much." DAVIES. "He is a most entertaining companion. And how can it be otherwise, when he has so much imagination, has read so much, and digested it so well?"

SUNDAY 26 DECEMBER. I went to Whitehall Chapel and heard service. I took a whim to go through all the churches and chapels in London, taking one each Sunday.

At one I went to Louisa's. I told her my passion in the warmest terms. I told her that my happiness absolutely depended upon her. She said it was running the greatest risk. "Then," said I, "Madam, you will show the greatest generosity to a most sincere lover." She said that we should take time to consider of it, and that then we could better determine how to act. We agreed that the time should be a week, and that if I remained of the same opinion, she would then make me blessed.

I this day received a letter from the Duke of Queensberry, in answer to one that I had wrote him, telling me that a commission in the Guards was a fruitless pursuit, and advising me to take to a civil rather than a military life. I was quite stupefied and enraged at this. I imagined my father was at the bottom of it. I had multitudes of wild schemes. I thought of enlisting for five years as a soldier in India, of being a private man either in the Horse or Footguards, &c. At last good sense prevailed, and I resolved to be cheerful and to wait and to ask it of Lady Northumberland.

MONDAY 27 DECEMBER. I went to Mrs. Gould's and told my lamentable story. I also told it to my friend Douglas. They advised me to apply to Lady Northumberland. I therefore wrote a letter to her Ladyship to the following purpose:

MADAM:—Your kindness to me upon many occasions makes me freely tell you anything that vexes me. Sympathy is the greatest cordial we can have. I have received a letter from the Duke of Queensberry informing me that a commission in the Guards cannot be got for me. What does your Ladyship think of a man who, notwithstanding of such a disappointment, can cry *vive la bagatelle!* and walk about contented, cheerful, and merry? Have not I spirit? Ought I not to be a soldier? Ought I not to have the honour of serving George the Third? When your Ladyship tore the skin of your leg and yet kept up your spirits, you had good reason to be vain. I think I may be so too. Your Ladyship may remember that I observed to you that people often fell into a great mistake: because people of consequence liked them as acquaintances and showed them civility, they applied to them for substantial favours, which is quite a different sort of a thing. To come to the point, Madam, here am I anxious to get a commission in the Guards. If you and my Lord can do the thing for me, I shall be very happy.

If your Ladyship tells me that it is not convenient, I shall neither be surprised nor fretted. I am much obliged to you for your goodness already. It just comes to this. If the representatives of the noble Percy choose to take a young man of a good old Scotch family by the hand, who will rather do credit to his friends than otherwise, and who will be very grateful, it will be extremely obliging. I remain, &c.

This I sent to her Ladyship.

THURSDAY 30 DECEMBER. I had Erskine with me at breakfast, after which he and I went to Lady Frances Erskine's, and then I went to Lady Northumberland's. In my letter to her I mentioned to her that I would not choose to be far from London; and therefore I would choose no other corps but the Guards or the Blues; that is to say, the Royal Horse Guards Blue. "Madam," said I, "I took the liberty to write you a letter." "Sir," said she, "I am sorry to find these Guards so difficult to be got. I have been speaking to some officers on that subject. I imagined that your father had wrote in such a way to the Duke of Queensberry that he had not been in earnest to get it. But I find that it really is a very difficult matter. As to the Blues again, I should hope that may be easier; and when the Marquis of Granby comes over, I shall apply to him." "So your Ladyship really intends to take a charge of me? Pray don't be upon ceremony. I have no title to ask such a thing of you. I really did not expect that you would have engaged in it." "Sir, I should not say so if I did not intend it."

I then went to Louisa's. I told her my happy prospect, which she rejoiced much at. She was very gentle and rather low-spirited this day. I was much at home with her. I talked of love connections very freely. We insensibly slid into our own story without mentioning parties. We said many tender delicate things. I told her that I was thinking according to our agreement. "Well, then," said she, "I hope you will think as I do." "Madam," said I, "I hope you will think as I do. However, we shall see when the time is elapsed."

FRIDAY 31 DECEMBER. I waited on Louisa. The conversation turned upon love, whether we would or not. She mentioned one consequence that in an affair of gallantry might be troublesome. "I suppose, Madam," said I, "you mean if a third person should be interested in the affair. Why, to be sure, if such a person should appear, he must be taken care of. For my own part, I have the strongest principles of that kind." "Well, Sir," said she, with a sweet complacency. "But we won't talk any more on the subject."

SATURDAY 1 JANUARY. I received for a suit of old clothes 11s., which came to me in good time. I went to Louisa at once. "Madam, I have been thinking seriously." "Well, Sir, I hope you are of my way of thinking." "I hope, Madam, you are of mine. I have considered this matter most seriously. The week is now elapsed, and I hope you will not be so cruel as to keep me in misery." (I then began to take some liberties.) "Nay, Sir—now—but do consider—" "Ah, Madam!" "Nay, but you are an encroaching creature!" (Upon this I advanced to the greatest freedom by a sweet elevation of the charming petticoat.) "Good heaven, Sir!" "Madam, I cannot help it. I adore you. Do you like me?" (She answered me with a warm kiss, and pressing me to her bosom, sighed, "O Mr. Boswell!") "But, my dear Madam! Permit me, I beseech you." "Lord, Sir, the people may come in." "How then can I be happy? What time? Do tell me." "Why, Sir, on Sunday afternoon my landlady, of whom I am most afraid, goes to church, so you may come here a little after three." "Madam, I thank you a thousand times." "Now, Sir, I have but one favour to ask of you. Whenever you cease to regard me, pray don't use me ill, nor treat me coldly. But inform me by a letter or any other way that it is over." "Pray, Madam, don't talk of such a thing. Indeed, we cannot answer for our affections. But you may depend on my behaving with civility and politeness."

SUNDAY 2 JANUARY. I had George Home at breakfast with me. He is a good honest fellow and applies well to his business as a merchant. He had seen me all giddiness at his father's, and was astonished to find me settled on so prudent a plan. As I have made it a rule to dine every Sunday at home, and have got my landlady to give us regularly on that day a piece of good roast beef with a warm apple pie, I was a little difficulted today, as our time of dining is three o'clock, just my hour of assignation. However, I got dinner to be at two, and at three I hastened to my charmer.

Here a little speculation on the human mind may well come in. For here was I, a young man full of vigour and vivacity, the favourite lover of a handsome actress and going to enjoy the full possession of my warmest wishes. And yet melancholy threw a cloud over my mind. I could relish nothing. I felt dispirited and languid. I approached Louisa with a kind of an uneasy tremor. I sat down. I toyed with her. Yet I was not inspired by Venus. I felt rather a delicate sensation of love than a violent amorous inclination for her. I was very miserable. I thought myself feeble as a gallant, although I had experienced the reverse many a time. Louisa knew not my powers. She might imagine me impotent. I sweated almost with anxiety, which made me worse. She behaved extremely well: did not seem to remember the occasion of our meeting at all. I told her I was very dull. Said she, "People cannot always command their spirits." The time of church was almost elapsed when I began to feel that I was still a man. I fanned the flame by pressing her alabaster breasts and kissing her delicious lips. I then barred the door of her dining-room, led her all fluttering into her bedchamber, and was just making a triumphal entry when we heard her landlady coming up. "O Fortune why did it happen thus?" would have been the exclamation of a Roman bard. We were stopped most suddenly and cruelly from the fruition of each other. She ran out and stopped the landlady from coming up. Then returned to me in the dining-room. We fell into each other's arms, sighing and panting, "O dear, how hard this is." "O Madam, see what you can contrive for me." "Lord, Sir, I am so frightened."

Her brother then came in. I recollected that I had been at no place of worship today. I begged pardon for a little and went to Covent

Garden Church, where there is evening service between five and six. I heard a few prayers and then returned and drank tea. She entertained us with her adventures when travelling through the country. Some of them were excellent. I told her she might make a novel. She said if I would put them together that she would give me material. I went home at seven. I was unhappy at being prevented from the completion of my wishes, and yet I thought that I had saved my credit for prowess, that I might through anxiety have not acted a vigorous part; and that we might contrive a meeting where I could love with ease and freedom.

MONDAY 3 JANUARY. I begged Louisa to invent some method by which we might meet in security. I insisted that she should go and pass the night with me somewhere. She begged time to think of it.

TUESDAY 4 JANUARY. Louisa told me that she would go with me to pass the night when she was sure that she would not be wanted at the playhouse next day; and she mentioned Saturday as convenient, being followed by Sunday, on which nothing is done. "But, Sir," said she, "may not this be attended with expense? I hope you'll excuse me." There was something so kind and so delicate in this hint that it charmed me. "No, Madam, it cannot be a great expense, and I can save on other articles to have money for this."

I then bethought me of a place to which Louisa and I might safely go. I went to my good friend Hayward's at the Black Lion, told him that I had married, and that I and my wife, who was to be in town on Saturday, would sleep in his house till I got a lodging for her. The King of Prussia says in one of his poems that gallantry comprises every vice. That of lying it certainly does, without which intrigue can never be carried on. But as the proverb says, in love and war all is fair. I who am a lover and hope to be a soldier think so. In this instance we could not be admitted to any decent house except as man and wife. Indeed, we are so if union of hearts be the principal requisite. We are so, at least for a time. How cleverly this can be done here.

WEDNESDAY 5 JANUARY. At nine Erskine and I went to Lord Eglinton's. His choice spirits were Lord Advocate, Sir James Macdonald, and Captain Johnstone of the Navy, son to Sir James. Erskine and I were most amazingly bashful and stupid. The conversation was all about the banks of Scotland; a method to burn ships at a distance, as by burning glasses; and other topics out of our way entirely. In short, we appeared to horrid disadvantage. Let never people form a character of a man from being a night in his company, especially a man of wit. George Selwyn, one of the brightest geniuses in England, of whom more good sayings are recorded than anybody, is often the dullest fellow that can be seen. He was a droll dog when at Oxford, and kept up a most earnest and grave correspondence with a reverend bishop on a point of controversial divinity: whether after receiving the Communion before Confirmation, he was in a reprobate state or in a state of grace. He kept up the disguise of mystical religion long and tormented the worthy prelate with his many grievous doubts. The letters he has by him. He was at last expelled the University for a piece of gross profanity, giving the sacrament to a dog. He did it literally, to a degree of craziness. He cut his arm and made the dog drink his blood, saying, "This is my blood, &c."

We stayed till near three. I was really uneasy going home. Robberies in the street are now very frequent. The night air, too, is very bad for the health, and always hurts me. I resolved to be determined against suppers, and always to be at home early, in spite of every temptation.

THURSDAY 6 JANUARY. I then walked into the City. I took a whim that between St. Paul's and the Exchange and back again, taking the different sides of the street, I would eat a penny Twelfth-cake at every shop where I could get it. This I performed most faithfully.

I drank tea at Dempster's. Erskine and Lady Anne were there. We laughed a good deal.

FRIDAY 7 JANUARY. Captain Maxwell and my brother breakfasted with me. I then waited on Louisa. She informed me that Saturday could not be the hoped-for time to bestow perfect felicity upon me. "Not," said she, "that I have changed my mind. But it cannot be." In short, I understood that Nature's periodical effects on the human, or more properly female, constitution forbade it. I was a little uneasy at this, though it could not be helped. It kept me longer anxious till my ability was known. I have, together with my vivacity and good humour, a great anxiety of temper which often renders me uneasy. My grandfather had it in a very strong degree.

SATURDAY 8 JANUARY. I dined at Gould's. Mrs. Douglas was there. She and I chatted away with much vivacity. I feel myself now quite easy at Colonel Gould's. He is a most amiable man. I like him much for his great degree of indolence. He loves to lie abed dearly, and gently grumbles at the thoughts of undergoing the fatigue of dressing. This is a pretty sort of account of my good friend. But I believe I have already mentioned his being a man of good sense, good temper, and regular conduct. I wish I could do him any good. He and I are growing better together every day. I asked him if he was severe upon the men. "No," said he. "I have too great an aversion at trouble myself to give them any."

Young Buckley, the son, takes me by the hand as his friend and there we talk away most intimately and most keenly. Miss Fanny runs smiling to me, sets her chair close by mine, directs her lively prattle with a most engaging vehemence to me, asks me many questions, and has a great respect for my opinion. And then we will read together a little tale, or a fable of Gay's, and sing some smart lively song. She is a very fine child, and will probably be one of the first beauties and clever women in England. She has a grandmother who may give her a very handsome fortune, and in that case she will be a most elegant match for a man of spirit. I call her sometimes Mrs. Boswell. She is very angry, to be sure; crests up her little head and tells me I am very impertinent. Then by and by takes me by the hand and throws out a sparkling sally of life. Were many people to read this leaf of my journal, they would hold me in great contempt as a very trifling fellow. But surely what Mr. Churchill calls *the grave triflers* are neither so wise nor so happy as he who can give his time and attention now and then to the rising sprouts of humanity and derive simplicity of feeling and gaiety of heart from children.

SUNDAY 9 JANUARY. I heard an excellent sermon at St. Martin's Church by Mr. Sumner, Master of Harrow School. His text was, "My yoke is easy." He showed that although religion might in some respects be called a yoke, as it laid some restraint upon the inclinations and passions of men, yet to a mind properly trained it was easy, nay delightful. The happiness of genuine piety he displayed in elegant language enforced by just and animated action.

After church I went in sober yet gay humour to Louisa and got her to fix Wednesday without fail as the happy night. I then called for Mr. Craufurd of Auchenames in Ayrshire and Errol in Fife, who received me with uncommon kindness, told me that he heard I was wanting to get into the Guards, and if he could do me any service, I might command him.

MONDAY 10 JANUARY. I waited on Lady Northumberland and expressed my joy at hearing that the Marquis of Granby was in a fair way of recovery, and would soon be over. "I hope, Madam," said I, "you will not forget me." "No, Sir," said she, "you may be sure I will not." As I hope to have the honour of a forenoon's conversation with her Ladyship every week, I shall enrich my journal with it in the form of the original dialogue.

LADY NORTHUMBERLAND. There was a gentleman presented yesterday on his getting a commission in the Guards. I thought of you, Mr. Boswell.

BOSWELL. Ay, the Guards. Madam; that is the thing. Really, I have been thinking on the subject since I saw you, and must tell your Ladyship that the Guards is the particular thing that I have always been fond of, just like the woman that a man is in love with.

LADY NORTHUMBERLAND. Why, Sir, I wish we may get you into the Guards.

BOSWELL. The thing is this, that I am anxious to live in London, and besides the exercise of the Horse would be disagreeable to me, whereas in the Guards my duty would be quite a pleasure to me.

LADY NORTHUMBERLAND. Indeed, Sir, that is of a good deal of consequence. I shall therefore present you to the Marquis as a friend of mine who is very desirous to serve in the Guards, and next to that in his own corps. He is a good-natured man and is therefore ready to give his promise.

BOSWELL. I wish I had this commission of mine.

LADY NORTHUMBERLAND. I wish you had. Could not you have the thing mentioned to your countryman, Lord Rothes?

BOSWELL. I was yesterday, Madam, with a Scotch Member, a brother of General Craufurd's, who is very intimate with Lord Rothes and promised to introduce me. But you know, Madam, there is a delicacy in talking to a colonel when a man is not to purchase, as he gets the profits of the commissions that are sold.

LADY NORTHUMBERLAND. Indeed, Sir, it would be the best thing for you to purchase if you could.

BOSWELL. But then, Madam, my father is rather averse to the scheme and would not advance the money; and by borrowing it, I should bring myself into difficulties. Indeed, I am determined to purchase if I cannot get in without it.

TUESDAY 11 JANUARY. I am amazed how I have neglected last Friday to mention a circumstance so very material to me as the payment of my allowance, which indeed elevated me to a most extraordinary pitch. Many a time did I lay the lovely shining pieces upon my table, count them over, put them in rank and file like the Guards, and place them in many different sorts of figures. In short, a boy at school could not be more childishly fond of sugar plums than I was of golden guineas.

This day I had some agreeable conversation with my dear Louisa. All was now agreed upon. I had been at Hayward's on Saturday morning and told that we could not be there that night, as my wife was not come to town. But that we would be there next week and take our chance for a bed. And here a hint or two of Louisa's history may well come in. She was born of very creditable parents in London. But being too strictly confined, she ran off and married heedlessly. She was obliged for subsistence to go upon the stage, and travelled in different companies. Her husband proved a harsh, disagreeable creature, with whom she led a terrible life; at last, as it was discovered that they were illegally married, they parted by consent, and she got into Covent Garden Theatre.

WEDNESDAY 12 JANUARY. Louisa and I agreed that at eight at night she would meet me in the Piazzas of Covent Garden. I was quite elevated, and felt myself able and undaunted to engage in the wars of the Paphian Queen.

At the appointed hour of eight I went to the Piazzas, where I sauntered up and down for a while in a sort of trembling suspense, I knew not why. At last my charming companion appeared, and I immediately conducted her to a hackney-coach which I had ready waiting, pulled up the blinds, and away we drove to the destined scene of delight. We contrived to seem as if we had come off a journey, and carried in a bundle our night-clothes, handkerchiefs, and other little things. We also had with us some almond biscuits, as they call them in London, macaroons, which looked like provision on the road. On our arrival at Hayward's we were shown into the parlour, in the same manner that any decent couple would be. I here thought proper to conceal my own name (which the people of the house had never heard), and assumed the name of Mr. Digges. We were shown up to the very room where he slept. I said my cousin, as I called him, was very well. That Ceres and Bacchus might in moderation lend their assistance to Venus, I ordered a genteel supper and some wine.

Louisa told me she had two aunts who carried her over to France when she was a girl, and that she could once speak French as fluently as English. We talked a little in it, and agreed that we would improve ourselves by reading and speaking it every day. I asked her if we did not just look like man and wife. "No," said she, "we are too fond for married people." No wonder that she may have a bad idea of that union, considering how bad it was for her. She has contrived a pretty device for a seal. A heart is gently warmed by Cupid's flame, and Hymen comes with his rude torch and extinguishes it. She said she found herself quite in a flutter. "Why, really," said I, "reason sometimes has no power. We have no occasion to be frightened, and yet we are both a little so. Indeed, I preserve a tolerable presence of mind." I rose and kissed her, and conscious that I had no occasion to doubt my qualifications as a gallant, I joked about it: "How curious would it be if I should be so frightened that we should rise as we lay down." She reproved my wanton language by a look of modesty. The bells of St. Bride's church rung their merry chimes hard by. I said that the bells in Cupid's court would be this night set a-ringing for joy at our union.

We supped cheerfully and agreeably and drank a few glasses, and then the maid came and put the sheets, well aired, upon the bed. I now contemplated my fair prize. Louisa is just twenty-four, of a tall rather than short figure, finely made in person, with a handsome face and an enchanting languish in her eyes. She dresses with taste. She has sense, good humour, and vivacity, and looks quite a woman in genteel life. As I mused on this elevating subject, I could not help being somehow pleasingly confounded to think that so fine a woman was at this moment in my possession, that without any motives of interest she had come with me to an inn, agreed to be my intimate companion, as to be my bedfellow all night, and to permit me the full enjoyment of her person.

When the servant left the room, I embraced her warmly and begged that she would not now delay my felicity. She declined to undress before me, and begged I would retire and send her one of the maids. I did so, gravely desiring the girl to go up to Mrs. Digges. I then took a candle in my hand and walked out to the yard. The night was very dark and very cold. I experienced for some minutes the rigours of the season, and called into my mind many terrible ideas of hardships, that I might make a transition from such dreary thoughts to the most gay and delicious feelings. I then caused made a bowl of negus, very rich of the fruit, which I caused be set in the room as a reviving cordial.

I came softly into the room, and in a sweet delirium slipped into bed and was immediately clasped in her snowy arms and pressed to her milk-white bosom. Good heavens, what a loose did we give to amorous dalliance! The friendly curtain of darkness concealed our blushes. In a moment I felt myself animated with the strongest powers of love, and from my dearest creature's kindness, had a most luscious feast. Proud of my godlike vigour, I soon resumed the noble game. I was in full glow of health. Sobriety had preserved me from effeminacy and weakness, and my bounding blood beat quick and high alarms. A more voluptuous night I never enjoyed. Five times was I fairly lost in supreme rapture. Louisa was madly fond of me; she declared I was a prodigy, and asked me if this was not extraordinary for human nature. I said twice as much might be, but this was not, although in my own mind I was somewhat proud of my performance. She said it was what there was no just reason to be proud of. But I told her I could not help it. She said it was what we had in common with the beasts. I said no. For we had it highly improved by the pleasures of sentiment. I asked her what she thought enough. She gently chid me for asking such questions, but said two times. I mentioned the Sunday's assignation, when I was in such bad spirits, told her in what agony of mind I was, and asked her if she would not have despised me for my imbecility. She declared she would not, as it was what people had not in their own power.

She often insisted that we should compose ourselves to sleep before

I would consent to it. At last I sunk to rest in her arms and she in mine. I found the negus, which had a fine flavour, very refreshing to me. Louisa had an exquisite mixture of delicacy and wantonness that made me enjoy her with more relish. Indeed I could not help roving in fancy to the embraces of some other ladies which my lively imagination strongly pictured. I don't know if that was altogether fair. However, Louisa had all the advantage. She said she was quite fatigued and could neither stir leg nor arm. She begged I would not despise her, and hoped my love would not be altogether transient. I have painted this night as well as I could. The description is faint; but I surely may be styled a Man of Pleasure.

THURSDAY 13 JANUARY. We awaked from sweet repose after the luscious fatigues of the night. I got up between nine and ten and walked out till Louisa should rise. I patrolled up and down Fleet Street, thinking on London, the seat of Parliament and the seat of pleasure, and seeming to myself as one of the wits in King Charles the Second's time. I then came in and we had an agreeable breakfast, after which we left Hayward's, who said he was sorry he had not more of our company, and calling a hackney-coach, drove to Soho Square, where Louisa had some visits to pay. So we parted. Thus was the conquest completed to my highest satisfaction. I can with pleasure trace the progress of this intrigue to its completion. I am now at ease on that head, having my fair one fixed as my own. As Captain Plume says, the best security for a woman's mind is her body. I really conducted this affair with a manliness and prudence that pleased me very much. The whole expense was just eighteen shillings.

FRIDAY 14 JANUARY. I drank tea with Louisa. There was one of the least men I ever saw at tea with us, on whom Louisa threw out many diverting jokes. At night I went to Lady Northumberland's. There was a very full meeting, and many people of my acquaintance, so that I was at my ease and had plenty of conversation. I strutted up and down, considering myself as a valiant man who could gratify a lady's loving desires five times in a night; and I satisfied my pride by considering that if this and all my other great qualities were known, all the women almost in the room would be making love to me. This evening I was accosted by a lady of quality whom I was a little acquainted with, and to whom I shall give the name of Lady Mirabel. Thus went our conversation:

LADY MIRABEL. You don't play, Mr. Boswell.
BOSWELL. No, Madam, I never do; and yet I am very well amused here. I can have a great deal of entertainment just by looking around me. A man,

Madam, who can be happy thus must either be very stupid or more clever than ordinary.

LADY MIRABEL. Indeed, Sir, he must be extremely clever.

BOSWELL. Well, Madam, I think I have made out what I wanted very well. But pray don't you think the meetings here of people of fashion very dull? There seems to be no communication between men and women. They seldom speak to each other.

LADY MIRABEL. True, but when they do speak, they speak to the purpose.

BOSWELL. Bravo! Indeed they do that. But they want sentiment.

LADY MIRABEL. And therefore it is that their connections last only for a winter. It is very different abroad.

BOSWELL. You must know, Madam, I run up and down this town just like a wild colt.

LADY MIRABELL. Why, Sir, then, don't you stray into my stable, amongst others?

BOSWELL. Madam, I shall certainly have that pleasure.

From this conversation and Lady Mirabel's looks, I entertained some notion that an intrigue would not be disagreeable to her Ladyship. Lady Mirabel is a widow of middle age, has a jointure sufficient to live genteelly upon; although not pretty she has a fine air and is very agreeable. In short, whether I succeed or not, this may be an amusing pursuit.

Lord Eglinton really paid court to me. He asked me how I had been this long time, and hoped that I heard of his being at my door several times. He insisted that I should sup with him. He said he had several very clever fellows, amongst whom was Erskine. But I told him that I never was abroad at night, for that I was in love with a fine woman and wanted to keep myself healthy, stout and strong.

SATURDAY 15 JANUARY. I then called at Louisa's, and begged to be allowed what I most desired. She would not consent today, as everybody was at home, but said that next day at one her landlady would be abroad, and I might come then. I begged to know if she had any intrigues since she parted with her husband. She confessed that she had one, but that it was now over, and the gentleman was not in Britain. My being afraid of a rival was a sure sign of a sincere passion.

SUNDAY 16 JANUARY. I then went to Louisa and was permitted the rites of love with great complacency; yet I felt my passion for Louisa much gone. I felt a degree of coldness for her and I observed an affectation about her which disgusted me. I had a strong proof of my own inconstancy of disposition, and I considered that any woman who married me must be miserable. Here I argued wrong. For as a licentious love is merely the child of passion, it has no sure ground to hope for a long continuance, as passion may be extinguished with the most sudden and trifling breath of wind; but rational esteem founded on just motives must in all probability endure, especially when the opinion of the world and many other considerations contribute to strengthen and preserve it. Louisa and I began this day to read French. Our book was a little light piece of French gallantry entitled *Journal Amoureux*. She pronounced best and I translated best. Between us we did very well.

TUESDAY 18 JANUARY. I then called for Lady Mirabel. She seemed to like me a good deal. I was lively, and I looked like the game. As it was my first visit, I was very quiet. However, it was agreed that I should visit her often. This elated me, as it afforded a fine, snug, and agreeable prospect of gallantry. Yet I could not think of being unfaithful to Louisa. But, then, I thought Louisa was only in the mean time, till I got into genteel life, and that a woman of fashion was the only proper object for such a man as me. At last delicate honour prevailed, and I resolved for some time at least to keep alive my affection for Louisa.

I this day began to feel an unaccountable alarm of unexpected evil: a little heat in the members of my body sacred to Cupid, very like a symptom of that distemper with which Venus, when cross, takes it into her head to plague her votaries. But then I had run no risks. I had been with no woman but Louisa; and sure she could not have such a thing. Away then with such idle fears, such groundless, uneasy apprehensions! When I came to Louisa's, I felt myself stout and well, and most courageously did I plunge into the fount of love, and had vast pleasure as I enjoyed her as an actress who had played many a fine lady's part. She was remarkably fond of me today, and sighing said, "What will become of me if I lose you now?"

At five I went to Sheridan's. In order to explain my errand there, I must give a narration of several sentences. Mrs. Sheridan some weeks ago asked me to write a prologue to her new comedy. She said there were very few good poets in this age; and she said that if they had been in good terms with Johnson, she would have asked him. Her applying to me after this no doubt flattered me a good deal. She said there were few who had sense and temper enough to allow a fair criticism on their verses, as they were too much attached to their favourite productions. But I told her she need be under no apprehension of making me angry, for that I was perfectly easy in that respect. Indeed, my ease proceeds not from the good sense it might be imputed to, but from a carelessness of fame and a happy indifference, from a thorough conviction of the vanity of all things. As I had written no verses for some months, the task appeared very formidable. However, I wrote one which she said had good lines but was too general. I therefore wrote another, which she said was near the mark, and with a little polishing would do. The thing now pleased me exceedingly. I thought it fine to have my lines spoken by Mr. Garrick and resounding through Drury Lane. I mentioned it to the Kellies and the Dempsters, and walked about elated, but would not let them hear it. To get a definite answer about this prologue was now my errand to Sheridan's. I must observe that from the first Sheridan himself never seemed hearty in the thing. I bid Mrs. Sheridan not show it him, as he was a severe critic. After sitting a little, he said, "Why, Sir, you don't ask about your prologue?" "Indeed," said I, "I am too indifferent."

> SHERIDAN. Well, but prepare your utmost philosophy.
> BOSWELL. How so?
> SHERIDAN. It is weighed in the balances and found light.
> BOSWELL. What, is not good?
> SHERIDAN. Indeed, I think it is very bad.
> BOSWELL. Pray, Mrs. Sheridan, what is the meaning of this?
> MRS. SHERIDAN. Mr. Sheridan, Sir, does not like it, and he has insisted upon me to write one which he thinks will do.

"Oho!" thought I, "is this it?" I then desired to hear the faults of mine. Sheridan pointed them out with an insolent bitterness and a clumsy ridicule that hurt me much, and when I answered them, bore down my words with a boisterous vociferation. It is incredible with what seeming good humour I behaved. I declared that I must either be a man of the finest temper or the nicest art. He then read Mrs. Sheridan's, which was much duller, as I thought.

We disputed about poems. Sheridan said that a man should not be a poet except he was very excellent; for that to be a *mediocris poeta* was but a poor thing. I said I differed from him. For the greatest part of those who read poetry have a mediocre taste; consequently one may please a great many. Besides, to write poems is very agreeable, and one has always people enough to call them good; so that a man of a tolerable genius rather gains than loses.

I returned to Lady Betty's at six really a good deal mortified, and in that sort of humour that made me consider writing as a dangerous thing and wish that I had never wrote and think I would not write again.

WEDNESDAY 19 JANUARY. This was a day eagerly expected by Dempster, Erskine, and I, as it was fixed as the period of our gratifying a whim proposed by me: which was that on the first day of the new tragedy called *Elvira*'s being acted, we three should walk from the one end of London to the other, dine at Dolly's, and be in the theatre at night; and as the play would probably be bad, and as Mr. David Malloch, the author, who has changed his name to David Mallet, Esq., was an arrant puppy, we determined to exert ourselves in damning it. I this morning felt stronger symptoms of the sad distemper, yet I was unwilling to imagine such a thing. However, the severe exercise of today, joined with hearty eating and drinking, I was sure would confirm or remove my suspicions.

We walked up to Hyde Park Corner, from whence we set out at ten. Our spirits were high with the notion of the adventure, and the variety that we met with as we went along is amazing. As the Spectator observes, one end of London is like a different country from the other in look and in manners. We eat an excellent breakfast at the Somerset Coffee-house. We turned down Gracechurch Street and went upon the top of London Bridge, from whence we viewed with a pleasing horror the rude and terrible appearance of the river, partly froze up, partly covered with enormous shoals of floating ice which often crashed against each other. Dempster said of this excursion from the road that our Epic Poem would be somewhat dull if it were not enlivened by such episodes. As we went along, I felt the symptoms increase, which was very confounding and very distressing to me. I thought the best thing I could do was not to keep it secret, which would be difficult and troublesome, but fairly to own it to Dempster and Erskine and ask their advice and sympathy. They really sympathized, and yet they could not help smiling a little at my catching a tartar so very unexpectedly, when I imagined myself quite safe, and had been vaunting most heroically of my felicity in having the possession of a fine woman, to whom I ascribed so many endearing qualities that they really doubted of her existence, and used to call her my *ideal lady*. We went half a mile beyond the turnpike at Whitechapel, which completed our course, and went into a little public house and drank some warm white wine with aromatic spices, pepper and cinnamon. We were pleased with the neat houses upon the road.

The evening was passed most cheerfully. When I got home, though, then came sorrow. Too, too plain was Signor Gonorrhoea. Yet I could scarce believe it, and determined to go to friend Douglas next day.

THURSDAY 20 JANUARY. I rose very disconsolate, having rested very ill by the poisonous infection raging in my veins and anxiety and vexation boiling in my breast. I could scarcely credit my own senses. What! thought I, can this beautiful, this sensible, and this agreeable woman be so sadly defiled? Can corruption lodge beneath so fair a form? Can she who professed delicacy of sentiment and sincere regard for me, use me so very basely and so very cruelly? No, it is impossible. I have just got a gleet by irritating the parts too much with excessive venery. And yet these damned twinges, that scalding heat, and that deep-tinged loathsome matter are the strongest proofs of an infection. But she certainly must think that I would soon discover her falsehood. But perhaps she was ignorant of her being ill. A pretty conjecture indeed! No, she could not be ignorant. Yes, yes, she intended to make the most of me. And now I recollect that the day we went to Hayward's, she showed me a bill of thirty shillings about which she was in some uneasiness, and no doubt expected that I would pay it. But I was too cautious, and she had not effrontery enough to try my generosity in direct terms so soon after my letting her have two guineas. And am I then taken in? Am I, who have had safe and elegant intrigues with fine women, become the dupe of a strumpet? Am I now to be laid up for many weeks to suffer extreme pain and full confinement, and to be debarred all the comforts and pleasures of life? And then must I have my poor pocket drained by the unavoidable expense of it? And shall I no more (for a long time at least) take my walk, healthful and spirited, round the Park before breakfast, view the brilliant Guards on the Parade, and enjoy all my pleasing amusements? And then am I prevented from making love to Lady Mirabel, or any other woman of fashion? O dear, O dear! What a cursed thing this is! What a miserable creature am I!

In this woeful manner did I melancholy ruminate. I thought of applying to a quack who would cure me quickly and cheaply. But then the horrors of being imperfectly cured and having the distemper thrown into my blood terrified me exceedingly. I therefore pursued my resolution of last night to go to my friend Douglas, whom I knew to be skillful and careful; and although it should cost me more, yet to get sound health was a matter of great importance, and I might save upon other articles. I accordingly went and breakfasted with him.

Mrs. Douglas, who has a prodigious memory and knows a thousand anecdotes, especially of scandal, told me that Congreve the poet lived in the family of old Lord Godolphin, who is yet alive, and that Lady Godolphin was notoriously fond of him. In so much that her lord having gone abroad upon an embassy for two years, on his return she presented him with a fine girl by the author of *Love For Love*, which he was so indulgent as to accept of; nay, after Congreve's death, he joined with her in grief, and allowed her to have an image of him in wax daily set at table and nightly in her bedcbamber, to which she spoke, believing it through heat of fancy, or believing it in appearnace, to be Congreve himself. The young lady was most tenderly educated, and it is a certain fact that she was never suffered to see the moon for fear she should cry for it. She is now Duchess of Leeds, and has turned out extremely well.

After breakfast Mrs. Douglas withdrew, and I opened my sad case to Douglas, who upon examining the parts, declared I had got an evident infection and that the woman who gave it me could not but know of it. I joked with my friend about the expense, asked him if he would take a draught on my arrears, and bid him visit me seldom that I might have the less to pay. To these jokes he seemed to give little heed, but talked seriously in the way of his business. And here let me make a just and true observation, which is that the same man as a friend and as a surgeon exhibits two very opposite characters. Douglas as a friend is most kind, most anxious for my interest, made me live ten days in his house, and suggested every plan of economy. But Douglas as a surgeon will be as ready to keep me long under his hands, and as desirous to lay hold of my money, as any man. In short, his views alter quite. I have to do not with him but his profession.

As Lady Northumberland was to have a great rout next day, I delayed beginning my course of medicine till Friday night. Enraged at the perfidy of Louisa, I resolved to go and upbraid her most severely; but this I thought was not acting with dignity enough. So I would talk to her coolly and make her feel her own unworthiness. But hearing the Duke of Queensberry was in town, I thought I would go and have one more brush at him and hear what he had to say.

When I entered, he looked somewhat abashed and timid, which encouraged me. "My Lord," said I, "I got your Grace's letter, and was sorry for the contents. Your Grace was pleased to mention my following a civil life. I should be glad to know what. The law I am not able for. If indeed I could be put upon the civil list for about a thousand a year, as Sir Francis Wronghead says, I should like it very well." At this he laughed. He then talked of the difficulty of getting a commission. "Certainly," said I, "my Lord Duke, it is very difficult. But your Grace has never yet mentioned me to Lord Ligonier. I should be sorry to give your Grace a great deal of trouble, but I should think that it would not be much to mention the thing once, so as I might be put upon Lord Ligonier's list." He promised to me that he would mention it. In short, I find that indolence was the matter with him, and that he must be pushed, although I have but little hopes from him.

I then went to Louisa. With excellent address did I carry on this interview, as the following scene, I trust, will make appear.

LOUISA. My dear Sir! I hope you are well today.

BOSWELL. Excessively well, I thank you. I hope I find you so.

LOUISA. No, really, Sir. I am distressed with a thousand things. (Cunning jade, her circumstances!) I really don't know what to do.

BOSWELL. Do you know that I have been very unhappy since I saw you?

LOUISA. How so, Sir?

BOSWELL. Why, I am afraid that you don't love me so well, nor have not such a regard for me, as I thought you had.

LOUISA. Nay, dear Sir! (Seeming unconcerned.)

BOSWELL. Pray, Madam, have I no reason?

LOUISA. No, indeed, Sir, you have not.

BOSWELL. Have I no reason, Madam? Pray think.

LOUISA. Sir!

BOSWELL. Pray, Madam, in what state of health have you been in for some time?

LOUISA. Sir, you amaze me.

BOSWELL. I have but too strong, too plain reason to doubt of your regard. I have for some days observed the symptoms of disease, but was unwilling to believe you so very ungenerous. But now, Madam, I am thoroughly convinced.

LOUISA. Sir, you have terrified me. I protest I know nothing of the matter.

BOSWELL. Madam, I have had no connection with any woman but you these two months. I was with my surgeon this morning, who declared I had got a strong infection, and that she from whom I had it could not be ignorant of it. Madam, such a thing in this case is worse than from a woman of the town, as from her you may expect it. You have used me very ill. I did not deserve it. You know you said where there was no confidence, there was no breach of trust. But surely I placed some confidence in you. I am sorry that I was mistaken.

LOUISA. Sir, I will confess to you that about three years ago I was very bad. But for these fifteen months I have been quite well. I appeal to God Almighty that I am speaking true; and for these six months I have had to do with no man but yourself.

BOSWELL. But by G—D, Madam, I have been with none but you, and here am I very bad.

LOUISA. Well, Sir, by the same solemn oath I protest that I was ignorant of it.

BOSWELL. Madam, I wish much to believe you. But I own I cannot upon this occasion believe a miracle.

LOUISA. Sir, I cannot say more to you. But you will leave me in the greatest misery. I shall lose your esteem. I shall be hurt in the opinion of everybody, and in my circumstances.

BOSWELL (to himself). What the devil does the confounded jilt mean by being hurt in her circumstances? This is the grossest cunning. But I won't take notice of that at all.—Madam, as to the opinion of everybody, you need not be afraid. I was going to joke and say that I never boast of a lady's *favours*. But I give you my word of honour that you shall not be discovered.

LOUISA. Sir, this is being more generous than I could expect.

BOSWELL. I hope, Madam, you will own that since I have been with you I have always behaved like a man of honour.

LOUISA. You have indeed, Sir.

BOSWELL (rising). Madam, your most obedient servant.

During all this conversation I really behaved with a manly composure and polite dignity that could not fail to inspire an awe, and she was pale as ashes and trembled and faltered. Thrice did she insist on my staying a little longer, as it was probably the last time that I should be with her. She could say nothing to the purpose. And I sat silent. As I was going, said she, "I hope, Sir, you will give me leave to inquire after your health." "Madam," said I, archly, "I fancy it will be needless for some weeks." She again renewed her request. But unwilling to be plagued any more with her, I put her off by saying I might perhaps go to the country, and left her. I was really confounded at her behaviour. There is scarcely a possibility that she could be innocent of the crime of horrid imposition. And yet her positive asseverations really stunned me. She is in all probability a most consummate dissembling whore.

Thus ended my intrigue with the fair Louisa, which I flattered myself so much with, and from which I expected at least a winter's safe copulation. It is indeed very hard. I cannot say, like young fellows who get themselves clapped in a bawdy-house, that I will take better care again. For I really did take care. However, since I am fairly trapped, let me make the best of it. I have not got it from imprudence. It is merely the chance of war.

I then called at Drury Lane for Mr. Garrick. He was vastly good to me. "Sir," said he, "you will be a very great man. And when you are so, remember the year 1763. I want to contribute my part towards saving you. And pray, will you fix a day when I shall have the pleasure of treating you with tea?" I fixed next day. "Then, Sir," said he, "the cups shall dance and the saucers skip."

What he meant by my being a great man I can understand. For really, to speak seriously, I think there is a blossom about me of something more distinguished than the generality of mankind. But I am much afraid that this blossom will never swell into fruit, but will be nipped and destroyed by many a blighting heat and chilling frost. Indeed, I sometimes indulge noble reveries of having a regiment, of getting into Parliament, making a figure, and becoming a man of consequence in the state. But these are checked by dispiriting reflections on my melancholy temper and imbecility of mind. Yet I may probably become sounder and stronger as I grow up.

I dined at Lady Betty's, as I resolved to live well these two days, knowing that severe starving would be my lot for some weeks after. I was now very sick and in very great pain. Yet we were merry enough.

FRIDAY 21 JANUARY. I then called on Lord Eglinton—no, I mistake, it was yesterday that I was there. I am scrupulous to a nicety about truth. He discovered by my looks that I was ill. I went with him into another room and confessed my misfortune. He was going to blame my rashness at first, but upon my telling him that my Dulcinea was an actress, he was silent. I told him I have had several intrigues within these two years, and that if I was taken in but once in four or five times, I was not unlucky. He agreed to all this. He was really kind today. I loved him.

I next went to Lady Northumberland's grand rout. I was in severe distress and grew very low-spirited. I cared for nothing, and I thought life very tiresome. I chatted a little with Lady Mirabel, but she was dissipated by the crowd and hurry. I got no speaking to Lady Northumberland, and I could scarce keep my dreary humour from persuading me that she despised me, a sure sign of the spleen, which makes us always imagine that we are despised. I chatted a while with Lord Eglinton. He promised that when I got sound, he would introduce me to some women of intrigue of the highest fashion. I came home in bad situation both of body and mind. I had informed my landlord of my misfortune, that everything might be got convenient for me, about which he was very obliging. I laid by my hat and sword, begun to take medicine, and coolly resolved to endure my ill chance patiently.

SATURDAY 22 JANUARY. Calmly and considerately did I sit down in my arm-chair this morning and endeavour to call up all the philosophy that I could. A distemper of this kind is more dreadful to me than most people. I am of a warm constitution: a complexion, as physicians say, exceedingly amorous, and therefore suck in the poison more deeply. I have had two visitations of this calamity. The first lasted ten weeks. The second four months. How severe a reflection is it! And, O, how severe a prospect! Yet let me take courage. Perhaps this is not a very bad infection, and as I shall be scrupulously careful of myself, I may get rid of it in a short time.

SUNDAY 23 JANUARY. I was very dull this day. I considered the Guards as a most improper scene of life for me. I thought it would yield me no pleasure, for my constitution would be gone, and I would not be able to enjoy life. I thought London a bad place for me. I imagined I had lost all relish of it. Nay, so very strange is wayward, diseased fancy that it will make us wish for the things most disagreeable to us merely to procure a change of objects, being sick and tired of those it presently has. I thought I would go immediately down to Edinburgh, and would be an advocate in the Parliament House, and so lead a comfortable life. I was vexed to find all my gay plans vanished, and I had a struggle between hope and despair.

MONDAY 24 JANUARY. What will now become of my journal for some time? It must be a barren desert, a mere blank. To relate gravely that I rose, made water, took drugs, sat quiet, read a book, saw a friend or two day after day, must be exceedingly poor and tedious. My journal must therefore, like the newspapers, yield to the times.

TUESDAY 25 JANUARY. This afternoon, by taking too much physic, I felt myself very ill. I was weak. I shivered, and I had flushes of heat. I began to be apprehensive that I was taking a nervous fever, a supposition not improbable, as I had one after such an illness when I was last in London. I was quite sunk. I looked with a degree of horror upon death. Some of my intrigues which in high health and spirits I valued myself upon now seemed to be deviations from the sacred road of virtue. My mind fluctuated, but grew more composed. I looked up to the beneficent Creator. I was resigned and more easy, and went to bed in hope.

SATURDAY 29 JANUARY. I amused myself with writing letters. I continued in a good way. I have lived all this week on bread and tea. I would fain say something to keep up the practice of writing journal, like the Highlander who stole his pockets full of hay to keep his hand in use. I put down mere trifles. I have now one great satisfaction, which is reading Hume's *History*. It entertains and instructs me. It elevates my mind and excites noble feelings of every kind.

SUNDAY 30 JANUARY. I regretted much my being kept from divine service. I was not so well. I had more inflammation, so I caused Douglas blood me, which gave me relief. I now began to take a little better diet. I had a pound of veal made into a large bowl of weak broth. This gave me better spirits, and cherished my nerves.

WEDNESDAY 2 FEBRUARY. I had a visit of Captain Erskine, eldest son to Lady Frances. Dempster drank tea with me. We talked of the House of Commons, and schemes of rising in the world. Dempster said he had a great deal of ambition, and yet much contentment. I asked him what his ambition extended to. He answered, "To be the first man in the Kingdom"—a fine idea no doubt but a chimerical one. I hinted that servility to the Court might be necessary: to stoop in order to rise. But he maintained that a man who kept himself quite independent, and who showed that he resolutely acted according to his conscience, would acquire respect, and would make his way honourably.

THURSDAY 3 FEBRUARY. I was not so well as yesterday. I was somewhat morose. I thought the treacherous Louisa deserved to suffer for her depravity. I therefore wrote her the following letter:

MADAM: —My surgeon will soon have a demand upon me of five guineas for curing the disease which you have given me. I must therefore remind you of the little sum which you had of me some time ago. You cannot have forgot upon what footing I let you have it. I neither *paid* it for prostitution nor *gave* it in charity. It was fairly borrowed, and you promised to return it. I give you notice that I expect to have it before Saturday sennight.

I have been very bad, but I scorn to upbraid you. I think it below me. If you are not rendered callous by a long course of disguised wickedness, I should think the consideration of your deceit and baseness, your corruption both of body and mind, would be a very severe punishment. Call not that a misfortune which is the consequence of your own unworthiness. I desire no mean evasions. I want no letters. Send the money sealed up. I have nothing more to say to you.

JAMES BOSWELL

This, I thought, might be a pretty bitter potion to her. Yet I thought to mention the money was not so genteel. However, if I get it (which is not probable), it will be of real service to me; and to such a creature as her a pecuniary punishment will give most pain. Am not I too vindictive? It appears so; but upon better consideration I am only sacrificing at the shrine of Justice; and sure I have chosen a victim that deserves it.

This day was the first representation of Mrs. Sheridan's comedy, *The Discovery*. As Dempster, Erskine, and I had made a resolution to be present at every first night, I determined to venture abroad, although I could not but hesitate for fear of being the worse of it. I had this forenoon visits from Lord Advocate and Dr. Pringle, so that I had two chariots in one day at my door. I told Lord Advocate that I could not do without employment; and that if I could not get into the Guards, I would go back to Scotland and join his society. But that in the mean time, I would take a full career of London, and perhaps roam a while abroad in France and Italy.

At three I swallowed an apple-tart, then wrapped myself well up in two pair of stockings, two shirts, and a greatcoat; and thus fortified against the weather, I got into a snug chair and was carried to Drury Lane. I took up my associates at the Rose Tavern, and we went into the pit at four, where, as they had not dined, they laid down their hats, one on each side of me, and there did I sit to keep their places. I was amused to find myself transported from my room of indisposition to the gay, gilded theatre. I put myself as much as possible into proper humour for seeing the play. Luckily, Dr. Goldsmith came into the seat behind me. I renewed my acquaintance with him, and he agreed to keep the same place for the night. His conversation revived in my mind the true ideas of London authors, which are to me something curious, and, as it were, mystical.

The evening went finely on. I felt a little pain when the prologue was spoke, considering how near I was to have had mine sounding away. We had several judicious and lively people round us, and kept up a clever enough chat. I wrought myself up to the imagination that it was the age of Sir Richard Steele, and that I was like him sitting in judgment on a new comedy.

This gave me much pleasure, in so much that I could have wished my two companions absent from me, as they brought down my ideas and made me imagine myself just at Edinburgh, which, though a kind of a comfortable idea, was not so high as what I was indulging. I find that I ought not to keep too much company with Scotch people, because I am kept from acquiring propriety of English speaking, and because they prevent my mind from being filled with London images, so that I might as well be in Scotland. For there is little or no difference between being with an entire Scotch company in a room in London and a room in Edinburgh.

This long digression has carried me quite away from the play. However, I may be glad now of any tolerable materials to furnish my journal with. The play really acted heavily. Dempster proposed its damnation. I would have agreed, had not I been tied up, as it would look like revenge for refusing my prologue. It was therefore allowed to jog through. Goldsmith said many smart acrimonious things. I stole quietly into a chair. As I was carried along and viewed the streets by the light of the lamps, I was amused by considering the variety of scenes going on in this metropolis with which I was now wholly unconnected during my state of confinement. Upon my coming home, I felt myself not so well. I dreaded the worse, and went to bed.

SUNDAY 6 FEBRUARY. Erskine drank tea with me.

We talked with relish on publishing and on the profits made by books and pamphlets. We both agreed that if we could get something worth while by our works, we would be very glad. Money got this way would be highly valued by us, and we would enjoy the pleasures which it purchased, with peculiar satisfaction. It is very agreeable to look forward and imagine that we shall probably write much, get much fame, and much gold.

I had now and then mentioned my journal to him. I read him a little of it this evening. To be sure it is very carelessly wrote, which he freely took notice, and said it might become a habit to me to write in that manner, so that I would learn a mere slatternly style. He advised me to take more pains upon it, and to render it useful by being a good method to practice writing: to turn periods and render myself ready at different kinds of expression. He is very right. I shall be more attentive for the future, and rather give a little neatly done than a good deal slovenly.

I am in spirits, you see. David Hume and John Dryden are at present my companions. Surely I am a man of genius. I deserve to be taken notice of. O that my grandchildren might read this character of me: "James Boswell, a most amiable man. He improved and beautified his paternal estate of Auchinleck; made a distinguished figure in Parliament; had the honour to command a regiment of footguards, and was one of the brightest wits in the court of George the Third."

As I formerly mentioned my giving orders to say that I was gone to the country, it may appear surprising that I should yet have so many visitors. But that surprise will soon vanish when I tell that these orders were countermanded. I found a little intercourse with the living world was necessary to keep my spirits from sinking into lethargic dulness or being soured to peevish discontent. My brother dined with me today. We did very well as companions.

WEDNESDAY 9 FEBRUARY. I got up excellently well. My present life is most curious, and very fortunately is become agreeable. My affairs are conducted with the greatest regularity and exactness. I move like very clock-work. At eight in the morning Molly lights the fire, sweeps and dresses my dining-room. Then she calls me up and lets me know what o'clock it is. I lie some time in bed indulging indolence, which in that way, when the mind is easy and cheerful, is most pleasing. I then slip on my clothes loosely, easily, and quickly, and come into my dining-room. I pull my bell. The maid lays a milk-white napkin upon the table and sets the things for breakfast. I then take some light amusing book and breakfast and read for an hour or more, gently pleasing both my palate and my mental taste. Breakfast over, I feel myself gay and lively. I go to the window, and am entertained with the people passing by, all intent on different schemes. To go regularly through the day would be too formal for this my journal. Besides, every day cannot be passed exactly the same way in every particular. My day is in general diversified with reading of different kinds, playing on the violin, writing, chatting with my friends.

Even the taking of medicines serves to make time go on with less heaviness. I have a sort of genius for physic and always had great entertainment in observing the changes of the human body and the effects produced by diet, labour, rest, and physical operations.

As I am now in tolerable health, my appetite is very good, and I eat my slender bit of dinner with great relish. I drink a great deal of tea. Between eleven and twelve my bed is warmed and I go calmly to repose. I am not at all unsatisfied with this kind of existence. It is passing my portion of time very comfortably. Most philosophically do I reason upon this subject, being certainly the most important one to me at present. I consider that although I want many pleasures which are to be had by being abroad, yet I also want many pains. I am troubled with no dirty streets nor no jostling chairmen. Multitudes of ideas float through my fancy on both sides of the question. I shall now and then put some of them down as they strike me strongly.

I now made a very near calculation of my expenses for the year, and found that I would be able to save £50 out of my allowance. This sum would be requisite for immediate necessaries in case of my getting a commission in the Guards, and I would have a pride to furnish it without any extraordinary assistance from my father, which it is reasonable he should allow in that event, as everybody thinks he should rig me out. However, if I can do without him, I must be called an excellent manager. Not satisfied with saving £50, I went to work still nearer, wishing to save £20 more, and with great thought and assiduity did I compute. In short, I found myself turning very fond of money and ruminating with a kind of transport on the idea of being worth £70 at the year's end. The desire of being esteemed a clever economist was no doubt mixed with it, but I seriously think that sheer love of coin was my predominant principle.

Upon my word my journal goes charmingly on at present. I was very apprehensive that there would be a dreary vacancy in it for some weeks, but by various happy circumstances I have been agreeably disappointed. I think, too, that I am making a good use of the hint which Captain Erskine gave me, and am taking more pains upon it, and consequently writing it in a more correct style. Style is to sentiment what dress is to the person.

How easily and cleverly do I write just now! I am really pleased with myself; words come skipping to me like lambs upon Moffat Hill; and I turn my periods smoothly and imperceptibly like a skillful wheelwright turning tops in a turning-loom. There's fancy! There's simile! In short, I am at present a genius: in that does my opulence consist, and not in base metal.

THURSDAY 10 FEBRUARY. This forenoon a maid from Louisa left a packet for me. It was most carefully sealed up, "by the hands of attention," but was not addressed to me. I opened it up and found my two guineas returned, without a single word written. I felt a strange kind of mixed confusion. My tender heart relented. I thought I had acted too harshly to her. I imagined she might—perhaps—have been ignorant of her situation. I was so foolish as to think of returning her the money and writing her a letter of atonement. I have too much of what Shakespeare calls "the milk of human kindness." I mentioned the thing to Dempster. He said it was just a piece of deep artifice in her. I resolved to think no more on the matter, and was glad that I had come off two guineas better than I expected.

FRIDAY 11 FEBRUARY. Nothing worth putting into my journal occurred this day. It passed away imperceptibly, like the whole life of many a human existence.

SUNDAY 13 FEBRUARY. This was a most terrible day. None of my friends could come abroad to see me. I was really a good deal low-spirited all the forenoon. In the evening my mind cleared up. I was pleased and lively, and my genius was in fine humour for composition. I wrote several fanciful little essays, which pleased me highly. Well, the human mind is really curious: I can answer for my own. For here now in the space of a few hours I was a dull and a miserable, a clever and a happy mortal, and all without the intervention of any external cause, except a dish of green tea, which indeed is a most kind remedy in cases of this kind. Often have I found relief from it. I am so fond of tea that I could write a whole dissertation on its virtues. It comforts and enlivens without the risks attendant on spirituous liquors. Gentle herb! Let the florid grape yield to thee. Thy soft influence is a more safe inspirer of social joy.

FRIDAY 18 FEBRUARY. At night I fell back into my melancholy mood. I was quite harassed with anxious discontent. I thought I would return to Scotland and drudge as a lawyer, which would please my father and gain me a character of prudence and also get me money and enable me to do good; and as I would not flatter myself with the expectation of much felicity, I would not be disappointed. But then I considered this scheme as the unripe fruit of vexatious thought and as what I would soon repent of. Then it pained me to the heart to think that all the gay schemes which I had planned were to prove abortive, and that all my intentions of seeing the world should be frustrated. Never was any man more upon the fret than I now was.

SATURDAY 19 FEBRUARY. This morning my guardian angel smiled

upon me and whispered soft notes into my glad ears. I loved the Guards and I longed for my commission. The Marquis of Granby had now been come home some time. I regretted my losing this fresh occasion of reminding Lady Northumberland of her promise. I considered that time was now precious, and as I thought an apology necessary for my long absence, I wrote her this letter:

MADAM: —I have been indisposed and confined to the house for some weeks, which has prevented me from having the honour and pleasure of paying my duty to your Ladyship. I am now better and hope to be abroad soon. In the mean time, Madam, as my Lord Granby is now come over, permit me to put your Ladyship in mind of my commission. I have the honour to be, Madam, your obliged and faithful humble servant,

JAMES BOSWELL

Crookshanks, who is Lord Eglinton's steward in England, comes now and then to see me. He came this forenoon and entered just on the same subject of the unhappiness of mortals. He is a spirited fellow, has read a good deal, and is much of a gentleman, but has at the same time much of what is called a *rattle*. He went on thus. "Damn me if I can see why God Almighty has created us all, just to complain and vex ourselves. By the Lord, I don't see who's happy, not I. And yet one may be happy with anything. I have been happy with buying a new gun, and have been in high spirits for a week with a new dog. By the Lord, Mr. Boswell, you have fine means of happiness by your turn for writing."

SUNDAY 20 FEBRUARY. I passed the day very comfortably. Captain Erskine was with me in the forenoon and we were very well together. Honest Captain Andrew! I must keep well with him. This forenoon I read the history of Joseph and his brethren, which melted my heart and drew tears from my eyes. It is simply and beautifully told in the Sacred Writings. It is a strange thing that the Bible is so little read. I am reading it regularly through at present. I dare say there are many people of distinction in London who know nothing about it. Were the history of Joseph published by some Genteel bookseller as an Eastern fragment and circulated amongst the gay world, I am persuaded that those who have any genuine taste might be taken in to admire it exceedingly and so by degrees have a due value for the oracles of GOD.

I set apart this day for taking medicine most effectually and keeping very warm, so was denied to everybody but those who were upon the footing of making good their way upstairs, notwithstanding of all my injunctions. I was quite in earnest to get quite free of this most terrible malady, which in my opinion is really a serious evil. I am sure it is so to me. But what I am most anxious about is to get it entirely eradicated, that I may recover perfect soundness of constitution and may not bring a race of poor sickly human beings into the world.

THURSDAY 24 FEBRUARY. This afternoon I was very high-spirited and full of ambition. I wanted much to be a man of consequence, and I considered that I could only be that in my own country, where my family and connections would procure it. I also considered that the law was my plain road to preferment. That if I would go to the Scotch bar I would soon be well employed, and as this confinement has made me see that I can sit in and labour very well, I thought I might be able very well to do business. By this means I would make money which would enable me to jaunt about wherever I pleased in the vacations. I would have an opportunity of being of much real use, of being of service to my friends by having weight in the country, and would make my father exceedingly happy.

I considered that my notions of an advocate were false. That I connected with that character low breeding and Presbyterian stiffness, whereas many of them were very genteel people. That I might have the wit and humour of Sir David Dalrymple, the jollity of Duncan Forbes, the whim of Baron Dalrymple, the show of Baron Maule, and the elegant taste of Baron Grant. I thought I might write books like Lord Kames and be a buck like Mr. James Erskine. That I might keep a handsome machine. Have a good agreeable wife and fine children and keep an excellent house. That I might show all the dull, vulgar, plodding young lawyers how easily superior parts can outstrip them.

I viewed this plan in every favourable light and become exceedingly fond of it. As I am most impetuous in whatever I take a fancy for, I was beginning to determine that I would write to my father and propose the thing to him, on condition that he made me a handsome settlement; that is to say, continued my £200 a year and agreed that I should have lodgings of my own and be quite an independent man. But then such a step taken precipitantly would not be the thing. I therefore thought I had better get his permission to go abroad for a year or two to Holland, where we have some Dutch relations, to France and to Italy; after which I would be better satisfied and more settled.

The law scheme appeared in another light. I considered it as bringing me back to a situation that I had long a rooted aversion to. That my father might agree to let me be upon the footing of independence, but when he had me under his eye, he would not be able to keep to it. I considered that I would at once embark myself for all my life in a labyrinth of care, and that my mind would be harassed with vexation. That the notion of being of consequence was not much, for that just now I knew from experience that just by strength of imagination I could strut about and think myself as great as any man. That the Guards was a situation of life that had always appeared most enchanting to me, as I could in that way enjoy all the elegant pleasures of the gay world, and by living in the Metropolis and having plenty of time, could pursue what studies and follow what whims I pleased, get a variety of acquaintances of all kinds, get a number of romantic adventures, and thus have my satisfaction of life. That if a man who is born to a fortune cannot make himself easier and freer than those who are not, he gains nothing. That if I should suddenly relinquish my favourite schemes, I should deservedly be considered as a man of no stability but inconstant and wavering with every breath. I considered that at present I was not a fair judge of a question of so much importance; that by a long course of confinement and medicine my animal spirits were necessarily tamed and my relish for pleasure and amusement and whim evaporated. That the mere satisfaction of ease after a situation of pain and the happy prospect of a recovery of health had elevated me too much and made me imagine nothing too difficult for me to compass. That indeed I had laboured hard, but it had been in writing my journal, letters, and essays, which were all works chiefly of the imagination. But that I would find it very irksome to sit for hours hearing a heavy agent explain a heavy cause, and then to be obliged to remember and repeat distinctly the dull story, probably of some very trivial affair.

I was anxious a little about my commission, and thought I should be disappointed in it and become peevish and turn a sort of misanthrope. But I summoned up more cheerful ideas and imagined that my noble Countess was pushing for me. At any rate, I determined to give it a year's run; and after that time I would be fully able to judge what to think of great people and what plan of life I should pursue.

SATURDAY 26 FEBRUARY. Last night Dempster came to me between ten and eleven and sat till one. He is really a most agreeable man; has fine sense, sweet dispositions, and the true manners of a gentleman. His sceptical notions give him a freedom and ease which in a companion is very pleasing, although to a man whose mind is possessed with serious thoughts of futurity, it is rather hurting to find them considered so lightly. He said he intended to write a treatise on the causes of happiness and misery.

SUNDAY 27 FEBRUARY. I had now kept the house five complete weeks, except that night when I was carried to *The Discovery*. My disorder was now over. Nothing but a gleet remained, which gave me no pain and which could be removed in three days. But I chose to give it a little longer time, that I might get clear of every the least tincture of infection. I thought, since I had been so much in earnest hitherto to have a complete cure, I would undoubtedly complete it. Douglas gave it as his opinion that I should confine myself no longer. There was no danger; and he thought a little air, exercise, and amusement would be of great use both to my health and spirits. This day the sun shone prettily, yet I doubted as to going abroad. However, a battalion of the Guards from Germany were this day to march into town; and when I heard the beat of their drums, I could not restrain my ardour, and thought this the happiest occasion for me to emerge from obscurity and confinement, to light and to life.

George Home was with me. I wrapped myself up in my greatcoat, and taking my staff in my hand, he accompanied me while I walked out to the Park. The Battalion was not drawn up on the Parade, as I expected, but was marched up to Lincoln's Inn Fields, so I lost that show. However, I was much obliged to my soldiers for bringing me fairly out. I might really have got a habit of laziness and become mopish altogether. The sweet elevation of spirits which I now felt is scarcely to be conceived. I was quite in an ecstasy. O how I admired all the objects around me! How I valued ease and health! To see the variety of people in the Park again put me all in a flutter. The sight of the Parade and the spendid Guards brought back my love to that profession with redoubled force. I was convinced that it was indeed the genuine object of my inclinations, and the only station in real life which (at least for some years) I could fill with pleasure.

I am now well and gay. Let me consider that the hero of a romance or novel must not go uniformly along in bliss, but the story must be chequered with bad fortune. Aeneas met with many disasters in his voyage to Italy, and must not Boswell have his rubs? Yes, I take them in good part. I am now again set a-going; let me be content and cheerful and pursue the chase of happiness.

MONDAY 28 FEBRUARY. I walked about half an hour in the Park very sweetly. The languor attendant on a man enfeebled with sickness has something in't not disagreeable to me. Then the taking care of one's self is amusing.

WEDNESDAY 2 MARCH. I called at Northumberland House, but my Lady was not at home. I now wished much for my commission, and hoped to push it with success.

THURSDAY 3 MARCH. I called again at Northumberland House. But

my Lady was again abroad. The porter promised to let her know that I
had been there and would call again next day. He is a fine civil fellow.

FRIDAY 4 MARCH. I called at Northumberland House a little after
ten. The porter said my Lady was not stirring, but would be up in half an
hour. I said I would call again. I then went to my banker's and received a
term's allowance. I had not such an exquisite relish for gold now as last
time, after my extreme poverty. At eleven I called again at Northumberland House but was told my Lady was just gone out but would be glad to
see me in the evening. This looked very ill. She could not possibly be
gone out so soon after she rose. She has found that she could not *easily*
do me any service with the Marquis of Granby, and so wants to shun a
conversation with me; and has asked me to come in the evening, as she is
then surrounded with company and I can have no opportunity to talk to
her.

I was much vexed and fretted, and began to despair of my
commission altogether and to ruminate whether it would not be better
just to lay aside thoughts of it.

SATURDAY 5 MARCH. I walked this day, as indeed I did yesterday, as
far as Holborn. I formerly, as it were, only coasted it, in the Park. But
now I launched into the wide ocean. I exulted in moving again freely
about. I was rather too keen, and had too great a hurry of spirits.

SUNDAY 6 MARCH. I heard prayers and sermon at Spring Garden
Chapel; I felt a calm delight in again being at divine service. I then went
and presented myself at Lady Betty's, where I was received with the
greatest kindness. I was very lively, and chatted with my former ease and
volatility; and they joked with great humour on my keeping the house.

FRIDAY 11 MARCH. Dempster took me into the House of Commons.
The novelty of being in the High Court of Parliament which I had heard
so much about pleased me exceedingly. My respect for it was greatly
abated by seeing that it was such a tumultuous scene. Yet I felt an
ambition to be a speaker there. I wish that may be the case. It must
afford very high satisfaction to make a figure as an orator before an
assembly of so much consequence. At night I was at Lady Northumberland's. She said that she had as yet only seen Lord Granby in public, but
would not forget me. She spoke rather slightly, and I imagined she had
no more thoughts of serving me. I was really depressed.

SATURDAY 12 MARCH. This was one of the blackest days that I ever
passed. I was most miserably melancholy. I thought I would get no
commission, and thought that a grievous misfortune, and that I was very
ill used in life. I ruminated of hiding myself from the world. I thought of
going to Spain and living there as a silent morose Don. Or of retiring to

the sweeter climes of France and Italy. But then I considered that I wanted money. I then thought of having obscure lodgings, and actually looked up and down the bottom of Holborn and towards Fleet Ditch for an out-of-the-way place. How very absurd are such conceits! Yet they are common. When a man is out of humour, he thinks he will vex the world by keeping away from it, and that he will be greatly pitied; whereas in truth the world are too busy about themselves to think of him, and "out of sight, out of mind."

I went to Lady Betty's. Lady Anne only was at home. She gave me some tea and we chatted gently. Then the rest came in. I valued them, as they were to go for Scotland on Monday. I stayed supper, after which we talked of death, of theft, robbery, murder, and ghosts. Lady Betty and Lady Anne declared seriously that at Allanbank they were disturbed two nights by something walking and groaning in the room, which they afterwards learnt was haunted. This was very strong. My mind was now filled with a real horror instead of an imaginary one. I shuddered with apprehension. I was frightened to go home. Honest Erskine made me go with him, and kindly gave the half of his bed, in which, though a very little one, we passed the silent watches in tranquillity.

SUNDAY 13 MARCH. Erskine and I took a walk to Covent Garden, and I carried him to Southampton Street and showed him the house in which I first paid my addresses to the Paphian Queen, where I first experienced the melting and transporting rites of Love.

In the evening I walked early and quietly home, and felt a most comfortable degree of sensation upon getting into my neat warm bed and resigning myself to repose.

TUESDAY 15 MARCH. I then went to Lord Eglinton's; he and I sauntered about all the forenoon. I had formed a scheme of writing a letter to Lord Bute about my commission, but thought it a wild conceit, so kept it to myself. Luckily Lord Eglinton hit upon the same, and proposed it to me. I appointed to meet him at his house this evening at eleven, when we might talk my affair over fully. He promised he would do everything in his power for me with Lord Bute. "But," said he, "Jamie, after all you will perhaps not believe me." "No, my Lord," said I. "Be not afraid of that. I always believe your Lordship in the past tense but never in the future. When you say, 'I *have* done so and so,' I make no doubt of it. But when you say, 'I *will* do so and so,' your Lordship must excuse me."

At night my Lord came as he promised. I ordered everything just as I pleased. I made it just an evening which we passed when I was first in London, which I described in my letter to his Lordship which was published in *The Scots Magazine:* "We sat down in the dining-room, to an enlivening bottle of old hock." I showed him a letter that I had written to Lord Bute, which he declared too long, too personal, and too circumstantial. He therefore wrote the following, which I just copied out:

MY LORD: —I am ashamed to trouble your Lordship, having nothing to recommend me but being the eldest son of a Scotch judge who is thought to serve his country honestly: I mean my Lord Auchinleck.

My father insisted on my following the law. I passed trials to please him, but having an utter detestation at that profession, beg your Lordship would recommend me to his Majesty to have a commission in the Army; which will be conferring the highest favour on one who is, with highest respect and esteem, my Lord, your Lordship's most obedient humble servant,

JAMES BOSWELL

THURSDAY 17 MARCH. I dined at Lord Advocate's, where was an invited contrived formal company. I was but dull. Wedderburn was there, who was overbearing and flippant. Mrs. Miller's abominable Glasgow tongue excruciated me. I resolved never again to dine where a Scotchwoman from the West was allowed to feed with us. At six I left them and met Erskine at Dempster's, where our society over the pleasant tea was very agreeable. Time galloped along. We stayed and had a little supper, and then getting into a deep speculative conversation about the immortality of the soul, human nature, the pursuits of men, and happiness, we did not part till near three, to the severe mortification of Maid Molly, who was obliged to sit up for me. Poor being!

FRIDAY 18 MARCH. Finding myself much dissipated and having a good deal to write, I kept the house all day and did my work, and became serene.

MONDAY 21 MARCH. I breakfasted with Fergusson. He said he had been constantly happy all his life, except one year that he was sick and three days that he was in love. We walked together. He told me that he had presented my *Ode on Ambition* to Lord Bute, which he read and liked. That he also presented my letter and told my story in the most favourable manner; but that Lord Bute told him it was impossible to give me a commission in the Guards, as people of the best parliamentary interest were pushing to purchase them. He then asked a commission in another regiment for me, which Lord Bute promised I should have.

When I went home in the evening, I felt myself quite dissipated by running about so much. I was indolent and careless and could not fix to anything. Even this my journal was in danger of being neglected. Near a whole week had elapsed without my writing a single page of it. By way therefore of penance for my idleness, and by way of making up for the time lost and bringing up my business, I determined to sit up all this night; which I accordingly did, and wrote a great deal. About two o'clock in the morning I inadvertently snuffed out my candle, and as my fire was long before that black and cold, I was in a great dilemma how to proceed. Downstairs did I softly and silently step to the kitchen. But, alas, there was as little fire there as upon the icy mountains of Greenland. With a tinder-box is a light struck every morning to kindle the fire, which is put out at night. But this tinder-box I could not see, nor knew where to find. I was now filled with gloomy ideas of the terrors of the night. I was also apprehensive that my landlord, who always keeps a pair of loaded pistols by him, might fire at me as a thief. I went up to my room, sat quietly till I heard the watchman calling, "Past three o'clock." I then called to him to knock at the door of the house where I lodged. He did so, and I opened it to him and got my candle relumed without danger. Thus was I relieved and continued busy till eight next day.

TUESDAY 22 MARCH. What a curious creature is man! With what a variety of powers and faculties is he endued! Yet how easily is he disturbed and put out of order! This night's watchfulness (or rather last night's) has quite stupefied and confused me. However, the day must be weathered out.

FRIDAY 25 MARCH. Erskine breakfasted with me. We parted in the forenoon, and I sauntered up and down the streets rather out of spirits. I drank tea at Sheridan's, where was Old Victor. We disputed much on systems of government. Sheridan stood up for monarchy, and Victor mumbled some stuff in favour of a republic. Surely a regular limited royal government is the best and the most conducive to the happiness of mankind. A republic is in my opinion a most confused, vulgar system, whereas a monarchy inspires us with gay and spirited ideas.

As I was coming home this night, I felt carnal inclinations raging through my frame. I determined to gratify them. I went to St. James's Park, and, like Sir John Brute, picked up a whore. For the first time did I engage in armour, which I found but a dull satisfaction. She who submitted to my lusty embraces was a young Shropshire girl, only seventeen, very well-looked, her name Elizabeth Parker. Poor being, she has a sad time of it!

SATURDAY 26 MARCH. Erskine and I sauntered up and down some hours. I should have mentioned some time ago that I said to him that if venereal delight and the power of propagating the species were permitted only to the virtuous, it would make the world very good. Our pulpits would then resound with noble descriptions of conjugal love. Preachers would incite the audience to goodness by warmly and lusciously setting before their imaginations the transports of amorous joy. This would render the pleasures of love more refined and more valuable, when they were participated only by the good. Whereas at present it is the common solace of the virtuous and the wicked, the man of taste and the man of brutality.

TUESDAY 29 MARCH. I was in miserable spirits. All was dark. I dined with Webster, who treated me as his guest at a military mess at the Tilt Yard. Really it must be observed that officers live rather better than any other society. They have less to do, so it is a more important object. I had this day the satisfaction of a very good dinner, genteelly served up in an elegant room, and a good company round me. Yet was I melancholy. I considered them all as unhappy, tired, slavish beings singled out from the rest of mankind for toil and pain. I disliked the idea of being a soldier. I thought of refusing a commission.

WEDNESDAY 30 MARCH. Erskine and I dined with Lord Eglinton, where we were very happy. My Lord and the Captain are growing better acquainted. We drank tea. We talked on human happiness. I said I wondered if any man ever passed a whole day pleasantly. Sir James said that a man in the gay life of London could scarcely do it, because a thousand accidents may cross and disappoint him. But that he had passed such days at Oxford, because his time was regularly laid out. Exactly at such hours he did such and such things, the doing of which in that manner was his pleasure, and could scarcely be interrupted, as he moved like clockwork.

THURSDAY 31 MARCH. Erskine this morning exhibited in a new capacity—that of a landlord. He promised me a breakfast; and a most excellent breakfast did he give, entertaining me not only with plenty of good tea and bread and butter but with that admirable viand, marmalade.

We were very cheerful and very cordial. I sauntered about all the day. I did not dine and was somewhat lowish. At night I strolled into the Park and took the first whore I met, whom I without many words copulated with free from danger, being safely sheathed. She was ugly and lean and her breath smelt of spirits. I never asked her name. When it was done, she slunk off. I had a low opinion of this gross practice and resolved to do it no more. I went and sat a while with Webster.

SATURDAY 2 APRIL. I dined at Cochrane's. He had two or three Scotch people with him, and we were very hearty. After dinner I sauntered in a pleasing humour to London Bridge, viewed the Thames's silver expanse and the springy bosom of the surrounding fields. I then went up to the top of the Monument. This is a most amazing building. It is a pillar two hundred feet high. In the inside, a turnpike stair runs up all the way. When I was about half way up, I grew frightened. I would have come down again, but thought I would despise myself for my timidity. Thus does the spirit of pride get the better of fear. I mounted to the top and got upon the balcony. It was horrid to find myself so monstrous a way up in the air, so far above London and all its spires. I durst not look round me. There is no real danger, as there is a strong rail both on the stair and balcony. But I shuddered, and as every heavy wagon passed down Gracechurch Street, dreaded that the shaking of the earth would make the tremendous pile tumble to the foundation.

MONDAY 4 APRIL. Temple breakfasted with me. I found him much more liberal in all his notions than when we were formerly together. We then walked in the Park a good time. We parted, and I went to Gould's, where I explained my scheme of accepting an ensigncy in a marching regiment. He pushed me to get it changed to a cornetcy, from which I might easily step into the Guards.

THURSDAY 7 APRIL. I breakfasted with Temple. This day was afterwards passed in dissipation which has left no traces on my brain.

SATURDAY 9 APRIL. Dr. Blair came and sat a while with me. I then went with Erskine to Holborn. At three I called on Blair, as we were engaged to go together to the English Opera of *Artaxerxes*. Nairne was with us. I conducted them to St. Clement's Chop-house, where we dined. I was diverted at walking the streets of London with Dr. Blair. I marched him down Southampton Street in the Strand, from the whimsical idea of passing under the windows of my first London lady of the town with an Edinburgh minister whom I had so often heard preach in the New Church. We were in good frame and talked agreeably serious.

The house at Covent Garden was much crowded; so I left my place to Nairne, went and drank tea with Mrs. Brown, then came to the Park, and in armorial guise performed concubinage with a strong, plump, good-humoured girl called Nancy Baker. I then went to Drury Lane gallery and saw the entertainment of *Thomas and Sally,* in which Mrs. Love appeared for the first time with pretty good applause. After the play I met Blair and Nairne at the great Piazza Coffee-house, where we had some negus and solaced our existences.

SUNDAY 10 APRIL. I breakfasted with Temple and then went to the Temple Church and heard a very good sermon on "Set thy house in order, for thou shalt shortly die."

I drank tea at Dempster's, from whence Erskine and I went to Lord Eglinton's and supped.

John Home was there; he was forward and priggish, but clever. I was arguing for the benefit of philosophy; how it soothed us in distress, and how, by hoping for future ease and pleasure, we might bear up under present distress. Said he, "If you was broiling upon a gridiron all this night, it would be no great consolation to you to know that you would be easy tomorrow." "Nay," said I, "but philosophy may be used to heal the mind as oil does a burnt finger." "But I'm afraid," said Home, "that philosophy is not such a specific as oil." "The true way," said Erskine, "to determine the thing, would be to burn both fingers and take philosophy to the one and oil to the other, and see which of them was first healed."

MONDAY 11 APRIL. I passed the forenoon with Lord Eglinton, sauntering about, and sitting at Mrs. Cadwaldin's the painter (for I believe her name is spelled thus). It was now fixed that Lord Northumberland should go Lord Lieutenant to Ireland. This I considered as a very fortunate thing for me, as I could go over as an aide-de-camp, get promotion in the Army in Ireland, and from thence step easily into the Guards. Lord Eglinton promised to do what he could to forward this scheme; and this forenoon we met my Lady Northumberland in her chair. Lord Eglinton stopped her and proposed the thing to her. She said she should like it much, but did not yet know whether my Lord and she were to go to Ireland. This looked ill, as if she wanted to shift doing anything. O these Great People! They are a sad set of beings. This woman who seemed to be cordially my friend and promised me her good offices so strongly is, I fear, a fallacious hussy. Thus do I philosophize, and thus do I lash such unworthy proceedings. However, let me not yet be too certain. She may perhaps be honest.

TUESDAY 12 APRIL. This was the greatest day that Erskine and I ever saw: the day of the publication of our *Letters*. We used to write lively humorous letters to one another. I thought we might make a very entertaining little volume of them, and proposed the scheme to Erskine, who at first opposed it much. But at last the inclination seized him and he became as fond of it as I. During my confinement the thing was resolved upon and set a-going. Flexney was pitched upon for bookseller and Mr. Chandler for printer. And this was the reason of our taking so many walks to Holborn, so often mentioned in this my journal, for both Flexney and Chandler live there. For a while we were in a sort of anxiety about the thing; dreaded censure and exposing ourselves; but by degrees we became well pleased with the plan. We were entertained with the printing of it. We kept our secret to a miracle. Not a single soul knew a word of it till it appeared in the newspapers.

Erskine went out of town today to St. Albans, where his regiment was to be broke. I went a little way in the chaise with him. He was more concerned this day by much than I was, and rejoiced at his being absent for the first week after the publication. For my part, I was pretty easy, and resolved just to bear the brunt.

WEDNESDAY 13 APRIL. I should have mentioned last night that I met with a monstrous big whore in the Strand, whom I had a great curiosity to lubricate, as the saying is. I went into a tavern with her, where she displayed to me all the parts of her enormous carcass; but I found that her avarice was as large as her a—,for she would by no means take what I offered her. I therefore with all coolness pulled the bell and discharged the reckoning, to her no small surprise and mortification, who would fain have provoked me to talk harshly to her and so make a disturbance. But I walked off with the gravity of a Barcelonian bishop. I had an opportunity tonight of observing the rascality of the waiters in these infamous sort of taverns. They connive with the whores, and do what they can to fleece the gentlemen. I was on my guard, and got off pretty well. I was so much in the lewd humour that I felt myself restless, and took a little girl into a court; but wanted vigour. So I went home, resolved against low street debauchery.

FRIDAY 22 APRIL. To make a fair trial of Lady Northumberland I had written to her as follows:

MADAM: —I am soon to have a commission in the Army. I beg leave to offer my attendance on Lord Northumberland to Ireland. Your Ladyship has it now in your power to serve me very much. I hope to be honoured with an answer. I am, &c.

This day I had her answer as follows:

SIR: —It is with very great pleasure I hear you are likely so soon to get a commission in the Army. I hope it is in the Guards, as I know that will be the most agreeable to you. My Lord is as well as myself extremely thankful to you for your polite offer of accompanying us into Ireland. Our establishment there was completed for some time before the King's destination of my Lord to the Lieutenancy of that Kingdom was made public; nor indeed is there any post in the Household fit for the acceptance of a man in your situation in life; but should anything happen in our power, we should be very happy to show our inclination to serve you, which I assure you we much wish to do. I am, with great truth, Sir, your most obedient humble servant,

ELIZABETH NORTHUMBERLAND.

I dined at Lord Eglinton's, where was John Home, with whom I argued against war for making so much bloodshed. "True," said he, "but consider by the exercise of how many virtues this bloodshed is brought about: by patience, by honour, by fortitude. And as to all the severities of a campaign, one day of the *ennui*, the low spirits of a man, in London is worse than them all." I don't know how far he was right. I am afraid that in a campaign I should have the low spirits and the severities into the bargain. I am sure I always feel myself rendered melancholy by any degree of these hardships.

FRIDAY 29 APRIL. The two Captain Erskines breakfasted with me. Captain Andrew and I dined with Houstoun Stewart. We were too extravagant in the ludicrous style, and I was not happy.

TUESDAY 3 MAY. I walked up to the Tower in order to see Mr. Wilkes come out. But he was gone. I then thought I should see prisoners of one kind or other, so went to Newgate. I stepped into a sort of court before the cells. They are surely most dismal places. There are three rows of 'em, four in a row, all above each other. They have double iron windows, and within these, strong iron rails; and in these dark mansions are the unhappy criminals confined. I did not go in, but stood in the court, where were a number of strange blackguard beings with sad countenances, most of them being friends and acquaintances of those under sentence of death. Mr. Rice the broker was confined in another part of the house. In the cells were Paul Lewis for robbery and Hannah Diego for theft. I saw them pass by to chapel. The woman was a big unconcerned being. Paul, who had been in the sea-service and was called Captain, was a genteel, spirited young fellow. He was just a Macheath. He was dressed in a white coat and blue silk vest and silver, with his hair neatly queued and a silver-laced hat, smartly cocked. An acquaintance asked him how he was. He said, "Very well"; quite resigned. Poor fellow! I really took a great concern for him, and wished to relieve him. He walked firmly and with a good air, with his chains rattling upon him, to the chapel.

Erskine and I dined at the renowned Donaldson's, where we were heartily entertained. All this afternoon I felt myself still more melancholy, Newgate being upon my mind like a black cloud. Poor Lewis was always coming across me. I felt myself dreary at night, and made my barber try to read me asleep with Hume's *History*, of which he made very sad work. I lay in sad concern.

WEDNESDAY 4 MAY. My curiosity to see the melancholy spectacle of the executions was so strong that I could not resist it, although I was sensible that I would suffer much from it. In my younger years I had read in the *Lives of the Convicts* so much about Tyburn that I had a sort of horrid eagerness to be there. I also wished to see the last behaviour of Paul Lewis, the handsome fellow whom I had seen the day before. Accordingly I took Captain Temple with me, and he and I got upon a scaffold very near the fatal tree, so that we could clearly see all the dismal scene. There was a most prodigious crowd of spectators. I was most terribly shocked, and thrown into a very deep melancholy.

I went to Lord Eglinton and begged he would try to relieve me. He made me dress and dine with him, and said he would take me at night to Ranelagh and introduce me to some pretty women. Dress and dinner gave me spirits. But at seven, he proposed to take a little boy, one Barron, in the coach with us. This is a boy of great genius both as a painter and a musician, and he will probably be a man of great eminence. But at present he is a little black trifling being, so that his being in my company is a punishment to me. My Lord therefore having gone out and promised to call with the coach and take us up, I made my escape very quietly. This was perhaps being too nice and capricious.

I went home and changed my clothes. But gloomy terrors came upon me so much as night approached that I durst not stay by myself; so I went and had a bed (or rather half a one) from honest Erskine, which he most kindly gave me.

THURSDAY 5 MAY. This was a Thanksgiving day for the Peace. But I did not go to church. Dempster, Erskine, and I walked out to Kensington to look for country lodgings to the great Orator (i.e., Dempster). It was a fine day, and the walking in the Garden delicious. We dined at the C-House, and came to Dempster's and passed the evening. I was still in horror, and so slept this night with him.

FRIDAY 6 MAY. I awaked as usual heavy, confused, and splenetic. Every morning this is the case with me. Dempster prescribed to me to cut two or three brisk capers round the room, which I did, and found attended with most agreeable effects. It expelled the phlegm from my heart, gave my blood a free circulation, and my spirits a brisk flow; so that I was all at once made happy. I must remember this and practice it.

When I went home at night, I was tired and went to bed and thought to sleep. But I was still so haunted with frightful imaginations that I durst not lie by myself, but rose and sallied straight to Erskine, who really had compassion on me, and as before shared his bed with me. I am too easily affected. It is a weakness of mind. I own it.

TUESDAY 10 MAY. At night I waited at Lord Eglinton's till he should come in. But the twelfth hour did not bring him. I therefore would wait no longer. At the bottom of the Haymarket I picked up a strong, jolly young damsel, and taking her under the arm I conducted her to Westminster Bridge, and then in armour complete did I engage her upon this noble edifice. The whim of doing it there with the Thames rolling below us amused me much. Yet after the brutish appetite was sated, I could not but despise myself for being so closely united with such a low wretch.

When I knocked at my lodgings, I could not get in. The poor girl, despairing of my approach, had gone to bed and fallen asleep. I returned to Lord Eglinton's, as Mr. Crookshanks was out of town and I might have his room. Accordingly, I was just shown into my old little chamber, which I slept in when I first lived at Lord Eglinton's. I was happy to get into it. But when I compared my ideas then with those I had now, the present seemed very dim and very tasteless. I went to bed at three. My Lord was still abroad.

FRIDAY 13 MAY. I breakfasted with Mr. Garrick. I was proud at being admitted to the society of so great an actor.

I parted with him, and then dined at Clifton's with Temple. We then went to his chambers, where he introduced me to a particular friend of his, a Mr. Nicholls who had been with him at Cambridge. I never saw anybody who engaged me more at the very first than this gentleman. He discovered an amiable disposition, a sweetness of manners, and an easy politeness that pleased me much. We went to Tom's and had a pot of coffee, and sat there for two hours. Our conversation took a literary turn. We talked of Helvétius, Voltaire, Rousseau, Hume. Mr. Nicholls I found to be sensible and elegantly learned; with an agreeable moderation of sentiment intermixed, his character was finely completed. I talked really very well. I have not passed so much rational time I don't know when. The degree of distance due to a stranger restrained me from my effusions of ludicrous nonsense and intemperate mirth. I was rational and composed, yet lively and entertaining. I had a good opinion of myself, and I could perceive my friend Temple much satisfied with me. Could I but fix myself in such a character and preserve it uniformly, I should be exceedingly happy. I hope to do so and to attain a constancy and dignity without which I can never be satisfied, as I have these ideas strong and pride myself in thinking that my natural character is that of dignity. My friend Temple is very good in consoling me by saying that I may be such a man, and that people will say, "Mr. Boswell is quite altered from the dissipated, inconstant fellow that he was. He is now a reserved, grave sort of a man. But indeed that was his real character; and he only deviated into these eccentric paths for a while." Well, then, let me see if I have resolution enough to bring that about.

SATURDAY 14 MAY. Every time that I sleep at the Earl's, I never fail to breakfast before I leave his house. I am really on an excellent plan at his house. I believe he is as fond of me as dissipation will allow him to be of any man. I must however complain against fate that Mrs. Brown stays in his house. For I really find her to be such a gawky, and so much of a low censorious Scots lass that I am just in a rage, or rather in a discontent, with her.

This forenoon I met Dempster. He has now taken country lodgings at Kensington for himself and sister. He and I called on Dr. Blair, where was Sir James, who asked if they could understand such a strange thing as this: Boswell and Macpherson got into a coach together; both exclaimed they were miserable; and both burst out in loud peals of laughter. This was literally true. Indeed, I have often found that when I vented my complaints of melancholy, it appeared somewhat ludicrous and I could not but laugh. Blair said that Macpherson must be miserable, because he was absolutely void of curiosity. Blair asked him why he was fond of staying in England, as he surely could not like John Bull. "Sir," said he, "I hate John Bull, but I love his daughters."

MONDAY 16 MAY. Temple and his brother breakfasted with me. I went to Love's to try to recover some of the money which he owes me. But, alas, a single guinea was all I could get. He was just going to dinner, so I stayed and eat a bit, though I was angry at myself afterwards. I drank tea at Davies's in Russell Street, and about seven came in the great Mr. Samuel Johnson, whom I have so long wished to see. Mr. Davies introduced me to him. As I knew his mortal antipathy at the Scotch, I cried to Davies, "Don't tell where I come from." However, he said, "From Scotland." "Mr. Johnson," said I, "indeed I come from Scotland, but I cannot help it." "Sir," replied he, "that, I find, is what a very great many of your countrymen cannot help." Mr. Johnson is a man of a most dreadful appearance. He is a very big man, is troubled with sore eyes, the palsy, and the king's evil. He is very slovenly in his dress and speaks with a most uncouth voice. Yet his great knowledge and strength of expression command vast respect and render him very excellent company. He has great humour and is a worthy man. But his dogmatical roughness of manners is disagreeable. I shall mark what I remember of his conversation.

He said that people might be taken in once in imagining that an author is greater than other people in private life. "Uncommon parts require uncommon opportunities for their exertion.

"In barbarous society superiority of parts is of real consequence. Great strength or wisdom is of value to an individual. But in more polished times you have people to do everything for money. And then there are a number of other superiorities, such as those of birth and fortune and rank, that dissipate men's attention and leave superiority of parts no extraordinary share of respect. And this is wisely ordered by Providence, to preserve a mediocrity.

"Lord Kames's *Elements* is a pretty essay and deserves to be held in some estimation, though it is chimerical.

"Wilkes is safe in the eye of the law. But he is an abusive scoundrel; and instead of sending my Lord Chief Justice to him, I would send a parcel of footmen and have him well ducked.

"The notion of liberty amuses the people of England and helps to keep off the *taedium vitae*. When a butcher says that he is in distress for his country, he has no uneasy feeling.

"Sheridan will not succeed at Bath, for ridicule has gone down before him, and I doubt Derrick is his enemy."

I was sorry to leave him there at ten, when I had engaged to be at Dr. Pringle's, with whom I had a serious conversation much to my mind.

LONDON
TO HOLLAND

17 May 1763 — 18 June 1764

INTRODUCTION

E IGHT DAYS AFTER THEIR MEETING, Boswell called upon Mr. Johnson at his "chambers." It was the first of many occasions of his doing so. On this day he arrived straight from the company of John Wilkes, whose politics Johnson considered scandalous, whom Johnson at their first meeting had designated "an abusive scoundrel," adding that "I would send a parcel of footmen and have him well ducked." Boswell, who was fascinated by extremes, might have reveled in the contrast of passing from the company of Wilkes to Johnson. He once amused himself by passing with a clergyman beneath the window of a prostitute.

To Mr. Johnson the young Boswell soon confided one of the principal problems of his life—his relationship with his father. Johnson reassuringly replied that Boswell at thirty would be the man his father wished him to be. He advised Boswell to "part" from his father for the present, to go abroad, "to perambulate Spain." He promised Boswell to assist him by putting him "upon a plan." Gratefully Boswell "put out my hand" upon hearing that Mr. Johnson would "really take a charge of me."

Boswell's appeal for advice undoubtedly was related to his receiving from Auchinleck his father's letter of May 30, 1763, so coolly saluting him "James," summarily dismissing ideas and projects so deeply valued by him and concluding abruptly by omitting an affectionate closing. Lord Auchinleck seemed to permit his anxiety for his son's future to take the form of intolerance of Boswell's present nature, as if he held no hope of growth. He did not see in his son the signs which Mr. Johnson saw.

In this letter Lord Auchinleck warned Boswell of the dangers of "mimicry, journals, and publications." Although Boswell would soon, by the study of law in Holland, temporarily please his father, he would never surrender his journal as a necessity of his life. He required it; it was a beneficial addiction. It was also the tool of a literary man, as he half hoped to be, and which, beyond his knowledge, and beyond anything his father understood about him, he inescapably was.

From the basis of his journal Boswell would form three books: his *Account of Corsica,* his *Journal of a Tour to the Hebrides,* and at last, of course, the triumphant *Life*. For Boswell, journal-keeping was not a simple or uncomplicated task. He or she who keeps a journal in depth lives constantly in a state of distraction and frustration. "In recollecting Mr. Johnson's conversation, I labour under much difficulty. It requires more parts than I am master of even to retain that strength of sentiment and perspicuity of expression for which he is remarkable. I shall just do my best and relate as much as I can."

But of what use, Lord Auchinleck asked, to record in the first place anyone's reflections upon topics remote from daily practical needs? Learn gardening, the father advised the son when the latter reached Holland. "You'll likewise see the method the Dutch manage their cattle, and take notes of it. I would wish to be informed of the method by which they keep their cows so clean, for my remembrance of it is dark. They had a contrivance for making their dung in no way offensive to them. . . ." It is hard to imagine Boswell, even at this tranquil hour of his life, preparing for that farther future when the care of his estate would indeed interest him. Of his father he wrote at this time a simple description: "He is perhaps too anxiously devoted to utility."

It was Johnson who saw Boswell off for his year of studying law in Holland. They had now been friends for three months. At Harwich "my revered friend walked down with me to the beach, where we embraced and parted with tenderness, and engaged to correspond by letters. I said, 'I hope, Sir, you will not forget me in my absence.' JOHNSON. 'Nay, Sir, it is more likely you should forget me, than that I should forget you.' As the vessel put out to sea, I kept my eyes upon him for a considerable time, while he remained rolling his majestick frame in his usual manner: and at last I perceived him walk back into the town, and he disappeared."

Soon after commencing his year of study in Holland, Boswell for his own governance composed an "Inviolable Plan," absorbing the counsel of both Mr. Johnson and his father. Perhaps he thought it wholly his own. Good advice, Mr. Johnson had told him, "if you will not take from others, you must take from your own reflections. . . ." I do not think Boswell read his Plan "every morning regularly at breakfast," as he had vowed, or even that he read it "frequently." Nevertheless, during no other period of his life do we find him so well controlled, so much master of himself, or so focused upon a goal his father considered useful and positive. During his months in Holland he was a disciplined and successful student, preparing himself for his livelihood; quite, in fact, devoted to utility.

TUESDAY 17 MAY. I sauntered up and down all this forenoon, and dined with Lord Eglinton, where was Sir James, who said he wondered how I could complain of being miserable who had always such a flow of spirits. Melancholy cannot be clearly proved to others, so it is better to be silent about it. I should have been at Lady Northumberland's rout tonight, but my barber fell sick; so I sallied to the streets, and just at the bottom of our own, I picked up a fresh, agreeable young girl called Alice Gibbs. We went down a lane to a snug place, and I took out my armour, but she begged that I might not put it on, as the sport was much pleasanter without it, and as she was quite safe. I was so rash as to trust her, and had a very agreeable congress.

WEDNESDAY 18 MAY. Much concern was I in from the apprehension of being again reduced to misery, and in so silly a way too. My benevolence indeed suggested to me to put confidence in the poor girl; but then said cool reason, "What abandoned, deceitful wretches are these girls, and even supposing her honest, how could she know with any certainty that she was well?" Temple was much vexed and dreaded the worst.

THURSDAY 19 MAY. I resolved to be merry while I could, and soon see whether the foul fiend of the genitals had again prevailed. We were plain and hearty and comfortable; much better than the people of high fashion. There was a Miss Rutherford there, a Scotch girl who had been long in America. She and I chatted very neatly.

We stayed and drank tea and coffee; and at seven, being in high glee, I called upon Miss Watts, whom I found by herself, neatly dressed and looking very well. I was free and easy with her, and begged that she would drink a glass of wine with me at the Shakespeare, which she complied with. I told her my name was Macdonald, and that I was a Scotch Highlander. She said she liked them much, as they had always spirit and generosity. We were shown into a handsome room and had a bottle of choice sherry. We sat near two hours and became very cheerful and agreeable to each other. I told her with a polite freedom, "Madam, I tell you honestly I have no money to give you, but if you allow me favours without it, I shall be much obliged to you." She smiled and said she would. Her maid then brought her a message that a particular friend from the country was waiting for her; so that I was obliged to give her up this night, as I determined to give her no money. She left me pleased, and said she hoped to have the pleasure of my company at tea when it was convenient. This I faithfully promised and took as a good sign of her willingness to establish a friendly communication with me.

I then sallied forth to the Piazzas in rich flow of animal spirits and burning with fierce desire. I met two very pretty little girls who asked me to take them with me. "My dear girls," said I, "I am a poor fellow. I can give you no money. But if you choose to have a glass of wine and my company and let us be gay and obliging to each other without money, I am your man." They agreed with great good humour. So back to the Shakespeare I went. "Waiter," said I, "I have got here a couple of human beings; I don't know how they'll do." "I'll look, your Honour," cried he, and with inimitable effrontery stared them in the face and then cried, "They'll do very well." "What," said I, "are they good fellow-creatures? Bring them up, then." We were shown into a good room and had a bottle of sherry before us in a minute. I surveyed my seraglio and found them both good subjects for amorous play. I toyed with them and drank about and sung *Youth's the Season* and thought myself Captain Macheath; and then I solaced my existence with them, one after the other, according to their seniority. I was quite *raised,* as the phrase is: thought I was in a London tavern, the Shakespeare's Head, enjoying high debauchery after my sober winter. I parted with my ladies politely and came home in a glow of spirits.

SATURDAY 21 MAY. I dined in the City with my honest friend Cochrane, and in the afternoon drank tea and sat a long time with Temple, who was in fine frame and talked to me seriously of getting out of a course of dissipation and rattling and of acquiring regularity and reserve, in order to attain dignity of character and happiness. He had much weight with me, and I resolved to be in earnest to pursue the course which he admired.

SUNDAY 22 MAY. I went to St. Andrew's Church in Holborn, which is a very fine building. At one end of it is a window of very elegant painted glass. I was in an excellent frame and heard service with true devotion.

TUESDAY 24 MAY. I received a very polite letter from Mr. Thornton, one of the authors of *The Connoisseur,* informing me that he had written the criticism on Erskine's and Boswell's *Letters* in *The Public Advertiser,* to which I had in return for their civility sent a little essay begging to know who had spoken so favourably of us. Mr. Thornton said he should be happy in our acquaintance. I wrote to him my thanks and said I would call upon him at eleven o'clock, which I did, and found him a well-bred, agreeable man, lively and odd. He had about £15,000 left him by his father, was bred to physic, but was fond of writing. So he employs himself in that way.

I went and waited upon Mr. Samuel Johnson, who received me very courteously. He has chambers in the Inner Temple, where he lives in literary state, very solemn and very slovenly. He had some people with him, and when they left him, I rose too. But he cried, "No, don't go away." "Sir," said I, "I am afraid that I intrude upon you. It is benevolent to allow me to sit and hear you." He was pleased with this compliment, which I sincerely paid him, and he said he was obliged to any man who visited him. I was proud to sit in such company.

He said that mankind had a great aversion at intellectual employment. But even supposing knowledge easily attained, most people were equally content to be ignorant.

"Moral good depends on the motive from which we act. If I fling half a crown at a beggar with intention to break his head, and he picks it up and buys victuals with it, the physical effect is good; but with respect to me, the action is very wrong. In the same way, religious services, if not performed with an intention to please GOD, avail us nothing. As our Saviour saith of people who perform them from other motives, 'Verily they have their reward.'

"The Christian religion has very strong evidences. No doubt it appears in some degree strange to reason. But in history we have many undoubted facts against which *a priori* in the way of ratiocination we have more arguments than we have for them; but then testimony has great weight, and casts the balance. I would recommend Grotius, Dr. Pearse on Miracles, and Dr. Clarke."

I listened to this great oracle with much satisfaction; and as I feel myself uneasy by reason of scepticism, I had great comfort in hearing so able an advocate for Revelation; and I resolved to read the books he mentioned. He pressed me to stay a second time, which I did. He said he went out at four in the afternoon and did not come home, for most part, till two in the morning. I asked him if he did not think it wrong to live so and not make use of his talents. He said it was a bad habit.

He said Garrick was the first man in the world for sprightly conversation.

I begged that he would favour me with his company at my lodgings some evening. He promised he would. I then left him, and he shook me cordially by the hand. Upon my word, I am very fortunate. I shall cultivate this acquaintance.

WEDNESDAY 25 MAY. Temple and his brother and I dined in their chambers, where we had dinner brought, thinking it a more genteel and agreeable way than in a chop-house. But we found it inconvenient, and so resolved to continue constant to Clifton's. I gave Bob a ticket to the play, and my worthy friend and I talked seriously. He advised me to force myself to be reserved and grave in a greater degree, otherwise I would just be Jamie Boswell, without any respect. And he said he imagined that my journal did me harm, as it made me hunt about for adventures to adorn it with, whereas I should endeavour to be calm and studious and regular in my conduct, in order to attain by habit a proper consistency of conduct. No doubt consistency of conduct is of the utmost importance. But I cannot find fault with this my journal, which is far from wishing for extravagant adventures, and is as willing to receive my silent and serious meditations as my loud and boisterous rhodomontades. Indeed, I do think the keeping of a journal a very excellent scheme if judiciously executed. To be sure, it may take up too much time from more serious concerns. But I shall endeavour to keep it with as much conciseness as possible.

SUNDAY 29 MAY. I breakfasted with Colonel Montgomerie. At three o'clock I went to Westminster Abbey and the verger politely showed me into one of the prebend's stalls, where I sat in great state with a purple silk cushion before me. I heard service with much devotion in this magnificent and venerable temple. I recalled the ideas of it which I had from *The Spectator*.

WEDNESDAY 1 JUNE. This morning the *Critical Review* on our *Letters* came out. Erskine breakfasted with me, and in great form did we read it. They did not use us with candour, but they were less abusive than we imagined they might be.

SATURDAY 4 JUNE. It was the King's birthnight, and I resolved to be a blackguard and to see all that was to be seen. I dressed myself in my secondmourning suit, in which I had been powdered many months, dirty buckskin breeches and black stockings, a shirt of Lord Eglinton's which I had worn two days, and little round hat with tarnished silver lace belonging to a disbanded officer of the Royal Volunteers. I had in my hand an old oaken stick battered against the pavement. And was not I a complete blackguard? I went to the Park, picked up a low brimstone, called myself a barber and agreed with her for sixpence, went to the bottom of the Park arm in arm, and dipped my machine in the Canal and performed most manfully. I then went as far as St. Paul's Church-yard, roaring along, and then came to Ashley's Punch-house and drank three threepenny bowls. In the Strand I picked up a little profligate wretch and gave her sixpence. She allowed me entrance. But the miscreant refused me performance. I was much stronger than her, and *volens nolens* pushed her up against the wall. She however gave a sudden spring from me; and screaming out, a parcel of more whores and soldiers came to her relief. "Bother soldiers," said I, "should not a half-pay officer r—g—r for sixpence? and here has she used me so and so." I got them on my side, and I abused her in blackguard style, and then left them. At Whitehall I picked up another girl to whom I called myself a highwayman and told her I had no money and begged she would trust me. But she would not. My vanity was somewhat gratified tonight that, notwithstanding of my dress, I was always taken for a gentleman in disguise. I came home about two o'clock, much fatigued.

MONDAY 6 JUNE. I must not omit to record in this my journal a most curious transaction. We have now in the house where I lodge a neat little maid called Nancy, newly imported from Cumberland. I had given her a frank of Lord Eglinton's, in which she had enclosed a letter to a companion in the country, but not having directed it fully, it was brought to my Lord, who opened it when I was with him. He gave it to me and put me upon the scheme of making her believe that I had the second sight. Accordingly, I picked out many circumstances from her letter about her friends and her journey to town and all her concerns, which I solemnly told her, and for two days she firmly believed that I had intelligence from the Devil. I then let her into the secret.

Nothing remarkable happened this day; and from henceforth I am determined to show more respect to this my journal. I shall never set down the mere common trifling occurrences of life, but say nothing at all, except when I have something worth while.

TUESDAY 7 JUNE. I just read, eat, drank, and walked.

WEDNESDAY 8 JUNE. I breakfasted with Mr. Coutts, and I sauntered about idly all forenoon, which gave me pain. At night I received a very kind letter from my father, in which he told me that he would allow me to follow any profession that I pleased, but at the same time said that the Army was but a poor scheme, and that if I would pursue the law, though moderately, and be in the style of his eldest son, that he would give all encouragement. It was a most sensible and indulgent letter. It made me think seriously, and I considered that I had now experienced how little I could depend on the favour of the great, which, when only founded on personal liking, is very slight. I considered too that I could have no prospect of rising in the Army. That my being in that way contrary to my parents' advice was uphill work, and that I could not long be fond of it. I considered that by getting into the plan of civil life, I should have all things smooth and easy, be on a respectful footing and of consequence in my own country, and please my worthy father, who, though somewhat narrow in his notions, is one of the best men in the world.

Auchinleck, 30 May 1763

JAMES:

My last letter, which was wrote in February, let you know how much I was displeased with some particulars of your conduct which had come to my knowledge. The answer you wrote me was telling me in pretty plain language you contemned what I could say or do. When I thereafter came to the country, I found that what I represented would probably be the consequence of your strange journals actually had happened. Mr. Reid came here, informed us he had seen them, and, having a good memory, repeated many things from them. He made these reflections, that he was surprised a lad of sense and come to age should be so childish as keep a register of his follies and communicate it to others as if proud of them. He added that if the thing were known, no man would choose to keep company with you, for who would incline to have his character traduced in so strange a manner, and this frequently after your receiving the greatest civilities and marks of friendship? When I went on my Circuit to Jedburgh, I received a fresh mortification. The news were brought to me, and therein was contained an account of the publishing some letters of yours; and one of them was insert as a specimen. I read it, and found that though it might pass between two intimate young lads in the same way that people over a bottle will be vastly entertained with one another's rant, it was extremely odd to send such a piece to the press to be perused by all and sundry. The gentlemen at Jedburgh imagined and endeavoured to persuade me that it had been somebody who put in that article in the news by way of jest, for they could not suspect the letter to be genuine. At the same time they said it was a cruel jest, as it was exposing you. From Jedburgh I came to Dumfries, where I found that while you were in that country you had given yourself up to mimicry, and had at different times and places taken off (as you called it) Lord Dumfries, Sir George Preston, and Logan. This, too, you may believe behoved to give me vast pain. To make a mock of others is not praiseworthy; besides, such things are seldom concealed. You create enemies to yourself and even to your friends, it being the way of the world to resent such impertinences against all who show any countenance to the person guilty of them. To all which I may add that mimicry has been justly considered as the lowest and meanest kind of wit.

After mentioning these particulars, if you'll at all reflect, you must be sensible what I suffer by your means. Is it not hard that after all the tenderness I have shown you and the expense and labour I have bestowed upon you, you should not only neglect your own reputation, but do what you can to bring me to shame on your account? The offices I hold entitle me to some respect, and I get it beyond my merit from all that know me except from you, who by the laws of God, nature, gratitude, and interest are bound to do what you can to make me happy, in place of striving, as it were, to find out the things will be most galling to me and making these your pursuit. What I have said will account for my not having wrote you these three months. Indeed, finding that I could be of no use to you, I had determined to abandon you, to free myself as much as possible from sharing your ignominy, and to take the strongest and most public steps for declaring to the world that I was come to this resolution. But I have been so much importuned by your excellent mother, the partaker of my distresses and shame on your account, again to write to you, and your last letter, which I received at Ayr when on the Circuit, is wrote in a strain that is becoming and speaks out that you are satisfied of some of your errors; therefore it is that you receive this from me in answer to those you sent me since the Session rose.

As in yours you desire me to give you my advice with freedom, you cannot be dissatisfied with the introduction to this letter. Every wise man would rather be informed for what things he is censured, that he may correct them, than be flattered when he don't deserve it; and he alone is a true friend who informs us of our faults. It is true such a friend is rarely to be met with, but you have had such friend in me.

You are under a mistake in your last when you write I have been struggling for authority over you. I have a right to it, indeed, but it is a thing I never wished or desired. And every step in my conduct has shown that to be the case. I always used you with lenity and tenderness; and though you were behaving in a way highly disrespectful to me, settled an annuity upon your life and so put you in a state of independency. You say that you was struggling for independency. What you mean by becoming independent I am at a loss to conceive, for it would seem to be something very different from what anybody else would aim at. Your notion of independency seems to consist in contemning your relations and your native country, where and from whom you have a natural right to receive regard and friendship, and to live in dependence upon strangers in another country, where you have no title to notice, and from whom you have nothing to expect but fair words. They have their relations to provide, their political connections to keep up, and must look on one who comes from Scotland as an idle person to have no right to share of their bounty; in the same way that we here would never think of bestowing anything upon a vaguing Englishman except a dinner or a supper.

To come more close to the point in your letter wherein you ask my advice as to what scheme of life you should follow, I shall convince you that I do not insist on authority, for though you tell me you will return to Scotland if I tell you your absence from it makes me unhappy, I will not insist either on one thing or another, but fairly and candidly lay matters before you. All that ever I insisted upon was that you should behave as the young gentlemen of your station do and act with prudence and discretion. If you set up in the character of my eldest son, you may expect regard and respect, but in the style of a vagrant must meet with the reverse. Be assured of this; for even I, who am your father and who, while you trod the paths of virtue and discretion was bound up in you and carried on all my projects with a view to you in whom I flattered myself to find a representative worthy of this respectable family—I say, even I by your strange conduct had come to the resolution of selling all off, from the principle that it is better to snuff a candle out than leave it to stink in a socket.

As for your manner of life, I never declared positively against any kind of life except that of dissipation and vice, and as a consequence against your going into the Guards. But I told you if you chose to be a soldier and make that your business in good earnest, though I did not like the business, I should procure you a commission in a marching regiment, and had one pressed upon me by my good friend General Sinclair, now no more. But you signified your unwillingness to serve in a marching regiment, so that scheme went over and you fell to the study of the law; and I can say with truth, showed as much genius for it when you applied as any ever I knew. Be assured that your following the study of the law, whether as a lawyer or as a gentleman, to fit you to be useful in the world, is what to me is most agreeable and what I verily think is the only thing will make you go through life agreeably; for as you well observe, without some pursuit that is rational, one of your turn can never be happy.

But be more on your guard for the future against mimicry, journals, and publications, still acting with prudence and discretion, which is as necessary for a soldier as for a man of any other employment. I would further recommend to you to endeavour to find out some person of worth who may be a friend, not one who will say as you say when with you and when he is away will make a jest of you as much as of any other.

Your mother is in her ordinary, so is Johnny. Both remember you with affection.

Farewell. It is in your power to make us all happy and yourself too. May God dispose you to the best.

FRIDAY 10 JUNE. At night, I went to Chelsea and saw Johnson ride, standing upon one and then two horses at full gallop, with all his feats of agility. I was highly diverted. It was a true English entertainment. The horses moved about to the tune of *Shilinagarie;* for music, such as it is, makes always a part of John Bull's public amusement.

While I stood gazing about, whom did I suddenly perceive but—Miss Sally Forrester, my first Lady of Venus's Bedchamber, whom I have sought for eagerly but could never find? I approached her with something like the air of a tragedy hero. She immediately knew me. I felt really a fine romantic sensation at meeting her. Miss Simson, who lodged in the house with her and was very civil to me, was with her tonight. We went into the Star and Garter, and I treated them with tea. We resumed our former adventures. I cannot express the curious feelings which I had when I looked back three years; called up my ideas then, and all that has happened to me since. Alas! my ideas have not now that giddy fervour which they had when I was first in London. However, I now walk on surer ground. She said she was married to Captain Peter Grant, a Scotch officer, and she would not allow me to renew my joy. But she promised to meet me at her companion's house, who also said she was married, and called herself Mrs. Tredwell. We walked into town together. The evening was delicious, and I glowed with pleasing imagination. I felt a great degree of satisfaction at thinking that my father would now be happy, and all things go well, and that I might indulge whim with a higher relish. I parted from them at Spring Gardens, and promised to see my dear Sally. They surely joked about their marriages.

MONDAY 13 JUNE. At night, Lord Eglinton and Bob Temple called in my Lord's coach and carried us to Vauxhall, which was quite delicious. There was a quarrel between a gentleman and a waiter. A great crowd gathered round and roared out, "*A ring—a ring,*" which is the signal for making room for the parties to box it out. My spirits rose, and I was exerting myself with much vehemence. At last the constable came to quell the riot. I seized his baton in a good-humoured way which made him laugh, and I rapped upon the people's heads, bawling out, "Who will resist the Peace? A ring, a ring."

TUESDAY 14 JUNE. I should have mentioned yesterday that I waited on Mr. Johnson, who was very civil to me. He said that such a man as Johnson the rider should be encouraged, as his performances showed the extent of the human powers in one instance and so tended to raise our opinion of the nature of man; and that he showed the great effects of industry and application. "So that every man might hope that by giving as much application, although perhaps he might never ride three horses at a time, or dance upon the wire, yet he might be equally expert in whatever profession he chose to pursue." Such is the views that Mr. Johnson has of the most trivial matters. I never am with this great man without feeling myself bettered and rendered happier.

He shook me by the hand at parting, and asked me why I did not call oftener. I said I was afraid of being troublesome. He said I was not; and he was very glad to see me. Can I help being vain of this? Nothing happened today.

FRIDAY 17 JUNE. I breakfasted at Mr. James Erskine's. The day was trifled away.

SATURDAY 18 JUNE. At night I took a streetwalker into Privy Garden and indulged sensuality. The wretch picked my pocket of my handkerchief, and then swore that she had not. When I got home, I was shocked to think that I had been intimately united with a low, abandoned, perjured, pilfering creature. I determined to do so no more; but if the Cyprian fury should seize me, to participate my amorous flame with a genteel girl.

THURSDAY 23 JUNE. Dempster and Erskine breakfasted with me, I then strolled about with them up and down the City, and then we went out to Dempster's and dined. In the evening we walked in Kensington Gardens, and talked of being abroad, and what was to be acquired. I said I wanted to get rid of folly and to acquire sensible habits. They laughed.

SATURDAY 25 JUNE. Mr. Johnson dined at Clifton's in the same room with me. He and an Irishman got into a dispute about the reason of some part of mankind being black. "Three ways have been taken to account for it: either that they are the posterity of Ham, who was cursed; or that God at first created two kinds of men, one black and another white; or that by the heat of the sun the skin is scorched, and so gets the sooty hue. This matter has been much canvassed among naturalists, but has never been brought to any certain issue." The Irishman grew very hot, and Johnson just rose up and quietly walked off. The Teague said he had a most ungainly figure and an affectation of pomposity unworthy of a man of genius.

At nine in the evening Mr. Johnson and I went to the Mitre Tavern in Fleet Street. He was vastly obliging to favour me with his company. I was quite proud to think on whom I was with.

I then told my history to Mr. Johnson, which he listened to with attention. I told him how I was a very strict Christian, and was turned from that to infidelity. But that now I had got back to a very agreeable way of thinking. That I believed the Christian religion; though I might not be clear in many particulars. He was much pleased with my ingenuous open way, and he cried, "Give me your hand. I have taken a liking to you."

I told him all my story. "Sir," said he, "your father has been wanting to make the man of you at twenty which you will be at thirty. Sir, let me tell you that to be a Scotch landlord, where you have a number of families dependent upon and attached to you, is perhaps as high a situation as humanity can arrive at. A merchant upon 'Change with a hundred thousand pounds is nothing. The Duke of Bedford with all his immense fortune is but a little man in reality. He has no tenants who consider themselves as under his patriarchal care.

"Sir, a father and a son should part at a certain time of life. I never believed what my father said. I always thought that he spoke *ex officio,* as a priest does.

"Sir, I am a friend to subordination. It is most conducive to the happiness of society. There is a reciprocal pleasure in governing and being governed.

"Sir, I think your breaking off idle connections by going abroad is a matter of importance. I would go where there are courts and learned men."

I then complained to him how little I knew, and mentioned study. "Sir," said he, "don't talk of study just now. I will put you upon a plan. It will require some time to talk of that." I put out my hand. "Will you really take a charge of me? It is very good in you, Mr. Johnson, to allow me to sit with you thus. Had I but thought some years ago that I should pass an evening with the Author of *The Rambler!*" These expressions were all from the heart, and he perceived that they were; and he was very complacent and said, "Sir, I am glad we have met. I hope we shall pass many evenings and mornings too together."

"Sir," said he, "there is a good deal of Spain that has not been perambulated; and a man of inferior parts to you might give us useful observations on that country." This pleased me. We sat till between one and two and finished a couple of bottles of port. I went home in high exultation.

SUNDAY 26 JUNE. I should have mentioned that Mr. Johnson said he thought I had a lucky escape from the Guards (*of* the Guards I mean), as I was past those puerilities.

This forenoon Mr. Cooper took me to the Chapel Royal, where I had a good seat and saw the King.

FRIDAY 1 JULY. Mr. Johnson, Dr. Goldsmith, and I supped together at the Mitre. I had curious ideas when I considered that I was sitting with London authors by profession.

Johnson allowed that it might have disadvantages, but affirmed that knowledge *per se* was certainly an object which every man would wish to attain, although perhaps he might not choose to take the trouble necessary for attaining it.

He said that Campbell who wrote the *Lives of the Admirals* is a man of much knowledge and a very good share of imagination; and he told us a diverting enough anecdote, that his wife was a printer's devil (as the cant word is), and when she used to bring him the proof-sheets, he fell in love with her and married her.

He began to lash Churchill. I said he was not a fair judge, as Churchill was a sort of enemy of his. "Sir," said he, "I am a very fair judge; because he turned my enemy when he found that I did not like his poetry. And, indeed, I have a better opinion of him now than I had at first, as he has shown more fertility than I expected. To be sure, he is a tree that cannot produce true fruit. He only bears crabs. But, Sir, a tree that produces a great many crabs is better than one which produces only a few crabs."

SATURDAY 2 JULY. I met Lord Eglinton today, whom I have not seen for near a week. "Jamie," said he, "I hear you are giving up all your bad company. But I beg I may not be included in the number."

SUNDAY 3 JULY. I then passed all the day with Temple, who advised me by all means to acquire habits of study and self-command, and then I will be happy in myself and respected by others. At night we walked in the Park.

MONDAY 4 JULY. This afternoon I went and saw Mrs. Salmon's famous wax-work in Fleet Street. It is excellent in its kind, and amused me very well for a quarter of an hour.

WEDNESDAY 6 JULY. What amazing universality of genius has Mr. Johnson, who has written *The English Dictionary*, a work of infinite labour and knowledge; *The Rambler*, which contains a rich store of morality and knowledge of human life, embellished with great imagination; *Rasselas*, where we find a humane preceptor delighting the fancy and mending the heart; *The Life of Savage*, which is distinguished for perspicuity of narration, and abounds with excellent reflection; *The Translations of the Third and Tenth Satires of Juvenal*, and *The Prologue spoken at Mr. Garrick's Opening Drury-Lane Theatre*, which display strong poetical genius, strength of sentiment, keenness of satire, vivaciousness of wit and humour, and manly power of versification. His conversation, too, is as great as his writing. He throws out all his powers with force of expression; and he mixes inimitable strokes of vivacity with solid goodsense and knowledge, so that he is highly instructive and highly entertaining.

I made myself easy as to my company by letting them know that they were to consider the Mitre Tavern as my lodgings for that night. Accordingly, I ordered supper there, and I had as my guests Mr. Samuel Johnson, Dr. Goldsmith, Mr. Ogilvie, Mr. Davies, bookseller, and Mr. Eccles, an Irish gentleman of fortune, a good ingenious sort of man. I was well dressed and in excellent spirits, neither muddy nor flashy. I sat with much secret pride, thinking of my having such a company with me. I behaved with ease and propriety, and did not attempt at all to show away; but gently assisted conversation by those little arts which serve to make people throw out their sentiments with ease and freedom.

Ogilvie was rapt in admiration of the Stupendous Johnson. Goldsmith was in his usual style, too eager to be right, and held a keen dispute with Johnson against that maxim in the British Constitution, "The King can do no wrong"; affirming that what was morally false could not be politically true. And as the King might command and cause the doing of what was wrong, he certainly could do wrong. Johnson showed that in our Constitution the King is the head, and that there is no power by which he can be tried; and therefore it is that redress is always to be had against oppression by punishing the immediate agents. "The King cannot force a judge to condemn a man wrongfully; therefore it is the judge that we pursue. Political institutions are formed upon the consideration of what will most frequently tend to the good of the whole, although now and then exceptions may occur. Thus it is better in general that a nation should have a supreme legislative power, although it may at times be abused. But, then, there is this consideration: that if the abuse be enormous, Nature will rise up, and claiming her original rights, overturn a corrupted political system."

In recollecting Mr. Johnson's conversation, I labour under much difficulty. It requires more parts than I am master of even to retain that strength of sentiment and perspicuity of expression for which he is remarkable. I shall just do my best and relate as much as I can.

We talked of Scotland. Ogilvie, who is a rank Scot, defended his native land with all the powers that could muster up. I was diverted to see how great a man a London wit is in comparison of one of your country swans who sing so *bonnily*. Ogilvie said there was very rich country round Edinburgh. "No, no," said Goldsmith, with a sneering laugh; "it is not rich country." Ogilvie then said that Scotland had a great many noble wild prospects. "Sir," said Johnson, "I believe you have a great many noble wild prospects. Norway too has some noble wild prospects; and Lapland is remarkable for prodigious noble wild prospects. But, Sir, I believe the noblest prospect that a Scotsman ever sees is the road which leads him to England!"

We gave a roar of applause to this most excellent sally of strong humour. At the same time, I could not help thinking that Mr. Johnson showed a want of taste in laughing at the wild grandeur of nature, which to a mind undebauched by art conveys the most pleasing awful, sublime ideas. Have not I experienced the full force of this when gazing at thee, O Arthur Seat, thou venerable mountain! whether in the severity of winter thy brow has been covered with snow or wrapped in mist; or in the gentle mildness of summer the evening sun has shone upon thy verdant sides diversified with rugged moss-clad rocks and rendered religious by the ancient Chapel of St. Anthony. Beloved hill, the admiration of my youth! Thy noble image shall ever fill my mind! Let me travel over the whole earth, I shall still remember thee; and when I return to my native country, while I live I will visit thee with affection and reverence!

Mr. Johnson was exceeding good company all this evening. We parted at one. I was very happy.

THURSDAY 7 JULY. Yesterday afternoon, before I went to the Mitre, I went to my lodgings in Downing Street, got Chetwynd, who has been a sort of prime minister to me, and packed up all my things. So curious a composition is the mind of man that I felt a degree of sorrow at leaving the room in which I had passed the winter, where I had been confined five weeks, and where this my journal and all my other little lucubrations have been written.

I then put my baggage into a hackney-coach, got into it myself, and drove to the Temple. My friend Temple was to go to Cambridge this morning, and kindly insisted that I should live in his chambers, which he has taken by the year. This morning he and I got up at five and breakfasted, after which I accompanied him to Bishopsgate Street, where the Cambridge machine inns. Nobody had taken a place besides himself, so I got in also, and rode till we were fairly out of London. The pleasing melancholy which possesses the mind when about to separate from a friend in the highest sense of the word had full power over us both. We recollected the many happy days which we have passed together, the long intimacy which has subsisted between us, and which continues as strong as ever. We expressed in the warmest manner our mutual cordiality and affection. We regretted that we were now to part for some years. (Good GOD! that is a very serious thought!) We promised to correspond as frequently as we could, and as fully. My friend advised me with much earnestness to study propriety of behaviour, and to acquire a habit of study, so that I might be independently happy and keep up the dignity of my character. He advised me to go to Utrecht, as my father wished me to do so. He said I might find it favourable to study and to getting rid of dissipation, so as to prepare me for travelling into the other parts of Europe with advantage. He said I might diversify the scene by trips to The Hague and other places; and if I found Holland very disagreeable, I might move away to some other place, such as Berlin or any other gayer capital. He said he hoped that I would return to England much improved, and that we might live much together with pleasure and comfort. He also advised me to follow virtue, which, upon the whole, would yield me most satisfaction. We then took leave of each other. My friend pursued his journey, and I walked calmly back to London.

SATURDAY 9 JULY. I dined this day at Lord Eglinton's. Lord March, Dr. Robertson, Dr. Jardine, and Dempster were there. Before dinner my Lord was roasting me about my publications. "Gentlemen," said I, "I let my Lord go on a while. But only think of a man's criticizing books who can scarcely read his own name."

SUNDAY 10 JULY. I went to Bow Church, the true centrical temple for the bluff citizens. I had many comfortable ideas. And here I must mention that some days ago I went to the old printing-office in Bow Church-yard kept by Dicey, whose family have kept it fourscore years. There are ushered into the world of literature *Jack and the Giants, The Seven Wise Men of Gotham,* and other story-books which in my dawning years amused me as much as *Rasselas* does now. I saw the whole scheme with a kind of pleasing romantic feeling to find myself really where all my old darlings were printed. I bought two dozen of the story-books and had them bound up with this title, *Curious Productions.* I thought myself like old Lord Somerville or some other man of whim, and wished my whims might be all as quiet.

WEDNESDAY 13 JULY. This afternoon I had some low debauchery with girls who patrol the courts in the Temple.

THURSDAY 14 JULY. Mr. Johnson and I met at the Mitre by ourselves. He was in most excellent humour, though the night was very rainy. I said it was good for the vegetable part of the creation. "Ay, Sir," said he, "and for the animals who eat those vegetables, and for the animals who eat those animals." We had a good supper, which made us very comfortable.

I said, "You and I, Sir, are very good companions, but my father and I are not so. Now what can occasion this? For you are as old a man as my father, and you are certainly as learned and as knowing." "Sir," said he, "I am a man of the world. I live in the world, and I take in some measure the colour of the world as it moves along. But your father is a judge in a remote part of the country, and all his notions are taken from the old world. Besides, there must always be a struggle between a father and son, while the one aims at power and the other at independency." I told him that I was afraid of my father's forcing me to be a lawyer. "Why, Sir," said he, "you need not be afraid of his forcing you to be a laborious practising lawyer. That is not in his power. For, as the proverb says, 'One man may lead a horse to the water, but twenty cannot make him drink.' He may be displeased, but it will not go far. If he only insists on your having as much law as is necessary for a man of property, and endeavours to get you into Parliament, he is quite in the right."

When we went into the Mitre tonight, Mr. Johnson said, "We will not drink two bottles of port." When one was drank, he called for another pint; and when we had got to the bottom of that, and I was distributing it equally, "Come," said he, "you need not measure it so exactly." "Sir," said I "it is done." "Well, Sir," said he, "are you satisfied? or would you choose another?" "Would you, Sir?" said I. "Yes," said he, "I think I would. I think two bottles would seem to be the quantity for us." Accordingly we made them out.

I take pleasure in recording every little circumstance about so great a man as Mr. Johnson. This little specimen of social pleasantry will serve me to tell as an agreeable story to literary people. He took me cordially by the hand and said, "My dear Boswell! I do love you very much"—I *will* be vain, there's enough.

SATURDAY 16 JULY. I carried Bob Temple with me to breakfast at Dempster's and introduced him to Dempster and his sister, where he was very well received. Since my being honoured with the friendship of Mr. Johnson, I have more seriously considered the duties of morality and religion and the dignity of human nature. I have considered that promiscuous concubinage is certainly wrong. It is contributing one's share towards bringing confusion and misery into society; and it is a transgression of the laws of the Almighty Creator, who has ordained marriage for the mutual comfort of the sexes and the procreation and right educating of children. Sure it is that if all the men and women in Britain were merely to consult animal gratification, society would be a most shocking scene. Nay, it would soon cease altogether. Notwithstanding of these reflections, I have stooped to mean profligacy even yesterday. However, I am now resolved to guard against it.

He advised me to keep a journal of my life, fair and undisguised. He said it would be a very good exercise, and would yield me infinite satisfaction when the ideas were faded from my remembrance. I told him that I had done so ever since I left Scotland. He said he was very

happy that I pursued so good a plan. And now, O my journal! art thou
not highly dignified? Shalt thou not flourish tenfold? No former
solicitations or censures could tempt me to lay thee aside; and now is
there any argument which can outweigh the sanction of Mr. Samuel
Johnson? He said indeed that I should keep it private, and that I might
surely have a friend who would burn it in case of my death. For my own
part, I have at present such an affection for this my journal that it shocks
me to think of burning it. I rather encourage the idea of having it
carefully laid up among the archives of Auchinleck. However, I cannot
judge fairly of it now. Some years hence I may. I told Mr. Johnson that I
put down all sorts of little incidents in it. "Sir," said he, "there is nothing
too little for so little a creature as man. It is by studying little things that
we attain the great knowledge of having as little misery and as much
happiness as possible."

He told me that he intended to give us some more imitations of
Juvenal. When I some time ago mentioned the universality of Mr.
Johnson's abilities and mentioned his Works, I am surprised how I
omitted *The Idler,* which is a more easy and lively paper than *The Rambler,*
but is distinguished for the same good sense and strong humour; and his
tragedy of *Irene,* which is far from deserving the indiscriminate censure
of frigidity which Dempster gave it in the beginning of winter, as may be
seen in a former page of this my journal.

At present we have an old woman called Mrs. Legge for a laundress,
who has breakfast set every morning, washes our linen, cleans the
chambers, wipes our shoes, and, in short, does everything in the world
that we can require of an old woman. She is perhaps as curious an
animal as has appeared in human shape. She presents a strong idea of
one of the frightful witches in *Macbeth;* and yet the beldame boasts that
she was once as handsome a girl as you could clap your eyes upon, and
withal exceedingly virtuous; in so much that she refused £500 from the
late Lord Hervey. She was servant in many great families, and then she
married for love a tall strapping fellow who died. She then owns that she
married Mr. Legge for money. He is a little queer round creature; and
claiming kindred with Baron Legge, he generally goes by the name of
The Baron, and fine fun we have with him. He serves as porter when we
have any message to send at a distance.

To give a specimen of Mrs. Legge, who is a prodigious prater. She
said to Bob this morning, "Ay, ay, Master Robert, you may talk. But we
knows what you young men are. Just cock-sparrows. You can't stand it
out. But the Baron! O Lord! the Baron is a staunch man. Ay, ay, did you
never hear that GOD never made a little man but he made it up to him in

something else? Yes, yes, the Baron is a good man, an able man. He laid a married woman upon the floor while he sent the maid out for a pint of porter. But he was discovered, and so I come to know of it."

MONDAY 18 JULY. At the head of St. James's Street I observed three Turks staring about in a strange manner. I spoke a little of English, French, and Latin to them, neither of which they understood a word of. They showed me a pass from a captain of a ship declaring that they were Algerines who had been taken by the Spaniards and made slaves. That they made their escape, got to Lisbon, and from thence were brought to England. I carried them with me to a French house, where I got a man who spoke a little Spanish to one of them, and learnt that they wanted to see the Ambassador from Tripoli, who though not from the same division of territory, is yet under the Grand Signior, as they are. I accordingly went with him to the Ambassador's house, where I found a Turk who could speak English and interpret what they said; and he told me that they had landed that morning and had already been with the Ambassador begging that he would get liberty for them from the Lords of the Admiralty; and that he had ordered them victuals. I gave them half a crown. They were very thankful, and my Turkish friend who spoke English said, "GOD reward you. The same God make the Turk that make the Christian. But the English have the tender heart. The Turk have not the tender heart."

I was anxious to have my poor strangers taken care of, and I begged that they might sleep in the house with the Ambassador. The landlady, a hard-hearted shrew, opposed this vehemently. "Indeed," said she, "I would not suffer one of 'em to lie in my beds. Who knows what vermin and nastiness they may have brought with them? To be sure I may allow them to sleep upon the floor, as they do in their own country; but for my beds, Sir, *as I'm a Christian,* I could not let them sleep in a bed of mine." Her Christian argument was truly conclusive. Abandoned wretch! to make the religion of the Prince of Peace, the religion which so warmly inculcates universal charity, a cloak for thy unfeeling barbarity!

At eleven I went to St. Paul's Church; walked up to the whispering gallery, which is a most curious thing. I had here the mortification to observe that the noble paintings in the ceiling of the Cupola are a good deal damaged by the moisture of winter. I then went up to the roof of the Cupola, and went out upon the leads, and walked around it. I went up to the highest storey of roof. Here I had the immense prospect of London and its environs. London gave me no great idea. I just saw a prodigious group of tiled roofs and narrow lanes opening here and there, for the streets and beauty of the buildings cannot be observed on account of the distance. The Thames and the country around, the beautiful hills of Hampstead and of Highgate looked very fine. And yet I did not feel the same enthusiasm that I have felt some time ago at viewing these rich prospects.

Mr. Johnson goes up to his library when he wants to study, as he will not allow his servant to say he is not at home when he is. I don't know but I may have mentioned before in my journal that he thinks that a servant's notions of truth would be hurt by such a practice. A philosopher may know that it is a mere form of denial, but few servants are such nice distinguishers. No place can be more favourable for meditation than such a retirement as this garret. I could not help indulging a scheme of taking it for myself many years hence, when its present great possessor will in all probability be gone to a more exalted situation.

WEDNESDAY 20 JULY. Dempster argued on Rousseau's plan, that the goods of fortune and advantages of rank were nothing to a wise man, who ought only to value internal merit. Replied Johnson: "If man were a savage living in the woods by himself, this might be true. But in civilized society we all depend upon each other, and our happiness is very much owing to the good opinion of others. Now, Sir, in civilized society, external advantages make us more respected by individuals. A man who has a good coat upon his back meets with a better reception than he who has a bad one.

"Go to the street and give one man a lecture of morality and another a shilling, and see who will respect you most. Sir, I was once a great arguer for the advantages of poverty, but I was at the same time very discontented. Sir, the great deal of arguing which we hear to represent poverty as no evil shows it to be evidently a great one. You never knew people labouring to convince you that you might live very happily upon a plentiful fortune. In the same way, you hear people talking how miserable a king must be. And yet every one of them would wish to have his place."

I said that in civilized society I considered distinction of rank of so much importance that if I were asked to dine with the Duke of Norfolk or with the first man for genius and instructive and agreeable conversation, I should hesitate which to prefer. Dempster looked odd at this. But Johnson said, "To be sure, Sir, if you were to dine only once, and if it were never to be known where you dined, you would choose to dine with the first genius. But in order to gain most respect, you would dine with the Duke of Norfolk. For nine people in ten that you meet with would have a higher opinion of you because you had dined with the Duke; and the great genius himself would receive you better in some degree because you had been with the great Duke."

Thus did Mr. Johnson show upon solid principles the necessity and the advantages of subordination, which gave much satisfaction to me, who have always had strong monarchical inclinations but could never give strong reasons in their justification.

THURSDAY 21 JULY. I remember nothing that happened worth relating this day. How many such days does mortal man pass!

FRIDAY 22 JULY. Mr. Johnson said that Mr. Hume and all other sceptical innovators were vain men; and finding mankind already in possession of truth, they could not gratify their vanity by supporting her; and so they have taken to error. "Sir," said he, "Truth is a cow which will yield such people no more milk, and so they are gone to milk the bull."

Mr. Johnson said he loved the acquaintance of young people. "Because," said he, "in the first place, I don't like to think myself turning old. In the next place, young acquaintances must last longest, if they do last; and in the next place, young men have more virtue than old men. They have more generous sentiments in every respect. I love the young dogs of this age: they have more wit and humour and knowledge of life than we had. But then the dogs are not so good scholars. Sir, in my early years I read very hard. It is a hard enough reflection, but a true one, that I knew almost as much at eighteen as I do now. My judgment, to be sure, was not so good, but I had all the facts. I remember very well when I was about five and twenty an old gentleman at Oxford said to me, 'Young man, ply your book diligently now and acquire a stock of knowledge; for when years come upon you, you will find that poring upon books will be but an irksome task.' "

I complained to Mr. Johnson that I was much afflicted with melancholy, which was hereditary in our family. He said that he himself had been greatly distressed with it, and for that reason had been obliged to fly from study and meditation to the dissipating variety of life. He advised me to have constant occupation of mind, to take a great deal of exercise, and to live moderately; especially to shun drinking at night. "Melancholy people," said he, "are apt to fly to intemperance, which gives a momentary relief but sinks the soul much lower in misery."

He insisted again on subordination of rank. "Sir," said he, "I would no more deprive a nobleman of his respect than of his money. I consider myself as acting a part in the great system, and do to others as I would have them do to me. Sir, I would behave to a nobleman as I would expect he should behave to me were I a nobleman and he Sam. Johnson. Sir, there is one Mrs. Macaulay in this town, a great republican. I came to her one day and said I was quite a convert to her republican system, and thought mankind all upon a footing; and I begged that her footman might be allowed to dine with us. She has never liked me since. Sir, your levellers count down only the length of themselves."

I told him that Sir James Macdonald had never seen him, but that he had a great respect, though at the same time a great terror, for him. "Sir," said he, "if he were to see me, it might lessen both."

He said he wished to visit the Western Isles of Scotland, and would go thither with me when I returned from abroad, unless some very good companion should offer when I was absent, which he did not think probable.

He said, "There are few people whom I take so much to as you"; and when I talked of leaving England, he said (with an affection that almost made me cry), "My dear Boswell! I should be very unhappy at parting, did I think we were not to meet again."

He maintained that a boy at school was the happiest being. I maintained that a man was more so. He said a boy's having his backside flogged was not so severe as a man's having the hiss of the world against him. He talked of the anxiety which men have for fame; and how the greater it is, the more afraid are they of losing it. I considered how wonderful it must be if even the great Mr. Johnson did not think himself secure.

TUESDAY 26 JULY. I called upon Mr. Johnson.

We talked of the education of children and what was best to teach them first. "Sir," said he, "there is no matter what you teach them first, any more than what leg you shall put into your breeches first. Sir, you may stand disputing which is best to put in first, but in the mean time your backside is bare. Sir, while you are considering which of two things you should teach your child first, another boy has learnt 'em both."

THURSDAY 28 JULY. I sat up all last night writing letters and bringing up my lagging journal, which, like a stone to be rolled up a hill, must be kept constantly going.

We then talked of Me. He said that I was very forward in knowledge for my age; that a man had no reason to complain who held a middle place and had many below him; and that perhaps I had not six above me. Perhaps not one. He did not know one. This was very high. I asked him, if he was my father, and if I did well at the law, if he would be pleased with me. "Sir," said he, "I should be pleased with you whatever way of life you followed, since you are now in so good a way. Time will do all that is wanting. Indeed, when you was in the irreligious way, I should not have been pleased with you." I returned him many thanks for having established my principles.

I begged Mr. Johnson's advice as to my method of study at Utrecht.

"Come," said he, "let us make a day of it. Let us go down to Greenwich and dine." Accordingly Saturday was fixed for that jaunt, if a sail on the river may be so expressed. It must be something curious for the people in the Turk's Head Coffee-house to see this great man and poor Me so often together by ourselves. My vanity is much flattered.

As we walked along the Strand tonight, arm in arm, a woman of the town came enticingly near us. "No," said Mr. Johnson, "no, my girl, it won't do." We then talked of the unhappy situation of these wretches, and how much more misery than happiness, upon the whole, is produced by irregular love. He parted from me at the Temple Gate, as he always does.

FRIDAY 29 JULY. Sound was the sleep which I enjoyed last night. As I am now determined to humour my father as much as I can, and may in time, perhaps, apply to the law in Scotland, I have written to Lord President, to whom I said that experience had now taught me that my father is as wise as myself, and that I am to follow his plan of life. I thank his Lordship for his former good offices while I was an idler, and hope he will not withhold them from me when I endeavour to be a man of business. To Pitfour I say that his prophecy that I would return to the law will be fulfilled; and I say that if a saint nowadays obtained the gift of prophecy, none can have a better chance for it than Pitfour. I bid him to tell his son to hasten on at the bar lest he be overtaken by a younger man. To Lord Advocate I talk in the easy style of a companion, as he and I were always easy, and mention with satisfaction my having more rational views. Such is the substance of these letters, which I expressed very neatly. I am sure they will do good, as they will be shown, or at least quoted, to my father. I have touched every man on the proper key, and yet have used no deceit.

SATURDAY 30 JULY. Mr. Johnson and I took a boat and sailed down the silver Thames.

We landed at the Old Swan and walked to Billingsgate, where we took oars and moved smoothly along the river. We were entertained with the immense number and variety of ships that were lying at anchor. It was a pleasant day, and when we got clear out into the country, we were charmed with the beautiful fields on each side of the river.

We talked of preaching, and of the great success that the Methodists have. He said that was owing to their preaching in a plain, vulgar manner, which was the only way to do good to common people, and which men of learning and genius ought to do, as their duty; and for which they would be praised by men of sense.

When we got to Greenwich, I felt great pleasure in being at the place which Mr. Johnson celebrates in his *London: a Poem*. I had the poem in my pocket, and read the passage on the banks of the Thames, and literally "kissed the consecrated earth."

We supped at the Turk's Head. Mr. Johnson said, "I must see thee go; I will go down with you to Harwich." This prodigious mark of his affection filled me with gratitude and vanity. I gave him an account of the family of Auchinleck, and of the Place. He said, "I must be there, and we will live in the Old Castle; and if there is no room remaining, we will build one." This was the most pleasing idea that I could possibly have: to think of seeing this great man at the venerable seat of my ancestors. I had been up all last night yet was not sleepy.

SUNDAY 31 JULY. In the forenoon I was at a Quakers' meeting in Lombard Street, and in the afternoon at St. Paul's, where I was very devout and very happy. After service, I stood in the center and took leave of the church, bowing to every quarter. I cannot help having a reverence for it. Mr. Johnson says the same. Mr. Johnson said today that a woman's preaching was like a dog's walking on his hinder legs. It was not done well, but you were surprised to find it done at all.

Johnson said that he always felt an inclination to do nothing. I said it was strange to think that the most indolent man in Britain had written the most laborious work, *The English Dictionary*. He said he took ten years to do it; but that if he had applied properly, he might have done it in three.

In the afternoon he carried me to drink tea with Miss Williams, who has a snug lodging in Bolt Court, Fleet Street. I found her a facetious, agreeable woman, though stone-blind. I was cheerful, and well received. He then carried me to what he called his walk, which is a paved long court overshadowed by some trees in a neighbouring garden. There he advised me when fixed in a place abroad to read with a keenness after knowledge, and to read every day an hour at Greek. And when I was moving about, to read diligently the great book of mankind. We supped at the Turk's Head. I was somewhat melancholy, but it went off. Mr. Johnson filled my mind with so many noble and just sentiments that the Demon of Despondency was driven away.

WEDNESDAY 3 AUGUST. I should have mentioned that on Monday night, coming up the Strand, I was tapped on the shoulder by a fine fresh lass. I went home with her. She was an officer's daughter, and born at Gibraltar. I could not resist indulging myself with the enjoyment of her. Surely, in such a situation, when the woman is already abandoned, the crime must be alleviated, though in strict morality, illicit love is always wrong.

I last night sat up again, but I shall do so no more, for I was very stupid today and had a kind of feverish headache. At night Mr. Johnson and I supped at the Turk's Head. He talked much for restoring the Convocation of the Church of England to its full powers, and said that religion was much assisted and impressed on the mind by external pomp. My want of sleep sat heavy upon me, and made me like to nod, even in Mr. Johnson's company. Such must be the case while we are united with flesh and blood.

THURSDAY 4 AUGUST. This is now my last day in London before I set out upon my travels, and makes a very important period in my journal. Let me recollect my life since this journal began. Has it not passed like a dream? Yes, but I have been attaining a knowledge of the world. I came to town to go into the Guards. How different is my scheme now! I am now upon a less pleasurable but a more rational and lasting plan. Let me pursue it with steadiness and I may be a man of dignity. My mind is strangely agitated. I am happy to think of going upon my travels and seeing the diversity of foreign parts; and yet my feeble mind shrinks somewhat at the idea of leaving Britain in so very short a time from the moment in which I now make this remark. How strange must I feel myself in foreign parts. My mind too is gloomy and dejected at the thoughts of leaving London, where I am so comfortably situated and where I have enjoyed most happiness. However, I shall be the happier for being abroad, as long as I live. Let me be manly. Let me commit myself to the care of my merciful Creator.

THE END OF MY JOURNAL BEFORE MY TRAVELS.

Boswell has passed now from London to Utrecht. In Holland, and through Europe, Boswell often kept his journals in French. The translation has been made by Professor Pottle. In an earlier volume Mr. Pottle observed that although Boswell "became fluent in French, he never became really idiomatic or even accurate in that language; and if one substitutes the literal English equivalents, the result is generally good Boswellian English."

SUNDAY 16 OCTOBER. You did a great deal yesterday. You made out your Plan, and you brought up near a whole week of journal. This day bring up the rest, and then you'll always after this be clear and easy. 'Tis true you sat up a little late, but that must now and then happen in important cases. Read your Plan every morning regularly at breakfast, and when you travel, carry it in trunk. Get commonplace-book. Be one week without talking of self or repeating. The more and oftener restraints, the better. Be steady.

Inviolable Plan

You have got an excellent heart and bright parts. You are born to a respectable station in life. You are bound to do the duties of a *Laird* of Auchinleck. For some years past you have been idle, dissipated, absurd, and unhappy. Let those years be thought of no more. You are now determined to form yourself into a man. Formerly all your resolutions were overturned by a fit of the spleen. You believed that you had a real distemper. On your first coming to Utrecht you yielded to that idea. You endured severe torment. You was pitiful and wretched. You was in danger of utter ruin. This severe shock has proved of the highest advantage. Your friend Temple showed you that idleness was your sole disease. The Rambler showed you that vacuity, gloom, and fretfulness were the causes of your woe, and that you was only afflicted as others are. He furnished you with principles of philosophy and piety to support the soul at all times. You returned to Utrecht determined. You studied with diligence. You grew quite well. This is a certain fact. You must never forget it. Nor attempt to plead a real incurable distemper; for you cured it, when it was at its very worst, merely by following a proper plan with diligence and activity. This is a great era in your life; for from this time you fairly set out upon solid principles to be a man.

Your worthy father has the greatest affection for you and has suffered much from your follies. You are now resolved to make reparation by a rational and prudent conduct. Your dear mother is anxious to see you do well.

You have been long without a fixed plan and have felt the misery of being unsettled. You are now come abroad at a distance from company with whom you lived as a frivolous and as a ludicrous fellow. You are to attain habits of study, so that you may have constant entertainment by yourself, nor be at the mercy of every company; and to attain propriety of conduct, that you may be respected.

Without a real plan, life is insipid and uneasy. You have an admirable plan before you. You are to return to Scotland, be one of the Faculty of Advocates, have constant occupation, and a prospect of being in Parliament, or having a gown. You can live quite independent and go to London every year; and you can pass some months at Auchinleck, doing good to your tenants and living hospitably with your neighbours, beautifying your estate, rearing a family, and piously preparing for immortal felicity.

SUNDAY 23 OCTOBER. Yesterday you was still too jocular and talked of yourself, particularly of your whoring, which was shameful; however, you continue your plan of study, and you make no great deviations. Lesser things must come by degrees. Try firmly this week never once to speak of yourself. It will be great.

SATURDAY 12 NOVEMBER. Yesterday was an irregular day. You passed three hours at Brown's with Miss de Zuylen. You was too much off guard, and gave way too much to instantaneous fancy, and was too keen about the Highlanders. You was a little lightheaded; however, you must not be too severe.

[Received 12 November, Lord Auchinleck to Boswell]

Auchinleck, ? October 1763

MY DEAR SON—Your letter of the 7th of October, which came in due course, gave me uncommon satisfaction, for as I know your veracity and can confide in the accounts you give of yourself, I now bless GOD that I have the prospect of having comfort in you and support from you; and that you will tread in the steps of the former Jameses, who in this family have been remarkably useful.

I quite approve of your plan of study. You may, by the assistance of Professor Trotz, come to be thoroughly master of the Pandects, which is the most rational system of law extant, and the reasonings in it the most acute and accurate.

SUNDAY 13 NOVEMBER. Yesterday you did extremely well. You received a letter from your worthy father which warmed your heart and gave you new vigour to pursue a proper course. . . .

THURSDAY 24 NOVEMBER. Yesterday you recovered very well after your riot with the Dutch students. But remember how near you was to getting drunk and exposing yourself, for if you had gone on a little longer, you could not have stopped. You have important secrets to keep. Though you are sorry for the crimes, yet preserve a warm affection and gratitude to the persons and show it when you meet, disinterestedly; and in the mean time always shun drinking, and guard lips. . . .

[C. 24-26 NOVEMBER. FRENCH THEMES] . . . Soon my Lord Bute was made Groom of the Stole, as they say in England, a very honourable office. He is master of the King's wardrobe. In these themes I can never resist anything laughable that presents itself, whether there is occasion for it or not. In this I follow the example of Rabelais, Tristram Shandy, and all those people of unbridled imagination who write their books as I write my themes—at random, without trying to have any order or method; and for that reason they have acquired great reputation among people of unregulated vivacity who do not wish to give themselves the trouble of thinking even in their amusements. . . .

MONDAY 28 NOVEMBER. Yesterday you did very well. You walked an hour. You was prudent at Mr. Brown's, and talked genteelly of your assemblies; after dinner you joked him too broadly on Calvinism. Let him alone. He is a very good man in his way. Behave politely to him, and you will reap advantage. Remember, you entrusted him with your story. Make him warn you. But be *retenu*. . . . You went at six to the Grand Bailiff's. . . . You played a party with a prince and Miss de Zuylen. You was shocked, or rather offended, with her unlimited vivacity.

TUESDAY 13 DECEMBER. . . . Consider what a different man you are now from what you have been for some years. Instead of idle dissipation, you read Greek, French, law; and instead of drollery, you have sensible conversation. You also mix gay amusement with study. . . .

[Received 14 December, Samuel Johnson to Boswell]

London, 8 December 1763

DEAR SIR:—You are not to think yourself forgotten or criminally neglected that you have had yet no letter from me. I love to see my friends, to hear from them, to talk to them, and to talk of them; but it is not without a considerable effort of resolution that I prevail upon myself to write. . . .

You know a gentleman, who, when first he set his foot in the gay world, as he prepared himself to whirl in the vortex of pleasure, imagined a total indifference and universal negligence to be the most agreeable concomitants of youth and the strongest indication of an airy temper and a quick apprehension. Vacant to every object and sensible of every impulse, he thought that all appearance of diligence would deduct something from the reputation of genius; and hoped that he should appear to attain, amidst all the ease of carelessness and all the tumult of diversion, that knowledge and those accomplishments which mortals of the common fabric obtain only by mute abstraction and solitary drudgery. He tried this scheme of life a while, was made weary of it by his sense and his virtue; he then wished to return to his studies; and finding long habits of idleness and pleasure harder to be cured than he expected, still willing to retain his claim to some extraordinary prerogatives, resolved the common consequences of irregularity into an unalterable decree of destiny, and concluded that Nature had originally formed him incapable of rational employment.

Let all such fancies, illusive and destructive, be banished henceforward from your thoughts for ever.

THURSDAY 15 DECEMBER. . . . You was indeed a great man yesterday. You received letters from Lord Auchinleck, Mr. Samuel Johnson, Sir David Dalrymple. Mr. Johnson's correspondence is the greatest honour you could ever imagine you could attain to. Look back only three years when you was first in London with Derrick. Consider. He is the first author in England. Let his counsel give you new vigour. Return still to the charge. . . .

FRIDAY 20 JANUARY. Yesterday you began Trotz. After dinner Brown and you, &c., went and heard Hahn on nitre. You said fatalists should be hanged and sceptics whipped. Greek went on. In the morning you visited Brouwer and saw Icelandic. You talked on scheme of Scots dictionary. Pursue it while here. Brown will assist you. It is not trifling. 'Twill be an excellent work. But be prudent with it. This day conclude letter to Johnston. Write Dutch song. Cheer up; take exercise and resume firmness; you must combat nervousness.

WEDNESDAY 1 FEBRUARY. . . . At Assembly you appeared in seagreen and silver and was really brilliant—much taken notice of and like an ambassador. You begin to be much at your ease and to take a true foreign polish. Madame Geelvinck was charming. You told her you expected to see her character by Zélide. She said, "It is not interesting." You said, "Oh, do not say that to me!" She said, "You, who are so sincere!" She saw what you meant. You played whist well. After it, you felt, for the first time in Holland, delicious love. O *la belle Veuve!* She talked low to you and close, perhaps to feel breath. All the *Heeren* looked blue. You took her hand to the coach, and your frame thrilled. . . .

[C. 2 FEBRUARY. FRENCH THEME] When I came home yesterday evening, I scolded my servant, not at all harshly but with proper restraint. I said, "Francois, really you don't know how to pack coats; just see how this one is wrinkled. You must fold the collar over and not this part, because although it gets a little crumpled at the neck, when one puts it on, the shoulders stretch it out and the wrinkles don't show; but it takes a long time for this part to come smooth. What do you call this part?" "Sir, it is the *pans* (skirts) of a coat. But I assure you that I packed them well on your trip. The coat was longer than the trunk, though not much, and I did fold it over a little at the collar. So I am sure that the skirts could not have been rumpled in the trunk. I must have folded it badly in the drawer here after you came back from The Hague." After a harangue like that I had nothing to say. I undressed in great tranquillity and set myself to read Monsieur Voltaire. . . .

I take credit to myself for having been so reasonable with my servant in a situation where passionate people like yourself would have beaten him. You say to me, "Why not strike a servant sometimes, when one feels like it? It is an amusement of a sort, it relieves one's spleen to punish the cause of it. The desire to avenge ourselves on those who have offended us is universal; and Nature herself shows us that it is right. You observe that a child, when he falls on a stone that hurts him, is angry and kicks it or beats it with a stick, and it is only afterwards that he is appeased."

SATURDAY 4 FEBRUARY. . . . At assembly . . . you spoke long time to *belle Veuve*. She stood up and she whispered and she corrected your French delightfully. She said she'd give you Zélide in her own writing. You told her 'twas strange—'twas the very thing you wished. She said, "I am glad that we meet." You said you was physiognomist. She said, "I reveal little, but I am very sincere." You are much in love. She perhaps wishes to marry rationally. But have a care.

SUNDAY 5 FEBRUARY. . . . You advance well in dictionary. At dinner you was really on guard and *retenu*, and spoke French.

THURSDAY 9 FEBRUARY (A triple memorandum). Yesterday you did not attend enough to Trotz. Amend this. At dinner you was on guard. It was fine, cheerful day. At four young De Zuylen came for you, and you went quite easy; was well with Mademoiselle, Bernard, and Rose, but was really hurt with her imprudent rattling and constant grin. You was angry for having thought of putting any confidence in her, for she blabbed, "It is your continual study to check your imagination." She is really foolish and *raised*. Be her friend, but trust her not. You had first been at *la Comtesse's*, who was snappish but polite enough; only pretended to understand your French worse than she did—vile spite, low cunning. At concert you was charmed with bassoon. You was timid, but at last went to Madame Geelvinck. She said, "Our faces are not unfamiliar to each other." A little after, you said, "Nor our sentiments." Love was introduced, how I know not; perhaps on such occasions the little god jumps in between the parties. She said, "I believe there is more evil than good in the world, and consequently more evil in love." You said, "There is only jealousy; that is horrible."

MME GEELVINCK. But after love comes *ennui*.

BOSWELL. Madame, I am too frank not to confess that I fear that too, yet I hope it is possible to guard against the evils of love.

MME GEELVINCK. I believe that one can truly love only once.

BOSWELL. Are you sure of that, Madame? I am not.

MME GEELVINCK. But you have been in love?

BOSWELL. I thought it was true love, but the lady was fickle. I am much indebted to you for having introduced me to true love.

MME GEELVINCK. Are you sincere?

BOSWELL. Yes, I assure you that I am. Are you sincere too? Come, will you make a pact of sincerity between us?

MME GEELVINCK. Yes.

BOSWELL. You see I speak without fear.

MME GEELVINCK. You are wrong if you are afraid of me.

BOSWELL. Well! I can speak to you quite openly?

MME GEELVINCK. Just as you speak when by yourself.

BOSWELL. Permit me merely to say, "I admire you," from time to time.—What must one do when one is in love?

MME GEELVINCK. I don't know.

BOSWELL. You are in a peculiar situation: beautiful, pleasant, and, what is generally more important, rich. Can you tell if people really love you?

MME GEELVINCK. It is difficult.—You must not repeat this conversation.

FRIDAY 10 FEBRUARY. Yesterday you did very well. On Wednesday you sat up very late, being all agitated with love and fiery imagination. You sprung out of bed, and upon your bare knees swore not to speak of yourself, except to Madame Geelvinck, for eight days. You forgot this once or twice yesterday. However, you'll keep to it more and more. You was hurt by want of rest. Your nerves were unhinged and spirits very low. But you kept it to self. Be more grave, and you'll support it with manly dignity. You must not tire at Brown's. All the world would seem insipid to each other after dining a number of months together. But you're at Utrecht to improve. So keep on.

SATURDAY 11 FEBRUARY. Yesterday you saw Prince and Princess pass. You was still cold and bad, really distemper of body. You told Brown you never would say where you dined, that he might not know when you fasted. Let this be observed. A message to dine with Monsieur d'Amerongen set you a-going. You dressed neat. At dinner you was gloomy, but kept your post and grew very cheerful, though still on guard, and spoke French and Dutch, and was temperate. You are growing firm. Amerongen, worthy man, said, "I invite you to our dinner, as you see, to show that we shall be happy to see you from time to time." He repeated this as you went away. 'Twill be an excellent house. Cultivate there. You went at five and read Greek—O noble! But you once or twice brought in self.

TUESDAY 14 FEBRUARY. Yesterday you got up in good time, and was fresh and healthy. You did not attend enough to Trotz. Go exact at the hour after this, and force attention. You fasted and stayed at home from one to five. You read Voltaire. You wrote journal. You had prayers. You renewed resolutions of virtue and piety. At the *partie* you was too merry in saying that Madame Roosmalen would *vous batter*. It seemed strange. They are stupid, low, censorious. Be not free with them. Take up, keep your own counsel, and show that you're quite independent. You supped elegant at Mademoiselle de Zuylen's with the General, &c. She said, "You write everything down." Have a care. Never speak on that subject.

[c.15 FEBRUARY. DUTCH THEME] It has been thirty years since my father studied at Leyden. He studied Dutch with great diligence and in a short time had mastered it so well that he was able to make himself understood. He took lodgings in a Dutch home. His landlady was a widow, and had a sister who lived with her. The widow was courted by a tailor, but the sister was no friend of the lover, which the widow took greatly amiss. One morning at four o'clock she waked my father in a state of great excitement "O Sir," said she, "Sister's dead." "What did you say, Ma'am?" answered he. "Is she dead?" "Yes, indeed, Sir," said the landlady. "She kept a bottle of brandy in her room every night, and I fear that she drank too much." My father got up in alarm and went downstairs and found Sister dead for certain; but he had suspicions that the widow had helped her out of the world when she married the tailor immediately afterwards.

SUNDAY 19 FEBRUARY. At four, Bailiff's in fine humour; heart rejoiced to see all the young folks; was quite at ease yet not too forward. Had long and important conversation with Madame Geelvinck:

> BOSWELL. At what age, &c., did you first truly fall in love?
>
> MME GEELVINCK. Really! That is certainly being frank.
>
> BOSWELL. Oh, how happy I am! And since you became a widow, have you been in love?
>
> MME GEELVINCK. No. Really!
>
> BOSWELL. But, Madame, I am very much in love. I adore you. Will you make a distinction between Madame Geelvinck and my friend, and give me your advice?
>
> MME GEELVINCK. Yes. But I am truly sorry. I advise you to cure your passion.
>
> BOSWELL. But, Madame, how?
>
> MME GEELVINCK. You have been in love before?
>
> BOSWELL. Yes, I have been in love before, but those passions had no foundation. I always had the help of reason to cure them. But I believe I have never really been in love before now.

MME GEELVINCK. Oh, fancy that!

BOSWELL. But, Madame, is it impossible for you to fall in love?

MME GEELVINCK. I shall never do so.

BOSWELL. There is more good than bad in love.

MME GEELVINCK. I am happy as things stand. I am free. I can go from one city to another. One ought not to give up a certainty.

BOSWELL. But, Madame, have you no thought of a pleasure you have not yet tasted? Only think how you could begin a new life.

MME GEELVINCK. Really, I am sorry that you are like this; it will make you unhappy. I will be your friend.

BOSWELL. Will you be my friend always, for the whole of your life?

MME GEELVINCK. Yes.

BOSWELL. But did you not know that I was in love with you?

MME GEELVINCK. No, really. I thought it was with Mademoiselle de Zuylen; and I said nothing about it.

BOSWELL. Oh, my dear Madame, what heavenly pleasure I have at this moment in looking at you. I am speaking as you told me to—as though I were alone. I can trust in you; you will not expose me?

MME GEELVINCK. No, I assure you on my conscience.

BOSWELL. You believe that I am in love? I swear it to you by all the hope I have of happiness in this existence or the other. You believe that I am sincere?

MME GEELVINCK. If you are not, you are horrible.

TUESDAY 21 FEBRUARY. Yesterday after a sad night of sickness from stomach disordered, you sprung up before seven, and taking dram, went out to St. Catherine Porte, where you made interest with honest German carabineer and got into his box and saw Madame pass. She looked angelic, and that glimpse was ravishing.

[C.20 FEBRUARY. FRENCH THEME] I like much to lie with my head very high. I think it is healthy to do so. At home I always have a couple of pillows, and if I am in a strange house, the first thing I ask is whether I can have a couple of pillows. I ask it without the least ceremony, whether of gentlemen or of ladies. When I was at Laird Heron's in Galloway, I said to the lady of the house, "I beg you, Madam, let me have your best bedroom and a couple of pillows." She could not grant me my first request, but she saw to the second. Likewise, when I was at the Earl of Galloway's, my Lord Garlies was so polite as to show me to my bedroom and say, "Mr. Boswell, you will have the goodness to mention it if there is anything you lack." I walked very softly over and looked at the bed. "My Lord," said I, "there is nothing lacking but a couple of pillows, and I hope I shall have enough interest to procure them." Sometimes I have forgotten to ask for my pillows, or have asked for them when it was too late; when the housekeeper had gone to bed and had her keys in her pocket carefully placed under her head. In such a case I have been extremely embarrassed. I have been at my wits' end. However, I have always found some expedient. I have sometimes put my clothes and sometimes a cushion in place of the pillows. I would rather use a stone than sleep without having my head well raised. It is said that to hold the head high is a sign of pride; and perhaps you will accuse me of hauteur even when I sleep. . . .

[C. 24 FEBRUARY. FRENCH THEME] . . . When I enter an assembly, I appear to be a young man of family on my travels, elegantly dressed in scarlet and gold. I am seen to chat pleasantly with the ladies of wit and beauty; I am seen to play a game of cards and to be as fashionable and as frivolous as the rest. No doubt, therefore, it would seem safe in talking to me to make fun of the author of a dictionary as being a heavy man; it might even be supposed that in talking thus one would be paying a compliment to a man of vivacity, and that he would be charmed to hear the most piquant witticisms directed against a man so different from himself. It might seem that in abusing the blockhead one would be praising the man of genius. But how taken in they are when they learn that the blockhead and the man of genius are one and the same! How surprised they are when they learn that I am writing a dictionary myself!

. . . It is a Scots dictionary. You must know, gentlemen, that Great Britain was peopled by the Gauls, the same people who came from Scythia and occupied a part of France, and then passed into Ireland and Britain. . . . Some centuries later, the barbarians of Scandinavia, especially the Saxons, invaded Great Britain, and having been victorious, the true ancient Britons were driven from the most fertile parts of the country and established themselves in the country of Wales, the neighbouring country of Cornwall, and the islands and mountains of the West and North of Scotland.

It is thus that has arisen the greatest difference between English and Scots. Half the words are changed only a little, but the result of that is that a Scot is often not understood in England. I do not know the reason for it, but it is a matter of observation that although an Englishman often does not understand a Scot, it is rare that a Scot has trouble in understanding what an Englishman says: and certainly *Sawney* has an advantage in that. It is ridiculous to give as the reason for it that a Scot is quicker than an Englishman and consequently cleverer in understanding everything. It is equally ridiculous to say that English is so musical that it charms the ears and lures men to understand it, while Scots shocks and disgusts by its harshness. I agree that English is much more agreeable than Scots, but I do not find that an acceptable solution for what we are trying to expound. The true reason for it is that books and public discourse in Scotland are in the English tongue.

There are several English dictionaries, especially the excellent work of Mr. Johnson; and doubtless to have such a work is a thing of great importance, for English in time will become the universal language of our isle. We have not a single Scots dictionary. Really, that is amazing.

I have spoken so much of my dictionary that you must surely be bored with it. I am dreadfully bored with it myself. Let us drop the subject. . . .

WEDNESDAY 29 FEBRUARY. This day, for the first time since 25 September 1763, I wrote no lines, having kept my bed with a cold.

FRIDAY 2 MARCH. Yesterday you got up better. You was however still distressed, and at Brown's was weakish and joked on *l'amour*.

SATURDAY 3 MARCH. Yesterday you lay too long. This cold is made an excuse for laziness. You finished Campbell and had clear proof for Christian miracles.

MONDAY 5 MARCH. Yesterday you was gloomy but better.

TUESDAY 6 MARCH. Yesterday you got up vigorous and well, your cold gone and health and joy bounding through your frame.

WEDNESDAY 7 MARCH. Yesterday you did very well. You thought that Smith's system was running mankind, melting them, into one mass in the crucible of Sympathy. Whereas they are separate beings, and 'tis their duty as rational beings to approach near to each other.

FRIDAY 9 MARCH. Yesterday you rose well; after breakfast you received a letter from Johnston with accounts of the death of the poor little child.* Alas, what is the world? You was distressed and sunk. Rose sympathized. You hesitated if to mourn. Rose said 'twas only external ceremony, and none but yourself knew.

SUNDAY 11 MARCH. Yesterday you was melted with tender distress. You walked musing in the Mall. You would fain have persuaded yourself that it was not true, that Charles was still alive. At dinner you was faint and gloomy, and you read Greek feebly.

MONDAY 12 MARCH. Yesterday you got up very dull. However, you dressed and went to the Jesuits' church, where the solemn worship put venerable ideas in your mind, not without many strange recollections of past life and philosophical ideas at present.

---

*The news Boswell had received was of the death of his natural son, Charles, about ten months old. The child's mother was Peggy Doig, apparently a servant. Boswell had provided funds for the child's support, and placed him in the care of a foster-mother.

THURSDAY 22 MARCH. Yesterday you was better. Rose and you walked after dinner. He said he was very lazy. You owned nothing. He drank coffee with you and talked of suicide. . . . You grew well at night. This day show that you are Boswell, a true soldier. Take your post. Shake off sloth and spleen, and just proceed. Nobody knows your conflicts. Be fixed as Christian, and shun vice. Go not to Amsterdam. Read more law. Write Father neat clear little letter. No metaphysics. Plain things. Be silent and polite always. Just resume Utrecht and expel antipathies.

FRIDAY 23 MARCH. Yesterday you got up bad. After dinner you grew better. At Society *chez* Peterson (Montesquieu's principle of honour), you recovered quite. You came home quite well. . . . You will make a man. Adore God and rejoice that you are virtuous. Reserve for wife except some Maintenon occur. Be good to Rose. Get little box for journal. Be a true soldier. Read more French. Saturday, journal. To keep nerves firm, shave fine. Have good humour.

SUNDAY 25 MARCH. Yesterday you awaked in great disorder, thinking that you was dying, and exclaiming, "There's no more of it! 'Tis all over." Horrid idea! You had sat up till four, writing.

[C. 27 MARCH. FRENCH THEME] [Indolence] attacks me especially in the morning. I go to bed at night with the most determined resolutions to get up early. Francois, my faithful servant, wakes me at half-past six. But when I open my eyes and see daylight again, a crowd of disagreeable ideas comes into my mind. I think gloomily of the vanity and misery of human life. I think that it is not worth while to do anything. Everything is insipid or everything is dark. The truth is that man is made for action. When he is busy, he fulfils the intention of his Creator, and he is happy. Sleep and amusement serve to refresh his body and his mind and qualify him to continue his course of action. How is it then that I feel so gloomy every morning, and that these convincing arguments have not the least influence on my conduct? I believe the explanation is some physical disorder. My nerves at that time are relaxed, the vapours have risen to my head. If I get up and move about a little, I am happy and brisk. But it is with the utmost difficulty that I can get up. I have thought of having my bed constructed in a curious fashion. I would have it so that when I pulled a cord, the middle of the bed would be immediately raised and me raised with it and gradually set up on the floor. Thus I should be gently forced into what is good for me.

THURSDAY 29 MARCH. Yesterday you was bad in the morning, but at one you talked to Trotz of new scheme for Scots law which put you in spirits.

SUNDAY 1 APRIL. Yesterday you was fine. You lay too long indulging.

You sat long with Trotz and found him to be *avarus*. Yet you was fond of the *scheme*. You walked with Rose. After dinner Brown advised you to *scheme,* if you can labour it enough. You thought yourself weak and not grand enough. You have always complaints. You wrote some of *scheme,* but found it very tedious. This day, Scots law till ten, and then eclipse, and at twelve, Trotz.

MONDAY 2 APRIL. Yesterday you was tolerable. You went to the Observatory, but could see nothing. You called on Trotz, who was clear for *scheme,* "Si tu pensam tuam prestare possis." You laboured six hours at it, and did much.

THURSDAY 5 APRIL. Yesterday you began hour with Trotz. You was not a little gloomy. You was distressed about the Scheme. Your mind was distracted. At last a lucky hint occurred. You wrote to Maclaine, and will have his advice. Go on with Scheme this week. You went to bed to see if ideas change.

FRIDAY 6 APRIL. Yesterday after four hours' confused sleep you bounced up.

[Received 7 April, the Reverend Archibald Maclaine to Boswell]

The Hague, 6 April 1764

YOUR SECOND LETTER demands a speedy answer; and to speak frankly, that answer might be contained in two words, *nosce teipsum.* Five hundred hours in one hundred days, employed upon an object where neither wit, genius, nor imagination can have the smallest exercise, and going cheek by jowl with a heavy recluse, called *privatissimum;* and this labour to be undertaken by the sprightly, brilliant, amiable philosopher whom I know and you, *at present,* know not—and this work to be done at a fixed time by a man that hates restraint, and that in conjunction with a sublime Professor who talks of guilders, *rascal counters,* profits, &c.—and by a man who loves change, wants often relaxation, and is subject to low spirits!—Surely you joke—or dream—or are inspired with a portion of the spirits of Cujas, who has appeared to you in a vision and taken the advantage of some foggy night, when the atmosphere loaded with heavy vapours has damped the wings of fancy, &c., &c., &c., &c.

Merriment aside, I should mightily approve of your plan were it to be executed with ease, liberty, and a proper mixture of amusement, polite literature, and *light summer reading.* The plan is good, must be useful and highly so to yourself, and *when executed,* will be a valuable present to the Republic of Letters; but if you thus measure your daily labour, as a weaver, by the yard, I will venture to foretell that before twenty days of the hundred are past, you will be wearied, *ennuyé,* you will begin to yawn, to grow drowsy, to curse plans, fixed time, measured tasks, ells of Civil Law, hundred guilders, profits of the edition; and tell Mr. Trotz that you are out of order, that your nerves are weak, your spirits low, and bid him (silently) go to the D__. My dear Boswell, the post will not wait.

A. MACLAINE.

SUNDAY 8 APRIL. Yesterday you awaked bad. You lay abed till nine. You sent apology to Trotz. You was uneasy. You received Maclaine's letter. It gave you pleasure. You read Greek well and did geography. You walked in Mall and played billiards. *Do so no more.* You called on Trotz; you said, "Sollicitudinem mihi dedit dubitatio." You told him, "Desinam."

MONDAY 9 APRIL. Yesterday you awaked very bad. You got up as dreary as a dromedary. . . .

WEDNESDAY 11 APRIL. Yesterday you got up as miserable as a being could be. All was insipid and dreary. But, blockhead that you are, have you not experienced this five hundred times? And can you not, as Sir William Temple says, "let such fits pass and return to yourself?" Remember this.

FRIDAY 13 APRIL. Yesterday you awaked shocked, having dreamt you was condemned to be hanged.

[Received 14 April, Lord Auchinleck to Boswell]

Auchinleck, 2 April 1764

MY DEAR SON,—Yours of the 20th of March came to hand on Friday. I looked for it with impatience, as I had not heard from you for a month.

I have the greatest feeling for you under these melancholy fits you are sometimes attacked with, but for your comfort know that numbers who have been subject to this distress in a much greater degree have made a good and an useful figure in life. You are not therefore to despond or despair; on the contrary, you must arm yourself doubly against them, as the poet directs: "Tu ne cede malis, sed contra audentior ito." Neither are you to imagine that variety of company and of diversions is the proper cure. I can assure you from the authority of several very sensible people who were subject to this disorder that it is just the reverse. It is like an opiate which allays the trouble for a little, but that is all; the trouble bursts out afterwards with double force. The only certain cure is to acquire the knowledge of as many things that you may constantly command as possible, for this is clear: that idleness to those who have a vicious turn is the mother of all manner of vice, and to those who have a virtuous turn, it commonly produces melancholy and gloom. The point therefore is still to be busy at something, and then melancholy cannot find a lodging.

My worthy father, whom you justly notice had a melancholic turn, was never troubled with it in Session time. Business drove it away.

As to the course you should steer when the college is over, and when I hope you shall emulate Sir David in reputation, I am at some loss what to advise. In general, I must tell you that travelling is a very useless thing, further than for one to say they have travelled; and therefore think you should spend very little time that way. You may think and advise whether it would be best to go through some of the German courts or go through Flanders and see Paris. The Prince of Brunswick, the Prince of Baden-Durlach, and the King of Prussia Lord Marischal recommends; and I can get him (whom I am to see at Aberdeen) to recommend to them all; and Mr. Mitchell, my friend at Berlin, will treat you kindly. I could wish to see you gainst winter at home.

ALEXR. BOSWEL.

SUNDAY 15 APRIL. Yesterday, after late sitting up, you rose with blood changed: all well, all gay. . . . You received excellent letter from worthy father, who sympathized with your distress and gave you noble ideas. His mention of *return* roused you.

[Boswell to Temple]

Utrecht, 17 April 1764

MY DEAR TEMPLE,

I wrote to my father an account of my late dreary state of mind. . . . Worthy man! I hope to give him satisfaction. He is perhaps too anxiously devoted to utility. He tells me that he thinks little time should be spent in travelling; and that he would have me make a tour through some of the German courts, or through Flanders and part of France, and return to Scotland against winter. You will agree with me in thinking this scheme greatly too confined. I laid my account with travelling for at least a couple of years after leaving this. I must however compound matters. I shall insist upon being abroad another winter, and so may pursue the following plan.

I shall set out from Utrecht about the middle of June. I shall make the tour of The Netherlands, from thence proceed to Germany, where I shall visit the Courts of Brunswick and Lüneburg, and about the end of August arrive at Berlin. I shall pass a month there. In the end of September I shall go to the Court of Baden-Durlach, from thence through Switzerland to Geneva. I shall visit Rousseau and Voltaire, and about the middle of November shall cross the Alps and get fairly into Italy. I shall there pass a delicious winter, and in April shall pass the Pyrenees and get into Spain, remain there a couple of months, and at last come to Paris. Upon this plan, I cannot expect to be in Britain before the autumn of 1765.

Miss Stewart is now Lady Maxwell. So much for that scheme, which I consulted you upon some months ago. There are two ladies here, a young, handsome, amiable widow with £4000 a year, and Mademoiselle de Zuylen, who has only a fortune of £20,000. She is a charming creature. But she is a *savante* and a *bel esprit,* and has published some things. She is much my superior. One does not like that. One does not like a widow, neither. . . .

WEDNESDAY 18 APRIL. Yesterday you continued in a kind of delirium. You wrote all day. At night you was at Monsieur de Zuylen's. You said one might trace resemblance in a young child as in a piece of wood, or a cinder, or the head of a staff. Zélide was *nervish.* You saw she would make a sad wife and propagate wretches.

[20 APRIL. FRENCH THEME] Really, Monsieur Reynst gave me a far from favourable idea of my dear Zélide. I would give a great deal to cure myself of my weakness of being too much affected by the opinions of others. Reynst changed to some extent my idea of Zélide. However, I fought like her champion. I said, "That young lady makes me feel very humble, when I find her so much above me in wit, in knowledge, in good sense." "Excuse me," said Reynst. "She lacks good sense and consequently she goes wrong; and a man who has not half her wit and knowledge may still be above her." I made no reply to that. I thought it very true, and I thought it was a good thing. For if it were not for that lack, Zélide would have an absolute power. She would have unlimited dominion over men, and would overthrow the dignity of the male sex.

[Received 28 April, Lord Auchinleck to Boswell]

Auchinleck, 15 April 1764

MY DEAR SON,—I have received yours of the 23d of March and commend your care and attention in writing it so speedily after your former, as you were under the apprehension that what you had wrote before would give me a desponding view of your situation; but the answer I made to your first letter would show you that I had no such apprehension from what you had wrote. It gave me indeed concern to find that you had been in distress, but that did not appear to me strange; the change from an idle dissipated life to a life of application and study was so great that it could not but affect your spirits. Any change we make as to our course of life naturally has that effect.

I remember to hear Lord Newhall tell that Dr. Cheyne, who was Physician at the Bath, having, by too full living, brought himself to that degree of corpulency that he had his coach made to open wholly on the side and was really become a burden to himself, came to the resolution to live abstemiously, and reduced his body thereby so much that he was obliged to be swaddled to make his loose skin clasp to his body. By this operation his intellectuals were reduced prodigiously and his spirits sunk to the greatest degree. However, as he had given a strict charge to his friends to keep him still in that abstemious way though he should alter his mind from the lowness of his spirits, they kept him at it; and the consequence was that by degrees he became inured to the new method of living and all his faculties, with his spirits, returned to him and he came out a clever agile man, and continued so with a high reputation and in great business till his death.

As to the course you are to follow after leaving Utrecht, I hinted my notion in my last. Travelling about from place to place is a thing extremely little improving except where one needs to rub off bashfulness, which is not your case. Your mother and Johnny remember you with affection. I am your affectionate father,

ALEXR. BOSWEL.

THURSDAY 3 MAY. Yesterday after twelve hours sleep you rose unrelaxed and refreshed and content. You read Greek, but that's all. At *five* you went . . . to Zélide. She sang and repeated verses, but was too *forced-meat.* She would never make wife. After dinner, Brown argued that Society is happiest by marriage and knowing that we have real descendants, &c., and all contrary practices are bad. You are to be husband to English lady, so keep yourself healthy. Concubinage is no dire sin, but never do it unless some very extraordinary opportunity of fresh girl that can do no harm; and such a case is impossible.

FRIDAY 25 MAY. Yesterday Brown said you reasoned exactly contrary to probability, for although you was well each day ere night, you imagined each morn you could never be well. He said Helvétius never mentioned our reasoning from probability, which is the greatest faculty of the mind and source of knowledge. Hahn was with you at six. You told him case. He pronounced gravely: bad nerves, acrimonious juices, lax solids. Sweeten, fortify, amuse. No metaphysics, plain common sense. No claps. Women are necessary when one has been accustomed, or retention will influence the brain.

Brown bid me judge of precepts about fornication as my reason directed; I saw then that irregular coition was not commendable but that it was no dreadful crime, and that as society is now constituted I did little or no harm in taking a girl, especially as my health required it. At night I went into the Amsterdam boat.

[SATURDAY 26 MAY] I came to Grub's, an English house. I was restless. I was fretful. I despised myself. At ten I waited on Longueville, one of the Scots ministers, a heavy, sulky dog, but born near Auchinleck. At eleven I went and called on Dr. Blinshall, the other Scots minister, a hearty, honest fellow, knowing and active, but Scotch to the very backbone. I next waited on Mr. James Boswell, glass-merchant, who has been here I believe forty years. He was very kind, and asked me to dinner next day. I strolled about very uneasy. I dined with Mr. Rich, merchant.

At five I went to a bawdy-house. I was shown upstairs, and had a bottle of claret and a *juffrouw*. But the girl was much fitter for being wrapped in the blankets of salivation than kissed between the sheets of love. I had no armour, so did not fight. It was truly ludicrous to talk in Dutch to a whore. This scene was to me a rarity as great as peas in February. Yet I was hurt to find myself in the sinks of gross debauchery. This was a proper way to consider the thing. But so sickly was my brain that I had the low scruples of an Edinburgh divine.

I ordered a genteel flowered-silk suit, and at eight I set out in the Leyden *roef*. I had with me two Brussels lawyers. One of them wanted much to convert me to the Popish religion. He was a learned, lively, pretty man. He told me what tranquillity, what joy, his holy religion gave him by its many aids to the imperfections of human nature, and how he had no doubts, but reposed in the bosom of his sacred Mother, the Church. I owned to him that I envied his situation. But for my part, I was pretty enlarged in my notions and was not afraid of my Creator. He seemed to have no difficulty at all with regard to transubstantiation. I went this far with him: "Sir, allow me to ask you one question. If the Church should say to you, 'Two and three make ten,' what would you do?" "Sir," said he, "I should believe it, and I should count like this: one, two, three, four, *ten*."

MONDAY 4 JUNE. In a genteel suit of flowered silk, I went this morning and paid my respects at the English Ambassador's, where was a very great crowd, it being King George's birthday. This morning was indeed a morning of joy. I received a large packet of letters, one from my Lord Marischal, informing me that I was to accompany him to Berlin, one from my father to the same purpose, and letters from my Scots and London bankers with a credit upon Berlin of £30 a month.

Never was man happier than I this morning. I was now to travel with a venerable Scots nobleman who had passed all his life abroad, had known intimately kings and great men of all kinds, and could introduce me with the greatest advantage at courts. A multitude of rich ideas filled my imagination.

WEDNESDAY 6 JUNE. I went in the *schuit* to Leyden. It was the *kermis* there, and all was gay. I found Monsieur Gronovius in his garden. I owned to him my melancholy. He bid me conceal it, and be always busy or amused. We passed this our last evening with much satisfaction. I took a hearty leave of him. I had engaged at The Hague a servant, his name Jacob Hänni, a *Bernois*, who spoke French and German. I took him with me, so that I had my two attendants. I own that I had little vanity enough to be pleased with this. One of my *schuit* companions asked me if my servant was German. "Sir," said I, "one of my servants is German and the other is French." My companion looked at me with a much more respectful eye.

MONDAY 11 JUNE. I had sat up all night. Reynst of The Hague met me, and carried me to Oblet's, where I found Monsieur and Madame Hasselaer, whom I have an antipathy against, and my dear Zélide, whom I have a sympathy with. My imbecility will never leave me. Zélide was in a fever of spirits. I drove about with her and Madame Hasselaer and had curious reflections to myself. In August last I was a gloomy, deplorable wretch in this dull city. Now I am a fine, gay gentleman, the gallant of fine, gay ladies. At eight Reynst came to me, and from many circumstances well interpreted, he persuaded me that Zélide was really in love with me. I believed it. But I was mild and *retenu*.

TUESDAY 12 JUNE. I had a room in the opposite side of my *Cour de l'Empereur* where I had Richardson lodged. At eleven I met Zélide at her music master's, where she played delightfully. I then walked with her and Bernard. I was touched with regret at the thoughts of parting with her. Yet she rattled so much that she really vexed me.

We drank tea at Brown's, where was Hahn, who said that Zélide would be always *une malheureuse demoiselle,* as she was quite governed by fancy. Richardson and I walked. He said he was surprised to find a physician talk so of his patient, for that from Hahn's manner of talking, Mademoiselle de Zuylen seemed to be crazy. I was vexed at this. Richardson's sound, hard knowledge entertained me well. We supped *tête à tête.*

WEDNESDAY 13 JUNE. I carried Richardson to dine at the Plaats Royaal, my old eating table. I was lumpish and dreary. I wished to be rid of Richardson. I thought my being obliged to entertain him a most laborious task. So discontented a mortal am I. My fancy forms plans. I execute them. They prove insipid. He and I walked. I complained to him of black ideas of religion. He said, "You think too much."

THURSDAY 14 JUNE. Zélide and I had a long conversation. She said she did not care for respect. She liked to have everybody free with her, and that they should tell her her faults. I told her that this was very wrong; for she would hardly find a husband of merit who had not some pride, and who would not be hurt at finding people so free with his wife. I owned to her that I was very sorry to leave her. She gave me many a tender look. We took a kind farewell, as I did of all the family. Monsieur de Zuylen and I talked a long time. I am sure he liked me. He has been exceedingly civil to me. Richardson could not well understand Zélide and me. "It is lucky," said Mr. Chaplain to me, "that you are to be no longer together; for you would learn her nonsense, and she would learn yours." He was right. Our airy speculating is not thinking.

SUNDAY 17 JUNE. At six Lord Marischal, Madame de Froment, Mademoiselle Kinloch, and I drove to Zuylen, where we drank tea before the gate in the open air. Zélide said to me, "Are you back again? We made a touching adieu." Zélide seemed much agitated, said she had never been in love, but said that *one* might meet with *un homme aimable,* &c., &c., &c., for whom *one* might feel a strong affection, which would probably be lasting, *but* this amiable man might not have the same affection for *one.* In short she spoke too plain to leave me in doubt that she *really* loved me. But then away she went with her wild fancy, saying that she thought only of the present moment. "I had rather feel than think. I should like to have a husband who would let me go away sometimes to amuse myself." In short, she seemed a frantic libertine. She said to me, "Sir, if you see the Count of Anhalt, don't speak to him of me. He may some day be my husband." She gave me her hand at parting, and the tender tear stood crystal in her eye. Poor Zélide! I took hearty leave at Brown's. I was sorry to leave the scene of much internal exercise. I sat up all night.

MONDAY 18 JUNE. My wakeful night well past, I was in glow of spirits. Zélide's letter was long and warm. She imagined me in love with her, and with much romantic delicacy talked of this having rendered her *distraite.* I was honest or simple enough to leave her a short letter, assuring her that I was not *amoureux,* but would always be her *fidèle ami.*

I had all my affairs in order. Honest Carron came and took leave of me. And next comes a most flagrant whim. Some days ago I called to me François, told him that he had served me honestly and well, and that I could give him a good character as a servant. I said I hoped that I had

been a good master. To know this certainly, I ordered him to write out a
full character of me, since he entered to my service, and charged him to
mark equally the bad and the good which he had observed, and to give it
me carefully sealed up. I accordingly received it this morning.

I took leave of my house in which I have had such an infinity of
ideas. At seven we set out in a coach and four. . . .

[Received 18 June 1764, François Mazerac to Boswell.
Original in French]

Utrecht, 17 June 1764

MONSIEUR:—My small ability makes it almost impossible for me to
comply with your orders, and I hope that Monsieur will take my remarks
kindly and regard them as coming from a person who is only trying to
obey you.

First: I have found that Monsieur is extremely negligent about his
money, his watch, and other effects, in leaving them on the table, or in
leaving the key on the bureau, and going out of the room leaving the
door open, as happened several times at The Hague. If it should ever
happen that you have the misfortune to lose something in this way, you
might entertain suspicions of your servant or some other innocent
person. There is a saying, "Opportunity makes the thief."

Secondly: I have found that Monsieur has a good heart, in doing
good to the poor: a virtue which is dictated by humanity and prescribed
by religion.

Thirdly: Monsieur is not at all given to backbiting, a vice very
common among great minds.

Fourthly: Very punctual in performing the duties of your religion,
by going to church, not swearing, and above all by saying your prayers
every morning.

Fifthly: I have found that when Monsieur has invited company, the
guests always arrived before you, which might expose you to some
reproach, especially in another country where they care more for social
formalities than they do here.

Sixthly: I have found that Monsieur applies himself too much to
study, which is noble in itself but ruinous to health if not done
judiciously.

Seventhly: I find that Monsieur goes to bed too late, which, with the
study, will make you lose your health, which Monsieur will regret when
it is too late and there is no help for it.

Eighthly and last item: I have found in Monsieur a really Christian
and noble heart, especially towards me, which I shall never forget. May
the Father of fathers take you under His holy protection, and keep His

eye on you, guarding you as a beloved child. May He guide your steps and direct your thoughts, so that no harm may come to you, and that when you have returned home safe and sound, you will bless Him therefor eternally.

I end by thanking Monsieur again for all his goodness, begging him to think of me sometimes. As for me, I believe I shall never forget Monsieur.—Permit me to beg you, Monsieur, that, should you ever have a chance, you will let me know how you are. Your very grieved and faithful servant,

FRANÇOIS MAZERAC.

PART III

BOSWELL
ON THE
GRAND TOUR

GERMANY AND SWITZERLAND

18 June 1764 — 16 December 1764

INTRODUCTION

JAMES BOSWELL, having completed his studies in Holland, now traveled over Europe. Had his father known how extensively Boswell was to travel, he would have opposed his plan more strenuously. "I could wish to see you 'gainst winter at home," Lord Auchinleck wrote, viewing travel, in any case, as "a very useless thing . . . a thing extremely little improving except where one needs to rub off bashfulness, which is not your case. . . ." Fifteen months later Lord Auchinleck complained in terms we can all appreciate that Boswell had spent in travel "much beyond what my income can afford, and much beyond what the sons of gentlemen near double my estate have spent on such a tour; and that makes it quite necessary now to put an end to peregrination."

Nevertheless, Boswell ended by traveling for a year beyond his father's stipulation—two and a half years altogether on the Continent —in itself a defiance his father might have tolerated, except that before Boswell was done he also would have brought himself to wide attention by taking up the cause of embattled Corsica. Lord Auchinleck, who cared, as we know, nothing for fame, cared as little for the Corsicans or their cause.

Departing from Utrecht, Boswell journeyed through Germany into Switzerland. "I would go where there are courts and learned men," Mr. Johnson had advised him, and so he did. He was guest and visitor in little kingdoms and at the palaces of international European society. He stopped as well beneath less commodious shelter. In exhaustion at one point of his passage through Germany, he "slept at every stage . . . throwing myself down" in stables. "This was very dangerous. I might easily have been robbed. The horses might have broken loose and trampled me to death in the dark." On another night "we were laid thirteen in a room, besides a Danish woman and three children. I could not bear this, so the postmaster gave me his own bed." We gain through Boswell close views of the pettiness of princes and the earthbound reality of plain people. We witness the whipping of a military deserter. "It made me sick to see it," Boswell writes, whose absorption with royalty is frequently leavened by his humaneness. In Dessau the hunting of a stag repulses him, as the cockfight had in London.

One of the great comic episodes bequeathed to us by Boswell is his series of meetings with Rousseau. As he approached Rousseau, a face-to-face meeting with "the wild philosopher" increasingly challenged him. He could not merely drop in, as one might drop in on princes. He had been reading Rousseau preparatory to their meeting, but to gain the meeting itself he must prepare a strategy. He felt it necessary to dramatize himself in a way to capture Rousseau's interest.

His journal reveals his plan, serving also as his rehearsal stage, and providing us during the process with an emerging portrait of a young man discovering himself. Indeed, he might not have known so completely who he was had he not written it down. Boswell was, above all, a young man still suspended between preparation and profession, still seeking identity, still painfully and comically divided: if he was on the whole one version of himself for his father, and another for the eyes of Mr. Johnson, he was yet another for M. Rousseau.

This is not to say that Boswell's intention in meeting Rousseau was simply to place himself in the presence of a famous man. Rousseau represented a democratic and skeptical spirit. Boswell was always responsive to unorthodox ideas. (As a very young man he had daringly and dangerously courted Roman Catholicism.) Rousseau was prophet and advocate of a world unlike the worlds envisioned by either Lord Auchinleck or Mr. Johnson. He rejected dogma and authority in culture and religion. Perhaps a brave new world might even at the last moment rescue Boswell from (as he saw it) provincial Edinburgh and the law court of his father. Prepared for the older world, he imagined another. "I am a Scots gentleman of ancient family," Boswell wrote to Rousseau to announce his imminence. "Now you know my rank. I am twenty-four years old. Now you know my age."

It was an age at which young men often invest in heroic leaders the power to change the world; and if one hero lacks that power, he will write a letter for the young man, introducing him to the next, as Rousseau did for Boswell, passing him along to General Paoli of the Corsicans.

One day in Germany, contemplating his journal, Boswell thought that "some years hence I shall perhaps abridge it in a more elegant style." Some of his journal was, of course, consciously converted by him to the more elegant style expected in a book—an example of that revision is his *Account of Corsica,* printed here. Wherever else we read Boswell's journal we may know that what we see is what he wrote. Passages of his journal have been destroyed or obliterated, but the wealth that remains was never revised.

Thus when Boswell rehearses his character as he means to present it to Rousseau, he reveals himself to himself, and to us, not by employing the calculations of an author but by an act of unrevised spontaneity. Boswell announced his approach to Rousseau with "a presentiment that a truly noble friendship will be born today." He promised to be so cordial that he would help Rousseau to forget his afflictions. Boswell's persistence vexed the older man, who called for his watch to prevent his visitor from lingering beyond the specified time. Nevertheless, Rousseau admitted Boswell five times to his company. Boswell was not easily put off; bashfulness was not his case. By such persistence he had won his way to Johnson's heart. He was a young man who attached himself to worthy subjects, writing them up for his journal and, as an accidental consequence, for posterity, into whose hands his journal eventually would be delivered.

Yet it was not history but self-clarification at the center of Boswell's purpose, and Rousseau was but one of several mentors or confidants to whom he applied and whose remarks he recorded. Once served in that way, Boswell was under no necessity to revise his writing for the sake of elegance. He was his own sole reader, whose Europe comes to us as he saw it in his passionate year. That it was something more was also true. "My wife, who does not like journalizing," Boswell wrote in his journal eleven years after his tour of Europe, "said it was leaving myself embowelled to posterity—a good strong figure. But I think it is rather leaving myself embalmed. It is certainly preserving myself."

MONDAY 18 JUNE 1764. . . . At seven we set out in a coach and four. My blood circulated just as briskly as in my days of youth. I was drowsy, and now and then nodded. My Lord Marischal was pretty silent. So was Madame de Froment. I laid my account with little conversation. We came at night to Nymwegen. I met Captain Mungo Graham of Gordon's regiment, who accompanied me round the ramparts. We saw a very ancient castle, in which it is said that Julius Caesar lived.

TUESDAY 19 JUNE. François has given me an excellent character. We dined at Kleve. I went and paid my respects to Monsieur and Madame Spaen at Bellevue, from whence there is indeed a fine prospect. It was pleasant to see the German baron's castle: a hall adorned with guns; an English clock that plays ten tunes and cost £1000. At night we came to Wesel, where we had a jolly, talking landlord. I find Madame de Froment very lively, although she has an indolence, or, as the French say, a *nonchalance,* that is terrible. She does not dress. Scarcely even will she speak. I talked with her in rather too gallant a strain.

We came at night to Herford. I found myself a new man. My ideas were altered. I had no gloomy fears. I talked with Madame de Froment, who had been educated Mahometan and who still believed that the Great Prophet was sent from God.

SUNDAY 24 JUNE. We came at night to an inn in the territory of Hanover. Thus was I laid. In the middle of a great German *salle,* upon straw spread on the floor, was a sheet laid; here "great Boswell lay." I had another sheet and a coverlet. On one side of me were eight or ten horses; on the other, four or five cows. A little way from me sat on high a cock and many hens; and before I went to sleep the cock made my ears ring with his shrill voice, so that I admired the wisdom of the Sybarites, who slew all those noisy birds. What frightened me not a little was an immense mastiff chained pretty near the head of my bed. He growled most horribly, and rattled his chain. I called for a piece of bread and made a friendship with him.

TUESDAY 26 JUNE. We arrived at Brunswick before dinner. My Lord dressed, dined, and went to Court. I strolled about; found it a large and handsome town, with a number of old buildings. At night Madame de

Froment and I supped tête-à-tête. She talked of the hypochondria, which she had severely felt. She understood it perfectly.

TUESDAY 3 JULY. Madame de Froment and I dined tête-à-tête, after which we went and were shown the Palace, which is magnificent.

At night Madame de Froment told me how hypochondriac she had been. "All my thoughts were gloomy. The beauties of Nature mocked me. I was in despair. Yet without any change in the external world I suddenly became perfectly happy. My imagination was gay. In the evening I found myself alone in my room; I wished for company, to tell them of my felicity. I opened my window. I was delighted with everything I saw: the moon, the stars, the fields, the lake, all bore their most cheerful aspect. I said to myself, 'Good heavens! is it possible? Where does all this joy come from?' The fact is, Sir, that our happiness depends on the way in which our blood circulates."

This description struck me very much. Some weeks ago at Utrecht when I felt an amazing flow of sudden felicity, I thought it quite singular; but I find that I have just had the very same distemper with my Turkish lady. This is curious, to find the same spleen over the whole globe. I was in the humour of gallantry tonight. I was pleased with the romantic idea of making love to a Turk. However, I talked morality at last and thought myself a Johnson. She seemed too indolent in body and too vivacious in mind to be a very rigid lady. Besides her ideas were quite different from mine. Her religion was of a kind very different from mine. Bless me! what are mortals?

THURSDAY 5 JULY. I hired post-horses for my Lord's coach, and set out free and happy to conduct Madame de Froment to Berlin. We had a pleasant jaunt, and arrived about two at Rufin's in the Post Straas. Here we found Monsieur de Froment, a lively Frenchman.

SUNDAY 8 JULY. I waited on Mr. Mitchell and found him a knowing, amiable, easy man. He was very polite. He talked of Mademoiselle de Zuylen: "She has a great deal of wit." "Yes," said I, "too much for the Dutch." And who was in the room but Mr. Verelst, the Dutch Envoy! Mr. Mitchell turned it off with a smiling reply: "Sir, you are paying a fine compliment to the Minister of Holland." Blockhead that I was! Let never man blunder out reflections against any country when he does not very well know his company.

MONDAY 9 JULY. Who will say that I am not a man of business, I who write my journal with the regularity of the German professor who wrote his folio every year?

WEDNESDAY 25 JULY. I am much pleased with my servant Jacob. He is a Bernois, a genteel, active fellow. I liked this specimen of him upon our journey to Potsdam from Utrecht. He was always alert and ready to put everything right. One day the postilions were at a loss for a machine to carry water in to cool the wheels. Jacob sprung away to the side of a brook, tore from its place a young tree that had fixed its roots in the humid soil, and bringing with it a lump of watery earth, he plashed against the wheels, as a London maid does against the stairs with her moistened mop. There was invention and execution, too, of the very epic kind. He is quite sober, has good Christian principles and even generous sentiments. He would fight for his master, and gold could not tempt him to marry a woman he did not like. He had a most extraordinary adventure before he left Holland. A young officer of the regiment where his master served was uncommonly civil to him, and even used him like a friend. He used to invite him of an evening to the tavern, and give him a bottle of wine, and show a strange fondness. He at last asked Jacob if he would come and live with him. Jacob began to suspect that the young dog was a man of Italian taste. The officer however told him, "I am not what you think me," and opening his breast discovered himself to be a woman. She was of a good family and fortune, but had run away from her friends. Jacob however would not marry her upon any account.

THURSDAY 26 JULY. I put my ladies of the family in a passion by affirming that I would not marry any woman whose fortune was less than £10,000. They were seriously shocked, and gave me all the goodcommon arguments against low interested matches. Very well. But my purpose is fixed: my wife shall have a handsome fortune and that will always be something sure. However, I need not say so. Let me above all strive to attain easy reserve.

SATURDAY 4 AUGUST. As I passed through a wood before I entered Potsdam, a branch struck my eye and hurt me a good deal. It made me muse on the risk I had run of losing the half of one of my senses. I had time in the dark silence of night to ruminate on the great question concerning Providence. Should I now have said that Providence preserved my eye? But, I pray you, why did Providence permit the branch to strike me? Oh, that was a natural event. Very well, and the degree of force was natural too; so that very naturally I have not lost my right eye. For shame, divines, how dare you bring in Providence on every trifling occasion? *Nec deus intersit nisi dignus vindice nodus.* 'Tis true, our heavenly Father sees every sparrow that falls to the ground. Yes, the universal eye perceives everything in the universe. But surely, the grand and extensive system employs the attention of God, and the minutiae are not to be considered as part of his care; at least, we are not to presume that he interests himself in every little accident. At Potsdam we stopped two hours. I laid myself down upon a timber stair and slept very sound.

THURSDAY 9 AUGUST. At night I was very gay at a pretty *opérette.* I sat in the Duke's *loge* and was fine with the ladies of the Court. Was not this quite as I could wish? My mind was clear and firm and fertile. It contained in itself both male and female powers: brilliant fancies were begotten, and brilliant fancies were brought forth. I saw my error in suffering so much from the contemplation of others. I can never be them, therefore let me not vainly attempt it in imagination; therefore let me not envy the gallant and the happy, nor be shocked by the nauseous and the wretched. I must be Mr. Boswell of Auchinleck, and no other.

Amidst all this brilliance, I sent forth my imagination to the Inner Temple, to the chambers of Mr. Samuel Johnson. I glowed with reverence and affection, and a romantic idea filled my mind. To have a certain support at all times, I determined to write to this great man, and beg that he might give me a "solemn assurance of perpetual friendship," so that I might march under his protection while he lived, and after his death, imagine that his shade beckoned me to the skies. Grand, yet enthusiastic, idea!

SATURDAY 11 AUGUST. After dining at Court I went to the French *comédie.* At night indolence made me think, why give myself so much labour to write this journal, in which I really do not insert much that can be called useful? Beg your pardon. Does it not contain a faithful register of my variations of mind? Does it not contain many ingenious observations and pleasing strokes which can afterwards be enlarged? Well, but I may die. True, but I may live; and what a rich treasure for my after days will be this my journal.

MONDAY 13 AUGUST. There came into my room this morning the sweetest girl I ever saw, a *blanchisseuse,* eighteen, fresh, gay. I spoke German to her with unusual ease, and told her that I would not for the world debauch her to give myself a few days' pleasure, but if she would go with me to England and then to Scotland, I would be very kind to her. She was really innocent. Her beauty thrilled my frame. I thought that I might be an old patriarch upon occasions and could not see any harm in taking her with me. She refused to go, but promised to come back from time to time.

After dinner I was at the noble entertainment of rope-dancing, at which was the Duke and all the Court. I have omitted in this my journal to mention that one day last week we had a ball at Court, where I danced most agreeably. I asked to dance a minuet with the Hereditary Princess. She graciously consented, but we had just made our reverence when the fiddles struck up a country dance which the Hereditary Prince was to begin. So we were stopped. Oh, I was a mortified gentleman. This evening was again a ball. No sooner did the amiable Princess perceive me than she came up to me with a smile celestial and said, "Mr. Boswell, let us finish our minuet." Accordingly I danced with Her Royal Highness, who danced extremely well. We made a very fine English minuet—or British, if you please, for it was a Scots gentleman and an English lady that performed it. What a group of fine ideas had I! I was dancing with a princess; with the grand-daughter of King George whose birthday I have so often helped to celebrate at Old Edinburgh; with the daughter of the Prince of Wales, who patronized Thomson and other votaries of science and the muse; with the sister of George the Third, my sovereign. I mark this variety to show how my imagination can enrich an object, so that I have double pleasure when I am well. It was noble to be in such a frame. I said to the Princess, "Madam, I return your Royal Highness a thousand thanks for the honour you have done me. This will serve me to talk of to my tenants as long as I live."

WEDNESDAY 15 AUGUST. I passed the morning with my worthy Abbé Jerusalem. He said the Duke was a worthy man, but passionate, and sometimes he gives way to terrible rages. I said, "The Prince seems pensive and even melancholy." "Sir," said he, "he has always loved war; from his youth he has been charmed by it. He has a restless spirit. He needs much occupation and great aims. At present he is not well. The greatest court is not equal to a camp. So he is not the great man that he was. After having had so much to do, he is now quite idle. Besides, he is obliged to please the Duke. Every morning regularly he must be at the parade; thus his morning disappears insensibly. Next he must dress, go to Court, receive people, go to the theatre: in short, he must spend his time in a manner which he finds beneath him."

This description pleased my discontented mind. I saw that all ranks must take their portion of evil. I saw the Prince was with his father just as I must be with mine.

THURSDAY 16 AUGUST. I passed the morning at home, in writing. I have attempted to write to Mr. Johnson every day since I formed the resolution of demanding a charter of his friendship, but have not yet been able to please myself.

TUESDAY 21 AUGUST. Cavalcabo paid me a visit. He told me that he had been "so wretched that if I had not had the care of my sister-in-law and her children, I should have been capable of blowing out my brains with a pistol." I told him, "Indeed, Sir, I was extremely gloomy. But I thought, what is the difference? It is all the same whether I suffer or not.

I am only a single individual." "Well, Sir," said he, "you had certainly fallen into a fine melancholy. It all comes from the body, and can be cured by diet. Happy is the man who knows his own body." I found him the true *bon catholique*, for he talked with ease of having women, and yet told me of a distemper that he had brought on himself by fasting.

This was my last day at Brunswick. I talked at Court, "I shall come back in twenty-five years to see who are dead and who are still living." I dined in a kind of luxurious sorrow. I must not forget to mark that I fell in love with the beauteous Princess Elizabeth. I talked of carrying her off from the Prince of Prussia, and so occasioning a second Trojan War. Madame de Boick was my confidante. I was also smitten by Lady Mary Coke. Madame de Boick would ask me, "Well, Sir, is it the English or the German lady who takes your fancy most this evening?" At the opera this evening, I was quite ravished. It made me recollect a story of Dr. Colquitt's, how at some fine music in London dukes and lords cried they'd dash out their brains against the wainscot. I owned to Feronce, "I could almost have wished that some one would cut my throat." Feronce agreed to correspond with me. So did Pless. I shall have a pretty correspondence in all at Brunswick.

I said to Cavalcabo, "People talk a great deal about the lightness and vivacity of the French, but indeed they have better judgment than the English. They always have *some* rules. The English have none at all." "Sir," said he, "the French appear to have more giddiness, but actually they do not have so much. A Frenchman jumps and sings in front of his mistress, but he is nevertheless master of himself. The Englishman, however, is all caprice; and with all the composure in the world he goes about setting the house on fire."

I was pensive at Court. I had taken leave of the Hereditary Princess. I mused on the life of a courtier here. Putting myself, by strong imagination, in every one's place, my gloomy temper found all their situations uneasy, even the Duke's. Yet I recalled the best ideas and felt pleasing regret. I took leave of the Duchess shortly. I have seen in her room a portrait of the King of Prussia, the only one for which His Majesty ever sat. It is very like, but it stoops too much.

When I took leave of the Duke, I said, "Sire, you have had people at your Court more brilliant than I, but never a better man, nor a man more sensible of the politeness which your Highness has shown to him." The Duke of Brunswick replied, "Sir, I am very glad that you have been pleased with your visit here." I expected still more civilities than I received, because forsooth the Duke spoke to me at Charlottenburg. I magnify all events in my own favour, and with the wind of vanity blow them up to size immense. I took a tender leave of the ladies and gentleman of the Court and said, "Is it not sad that we shall never see one another again?"

WEDNESDAY 22 AUGUST. I was hippish. I went upon the Parade and saw the Duke once more. I wondered how he could plague himself every morning with making men march about. I was convinced that all situations are judged of by comparison, so that he who has been Laird of Auchinleck ten years feels himself as great as he who has been Duke of Brunswick ten years. I then took leave of Ap Herusalem, as they call him here. I don't know how it is, but I am always gloomy on leaving a room where I have lodged. I could get no extra post, which vexed me a little. I however hoped the Court would suppose me gone in some company. I mounted the post-wagon without the gate, and away we went.

THURSDAY 23 AUGUST. Rumbled along.

FRIDAY 24 AUGUST. Why relate that I had blackguards with me, that I was sorely shaken, that the night air began to grow cold, that I slept at every stage? I had, however, a very bad custom of running always to the stable, making a bed of straw or of lint, throwing myself down, and making Jacob call me when the horn sounded. This was very dangerous. I might have easily been robbed. The horses might have broke loose and trampled me to death in the dark.

MONDAY 3 SEPTEMBER. At night I was the guest of Stoltz at an ordinary for supper. I did not like it much. After supper, Hübner and Blanchot and some more of us went to a Berlin bawdy-house, which I was curious to see. We found a poor little house, an old bawd, and one whore. I was satisfied with what I saw.

TUESDAY 4 SEPTEMBER. Hübner went with me to the Park, where I saw a Prussian regiment exercised. The soldiers seemed in terror. For the least fault they were beat like dogs. I am, however, doubtful if such fellows don't make the best soldiers. Machines are surer instruments than men. Were I to knock down a scoundrel, I would rather take a stick than take a child by the heels to give him a blow with. I also saw a deserter pass the *baguette* twelve times. He was much cut. It made me sick to see it.

THURSDAY 6 SEPTEMBER. I waited on Lord Marischal. I had written to him from Berlin, complaining of his coldness of manner which prevented me from enjoying with ease his excellent conversation, telling him what esteem I had for him, and how I had "old-fashioned ideas" which made me have a particular veneration for the "representative of the illustrious family of Keith." I also begged his advice as to my travels. I found that my letter had pleased him. He was more affable than usual.

I owned to him that I was afraid I could not do great things as a Scots lawyer, and could wish to be in some other employment. "As for the Army," said he, "it is too late." "Then, my Lord, might I not be employed abroad?" "Sir, you must begin as secretary, and if you are not with a man to your mind, you are very unhappy. Then, if you should be sent Envoy, if you are at a place where there is little to do, you are idle and unhappy. If you have much to do, you are harassed with anxiety." "Well then, my Lord, I would get into Parliament." "No, Sir, you would be obliged to stick to a party, right or wrong, through thick and through thin, or you must be singular, and be thought absurd." "My Lord, if you go on, you'll chase me out of existence altogether. What say you to my following the law in Scotland moderately? jogging on between the Parliament House and Auchinleck, and so doing pretty well?" "Indeed, Sir, I'm for your jogging on. Your father will see that you do your best. He has a great liking for you, and you'll do very well together." "Then, my Lord, will you write to him, that in the mean time he may allow me to travel a year?" "I will." His Lordship then gave me my route by Switzerland, Italy, and France.

MONDAY 10 SEPTEMBER. I took leave of the riding-school. I was glad to do so, for I had the spleen. I drove it off by writing all day. At night I supped with the family. Mademoiselle made me a present of a book to keep an *album amicorum,* a great custom in Holland and Germany and the northern countries. You present your book to a friend, who writes something in it of his own, or a quotation from some author, and writes his name below; or, if he can draw, designs you something. Thus you have a remembrance of your friends. It is not a bad contrivance, but a little ridiculous.

[Received *c.* 10 September, Lord Marischal to Boswell]

Sunday [9 September 1764]

SIR:—I have writ as you desire to try if your father will indulgence you in your project of travelling a year more. I have also told him that as travelling is dearer than only short excursions, I think you will want two hundred pounds sterling extraordinary, which I dare say will do. In Italy one can have a chaise for two at about a gold ducat a day, horse, chaise, eating, and all included. I remember I paid a ducat (per head) from Venice to Augsburg. I heartily wish you a good journey, having the honour to be, with particular regard, Sir, your most humble and obedient servant,

MARISCHAL.

TUESDAY 11 SEPTEMBER. To punish my extravagant rodomontading, and to bring up my affairs and compose my spirit, I had sitten up all night. Grievous was it to the flesh till seven in the morning, when my blood took a fine flow. I was quite drunk with brisk spirits, and about eight, in came a woman with a basket of chocolate to sell. I toyed with her and found she was with child. Oho! a safe piece. Into my closet. "Habs er ein Man?" "Ja, in den Gards bei Potsdam." To bed directly. In a minute—over. I rose cool and astonished, half angry, half laughing. I sent her off. Bless me, have I now committed adultery? Stay, a soldier's wife is no wife. Should I now torment myself with speculations on sin, and on losing in one morning the merit of a year's chastity? No: this is womanish. Nay, your elegant mystics would not do so. Madame Guyon was of opinion that sin should be forgotten as soon as possible, as being an idea too gross for the mind of a saint, and disturbing the exercise of sweet devotion. Her notion is ingenious. I am sorry that this accident has happened, I know not how. Let it go. I'll think no more of it. Divine Being! Pardon the errors of a weak mortal. Give me more steadiness. Let me grow more perfect. What a curious thing is it to find a strict philosopher speculating on a recent fault! Well, I shall not be proud. I shall be a mild and humble Christian.

THURSDAY 13 SEPTEMBER. I then went to Madame de Brandt's, where I imagined I was invited. But I had mistaken Tuesday for Thursday, and she punished me by a recital of the fine *partie* that she had, as it was her daughter's birthday. How she had a fine supper and a fine ball and all the company were dressed *à la turque;* and how a dress was ready for me. She asked me to stay this evening with her. Much she talked of gallantry and of the Duke of Portland, who was here some years ago. Young Comte Schaffgotsch supped with us, and after supper we played at "seek the pin." One is sent out of the room till the pin is hid, and when he enters he must seek it. In proportion as he approaches it, one beats harder and harder upon the table, till at last he finds it.

FRIDAY 14 SEPTEMBER. At four Castillon and I went and saw old Marggraf, the chemical professor, a very industrious and able man in his profession. But a strange old fellow. It thundered and lightened. He cried, "I love to see my God in flames," and he laughed always when he spoke. Such is man. He must have defects. He may have health and manners. But then he is ignorant. He may have knowledge. But then he is sick or awkward.

SATURDAY 22 SEPTEMBER. The Hereditary Prince of Brunswick was now at Potsdam. I waited upon him in the Palace, and talked some time. On the Parade I stood by Wylich, who had promised that if it was possible he would present me to the King. But an opportunity did not present itself. This King is feared like a wild beast. I am quite out of conceit with monarchy.

[Lord Marischal to Boswell. Original in French]

[Potsdam, *c.* 23 September 1764]

LORD MARISCHAL sends Mr. Boswell his wishes for a good trip, and hopes he will have health, pleasure, and profit from the fine things he will see in Italy.

He begs him if he sees Monsieur Rousseau to pay him many compliments on Lord Marischal's part, and to inform Lord Marischal of the state of Monsieur Rousseau's health.

MONDAY 24 SEPTEMBER. About noon I arrived at Coswig, the residence of the Prince of Zerbst, who is a strange, wrong-headed being. He has got his troops, forsooth, to the number of 150 foot and 30 horse, and, during the last war, he took a fancy that the King of Prussia was coming to attack him. So he put in readiness his little battery of cannon, and led out his 180 to make head against the armies of Frederick. He was not here at present, but at Vienna, as he has a regiment in the Austrian service. So I had no opportunity of paying my court to him. The appearance of his little dirty town, his castle, and his sentinels with sentry-boxes painted in lozenges of different colours, like the stockings of Harlequin, diverted me a good deal. I walked about, and, to have a little German talk, I asked every sentry, "Vie veel troepen hebt der Furst?" One soldier, whose head resembled that of his prince, had marked me with serious political attention, and, dreading that a foreign spy had got into his Highness's dominions, and that a conspiracy was forming against the state, followed me close, and at last when I came to the grenadier before the Castle-gate, he laid hold of me, charged the sentry with me, and bringing a party, conducted me to the main Guard. I was heartily entertained with this adventure, and marched with all the formal composure of a state prisoner. When I arrived at the Guard, there was a hue and cry around me as if I had entered a kennel of dogs. I could not explain myself well enough in German, and stood for some time like the stag at bay. At last a blackguard dog of a soldier said, "Dominus forsitan loquitur Latine." I told this fellow that I was a stranger, a gentleman of Scotland, and that I had asked the number of his prince's troops to amuse my curiosity, and that I supposed I had done no harm. He repeated this in German, and most of the troops seemed content. But my foolish fellow of an accuser would see more into the matter, and so away they carried me before the Burgmeester, while I laughed and cried "Beast." My interpreter repeated my defence to the Burgmeester, and this judicious magistrate smiled at the fellow and dismissed me immediately.

> Solvuntur risu tabulae, tu missus abibis.
>
> My Lords the judges laugh, and you're dismissed.

FRIDAY 28 SEPTEMBER. Again we went a-hunting. We went to another part of the forest from that where we were last day. We were obliged to wait a long time till the stag was found. I went into a farm-house, where I learnt a piece of German housewifery. The country people here have in their gardens a great many plums of the bluish-red kind which we call burnets at Auchinleck. They skin them and take out their stones and then throw them into a great cauldron with a certain quantity of water. They put them over a brisk fire of wood, and keep stirring them till they are sufficiently boiled. They mix no sugar with them, as their juice makes them sweet enough, and being well boiled they can be kept a great while. They throw this rustic jelly into a large tub. They call it *Floum Moose*. When butter is dear, they spread it very thick on their brown bread, and a very good relish it makes. I took a hearty bit of it, for which, bread and all, I paid a groschen.

At last the stag was put up, and a glorious chase we had, much better than the first. I acquired venatic courage, took made roads no more, but rushed boldly along with the Herr Overstalmeester, as they called my friend Neitschütz. The stag did not get to the river. But when run down, he couched three several times, and three several times took another race, and stood at last at bay. Of all this we had a full view. At last he sunk, the dogs laid hold of him, and the *coup de grâce* laid him dead on the field. Poor animal! the agitation of sport prevented us from pitying him so much as we ought.

SUNDAY 30 SEPTEMBER. I saw the convent where Luther lived, and I went to the old church in which he first preached the Reformation. It has been miserably shattered by the bombardments. But the tomb of Luther is still entire, as is that of Melanchthon, just opposite to it. They are nothing more than two large plates of metal fixed on the floor. They have inscriptions in raised letters.

LUTHER'S:

Martini Luteri S. Theologiae D. Corpus H.L.S.E.
Qui An. Christi MDXLVI. XII. Cal. Martii Eyslebii in Patria S.
M.O.C.V. Ann. LXIII. M.II. D.X.

MELANCHTHON'S:

Philippi Melanchthonis S.V. Corpus H.L.S.E.
Qui An. Christi MDLX. XIII. Cal. Maii in Hac Urbe
M.O.C.V. Ann. LXIII. M.II. D.II

I was in a true solemn humour, and a most curious and agreeable idea presented itself, which was to write to Mr. Samuel Johnson from the tomb of Melanchthon. The woman who showed the church was a good obliging body, and very readily furnished me with pen and ink. That my paper might literally rest upon the monument, or rather the simple epitaph, of this great and good man, I laid myself down and wrote in that posture. The good woman and some more simple beings gathered round and beheld me with wonder. I dare say they supposed me a little mad. Tombs have been always the favourite resort of gloomy, distracted mortals. I said nothing of hot-headed Luther. I only mentioned the mild Melanchthon, and that at his tomb I vowed to Mr. Johnson an eternal attachment. This letter must surely give him satisfaction. I shall not send it till I see if he gives me a favourable answer to my two last letters.

[Boswell to Samuel Johnson]

[Wittenberg] Sunday 30 September 1764
MY EVER DEAR AND MUCH RESPECTED SIR:—You know my solemn enthusiasm of mind. You love me for it, and I respect myself for it, because in so far I resemble Mr. Johnson. You will be agreeably surprised when you learn the reason of my writing this letter. I am at Wittenberg in Saxony. I am in the old church where the Reformation was first preached and where some of the Reformers lie interred. I cannot resist the serious pleasure of writing to Mr. Johnson from the tomb of Melanchthon. My paper rests upon the gravestone of that great and good man, who was undoubtedly the worthiest of all the Reformers. He wished to reform abuses which had been introduced into the Church, but had no private resentment to gratify. So mild was he that when his aged mother consulted him with anxiety on the perplexing disputes of the times, he advised her to keep to the old religion. At this tomb, then, my ever dear and respected friend, I vow to thee an eternal attachment. It shall be my study to do what I can to render your life happy, and if you die before me, I shall endeavour to do honour to your memory and, elevated by the remembrance of you, persist in noble piety. May God, the Father of all beings, ever bless you! And may you continue to love your most affectionate friend and devoted servant,

JAMES BOSWELL

WEDNESDAY 3 OCTOBER. As it was Fair time, the town was full. I was obliged to pay a ducat a day for lodging for myself and servant. The people were very civil and of the better sort. I had a damp alcove to sleep in, but a very handsome chamber. So I caused Jacob spread my bed on the floor of the chamber, and thus I lay with my clothes on, a good coverlet above me, and my head reposed on a pillow laid on one of my trunks. This operation however was performed after the good folks of the house were abed, for I would not shock them by letting them know that I could not bear their dormitory. This is in some degree benevolence.

THURSDAY 4 OCTOBER. Lying on the floor did me much good. I sprung up cheerful. Experience shall ever be my great guide. I find that to sleep on a very hard bed prevents my nervous system from being totally unstrung, and so prevents me from being clouded, except when I have eat too much and so caused obstructions.

I then went and called on the Professor Gottsched, one of the most distinguished *literati* in this country. It was he who set a-going the true cultivation of the German language, of which he has given an excellent grammar. He has also written several pieces, both in verse and prose. I found him a big, stately, comely man, with an ease of manners like a man of the world. Although I had no recommendation, he received me with a perfect politeness. We talked of Scotland, of its language and the difference between it and English. I mentioned to him my plan of a Scots dictionary, and promised to show him a specimen of it. He said the Preface to Johnson's *Dictionary* was one of the best pieces he had ever read. Said he, "He knows his subject to the bottom."

FRIDAY 5 OCTOBER. At three I went to Gellert. They call him the Gay of Germany. He has written fables and little dramatic pieces. I found him to be a poor, sickly creature. He said he had been twenty years hypochondriac. He said that during a part of his life, every night he thought to die, and every morning he wrote a fable. He said, "My poetry is at an end. I no longer have the power of mind." He spoke bad Latin and worse French, so I did my best with him in German. He translated to me in Latin one of his fables, and I promised to learn German so as to read him well. Yet alas! how unpersevering am I! Where is my Greek? Where is my translation of Scots law? Well, all will come about yet.

SATURDAY 6 OCTOBER. We had with us Herr Rogler, M.A., who has made a surprising progress in the English language. He has given a dictionary, German and English, which is properly a translation of the *Dictionary* of Mr. Samuel Johnson, as he says in his title-page. But from the unlucky inclination to be voluminous, which is so remarkable in Germans, he has *enriched* it forsooth with three thousand words taken from *others,* so that he has amassed all the rubbish which Mr. Johnson has with so much judicious care kept out of his book.

SUNDAY 7 OCTOBER. I must take the liberty to think otherwise upon the evidence of facts. My father's friends have been ever ready to oblige him. I have surely more people who would be ready to oblige me. The difference is that my father formed his friendships very slowly, whereas I have formed mine quickly. Can I help it if I find mankind take an affection for me at once? Besides, my father's friends are only rational connections. He has no friends for whom he feels that enthusiasm of affection which I feel for Temple or for Johnston.

TUESDAY 9 OCTOBER. This morning I was in delicious spirits. I stood calm in my chamber, while the sun shone sweet upon me, and was *sure* that after gloom I may be *quite well.* This is a corporeal change. No matter. No philosophizing. Mr. Stanhope sent me his compliments, and said he'd carry me to Court at twelve. He came very politely, and took me in his coach. Scarcely had we gone two yards when he called out, "Stop!" and catching hold of me, said, "You can't go to Court." In short the Court of Saxony was in mourning, and I had not a black coat. As I intended staying here only three or four days, Mr. Stanhope said it was not worth my while to make a suit of mourning. But he advised me never to be without a black coat, as so many accidents may happen.

THURSDAY 11 OCTOBER. I must remark that at Dresden strangers pay monstrously dear for seeing the fine things, which is shameful when they are the property of a prince. My *valet de louage* told me that I must pay a ducat to the library-keeper and a florin to his man, which I was fool enough to do, as I would be genteel, forsooth. It seems, too, I must pay at the museum a louis to the principal keeper, two écus to another, and a guilder to the servant. Instead of this I made two guilders do the business. I know not how I divided it between the upper keeper and the servant. I forget, but no matter. The fellows looked strange and I saved six écus. The museum has indeed many great curiosities, but some of its richest pieces have been sold to repair the ruins of the war. I then walked to the garden, where I saw some fine antiques in bronze. I went to the French *comédie,* which is very pretty here. I saw the Elector, Prince Xavier, and several more of the Court. I was enlivened with new ideas. Yet again I went with those easy street girls, and between their thighs—, merely for health. I would not embrace them. First, because it was dangerous. Next, because I could not think of being so united to miscreants. Both last night and this they picked my pocket of my handkerchief. I was angry at myself. I was obliged to own to my servant that I had been *avec des filles.* Man is sometimes low.

MONDAY 15 OCTOBER. I was obliged to go on very slowly, as they sometimes made me wait five hours for horses to my machine. I resolved never again to take an extra. I strolled about in a village in search of the ugliest woman I could find. I restrained myself. Such inclinations are caused by disease.

FRIDAY 19 OCTOBER. I went and saw the Duke's Library, which is very large, in excellent order, and contains some curious pieces. There is also a German Bible which formerly belonged to the Elector of Bavaria. It is a manuscript written an age before the Reformation. It is in two volumes. The first contains the historical books of the Old Testament. It is probable that there has been another volume in which the rest of the Old Testament has been written. This first volume is decorated with paintings in an odd taste, but finely illuminated and richly gilded in the manner of that ancient art, which is now totally lost. Some of the designs are truly ludicrous. When Adam and Eve perceive that they are naked, God comes in the figure of an old man with a pair of breeches for Adam and a petticoat for Eve. One would almost imagine that the painter intended to laugh at the Scriptures. But in those days it was not the mode to mock at the religion of their country. The genius which is now employed to support infidelity was then employed to support piety. The imagination which now furnishes licentious sallies was then fertile in sacred emblems. Sometimes superstition rendered them extravagant, and sometimes weakness made them ridiculous, as I have now given an example.

I was this day dressed in a suit of flowered velvet of five colours. I had designed to put on this suit first at Saxe-Gotha. I did so. It is curious, but I had here the very train of ideas which I expected to have. At night the Princess made me come to the table where she sat at cards, and said, "Mr. Boswell! Why, how fine you are!" She is a good, lively girl. I am already treated here with much ease. My time passes pleasantly on. Between dinner and evening court I read the *Nouvelle Héloïse;* I write; I think.

SUNDAY 21 OCTOBER. I got up at six. I heard the noise of an organ. I entered the great church. I found there a numerous congregation, a great many well-dressed people, lustres lighted. This morning worship had a fine effect. I then mounted my old friend the post-wagon. I was in the sweetest spirits. 'Tis strange that want of sleep should produce such an effect. But so I find it. I drove two miles to Langensalza, where the wagon was to stop all day. I dismounted, went to my inn, and sent a card to the Grand Maître of the Princesse Frédérique of Saxe-Gotha, Douairière de Saxe-Weissenfels, a house now sunk into that of the Elector. I was here quite at my ease in the house of the sister of the

Princess of Wales, and the aunt of my king. After dinner I took leave politely, saying I should be happy to tell the Princess of Wales that I had the honour of paying my respects here. I had one of her Highness's coaches to conduct me to my inn. Was not this a rare adventure? I called this "shooting a princess flying." I was indeed the person in motion and her Highness the person at rest. I was in a moment again in my travelling-dress. Her Highness's chaplain, who had dined with us, waited upon me, and carried me to take a walk and see the town. It is the dirtiest that I ever saw. Its streets are overflowed with liquid mud, and with difficulty you step along a narrow path on each side. The chaplain was a laughing fellow, tolerably knowing.

At six we parted. I was somewhat splenetic, and dreary apprehensions as to my conduct distressed me. I swore solemnly neither to talk as an infidel nor to enjoy a woman before seeing Rousseau. So I am bound a month at least. I was very heavy-headed from having had no sleep last night; and as I did not know when the wagon might set out, I threw myself on the bed, leaving orders to Jacob to call me. I slept till eleven, and got up unhinged. But a glass of cold water and a walk up and down the room set me to rights. By long study I shall be quite master of spleen. Between eleven and twelve at night I set out.

MONDAY 22 OCTOBER. Sad travelling. About twelve at night as the wagon was rumbling down a hill, one of its wheels fell into a deep hole, and there we stuck fast and had almost been overturned. We could not get the horses to pull out the wagon. Luckily we were within a little of our station, the village of Helsa. The postilion went to bring help. He returned with a man and a horse. Still it would not do. He went once more. He was an old creature and mighty slow. It was a dreadful rain. We remained upon the hill more than two hours. It was quite serving a campaign. The postilion, I do believe, would have allowed us to remain a-soaking till daybreak. But at last we walked to the village, and sent a man to watch our baggage. I kept my temper. I went to bed and slept pretty sound.

WEDNESDAY 24 OCTOBER. I then called on Monsieur de La Porte, French minister here, brother to Monsieur de La Porte whom I knew at Utrecht. He carried me to see the Maison des Modèles, which is a singular thing. You have here models of all the buildings and gardens of the Prince, in particular, however, of the grand waterfall, which is not yet completely executed. But there are here many pieces yet unexecuted. The waterfall must be a work of prodigious expense. The water issues from a hill and flows down a flight of steps till it reaches a basin; from thence it again is conveyed to a flight of steps. In short, this alternation will be carried on a vast way. On each side of the fall are evergreens, verdant banks, and a serpentine stair. On the top of the hill, or rock, is a large statue of Hercules, in the inside of which is a stair. The statue is so large that a man may stand in the head of it. It was the grand-uncle of this Landgrave who caused make the waterfall. His son, the King of Sweden, came to see him, and was immediately carried to view the fall. His father asked him, "Is it not beautiful? Can you imagine anything that is lacking here?" The King replied, "Nothing, except a gibbet for the man who planned this for your Highness."

THURSDAY 25 OCTOBER. All the morning I wrote. My method is to make a memorandum every night of what I have seen during the day. By this means I have my materials always secured. Sometimes I am three, four, five days without journalizing. When I have time and spirits, I bring up this my journal as well as I can in the hasty manner in which I write it. Some years hence I shall perhaps abridge it in a more elegant style.

FRIDAY 26 OCTOBER. I supped at Court. Before supper I took leave of the Landgrave. He was very hypochondriac. For most part, he talks too freely. But all he said to me when presented first, was, "Where do you come from last?" and when I took leave, "Where do you go from here?"

SATURDAY 27 OCTOBER. I had with me in the wagon a French servant, a blackguard, impudent dog. Yet at night I supped with him and my servant. Such is my hardy plan on my German travels. I also lay down with them on the straw. It was terrible. The heat of an iron stove rendered the straw musty and the air hot, and this, joined to the breaths of a good many people by no means of the most clean race, rendered the room most abominable. I could not sleep. One sad circumstance in the *Stube,* or common room of a German inn, is being obliged to sleep with a tallow candle or a coarse lamp a-burning. I had recourse to the Stall Knecht and got a place in the hayloft, where I slept sound though cold.

MONDAY 29 OCTOBER. We jogged well on. At night we were laid thirteen in a room, besides a Danish woman and three children. I could not bear this, so the postmaster gave me his own bed.

SATURDAY 3 NOVEMBER. I was well amused for some hours, and then returned to my inn, and read English newspapers which old Harold sent me. While abroad, I am often long without seeing a London paper. Now and then I come to a place where I get a budget of them. At Dresden I got one. Here I got one. It is curious how ideas are effaced and renewed. I had not thought of Chace Price since I left England, till I read tonight in the papers that his house had been robbed.

WEDNESDAY 7 NOVEMBER. I then went to see the Jesuits' College. I had heard that there was here a French Jesuit, Père Monier. I asked for him. He came to me immediately. He was a black, handsome man, between thirty and forty. He showed me their *réfectoire*, but told me that although their college had a good outside, it was but poor within. He showed me their garden, where he and I walked an hour. He had been in Canada. He asked me if I was Catholic. I told him, "No. But I hope I shall not be damned for that" (striking him gently on the shoulder). "Do you really believe that I shall be damned?" He replied, "Sir, it is hard; but it is absolutely necessary for me to believe it. You have not the excuse of a poor peasant. You are enlightened." I smiled modestly. He immediately entered on the favourite subject of Jesuits, the Catholic controversy. He run on with arguments which I do not conceive any Protestant, truly attached to his religion as the only means of salvation, could answer. I told Père Monier that I was of no sect. That I took my faith from Jesus, that I endeavoured to adore God with fervency; that I found my devotion excited by grand worship, and that I was happy to worship in a Romish church. I said my notions of God made me not fear him as cruel. The Père said, "I am really sorry that you are not a Catholic." He was so agreeable I almost regretted that I could not make him happy by thinking as he did. But I took him by the hand, and said, "Sir, I shall have the pleasure of meeting you in heaven."

MONDAY 12 NOVEMBER. I have quite the disposition for travelling. When I find a court agreeable, I wish to remain there for life. I would be *attaché*. Were I but so fixed, O how tired would I be! I must however learn to keep my place at Auchinleck. It is my duty, as I am born a laird. Were all the German princes to go and live in the delicious Spain, their families would fall, and I would find no courts. This day I talked with the Prince on fate and free will. I was clear and lively and strong. His Highness talked with me today a long time. My morning was passed among the medals and books. My evening in reading Rousseau, and supping at the Marshal's table.

TUESDAY 13 NOVEMBER. It is needless for me to mention every day the medals and the Maréchal's table. I had much conversation today with the Prince. I told him how I obtained the acquaintance of Mr. Samuel Johnson. I told him how I had formerly been an excellent mimic, but that I had given it up absolutely, as it debased my character and procured me enemies.

FRIDAY 16 NOVEMBER. And now let me record my talents as a courtier. From my earliest years I have respected the great. In the groves of Auchinleck I have indulged pleasing hopes of ambition. Since

I have been in Germany it has been my ardent wish to find a prince of merit who might take a real regard for me, and with whose ennobling friendship I might be honoured all my life. I pleased myself with thinking that among the variety of princes whom I intended to visit such a one might be found. After having been at a number of courts, I had almost given up my idea. At the last court but one, my utmost wish has been fulfilled. I have found a grave, a knowing, and a worthy prince. He has seen my merit. He has shown me every mark of distinction. He has talked a great deal with me. Some days ago, I said to him, "Is it possible, Sir, that after I am gone from this I may give you any mark of my gratitude?" He answered, "I shall write to you sometimes; I shall be very glad to receive your letters." The Prince of Baden-Durlach has an order to give. He creates Knights of the Order of Fidelity. They wear a star and a ribbon hanging from their necks. My Lord Wemyss has this order. I fixed my inclination upon it. I was determined if possible to obtain it. When the Prince honoured me so far as to grant me his correspondence, I thought he would surely grant me his order. I asked him once *en passant* if only counts could have it. He said, "It is enough to be a good gentleman." Munzesheim had told me that the Prince was a little nice in giving it. This being my last day here, I was presented to take leave. The Prince said, "I cannot ask you to stay longer, as I am afraid you would tire." I said, by no means, but I was a little hurried at present, and would return again and pass a longer time. I then took courage and said, "Sir, I have a favour to ask of you, a very great favour. I don't know whether I should mention it." I was quite the courtier, for I appeared modest and embarrassed, when in reality I was perfectly unconcerned. He said, "What, Sir?" I replied, "Your Highness told me that a good gentleman might have your Highness's order. Sir, might I presume to ask you that, if I bring you proof of my being a very good gentleman, I may obtain the order?" He paused. I looked at him steadily. He answered, "I shall think of it." I said, "Sir, you have already been so good to me that I flatter myself that I have the merit for obtaining such a favour. As to my rank, I can assure you that I am a very old gentleman" (some days ago I had given his Highness a history of my family) "and it may sound strange, but, Sir, I can count kindred with my sovereign from my being related to the family of Lennox and the royal family of Stuart. Sir, I am one of your old proud Scots. If you grant me this favour, you will make me happy for life, in adding honour to my family; and I shall be proud to wear in my own country the Order of Fidelity of such a prince." He seemed pleased. I said, "I hope, Sir, you do not take amiss my having mentioned this. I was anxious to obtain it, and I thought it was pity to want what I valued so highly, for want of boldness to ask it." He said, "Let me have your genealogy attested, and when you return, we shall see." Oh, I shall have it. I took leave of his Highness with much respect.

I then went to President Gemmingen's, where I heard music and danced and was gay. I have a weakness of mind which is scarcely credible. Here amidst music and dancing I am as cheerful as if nothing had ever vexed me. My mind is like an air-pump which receives and ejects ideas with wonderful facility.

SATURDAY 17 NOVEMBER. I had sitten up all night to journalize. As usual I felt myself immediately bettered by it.

At six we went to a little theatre in the Palace, and saw a German play. One scene was ludicrous enough. A sort of Drawcansir made a row of lubberly fellows stand behind each other and each take the left foot of his neighbour under his arm. Thus ranged, he bastinadoed them, and made them hop off the stage in a group. As I understood very little of the play and had been a night out of bed, drowsiness overpowered me and I fell sound asleep by the side of a very pretty young lady. We had a splendid supper.

SUNDAY 18 NOVEMBER. I lost a louis at faro. Cards make me always melancholy. It is an instantaneous effect like a Presbyterian sermon.

Lest I may have forgotten it in its place, I now record that when at Berlin I made a most extraordinary experiment. I composed a discourse against fornication quite like an old Scots minister. I said to myself, what damned stuff is this! and was clearly convinced that I said what was certainly true. I then read it aloud with the Presbyterian tone, and upon my word frightened myself. Ought not this to prevent me from being any more rendered dismal by a *domine?* No; for, as my Lord Marischal said, "A sermon is to me like a doleful tune, which I cannot resist."

MONDAY 19 NOVEMBER. This night I took leave here. I remember Mr. Brown told me that I should see a prodigious difference between the Protestant and Popish towns of Baden. I could not perceive it.

SATURDAY 24 NOVEMBER. We now entered Switzerland. Imhof, our landlord, was a most original fellow. He was prodigiously fluent in the praises of his town, which he said deserved to be seen at great length, so that I should stay with him several days. He went out and took a turn with us, expatiating on all that he saw. We supped at his table d'hôte, where he harangued on the number of people and on the distinguished savants who had been in his house. He said, "Voltaire came here. He went to bed. I asked his servant, 'Does your master wish any supper?' 'I don't know. It all depends. Perhaps yes, perhaps no.' Well, I had some good soup made, and a chicken dressed. Monsieur Voltaire wakes up; he asks for supper. I serve him the soup. He takes it. He refuses it. Then he takes it again. 'It is excellent soup!' A gentleman had come in, and I gave him half the chicken. I serve the other half to Monsieur Voltaire. He takes it. He refuses it. Then he takes it again. 'It is an excellent chicken!' He is annoyed because he has not a whole chicken, and keeps saying, 'Half a chicken is no chicken! Half a chicken is no chicken!' In short, he was very well pleased with my house."

SUNDAY 25 NOVEMBER. I read with attention Rousseau's "Creed of the Savoyard." I was struck with its clearness, its simplicity, and its piety.

He told me a most curious anecdote. The clock of the city of Bâle is about an hour before all the clocks in the country, and indeed before the sun himself, by which they are regulated; so that when a stranger sets out from Bâle at noon, after travelling a league, he finds it noon still. Various are the causes assigned for this particularity of the Bâle clock. Some say that there was a conspiracy of the citizens to rise in arms at a certain hour, and that the magistrates, having had notice of it, advanced the clock an hour; so that some of the conspirators came to the rendezvous too late, and others too soon, and in short were all in confusion. Some again maintain that the enemy was at their gates, and were to be let in at a certain time by some wicked malcontents, but that a miracle was wrought in the favour of Bâle, and the clock advanced an hour. This tradition is highly natural. It flatters their vanity and pleases their superstition to suppose such an interposition of Providence.

I must give a specimen of Wolleb's wit. When in England he said, "You English don't love the foreigners; and yet had it not been for a foreigner, you would be damned. You own there is no salvation but through Jesus Christ."—"Yes, sure."—"Well, Jesus Christ was a foreigner. Ha! ha!" This is wit like Kennicott's.

MONDAY 26 NOVEMBER. Bâle makes me think of my worthy father, as Erasmus and Frobenius lived here. Wolleb waited upon me. We talked of Rousseau's idea of teaching nothing to a child before twelve or fourteen, because before that age a child has no inclination to learn, and he should never be forced. "But," said Wolleb, "a child may have an inclination to learn earlier. For example, I have a daughter. I always used to say, 'Are you in the humour?' If she said yes, I taught her something; if not, I left her alone." I asked him if he took no method to force her inclination. "I own that I said to her, 'You must not often be out of the humour.'" "Ah, Sir," said I, "you spoil everything."

I went and saw a private collection of pictures, some of which were good. I then saw at the Maison de Ville a picture by Holbein, the Sufferings of Christ, in eight pieces. I wrote a description of it. I then saw the Cathedral Church, one of the venerable Gothic buildings. The pulpit is of stone curiously carved. In those times when this church was built, superstition run high, but morals were at a very low ebb. There is carved in this church a monk in most gross copulation with a nun. Wolleb also showed me an old Popish chapel on the Pont du Rhin. Above the door was a niche in which was formerly placed a statue of the Virgin, and under this niche, by way of ornament, was carved a woman's thighs wide open and all her nakedness fully displayed. It has appeared so indecent that they have effaced it a little, yet still the *ipsa res* appears. At two we went and saw the College Library, which is very numerous, and has a good many manuscripts.

THURSDAY 29 NOVEMBER. At five I set out and had a pleasant drive to Berne. Jacob rejoiced not a little to find himself in his own capital, within two miles of which he was born. I put up at the Faucon. Berne is a pretty town. The houses are excellent; good stone without and wood within. They are very warm. This town has a singular convenience in having on each side of the principal streets spacious piazzas, so that one can traverse the whole town in the worst weather without suffering any inconvenience. This afternoon I had a return of my gloom. I walked out and was very uneasy. I returned to my inn, journalized, and recovered.

FRIDAY 30 NOVEMBER. I must here remark that in this and all the principal libraries that I have seen abroad, they have shown me a present of books sent them by a certain unknown whimsical Englishman. He is no doubt a most prodigious Whig, for he has sent Milton's prose works (which I suppose he prefers to his poetry), Toland's *Life of Milton*, Algernon Sidney's works, and several other such dainty pieces of British republican writing. The books are bound in red morocco, and adorned with gilded stamps of the cap of liberty, pitchforks, swords, and I know not what other terrible instruments of fury. I am surprised that he has not thought of introducing the scaffold, the block, and the axe. He might have adorned a whole board with a representation of the murder of King Charles. He has, however, a stamp of Great Britain, as she is usually seen portrayed upon our halfpence; to render her, however, complete, he has subjoined this sensible and sublime inscription, "O Fair Britannia! Hail!" Lest Sidney, Milton, and Toland should not be strong enough in the good cause, our enthusiast has now and then added notes of his own, and quotations from others like himself. He has taken care to copy an apt passage in the poetry of Mr. Richard Glover. In short, he has made me laugh very heartily.

As Jacob's friends are only two leagues from this, he had written to them to come and meet him. This day his mother, his sister, and three brothers arrived. He entertained them well. He insisted that I should show myself to them. I did so, and was highly pleased to see this picture of family affection.

MONDAY 3 DECEMBER. I let Jacob go for a week to see his relations, which made him very happy. One great object which I have ever had in view since I left Britain has been to obtain the acquaintance, and if possible the regard, of Rousseau. I was informed that he lived in a wild valley, five leagues from Neuchâtel. I set out early this morning, mounted on a little horse, with a *Reysesac* which held some shirts. I was joined by Abraham François, a merchant here. My horse was lazy; he lent me a spur and a whip, and on we jogged very cordially. He taught me a French song, "Sous le nom de l'amitié, Phillis, je vous adore," to a minuet tune. I amused myself with him, and this amusement formed an excellent contrast to the great object which occupied my mind.

We had a fine, hard road amidst mountains covered with snow. We stopped at Brot, the half-way inn. Monsieur Sandoz, the landlord, had a handsome daughter, very lively and very talkative, or rather chatty, to give the young lady a lighter word. She told us, "Monsieur Rousseau often comes and stays here several days with his housekeeper, Mademoiselle Le Vasseur. He is a very amiable man. He has a fine face. But he doesn't like to have people come and stare at him as if he were a man with two heads. Heavens! the curiosity of people is incredible. Many, many people come to see him; and often he will not receive them. He is ill, and doesn't wish to be disturbed. Over there is a pass where I have gone with him and Mademoiselle Le Vasseur. We have dined there. He will walk in such wild places for an entire day. Gentlemen who have come here have asked me a thousand questions: 'And his housekeeper, is she young? Is she pretty?'" All this chat of Mademoiselle helped to frighten me.

There was here a stone-cutter who had wrought for Voltaire. The most stupid of human beings will remember some anecdote or other of a great man whom he has had occasion to see. This stone-cutter told me, "Sir, there used to be a horse that pulled a cart at Ferney, and Monsieur Voltaire always said, 'Poor horse! you are thin, you are like me.'" Any trifle of such a genius has a value.

Abraham François and I drank a glass of good wine and pursued our journey. We passed one place exactly like Killiecrankie and another where a group of broken rocks seemed every moment ready to tumble down upon us. It will most certainly tumble ere long. Monsieur Rousseau lives in the village of Môtiers. A league on this side of it, Abraham parted from me, after I had returned him his whip and his spur. I advanced with a kind of pleasing trepidation. I wished that I might not see Rousseau till the moment that I had permission to wait upon him. I perceived a white house with green window-boards. He mentions such a one in *Émile*. I imagined it might perhaps be his, and turned away my eyes from it. I rode calmly down the street, and put up at the Maison de Village. This inn is kept by Madame Grandpierre, a widow, and her two daughters, fat, motherly maidens. The eldest received me. I told her, "I have let my servant go and see his friends and relations, so I am alone. You must take good care of me." Said she, "We shall do our best."

I asked for Monsieur Rousseau. I found he kept himself very quiet here, as my landlady had little or nothing to chatter concerning him. I had heard all that could be said as to his being difficult of access. My Lord Marischal had given me a card with compliments to him, which I was sure would procure me admission. Colonel Chaillet had given me a letter to the Châtelain, Monsieur Martinet, the Principal Justice of the place, who could introduce me without difficulty. But my romantic genius, which will never be extinguished, made me eager to put my own merit to the severest trial. I had therefore prepared a letter to Monsieur Rousseau, in which I informed him that an ancient Scots gentleman of twenty-four was come hither with the hopes of seeing him. I assured him that I deserved his regard, that I was ready to stand the test of his penetration. Towards the end of my letter I showed him that I had a heart and a soul. I have here given no idea of my letter. It can neither be abridged nor transposed, for it is really a masterpiece. I shall ever preserve it as a proof that my soul can be sublime. I dressed and dined and sent my letter *chez* Monsieur Rousseau, ordering the maid to leave it and say she'd return for the answer, so that I might give him time to consider a little, lest perhaps he might be ill and suddenly refuse to see me. I was filled with anxiety. Is not this romantic madness? Was I not sure of admittance by my recommendations? Could I not see him as any other gentleman would do? No: I am above the vulgar crowd. I would have my merit fairly tried by this great judge of human nature. I must have things in my own way. If my bold attempt succeeds, the recollection of it will be grand as long as I live. But perhaps I may appear to him so vain, or so extraordinary, that he may be shocked by such a character and may not admit me. I shall then be in a pretty situation, for I shall be ashamed to present my recommendations. But why all this doubt and uneasiness? It is the effect of my melancholy timidity. What! can the author of *Eloisa* be offended at the enthusiasm of an ingenuous mind? But if he does admit me, I shall have a very difficult character to support; for I have written to him with unusual elevation, and given him an idea of me which I shall hardly come up to.

[Boswell to Rousseau. Original in French]

[Môtiers] Val de Travers, 3 December 1764

Sir:—I am a Scots gentleman of ancient family. Now you know my rank. I am twenty-four years old. Now you know my age. Sixteen months ago I left Great Britain a completely insular being, knowing hardly a word of French. I have been in Holland and in Germany, but not yet in France. You will therefore excuse my handling of the language. I am travelling with a genuine desire to improve myself. I have come here in the hope of seeing you.

I have heard, Sir, that you are very difficult, that you have refused the visits of several people of the first distinction. For that, Sir, I respect you the more. If you admitted all those who from vanity wished to be able to say, "I have seen him," your house would no longer be the retreat of exquisite genius or elevated piety, and I should not be striving so eagerly to be received into it.

I present myself, Sir, as a man of singular merit, as a man with a feeling heart, a lively but melancholy spirit. Ah, if all that I have suffered does not give me singular merit in the eyes of Monsieur Rousseau, why was I made as I am? Why did he write as he has written?

Do you ask if I have recommendations? Surely you do not need them? In the commerce of the world a recommendation is necessary in order to protect people who lack penetration from impostors. But you, Sir, who have made such deep study of human nature, can you be deceived in a character? I think of you thus: excepting for the incomprehensible essence of the soul, you have a perfect knowledge of all the principles of body and mind, of their movements, their sentiments; in short, of everything they can do, of everything they can acquire which truly affects man as man. And yet, Sir, I dare present myself before you. I dare to put myself to the test. In cities and in courts, where there are numerous companies, one can disguise one's self, one can sometimes dazzle the eyes of the greatest philosophers. But for my part, I put myself to the severest test. It is in the silence and the solitude of your sacred retreat that you shall judge of me, and think you in such circumstances I shall be able to dissimulate?

Your writings, Sir, have melted my heart, have elevated my soul, have fired my imagination. Believe me, you will be glad to have seen me. You know what Scots pride is. Sir, I am coming to see you in order to make myself more worthy of a nation that has produced a Fletcher of Saltoun and a Lord Marischal. Forgive me, Sir, I feel myself moved. I cannot restrain myself. O dear Saint-Preux! Enlightened Mentor! Eloquent and amiable Rousseau! I have a presentiment that a truly noble friendship will be born today.

I learn with deep regret, Sir, that you are often indisposed. Perhaps you are so at present. But I beg you not to let that prevent you from receiving me. You will find in me a simplicity that will put you to no trouble, a cordiality that may help you forget your pains.

I have much to tell you. Though I am only a young man, I have experienced a variety of existence that will amaze you. I find myself in serious and delicate circumstances concerning which I eagerly hope to have the counsel of the author of the *Nouvelle Héloïse*. If you are the charitable man I believe you to be, you cannot hesitate to grant it to me. Open your door, then, Sir, to a man who dares to tell you that he deserves to enter it. Place your confidence in a stranger who is different. You will not regret it. But I beg you, be alone. In spite of all my enthusiasm, after having written to you in this fashion, I know not if I would not prefer never to see you than to see you for the first time in company. I await your reply with impatience.

BOSWELL.

MONDAY 3 DECEMBER [continued]. To prepare myself for the great interview, I walked out alone. I strolled pensive by the side of the river Reuse in a beautiful wild valley surrounded by immense mountains, some covered with frowning rocks, others with clustering pines, and others with glittering snow. The fresh, healthful air and the romantic prospect around me gave me a vigorous and solemn tone. I recalled all my former ideas of J. J. Rousseau, the admiration with which he is regarded over all Europe, his *Héloïse*, his *Émile:* in short, a crowd of great thoughts. This half hour was one of the most remarkable that I ever passed.

I returned to my inn, and the maid delivered to me a card with the following answer from Monsieur Rousseau: "I am ill, in pain, really in no state to receive visits. Yet I cannot deprive myself of Mr. Boswell's, provided that out of consideration for the state of my health, he is willing to make it short."

My sensibility dreaded the word "short." But I took courage, and went immediately. I found at the street door Mademoiselle Le Vasseur waiting for me. She was a little, lively, neat French girl and did not increase my fear. She conducted me up a darkish stair, then opened a door. I expected, "Now I shall see him"—but it was not so. I entered a room which serves for vestibule and for kitchen. My fancy formed many, many a portrait of the wild philosopher. At length his door opened and I beheld him, a genteel black man in the dress of an Armenian. I entered saying, "Many, many thanks." After the first looks and bows were over, he said, "Will you be seated? Or would you rather take a turn with me in the room?" I chose the last, and happy I was to escape being formally placed upon a chair. I asked him how he was. "Very ill. But I have given up doctors." "Yes, yes; you have no love for them." As it is impossible for me to relate exactly our conversation, I shall not endeavour at order, but give sentences as I recollect them.

BOSWELL. "The thought of your books, Sir, is a great source of pleasure to you?" ROUSSEAU. "I am fond of them; but when I think of my books, so many misfortunes which they have brought upon me are revived in my memory that really I cannot answer you. And yet my books have saved my life." He spoke of the Parlement of Paris: "If any company could be covered with disgrace, that would be. I could plunge them into deep disgrace simply by printing their edict against me on one side, and the law of nations and equity on the side opposite. But I have reasons against doing so at present." BOSWELL. "We shall have it one day, perhaps?" ROUSSEAU. "Perhaps."

I was dressed in a coat and waistcoat, scarlet with gold lace, buckskin breeches, and boots. Above all I wore a greatcoat of green camlet lined with fox-skin fur, with the collar and cuffs of the same fur. I held under my arm a hat with a solid gold lace, at least with the air of being solid. I had it last winter at The Hague. I had a free air and spoke well, and when Monsieur Rousseau said what touched me more than ordinary, I seized his hand, I thumped him on the shoulder. I was without restraint. When I found that I really pleased him, I said, "Are you aware, Sir, that I am recommended to you by a man you hold in high regard?"

ROUSSEAU. "Ah! My Lord Marischal?" BOSWELL. "Yes, Sir; my Lord furnished me with a note to introduce me to you." ROUSSEAU. "And you were unwilling to take advantage of it?" BOSWELL. "Nay, Sir; I wished to have proof of my own merits." ROUSSEAU. "Sir, there would have been no kind of merit in gaining access to me by a note of Lord Marischal's. Whatever he sends will always find a welcome from me. He is my protector, my father; I would venture to say, my friend." One circumstance embarrassed me a little: I had forgotten to bring with me from Neuchâtel my Lord's billet. But a generous consciousness of innocence and honesty gives a freedom which cannot be counterfeited. I told Monsieur Rousseau, "To speak truly, I have forgotten to bring his letter with me; but you accept my word for it?"

ROUSSEAU. "Why, certainly. Numbers of people have shown themselves ready to serve me in their own fashion; my Lord Marischal has served me in mine. He is the only man on earth to whom I owe an obligation." He went on, "When I speak of kings, I do not include the King of Prussia. He is a king quite alone and apart. That force of his! Sir, there's the great matter, to have force—revenge, even. You can always find stuff to make something out of. But when force is lacking, when everything is small and split up, there's no hope. The French, for example, are a contemptible nation." BOSWELL. "But the Spaniards, Sir?" ROUSSEAU. "Yes, you will find great souls in Spain." BOSWELL. "And in the mountains of Scotland. But since our cursed Union, ah—" ROUSSEAU. "You undid yourselves." BOSWELL. "Truly, yes. But I must tell you a great satisfaction given me by my Lord. He calls you Jean Jacques out of affection. One day he said to me, 'Jean Jacques is the most grateful man in the world. He wanted to write my brother's life; but I begged him rather to write the life of Mr. Fletcher of Saltoun, and he promised me he would do so.'" ROUSSEAU. "Yes, Sir; I will write it with the greatest care and pleasure. I shall offend the English, I know. But that is no matter. Will you furnish me with some anecdotes on the characters of those who made your Treaty of Union, and details that cannot be found in the historians?" BOSWELL. "Yes, Sir; but with the warmth of an ancient Scot." ROUSSEAU. "By all means."

He spoke of ecclesiastics. "When one of these gentlemen provides a new explanation of something incomprehensible, leaving it as incomprehensible as before, every one cries, 'Here's a great man.' But, Sir, they will tell you that no single point of theology may be neglected, that every stone in God's building, the mystic Jerusalem, must be considered as sacred. 'But they have added stones to it.—Here, take off this; take off that! Now you see, the building is admirably complete, and you have no need to stand there to hold it up.' 'But *we* want to be necessary!' Ah!—

"Sir, you don't see before you the bear you have heard tell of. Sir, I have no liking for the world. I live here in a world of fantasies, and I cannot tolerate the world as it is." BOSWELL. "But when you come across fantastical men, are they not to your liking?" ROUSSEAU. "Why, Sir, they have not the same fantasies as myself.—Sir, your country is formed for liberty. I like your habits. You and I feel free to stroll here together without talking. That is more than two Frenchmen can do. Mankind disgusts me. And my housekeeper tells me that I am in far better humour on the days when I have been alone than on those when I have been in company." BOSWELL. "There has been a great deal written against you, Sir." ROUSSEAU. "They have not understood me. As for Monsieur Vernet at Geneva, he is an Arch-Jesuit, that is all I can say of him."

BOSWELL. "Tell me, Sir, do you not find that I answer to the description I gave you of myself?" ROUSSEAU. "Sir, it is too early for me to judge. But all appearances are in your favour." BOSWELL. "I fear I have stayed too long. I shall take the honour of returning tomorrow." ROUSSEAU. "Oh, as to that, I can't tell." BOSWELL. "Sir, I shall stay quietly here in the village. If you are able to see me, I shall be enchanted; if not, I shall make no complaint." ROUSSEAU. "My Lord Marischal has a perfect understanding of man's feelings, in solitude no less than in society. I am overwhelmed with visits from idle people." BOSWELL. "And how do they spend their time?" ROUSSEAU. "In paying compliments. Also I get a prodigious quantity of letters. And the writer of each of them believes that he is the only one." BOSWELL. "You must be greatly surprised, Sir, that a man who has not the honour of your acquaintance should take the liberty of writing to you?" ROUSSEAU. "No. I am not at all surprised. For I got a letter like it yesterday, and one the day before yesterday, and others many times before that." BOSWELL. "Sir, your very humble servant. —What, you are coming further?" ROUSSEAU. "I am not coming with you. I am going for a walk in the passage. Good-bye."

TUESDAY 4 DECEMBER. After taking a walk in the *vallon,* I went to the door of Monsieur Rousseau. Mademoiselle Le Vasseur was abroad, and I could not get in. I met her on the street, and she said, "Monsieur Rousseau will let you know this afternoon at what hour he can see you."

At five I went to Monsieur Rousseau, whom I found more gay than he had been yesterday. We joked on Mademoiselle Le Vasseur for keeping him under lock and key. She, to defend herself, said he had another door to get out at. Said he, "Ah, Mademoiselle, you can keep nothing to yourself."

He gave me the character of the Abbé de Saint-Pierre, "a man who did good, simply because he chose to do good: a man without enthusiasm. One might say that he was passionately reasonable. If you become a Member of Parliament, you must resemble the Abbé de Saint-Pierre. You must stick to your principles." BOSWELL. "But, then, one must be very well instructed." ROUSSEAU. "Ah, sure enough. You must have a well-furnished head." BOSWELL. "But, Sir, a Member of Parliament who behaves as a strictly honest man is regarded as a crazy fool." ROUSSEAU. "Well then, you must be a crazy fool of a Member; and believe me, such a man will be respected—that is, if he holds consistently by his principles. A man who changes round on every occasion is another affair."

He talked of his *Plan for Perpetual Peace, taken from the Abbé de Saint-Pierre.* I frankly owned that I had not read it. "No?" said he—then took one down from his bookcase and gave it me. I asked him smilingly if he would not put his name upon it. He laughed heartily at me. I talked to him of the German album and how I had been forced to take one; but that except what was written by the person who gave it me, there was nothing in it. Said he, "Then your album is *album*." There was a sally for you. A precious pearl; a pun made by Rousseau. He said, "I have seen the Scottish Highlanders in France. I love the Scots; not because my Lord Marischal is one of them but because he praises them. *You* are irksome to me. It's my nature. I cannot help it." BOSWELL. "Do not stand on ceremony with me." ROUSSEAU. "Go away."

Mademoiselle always accompanies me to the door. She said, "I have been twenty-two years with Monsieur Rousseau; I would not give up my place to be Queen of France. I try to profit by the good advice he gives me. If he should die, I shall have to go into a convent." She is a very good girl, and deserves to be esteemed for her constancy to a man so valuable. His simplicity is beautiful. He consulted Mademoiselle and her mother on the merits of his *Héloïse* and his *Émile*.

WEDNESDAY 5 DECEMBER. When I waited upon Monsieur Rousseau this morning, he said, "My dear Sir, I am sorry not to be able to talk with you as I would wish." I took care to waive such excuses, and immediately set conversation a-going. I told him how I had turned Roman Catholic and had intended to hide myself in a convent in France. He said, "What folly! I too was Catholic in my youth. I changed, and then I changed back again. I returned to Geneva and was readmitted to the Protestant faith. I went again among Catholics, and used to say to them, 'I am no longer one of you'; and I got on with them excellently." I stopped him in the middle of the room and I said to him, "But tell me sincerely, are you a Christian?" I looked at him with a searching eye. His countenance was no less animated. Each stood steady and watched the other's looks. He struck his breast, and replied, "Yes. I pique myself upon being one." BOSWELL. "Sir, the soul can be sustained by nothing save the Gospel." ROUSSEAU. "I feel that. I am unaffected by all the objections. I am weak; there may be things beyond my reach; or perhaps the man who recorded them made a mistake. I say, God the Father, God the Son, God the Holy Ghost."

BOSWELL. "But tell me, do you suffer from melancholy?" ROUSSEAU. "I was born placid. I have no natural disposition to melancholy. My misfortunes have infected me with it." BOSWELL. "I, for my part, suffer from it severely. And how can I be happy, I, who have done so much evil?" ROUSSEAU. "Begin your life anew. God is good, for he is just. Do good. You will cancel all the debt of evil. Say to yourself in the morning,

'Come now, I am going to *pay off* so much evil.' Six well-spent years will pay off all the evil you have committed." BOSWELL. "But what do you think of cloisters, penances, and remedies of that sort?" ROUSSEAU. "Mummeries, all of them, invented by men. Do not be guided by men's judgments, or you will find yourself tossed to and fro perpetually. Do not base your life on the judgments of others; first, because they are as likely to be mistaken as you are, and further, because you cannot know that they are telling you their true thoughts; they may be impelled by motives of interest or convention to talk to you in a way not corresponding to what they really think." BOSWELL. "Will you, Sir, assume direction of me?" ROUSSEAU. "I cannot. I can be responsible only for myself." BOSWELL. "But I shall come back." ROUSSEAU. "I don't promise to see you. I am in pain. I need a chamber-pot every minute." BOSWELL. "Yes, you will see me." ROUSSEAU. "Be off; and a good journey to you."

About six I set out.

[Boswell to Rousseau]

Môtiers, Val de Travers, 5 December 1764
SIR:—I am as grateful as man can be for your really gracious reception.

If you can, I beseech you to help me. I am leaving you a sketch of my life. It is hastily written. In it you have facts merely; had I entered on feelings, it would have been too diffuse. You do not love to be bothered by any one's company, but my papers may perhaps be admitted. After all that I have done, I still have my health; I still have for the most part a very healthy mind; I have a soul that incites me to be a man. Oh, vouchsafe to preserve a true Scot! My Lord Marischal is old. That illustrious Scottish oak-tree must soon fall. You love that ancient country. Preserve a sapling from it. I shall return with my Lord's portrait. You will see me, and I shall go out from your retreat into the world with two or three simple and noble principles, and I shall be a man all the rest of my days. You will be so generous as to keep my secret. Imperfect as I am, I consider myself an excellent man in the world as it exists. But I have an idea that it is possible to rise above the world as it is; and until I do, I shall not be content.

[5 December, Extract from "Sketch of My Life."
Original in French]

. . . I loved the daughter of a man of the first distinction in Scotland. She married a gentleman of great wealth. She allowed me to see that she loved me more than she did her husband. She made no difficulty of granting me all. She was a subtle philosopher. She said, "I love my husband as a husband, and you as a lover, each in his own sphere. I perform for him all the duties of a good wife. With you I give myself up to delicious pleasures. We keep our secret. Nature has so made me that I shall never bear children. No one suffers from our loves. My conscience does not reproach me, and I am sure that God cannot be offended by them." Philosophy of that sort in the mouth of a charming woman seemed very attractive to me. But her father had heaped kindnesses on me. Her husband was one of the most amiable of men. . . . I was seized with the bitterest regrets. I was sad. I was almost in despair, and often wished to confess everything to Monsieur de _____, in order to compel him to deprive me of my wretched life. But that would have been the most fatal of follies. I opened my heart to Madame de _____. Although she was affectionate and generous, she was set in her ideas. She reproached me for my weakness. What could I do? I continued my criminal amour, and the pleasures I tasted formed a counterpoise to my remorse. Sometimes even in my transports I imagined that heaven could not but smile on so great a happiness between two mortals. At twenty-two, my father permitted me to go to London. I was glad to escape from Madame de _____'s vicinity. I made a resolve never to write to her, and for two years we have had no news of each other, except that we are in good health. . . . Sir, I have given you in haste a record of all the evil I have done. I have told you of all there is good in me. Tell me, is it possible for me yet to make myself a man?

THURSDAY 6 DECEMBER. I had not heard from my father for three months, and was very uncertain if he would allow me to go to Italy. His letter this night was most kind. He agreed to my going to Italy for four months, and wrote to me as to a man. I was penetrated with his goodness. I had a letter from Sir David Dalrymple in which he scourged me with humorous severity till I was almost angry;

[Received 6 December, Sir David Dalrymple to Boswell]

First, you must not be a *true young laird.* You say you would rather die, and this you solemnly swear.—This depends not upon your father but upon yourself, for if you are a man of business, fill up your time and think of contributing any usefulness to society, you will not be a *young laird* in your sense of the word. There are *young lairds* of your acquaintance, and those of considerable rank, who continue so although their fathers have been long at rest. They are the idle and dissipated, who depend for their pleasure upon every trifling amusement and upon every companion as idle and dissipated as themselves and as trifling as their amusements.

Your next condition is that you shall while in Edinburgh worship

God according to the rites of the Church of England, which make you think of heaven, whereas the Presbyterian worship makes you think of hell, as you once told David Hume.—For my own part, I do not consider it as a matter of much moment in which of the two ways God is worshipped, provided that he is worshipped, the difference of the rites being in my poor opinion very inconsiderable. Perhaps I do not totally approve of either, but what then? Ought I to expect that every one should dress according to my fancy?

Your third condition is *ménage à part*. My answer is, marry some woman of family and tolerable sense in your own country, and then the rest will follow of course. Believe me, without this your plan of separate family will sound ridiculous to others and in a few weeks be irksome to yourself.

The last condition is the worst of all: a journey to London once a year. But this is not your own, you got it in *Tristram Shandy*. If you were my son, I would never consent to such a journey. You mean to wind up the watch backwards, and thus undo what had been done and break the spring. If your duty as a lawyer called you to London, good. Your father then would not have the power of preventing your journey. If you was in Parliament, *vir bonus ac discretus,* as the writs bear, it would be a breach of privilege to keep you away. But to stipulate that you should go annually to London whether you have anything to do there or not—if you were my son, I would as soon agree to your making an annual jaunt to Sodom and Gomorrah.

MONDAY 10 DECEMBER. I went to the Maison de Village, kept by the father of Madame Froment's Lisette. Her sister Caton served me up a good Swiss dinner. I asked her, "Would you like to go to Scotland?" She said, "Yes, Sir. I don't want to stay here." She pleased me.

TUESDAY 11 DECEMBER. I went to the inn and found Caton. "Were you serious when you said you would go with me to Scotland?" "Yes, Sir. When I was still a young girl, in the house of Monsieur ———, an attempt was made to force me. I escaped. I married through vexation. I never loved my husband. He spent all his money. He ran off. I can have a divorce. I should like to be far away from here. I would go with a gentleman to whom I was attached. I believe you to be a perfectly honourable man." "But you understand on what footing you will be with me? I do not wish to deceive you." "Yes, Sir; you will dispose of me as you see fit." She had two pretty children and was a fine fresh Swiss lass. I said, "Well, I make no promises; but if I find it suitable, I shall write to you."

13 OR 14 DECEMBER. Suicide. Hypochondria. A real malady: family madness. Self-destruction: your arguments, not answered.—Was poet,

praised in journals.—Suppose not slave to appetites, more than in marriage, but will have Swiss girl, amiable, &c. Quite adventure. [I would name my natural sons] Marischal Boswell, Rousseau Boswell. Court of London? No. Envoy? No. Parliament or home, and lawyer. Old estate, good principle. Propagate family great thing of all. Shall I suffer gloom as [expiation of] evil? And you, O great philosopher, will you befriend me?

FRIDAY 14 DECEMBER. At eight I got on horseback and had for my guide a smith called Dupuis. I said, "Since when (*depuis quand*) have you had that name?" I passed the Mountain Lapidosa, which is monstrously steep and in a great measure covered with snow. I was going to Rousseau, which consideration levelled the roughest mountains. I arrived at Môtiers before noon. I alighted at Rousseau's door. Up and I went and found Mademoiselle Le Vasseur, who told me, "He is very ill." "But can I see him for a moment?" "I will find out. Step in, Sir." I found him sitting in great pain.

ROUSSEAU. "I am overcome with ailments, disappointments, and sorrow. I am using a probe.—Every one thinks it my duty to attend to him." BOSWELL. "That is most natural; and are you not pleased to find you can be of so much help to others?" ROUSSEAU. "Why—"

I had left with him when I was last here what I called a "Sketch of My Life," in which I gave him the important incidents of my history and my melancholy apprehensions, and begged his advice and friendship. It was an interesting piece. He said, "I have read your Memoir. You have been gulled. You ought never to see a priest." BOSWELL. "But can I yet hope to make something of myself?" ROUSSEAU. "Yes. Your great difficulty is that you think it so difficult a matter. Come back in the afternoon. But put your watch on the table." BOSWELL. "For how long?" ROUSSEAU. "A quarter of an hour, and no longer." BOSWELL. "Twenty minutes." ROUSSEAU. "Be off with you!—Ha! Ha!" Notwithstanding the pain he was in, he was touched with my singular sally and laughed most really. He had a gay look immediately.

At four I went to Monsieur Rousseau. "I have but a moment allowed me; I must use it well.—Is it possible to live amongst other men, and to retain singularity?" ROUSSEAU. "Yes, I have done it." BOSWELL. "But to remain on good terms with them?" ROUSSEAU. "Oh, if you want to be a wolf, you must howl.—I attach very little importance to books." BOSWELL. "Even to your own books?" ROUSSEAU. "Oh, they are just rigmarole." BOSWELL. "Now you are howling." ROUSSEAU. "When I put my trust in books, I was tossed about as you are—though it is rather by talking that you have been tossed. I had nothing stable here" (striking his head) "before I began to meditate." BOSWELL. "But you would not have meditated to such good purpose if you had not read." ROUSSEAU. "No. I should have meditated to better purpose if I had begun sooner." BOSWELL. "But I, for example, would never have had the agreeable ideas I possess of the Christian religion, had I not read 'The Savoyard's Creed.' Yet, to tell the truth, I can find no certain system. Morals appear to me an uncertain thing. For instance, I should like to have thirty women. Could I not satisfy that desire?" ROUSSEAU. "No!" BOSWELL. "Why?" ROUSSEAU. "Ha! Ha! If Mademoiselle were not here, I would give you a most ample reason why." BOSWELL. "But consider: if I am rich, I can take a number of girls; I get them with child; propagation is thus increased. I give them dowries, and I marry them off to good peasants who are very happy to have them. Thus they become wives at the same age as would have been the case if they had remained virgins, and I, on my side, have had the benefit of enjoying a great variety of women." ROUSSEAU. "Oh, you will be landed in jealousies, betrayals, and treachery." BOSWELL. "But cannot I follow the Oriental usage?" ROUSSEAU. "In the Orient the women are kept shut up, and that means keeping slaves. And, mark you, their women do nothing but harm, whereas ours do much good, for they do a great deal of work." BOSWELL. "Still, I should like to follow the example of the old Patriarchs, worthy men whose memory I hold in respect." ROUSSEAU. "But are you not a citizen? You must not pick and choose one law here and another law there; you must take the laws of your own society. Do your duty as a citizen, and if you hold fast, you will win respect. I should not talk about it, but I would do it.—And as for your lady, when you go back to Scotland you will say, 'Madam, such conduct is against my conscience, and there shall be no more of it.' She will applaud you; if not, she is to be despised." BOSWELL. "Suppose her passion is still lively, and she threatens to tell her husband what has happened unless I agree to continue our intrigue?" ROUSSEAU. "In the first place, she will not tell him. In the second, you have no right to do evil for the sake of good." BOSWELL. "True. None the less, I can imagine some very embarrassing situations. And pray tell me how I can expiate the evil I have done?" ROUSSEAU. "Oh, Sir, there is no expiation for evil except good."

BOSWELL. "Upon my word, I am at a loss how to act in this world; I cannot determine whether or not I should adopt some profession." ROUSSEAU. "One must have a great plan." BOSWELL. "What about those studies on which so much stress is laid? Such as history, for instance?" ROUSSEAU. "They are just amusements." BOSWELL. "My father desires me to be called to the Scottish bar; I am certainly doing right in satisfying my father; I have no such certainty if I follow my light inclinations. I must therefore give my mind to the study of the laws of Scotland." ROUSSEAU. "To be sure; they are your tools. If you mean to be a carpenter, you must have a plane." BOSWELL. "I do not get on well with my father. I am not at my ease with him." ROUSSEAU. "To be at ease you need to share some amusement." BOSWELL. "We look after the planting together." ROUSSEAU. "That's too serious a business. You should have some amusement that puts you more on an equal footing: shooting, for example. A shot is missed and a joke is made of it, without any infringement of respect."

(I should have observed that when I pushed the conversation on women, Mademoiselle went out, and Monsieur Rousseau said, "See now, you are driving Mademoiselle out of the room." She was now returned.) He stopped, and looked at me in a singular manner. "Are you greedy?" BOSWELL. "Yes." ROUSSEAU. "I am sorry to hear it." BOSWELL. "Ha! Ha! I was joking, for in your books you write in favour of greed. I know what you are about to say, and it is just what I was hoping to hear. I wanted to get you to invite me to dinner. I had a great desire to share a meal with you." ROUSSEAU. "Well, if you are not greedy, will you dine here tomorrow? But I give you fair warning, you will find yourself badly off." BOSWELL. "No, I shall not be badly off; I am above all such considerations." ROUSSEAU. "Come then at noon; it will give us time to talk." BOSWELL. "All my thanks." ROUSSEAU. "Good evening."

Mademoiselle carried me to the house of a poor woman with a great many children whom Monsieur Rousseau aids with his charity. I contributed my part. I was not pleased to hear Mademoiselle repeat to the poor woman just the common consolatory sayings. She should have said something singular.

SATURDAY 15 DECEMBER. I was full of fine spirits. Gods! Am I now then really the friend of Rousseau? What a rich assemblage of ideas! I relish my felicity truly in such a scene as this. Shall I not truly relish it at Auchinleck? I was quite gay, my fancy was youthful, and vented its gladness in sportive sallies. I supposed myself in the rude world. I supposed a parcel of young fellows saying, "Come, Boswell, you'll dine with us today?" "No, gentlemen, excuse me; I'm engaged. I dine today with Rousseau."

I then went to Monsieur Rousseau. "I hope your health is better today." ROUSSEAU. "Oh, don't speak of it." He seemed unusually gay. Before dinner we are all so, if not made to wait too long. A keen appetite gives a vivacity to the whole frame.

I said, "You say nothing in regard to a child's duties towards his parents. You tell us nothing of your Émile's father." ROUSSEAU. "Oh, he hadn't any. He didn't exist." It is, however, a real pity that Monsieur Rousseau has not treated of the duties between parents and children. It is an important and a delicate subject and deserves to be illustrated by a sage of so clear a judgment and so elegant a soul.

He praised *The Spectator*. He said, "One comes across allegories in it. I have no taste for allegories, though your nation shows a great liking for them."

I gave him very fully the character of Mr. Johnson. He said with force, "I should like that man. I should respect him. I would not disturb his principles if I could. I should like to see him, but from a distance, for fear he might maul me." I told him how averse Mr. Johnson was to write, and how he had his levee. "Ah," said he, "I understand. He is a man who enjoys holding forth." I told him Mr. Johnson's *bon mot* upon the innovators: that truth is a cow which will yield them no more milk, and so they are gone to milk the bull. He said, "He would detest me. He would say, 'Here is a corrupter: a man who comes here to milk the bull.' "

I had diverted myself by pretending to help Mademoiselle Le Vasseur to make the soup. We dined in the kitchen, which was neat and cheerful. There was something singularly agreeable in this scene. Here was Rousseau in all his simplicity, with his Armenian dress, which I have surely mentioned before now. His long coat and nightcap made him look easy and well.

Our dinner was as follows: 1. A dish of excellent soup. 2. A *bouilli* of beef and veal. 3. Cabbage, turnip, and carrot. 4. Cold pork. 5. Pickled trout, which he jestingly called tongue. 6. Some little dish which I forget. The dessert consisted of stoned pears and of chestnuts. We had red and white wines. It was a simple, good repast. We were quite at our ease. I sometimes forgot myself and became ceremonious. "May I help you to some of this dish?" ROUSSEAU. "No, Sir. I can help myself to it." Or, "May I help myself to some more of that?" ROUSSEAU. "Is your arm long enough?"

BOSWELL. "You are so simple. I expected to find you quite different from this: the Great Rousseau. But you do not see yourself in the same light as others do. I expected to find you enthroned and talking with a grave authority." ROUSSEAU. "Uttering oracles? Ha! Ha! Ha!" BOSWELL. "Yes, and that I should be much in awe of you. And really your simplicity might lay you open to criticism; it might be said, 'Monsieur Rousseau does not make himself sufficiently respected.' In Scotland, I assure you, a very different tone must be taken to escape from the shocking familiarity which is prevalent in that country. Upon my word, I cannot put up with it. Should I not be justified in forestalling it by fighting a duel with the first man who should treat me so, and thus live at peace for the rest of my life?" ROUSSEAU. "No. That is not allowable. It is not right to stake one's life on such follies. Life is given us for objects of importance. Pay no heed to what such men say. They will get tired of talking to a man who does not answer them." BOSWELL. "If you were in Scotland, they would begin at the very start by calling you Rousseau; they would say, 'Jean Jacques, how goes it?' with the utmost familiarity." ROUSSEAU. "That is perhaps a good thing."

BOSWELL. "Yesterday I thought of asking a favor of you, to give me credentials as your ambassador to the Corsicans. Will you make me his Excellency? Are you in need of an ambassador? I offer you my services: Mr. Boswell, Ambassador Extraordinary of Monsieur Rousseau to the Isle of Corsica." ROUSSEAU. "Perhaps you would rather be King of Corsica?" BOSWELL. "On my word! Ha! Ha! Not I. It exceeds my powers" (with a low bow). "All the same, I can now say, 'I have refused a crown.' "

Mademoiselle said, "Shall you, Sir, see Monsieur de Voltaire?" BOSWELL. "Most certainly." (To Rousseau.) "Monsieur de Voltaire has no liking for you. That is natural enough." ROUSSEAU. "Yes. One does not like those whom one has greatly injured. His talk is most enjoyable; it is even better than his books." BOSWELL. "Have you looked at the *Philosophical Dictionary?*" ROUSSEAU. "Yes." BOSWELL. "And what of it?" ROUSSEAU. "I don't like it. I am not intolerant, but he deserves—" (I forget his expression here.) "It is very well to argue against men's opinions; but to show contempt, and to say, 'You are idiots to believe this,' is to be personally offensive.—Now go away." BOSWELL. "Not yet. I will leave at three o'clock. I have still five and twenty minutes." ROUSSEAU. "But I can't give you five and twenty minutes." BOSWELL. "I will give you even more than that." ROUSSEAU. "What! of my own time? All the kings on earth cannot give me my own time." BOSWELL. "But if I had stayed till tomorrow I should have had five and twenty minutes, and next day another five and twenty. I am not taking those minutes. I am making you a present of them." ROUSSEAU. "Oh! You are not stealing my money, you are giving it to me." He then repeated part of a French satire ending with "And whatever they leave you, they count as a gift." BOSWELL. "Pray speak for me, Mademoiselle." (To Rousseau.) "I have an excellent friend here." ROUSSEAU. "Nay, but this is a league." BOSWELL. "No league at all." Mademoiselle said, "Gentlemen, I will tell you the moment the clock strikes." ROUSSEAU. "Come; I need to take the air after eating."

ROUSSEAU. "The roads are bad. You will be late." BOSWELL. "I take the bad parts on foot; the last league of the way is good.—Do you think that I shall make a good barrister before a court of justice?" ROUSSEAU. "Yes. But I regret that you have the talents necessary for defending a bad case."

BOSWELL. "Have you any commands for Italy?" ROUSSEAU. "I will send a letter to Geneva for you to carry to Parma." BOSWELL. "Can I send you anything back?" ROUSSEAU. "A few pretty tunes from the opera." BOSWELL. "By all means. Oh, I have had so much to say, that I have neglected to beg you to play me a tune." ROUSSEAU. "It's too late."

MADEMOISELLE. "Sir, your man is calling for you to start." Monsieur Rousseau embraced me. He was quite the tender Saint-Preux. He kissed me several times, and held me in his arms with elegant cordiality. Oh, I shall never forget that I have been thus. ROUSSEAU. "Good-bye. You are a fine fellow." BOSWELL. "You have shown me great goodness. But I deserved it." ROUSSEAU. "Yes. You are malicious; but 'tis a pleasant malice, a malice I don't dislike. Write and tell me how you are." BOSWELL. "One word more. Can I feel sure that I am held to you by a thread, even if of the finest? By a hair?" (Seizing a hair of my head.) ROUSSEAU. "Yes. Remember always that there are points at which our souls are bound." BOSWELL. "It is enough. I, with my melancholy, I, who often look on myself as a despicable being, as a good-for-nothing creature who should make his exit from life,—I shall be upheld for ever by the thought that I am bound to Monsieur Rousseau. Good-bye. Bravo! I shall live to the end of my days." ROUSSEAU. "That is undoubtedly a thing one must do. Good-bye."

Mademoiselle accompanied me to the outer door. Before dinner she told me, "Monsieur Rousseau has a high regard for you. The first time you came, I said to him, 'That gentleman has an honest face. I am sure you will like him.'" I said, "Mademoiselle is a good judge." "Yes," said she, "I have seen strangers enough in the twenty-two years that I have been with Monsieur Rousseau, and I assure you that I have sent many of them packing because I did not fancy their way of talking." I said, "You have promised to let me have news of you from time to time." "Yes, Sir." "And tell me what I can send you from Geneva. Make no ceremony." "Well, if you will, a garnet necklace."

We shook hands cordially, and away I went to my inn.

PART IV

CORSICA BOSWELL

24 December 1764 – 13 February 1766

INTRODUCTION

O N THE DAY BEFORE CHRISTMAS, 1764, Boswell announced himself to Voltaire, who was "much annoyed at being disturbed." He received Boswell nevertheless. Boswell records his wit for us, bringing smiles to our faces down two centuries. "I told him that Mr. Johnson and I intended to make a tour through the Hebrides, the Northern Isles of Scotland. He smiled, and cried, 'Very well; but I shall remain here. You will allow me to stay here?' 'Certainly.' 'Well then, go. I have no objections at all.' "

Boswell had now been abroad sixteen months, and he was to be yet another year in Europe, part of that time in Corsica. Of the experience of Corsica he would say afterward to the Corsican leader, General Paoli, "I had got upon a rock in Corsica, and jumped into the middle of life." His adventures in Corsica were to provide him with his first experience of literary success. This was important to him in defining himself, in holding before him a sense of himself as literary person even as he plunged into the practice of the law.

His son's literary success would never cheer Lord Auchinleck nor improve relations between them. "Dear Son," he wrote, even before he learned of Boswell's traveling to Corsica, "Your conduct astonishes and amazes me. You solicited liberty to go four months to Italy. I opposed it as altogether useless; but upon your pressing importunity, contrary to my own opinion, I agreed to it, and thereafter allowed you one month more. . . . But when I heard of Lord Mountstuart's coming over, how surprised was I that you had not come along with him, but stayed in a country where you had nothing to do, and where all you could learn could be of no use in after life."

When Lord Auchinleck finally learned of Boswell's journey to Corsica, he was especially dismayed that his knowledge came only from newspaper accounts. Possibly Boswell's decision to go to Corsica was somewhat sudden, quickened by his visit with Rousseau, who had praised Corsica as the "one country in Europe capable of legislation." The Corsicans, wrote Rousseau, were people of "valour" and "constancy" in defense of "liberty." As Boswell had a "presentiment" of friendship with Rousseau, so Rousseau had a "presentiment" that

Corsica would one day "astonish Europe." If Corsica were to be the model of perfectible society, Boswell would provide all interested readers with a report of that place. He became the first Englishman to travel in the interior of that island, and his report of his visit was seized with interest in England and Europe. He was often thereafter referred to as "Corsica Boswell."

Although Boswell wrote to Rousseau a half-hour before embarking for Corsica that "Death is nothing to me" he was in fact supplied with letters of reference and protection—"recommendations in plenty," he said in the same letter. He passed from Rousseau to General Paoli, learned and benevolent leader of the Corsicans, who, after his defeat by the French four years later, removed to exile in London. In October, 1769, Boswell arranged a meeting between Paoli and Johnson, for which he served as interpreter, comparing himself on that occasion "to an isthmus which joins two great continents."

Mr. Johnson had not at first been encouraging on the subject of Corsica. "As to your History of Corsica," he wrote to Boswell six months before Boswell sat to prepare it for the press, "you have no materials which others have not, or may not have. You have, somehow or other, warmed your imagination. I wish there were some cure, like the lover's leap, for all heads of which some single idea has obtained an unreasonable and irregular possession. Mind your own affairs, and leave the Corsicans to theirs." A year and a half later, completed book in hand, Johnson's response was to express his irritation over Boswell's having quoted him without permission. "I have omitted a long time to write to you, without knowing very well why. I could now tell you why I should not write; for who would write to men who publish the letters of their friends, without their leave?" He again expressed the wish that Boswell "would empty your head of Corsica," concluding with a renewal of affection which Boswell preferred to remember above the reproach.

Yet another eighteen months passed, but at last Mr. Johnson wrote of *Account of Corsica* in a way to please its author, distinguishing between its merely conventional aspects and that more audacious text which had been formed from Boswell's journal. "Your History is like other histories," Mr. Johnson wrote with some surprise, "but your Journal is in a very high degree curious and delightful. There is between the History and the Journal that difference which there will always be found between notions borrowed from without, and notions generated within. Your History was copied from books; your Journal rose out of your own experience and observation. You express images which operated strongly upon yourself, and you have impressed them with great force upon your readers. I know not whether I could name any narrative by which curiosity is better excited, or better gratified."

The portion of *Account of Corsica* republished here is of course the Journal, not the History, upon the recommendation of Samuel Johnson.

Between Genoa and Paris, through southern France, during the weeks immediately following his departure from Corsica, Boswell seems to have sunk to depression and rage. Neither his servant nor his dog nor his accommodations en route satisfied him. Indeed, his relationship with his dog—a gift of General Paoli—was sufficiently irrational that in a balanced mood Boswell attempted afterward to expunge from his journal the evidence of his own brutal behavior. To hang a dog! But he was fatigued. He had been two and a half years on the continent, much of that time traveling. In Corsica he had concentrated intensely upon recording all he saw, and he carried with him now not only the material record of his visit but the psychic burden of suspecting that he was carrying home, in the form of his journal, the makings of a noteworthy book. His feet troubled him dismally ("Both the nails of my great toes were now in the flesh and made me suffer sadly"). And before him lay the prospect of reunion with his father.

On January 27, 1766, the quality of Boswell's anguish dramatically altered. In John Wilkes's chambers in Paris he read in a newspaper already nine days old of the death of his mother, in Edinburgh. "Stunned," truly grieved, he hastened, before hastening home, to a prostitute named Constance. In Paris he also learned that Rousseau, whom he had perhaps hoped to call upon again, had departed for England, pursued by enemies real or imagined, but that Thérèse, who soon would follow him there, remained for the moment behind. With the kind intention of offering to escort her to England, Boswell called upon her. She had anticipated his thought. "Mon Dieu, Monsieur, if we could go together!" Boswell had last communicated with her more than a year before, when he had sent her a garnet necklace and saluted her with a kiss.

MONDAY 24 DECEMBER. After calling on my bankers, Cazenove, Clavière et fils, from whom I received payment of a bill granted me by Splitgerber and Daum, and on Chappuis et fils, to whom I was addressed by Messrs. Herries and Cochrane, I took a coach for Ferney, the seat of the illustrious Monsieur de Voltaire. I was in true spirits; the earth was covered with snow; I surveyed wild nature with a noble eye. I called up all the grand ideas which I have ever entertained of Voltaire. The first object that struck me was his church with this inscription: "Deo erexit Voltaire MDCCLXI." His château was handsome. I was received by two or three footmen, who showed me into a very elegant room. I sent by one of them a letter to Monsieur de Voltaire which I had from Colonel Constant at The Hague. He returned and told me, "Monsieur de Voltaire is very much annoyed at being disturbed. He is abed." I was afraid that I should not see him. Some ladies and gentlemen entered, and I was entertained for some time. At last Monsieur de Voltaire opened the door of his apartment, and stepped forth. I surveyed him with eager attention, and found him just as his print had made me conceive him. He received me with dignity, and that air of the world which a Frenchman acquires in such perfection. He had a slate-blue, fine frieze greatcoat nightgown, and a three-knotted wig. He sat erect upon his chair, and simpered when he spoke. He was not in spirits, not I neither. All I presented was the "foolish face of wondering praise."

We talked of Scotland. He said the Glasgow editions were "très belles." I said, "An Academy of Painting was also established there, but it did not succeed. Our Scotland is no country for that." He replied with a keen archness, "No; to paint well it is necessary to have warm feet. It's hard to paint when your feet are cold." Another would have given a long dissertation on the coldness of our climate. Monsieur de Voltaire gave the very essence of raillery in half a dozen words.

I mentioned the severe criticism which the *Gazette littéraire* has given upon Lord Kames's *Elements*. I imagined it to be done by Voltaire, but would not ask him. He repeated me several of the *bons mots* in it, with an air that confirmed me in my idea of his having written this criticism. He called my Lord always "ce Monsieur Kames."

I told him that Mr. Johnson and I intended to make a tour through the Hebrides, the Northern Isles of Scotland. He smiled, and cried, "Very well; but I shall remain here. You will allow me to stay here?" "Certainly." "Well then, go. I have no objections at all."

I asked him if he still spoke English. He replied, "No. To speak English one must place the tongue between the teeth, and I have lost my teeth."

As we talked, there entered Père Adam, a French Jesuit, who is protected in the house of Voltaire. What a curious idea. He was a lively old man with white hair. Voltaire cried in English, "There, Sir, is a young man, a scholar who is learning your language, a broken soldier of the Company of Jesus." "Ah," said Père Adam, "a young man of sixty."

Monsieur de Voltaire did not dine with us. Madame Denis, his niece, does the honours of his house very well. She understands English. She was remarkably good to me. I sat by her and we talked much. I became lively and most agreeable. We had a company of about twelve. The family consists of seven. The niece of the great Corneille lives here. She is married to a Monsieur Dupuits. The gates of Geneva shut at five, so I was obliged to hasten away after dinner without seeing any more of Monsieur de Voltaire.

At Geneva I called for Monsieur Constant Pictet, for whom I had a letter from his sister-in-law, Madame d'Hermenches. I found his lady, who asked me to stay the evening. There was a company here at cards. I saw a specimen of Genevoises, and compared them with Rousseau's drawings of them. Constant, the husband, was lively without wit and polite without being agreeable. There were a good many men here who railed against Rousseau on account of his *Lettres écrites de la montagne.* Their fury was a high farce to my philosophic mind. One of them was arrant idiot enough to say of the illustrious author, "He's a brute with brains, a horse with brains, an ox with brains." "Rather, a snake," said a foolish female with a lisping tone. Powers of absurdity! did your influence ever extend farther? I said, "On my word, it is time for me to leave this company. Can *women* speak against the author of the *Nouvelle Héloïse?*"

[Boswell to Madame Denis]

I MUST BEG your interest, Madam, in obtaining for me a very great favour from Monsieur de Voltaire. I intend to have the honour of returning to Ferney Wednesday or Thursday. The gates of this sober city shut at a most early, I had very near said a most absurd, hour, so that one is obliged to post away after dinner before the illustrious landlord has had time to shine upon his guests. Besides, I believe Monsieur de Voltaire is in opposition to our sun, for he rises in the evening. Yesterday he shot forth some rays. Some bright sparks fell from him. I am happy to have seen so much. But I greatly wish to behold him in full blaze.

Is it then possible, Madam, that I may be allowed to lodge one night under the roof of Monsieur de Voltaire? I am a hardy and a vigorous Scot. You may mount me to the highest and coldest garret. I shall not even refuse to sleep upon two chairs in the bedchamber of your maid. I saw her pass through the room where we sat before dinner.

I have the honour to be, Madam, your very humble servant,

BOSWELL

[Received 25 December, Voltaire to Boswell]

[Ferney, 25 December 1764]

SR You will do us much honour and pleasure. We have few beds, but you will not sleep on two chairs. My uncle, tho very sick, hath guess'd at yr merit. j know it more, because j have seen you longer.

THURSDAY 27 DECEMBER. I then went to Ferney, where I was received with complacency and complimented on my letter. I found here the Chevalier de Boufflers, a fine, lively young fellow and mighty ingenious. He was painting in crayon a Madame Rilliet, a most frolicsome little Dutch Genevoise. There was here a Monsieur Rieu, a Genevois, a heavy, knowing fellow. Monsieur de Voltaire came out to us a little while, but did not dine with us.

Between seven and eight we had a message that Voltaire was in the drawing-room. He always appears about this time anight, pulls his bell and cries, "Fetch Père Adam." The good Father is ready immediately, and they play at chess together. I stood by Monsieur de Voltaire and put him in tune. He spoke sometimes English and sometimes French. He gave me a sharp reproof for speaking fast. "How fast you foreigners speak!" "We think that the French do the same." "Well, at any rate, *I* don't. I speak slowly, that's what I do"; and this he said with a most keen tone. He got into great spirits. I would not go to supper, and so I had this great man for about an hour and a half at a most interesting tête-à-tête. I have written some particulars of it to Temple, and as our conversation was very long, I shall draw it up fully in a separate paper. When the company returned, Monsieur de Voltaire retired. They looked at me with complacency and without envy. Madame Denis insisted that I should sup; I agreed to this, and a genteel table was served for me in the drawing-room, where I eat and drank cheerfully with the gay company around me. I was very lively and said, "I am magnificence itself. I eat alone, like the King of England." In short this was a rich evening.

FRIDAY 28 DECEMBER. Last night Monsieur de Voltaire treated me with polite respect: "I am sorry, Sir, that you will find yourself so badly lodged." I ought to have a good opinion of myself, but from my unlucky education I cannot get rid of mean timidity as to my own worth. I was very genteelly lodged. My room was handsome. The bed, purple cloth lined with white quilted satin; the chimney-piece, marble, and ornamented above with the picture of a French toilet. Monsieur de Voltaire's country-house is the first I have slept in since I slept in that of some good Scots family—Kellie, indeed. I surveyed every object here with a minute attention and most curiously did I prove the association of ideas. Everything put me fully in mind of a decent Scots house, and I thought surely the master of the family must go to church and do as public institutions require; and then I made my transition to the real master, the celebrated Voltaire, the infidel, the author of so many deistical pieces and of the *Pucelle d'Orléans*.

I awaked this morning bad, even here. Yet I recovered, and as I was here for once in a lifetime, and wished to have as much of Voltaire as possible, I sent off Jacob to Geneva, to stop my coach today and to bring it out tomorrow. I then threw on my clothes and ran like the Cantab in the imitation of Gray's *Elegy*, "with hose ungartered," to Voltaire's church, where I heard part of a mass and was really devout. I then walked in his garden, which is very pretty and commands a fine prospect. I then went to my room, got paper from Voltaire's secretary, and wrote to my father, to Temple, and to Sir David Dalrymple. I sent to Monsieur de Voltaire a specimen of my poem called *Parliament*. I also wrote a fair copy of my *Ode on Ambition* for him, and inscribed it thus: "Most humbly presented to Monsieur de Voltaire, the glory of France, the admiration of Europe, by Mr. Boswell, who has had the honour of regarding and loving him in private life at his Château de Ferney."

He was bad today and did not appear before dinner. We dined well as usual. It was pleasant for me to think I was in France. In the afternoon I was dullish. At six I applied to the secretary for a volume of Voltaire's plays, and went to my room, and read his *Mahomet* in his own house. It was curious, this. A good, decent, trusty servant had fire and wax candles and all in order for me. There is at Ferney the true hospitality. All are master of their rooms and do as they please. I should have mentioned yesterday that when I arrived, Monsieur Rieu carried me to a room where the maids were and made me point out which of them I meant in my letter to Madame Denis. Monsieur de Voltaire was sick and out of spirits this evening, yet I made him talk some time.

[Boswell to Temple]

Château de Ferney, 28 December 1764

MY DEAR TEMPLE, And whence do I now write to you, my friend? From the château of Monsieur de Voltaire. I had a letter for him from a Swiss colonel at The Hague. I came hither Monday and was presented to him. He received me with dignity and that air of a man who has been much in the world which a Frenchman acquires in perfection. I saw him for about half an hour before dinner. He was not in spirits. Yet he gave me some brilliant sallies.

I returned yesterday to this enchanted castle. The magician appeared a very little before dinner. But in the evening he came into the drawing-room in great spirits. I placed myself by him. I touched the keys in unison with his imagination. I wish you had heard the music. He was all brilliance. He gave me continued flashes of wit. I got him to speak English, which he does in a degree that made me now and then start up and cry, "Upon my soul this is astonishing!" When he talked our language he was animated with the soul of a Briton. He had bold flights. He had humour. He had an extravagance; he had a forcible oddity of style that the most comical of our *dramatis personae* could not have exceeded. He swore bloodily, as was the fashion when he was in England. He hummed a ballad; he repeated nonsense. Then he talked of our Constitution with a noble enthusiasm. I was proud to hear this from the mouth of an illustrious Frenchman. At last we came upon religion. Then did he rage. The company went to supper. Monsieur de Voltaire and I remained in the drawing-room with a great Bible before us; and if ever two mortal men disputed with vehemence, we did. Yes, upon that occasion he was one individual and I another. For a certain portion of time there was a fair opposition between Voltaire and Boswell. The daring bursts of his ridicule confounded my understanding. He stood like an orator of ancient Rome. Tully was never more agitated than he was. He went too far. His aged frame trembled beneath him. He cried, "Oh, I am very sick; my head turns round," and he let himself gently fall upon an easy chair. He recovered. I resumed our conversation, but changed the tone. I talked to him serious and earnest. I demanded of him an honest confession of his real sentiments. He gave it me with candour and with a mild eloquence which touched my heart. I did not believe him capable of thinking in the manner that he declared to me was "from the bottom of his heart." He expressed his veneration —his love—of the Supreme Being, and his entire resignation to the will of Him who is All-wise. He expressed his desire to resemble the Author of Goodness by being good himself. His sentiments go no farther. He does not inflame his mind with grand hopes of the immortality of the soul. He says it may be, but he knows nothing of it. And his mind is in perfect tranquillity. I was moved; I was sorry. I doubted his sincerity. I called to him with emotion, "Are you sincere? are you really sincere?" He answered, "Before God, I am." Then with the fire of him whose tragedies have so often shone on the theatre of Paris, he said, "I suffer much. But I suffer with patience and resignation; not as a Christian —but as a man."

Temple, was not this an interesting scene? Would a journey from Scotland to Ferney have been too much to obtain such a remarkable interview? I have given you the great lines. The whole conversation of the evening is fully recorded, and I look upon it as an invaluable treasure. One day the public shall have it. It is a present highly worthy of their attention. I told Monsieur de Voltaire that I had written eight quarto pages of what he had said. He smiled and seemed pleased. Our important scene must not appear till after his death. But I have a great mind to send over to London a little sketch of my reception at Ferney, of the splendid manner in which Monsieur de Voltaire lives, and of the brilliant conversation of this celebrated author at the age of seventy-two. The sketch would be a letter, addressed to you, full of gaiety and full of friendship. I would send it to one of the best public papers or magazines. But this is probably a flight of my over-heated mind. I shall not send the sketch unless you approve of my doing so.

Before I left Britain, I was idle, dissipated, ridiculous, and regardless of reputation. Often was I unworthy to be the friend of Mr. Temple. Now I am a very different man. I have got a character which I am proud of. Speak, thou who hast known me from my earliest years! Couldst thou have imagined eight years ago that thy companion in the studies of Antiquity, who was debased by an unhappy education in the smoke of Edinburgh, couldst thou have imagined him to turn out the man that he now is?

My worthy father has consented that I shall go to Italy. O my friend, what a rich prospect spreads before me! My letter is already so long that I shall restrain my enthusiastic sallies. Imagine my joy. On Tuesday morning I set out for Turin. I shall pass the rigorous Alps with the resolution of Hannibal. I shall be four months in Italy and then return through France. I expect to pass some time at Paris.

SATURDAY 29 DECEMBER. I was dressed the first time at Ferney in my sea-green and silver, and now in my flowered velvet. Gloom got hold of me at dinner, in so much that I thought I would not be obliged to stay here for a great deal of money. And yet in reality I would be proud and pleased to live a long time *chez* Monsieur de Voltaire. I was asked to return when I should be at Lyons. I took an easy leave of the company. Monsieur de Voltaire was very ill today, and had not appeared. I sent my respects to him, and begged to be allowed to take leave of him. He sent to me his compliments and said he would see me. I found him in the drawing-room, where I had near half an hour more with him; at least, more than a quarter. I told him that I had marked his conversation. He seemed pleased. This last conversation shall also be marked. It was truly singular and solemn. I was quite in enthusiasm, quite agreeably mad to a certain degree. I asked his correspondence. He granted it. Is not this great?

BOSWELL. "Would you have no public worship?" VOLTAIRE. "Yes, with all my heart. Let us meet four times a year in a grand temple with music, and thank God for all his gifts. There is one sun. There is one God. Let us have one religion. Then all mankind will be brethren." BOSWELL. "May I write in English, and you'll answer?" VOLTAIRE. "Yes. Farewell."

SUNDAY 30 DECEMBER. I sat at home all forenoon writing. After tea and coffee was a ball. I played a hand at whist, and after we had played and danced enough, we went to supper. I say *we* danced, for, although I was not much in spirits, I danced a minuet with Madam Rilliet, whom I had seen and grown fond of at Ferney; and thus I solaced myself with the downfall of Presbyterian strictness. We supped in a great town hall, and eat and drank considerably. After which they pelted each other with the crumb of their bread formed into little balls. This was rather rude in a large company and in presence of a stranger. I however threw with the rest, partly to keep them in countenance, partly to indulge my whim. I asked if this was the common custom at Geneva. They said they did so only among friends. They were monstrously familiar, the men pawing the sweaty hands of the women, and kissing them too, as the minister slabbered the greasy, unwashen hands of a married woman. Had I been the husband, I should have kicked the fellow downstairs. I was disgusted much, and only consoled myself that I beheld a nauseous example of the manners of republicans. I was glad to get home.

[Boswell to Rousseau. Original in French]

Geneva, 31 December 1764

I have been with Monsieur de Voltaire. His conversation is the most brilliant I have ever heard. I had a conversation alone with him lasting an hour. It was a very serious conversation. He spoke to me of his natural religion in a way that struck me. In spite of all that has happened, you would have loved him that evening.

Here I am in the city of which you were once proud to be a citizen, and which you will never be able to deprive of the glory of having borne you. Your *Letters from the Mountain* are making a tremendous noise here. I have for the most part found myself among the partisans of the magistracy, consequently among your furious enemies. I should be ashamed to repeat to you what I have heard them say in their rage against "that scoundrel Rousseau." You are the cause of a terrible ferment in this seat of learning. I consider Geneva like Athens, but an Athens during the persecution of Socrates.

I set out for Italy tomorrow. I beg you to give me your advice as to how to conduct myself so as to profit most in that country of the fine arts. I love antiquities. I love painting. I shall have the best opportunities for perfecting myself in both. I have a real taste for music. I sing tolerably well. I play on the flute a little, but I think it beneath me. Two years ago I began to learn to play the violin, but I found it so difficult that I gave it up. That was a mistake. Tell me, would I not do well to apply seriously to music—up to a certain point? Tell me what instrument I should choose. It is late, I admit. But shall I not have the pleasure of making steady progress, and shall I not be able to soothe my old age with the notes of my lyre?

You will not object if I write occasionally to Mademoiselle Le Vasseur. I assure you that I have formed no scheme of abducting your housekeeper. I often form romantic plans but never impossible ones. Tell me, can I hope to be able to write French some day?

I am truly yours,

BOSWELL.

[Boswell to Thérèse Le Vasseur. Original in French]

Geneva, 31 December 1764

I TAKE THE LIBERTY, MY DEAR MADEMOISELLE, of sending you a garnet necklace, which you will have the goodness to keep as a slight remembrance of a worthy Scot whose face you found honest.

I shall never forget your worth. I shall never forget your feats of legerdemain. You weave lace. You do the cooking. You sit down at table. You make easy, cheerful conversation. Then you rise, the table is cleared, the dishes are washed, all is put in order, Mademoiselle Le Vasseur is with us again. Only a juggler could perform such feats.

Deign to write to me sometimes and to give me a particular account of what is happening to you. You have promised me that you will. You have doubtless always believed that a promise ought to be sacred. And the Philosopher with whom you dwell teaches you no other doctrine in that regard.

Farewell, Mademoiselle. Allow me to salute you with a kiss.

BOSWELL.

TUESDAY 1 JANUARY. Voltaire had solemnly assured me that he never was afraid of death, and had desired me to ask the famous Dr. Tronchin, his physician, if he had ever seen him so. I found him a stately, handsome man, with a good air and great ease. I said, "Sir, I am not ill, but if a man in good health may pay you his respects—" He replied, "One must indeed be at home to such men," and smiled. He said Rousseau was "a haughty, ambitious, wicked rascal, who has written with a dagger dipped in the blood of his fellow citizens. A man ruined by venereal diseases, a man who affects a severity of manners and at the same time keeps a mistress. This shocked me; but I recollected that Tronchin was connected with the Geneva magistracy, whom Rousseau has so keenly attacked. Tronchin saw that I was hurt at hearing such a character of my admired Rousseau, and said, "I have plucked a feather from your happiness." I replied, "It will grow again."

I then talked of Voltaire. He said, "He is very amiable, but is never the same for two days. Sometimes he is a very good deist. But if he is vexed, if he has received a letter which has annoyed him, he hurls his shafts at Providence. I have always regarded him as an astronomer regards a phenomenon." BOSWELL. "It is curious to see great men close at hand." TRONCHIN. "Sir," there are few men who can keep their glory when they are examined under the microscope. I have sent off my son on his travels. He will see all the great men in Europe, and he will learn to judge without prejudice.—I once asked Monsieur de Voltaire why he did not act with more constancy according to his principles. He replied, 'If I had as strong a body as you, I should be more constant.' "

I set out at eleven in a chaise mounted so high before that I was thrown back like a bishop in his studying-chair. All the chaises for passing the Alps are hung in this way. I jogged on, mighty deliberate.

[Boswell to Voltaire]

Turin, 15 January 1765

SIR: I reflect with great satisfaction on my spirited candour when we talked of religion. I told you upon this occasion, "Sir, you are one individual and I another." You may remember that I showed no mean timidity; and while I maintained the immortality of my soul, did I not glow with a fire that had some appearance of being divine? I am exceedingly happy that I have had an important conversation with you. Before that, my admiration of your genius was obscured by the horror with which I had been taught to consider your character as a man. Had I not waited upon you at Ferney, I should have had a very honest detestation of you while I lived. But, Sir, since that time I have thought of you very differently. Although I am sincerely sorry at your being prejudiced against the doctrines of consolation and hope, I shall ever esteem your humanity of feeling and generosity of sentiment. I know you must be changeable. But were not the general tenor of your mind excellent, you could not have talked to me as you did during our serious evening. When I returned to Geneva, I waited upon Dr. Tronchin, and according to your desire I asked him if you had ever shown those fears of death which the zealous orthodox have affirmed to be a certain proof of your insincerity. Dr. Tronchin assured me that you never had such fears. He said of you, "The nearer death he believes himself to be, the better deist he becomes." I am now fully satisfied as to your character; and in my presence Falsehood and Folly shall no longer blacken it. I have already had more than one occasion of vindicating you. Your faults must be allowed, but I will suffer no additions.

THURSDAY 3 JANUARY. I can record nothing but that Jacob, who observes me writing much, said, "Sir, I think you are making books like M. Rousseau."

FRIDAY 4 JANUARY. I now began to be really among the Alps. Jacob said, "If one were to transport these mountains to Holland, they wouldn't stay there. The watery earth could not support them. They would sink at once."

SATURDAY 5 JANUARY. A poor *piémontais*, or Italian of some kind, who had been a Spanish officer (as he said) and was now going to see his friends, had lost his money upon the road by gaming, and was obliged to walk to Turin. He begged leave to put his cloak-bag behind my chaise, which I granted, although this might have been a trick of some rogue who wanted a snug opportunity to rob me. He trudged along till he was quite knocked up, although I now and then walked and let him into the chaise. Today I gave him a horse till the stage of dinner.

TUESDAY 8 JANUARY. I got up very fretful, but drove off the fiend. I got my coach and *valet de louage* and went to M. Torraz, my banker, a good, brisk, civil fellow. I received a letter from my dear mother, which gave me great comfort, for I had not heard from her since I left England and had formed to myself dreary ideas of her being dead, or sick, or offended with me.

I sent a letter of recommendation from Colonel Chaillet to the Comtesse de St. Gilles. She received me at four o'clock. She was past fifty and had long been *hackneyed in the ways of men,* but, being strong, was still well enough. She talked of Duke Hamilton who had been a great gallant of hers. She had animal spirits and talked incessantly. She carried me out in her coach to take the air. I was already then quite in the Italian mode. We returned to her house, where was a stupid *conversazione,* all men. After this we all went to a public ball at the Théâtre de Carignan. It was very handsome and gay. I danced a minuet with the Spanish Ambassadress. There was here many fine women. The counts and other pretty gentlemen told me whenever I admired a lady, "Sir, you can have her. It would not be difficult." I thought at first they were joking and waggishly amusing themselves with a stranger. But I at last discovered that they were really in earnest and that the manners here were so openly debauched that adultery was carried on without the least disguise. I asked them, "But why then do you marry?" "Oh, it's the custom; it perpetuates families."

THURSDAY 10 JANUARY. I tried to write this morning, but could do nothing. I drove about in the environs. At three I called on M. Bartoli, the King's Antiquary, whom M. Schmidt at Karlsruhe had advised me to see. I was courteously received. I found him confusedly learned and lively. He improved the more I talked with him. I gave him anecdotes of Voltaire and Rousseau. He did not approve of the writings of either of the two, for he was a man attached to the Catholic religion. I told him that Rousseau said, "I live in a world of chimeras." He replied, "Then let him keep his books there, and not be sending them out into the real world." He offered me his services while I remained at Turin.

I then went to Mme. St. Gilles'. The whim seized me of having an intrigue with an Italian countess, and, as I had resolved to stay very little time here, I thought an oldish lady most proper, as I should have an easy attack. I began throwing out hints at the opera. I sat vis-à-vis to her and pressed her legs with mine, which she took very graciously. I began to lose command of myself. I became quite imprudent. I said, "Surely there will be another world, if only for getting the King of Prussia flogged"; against whom I raged while the Imperial Minister sat by us. Billon carried me to the box of the Countess Burgaretta, and introduced me to her. She was a most beautiful woman. Billon told me I might have her. My mind was now quite in fermentation. I was a sceptic, but my devotion and love of decency remained. My desire to know the world made me resolve to intrigue a little while in Italy, where the women are so debauched that they are hardly to be considered as moral agents.

SATURDAY 12 JANUARY. I called this morning on Gray, who lived at the Academy. I found there Mr. Needham of the Royal Society, whose acquaintance I much wished for. When I hear of such a man's being in a place where I arrive at, I go immediately and make him the first visit, although I stand upon the very pinnacle of punctilios with the British in general. I found him a learned, accurate, easy man. He said he followed just the study which pleased him at the time, and went on calm and moderate, finding every part of knowledge add to the general stock. We talked of vanity, which I defended, and owned I felt a good deal. "Yes," said he, smiling, "you never hear of a great man but you would wish to be him. I am not so, for I have observed the condition of such men. I love fame only as an ingredient in happiness."

At night I sat a long time in the box of Mme. B., of whom I was now violently enamoured. I made my declarations, and was amazed to find such a proposal received with the most pleasing politeness. She however told me, "It is impossible. I have a lover" (showing him), "and I do not wish to deceive him." Her lover was the Neapolitan Minister, Comte Pignatelli, in whose box she sat. He was a genteel, amiable man. He went away, and then I pursued my purpose. Never did I see such dissimulation, for she talked aloud that I should think no more of my passion, and the *piémontais* around us heard this and said without the least delicacy, "A traveller expects to accomplish in ten days as much as another will do in a year." I was quite gone. She then said to me, "Whisper in my ear," and told me, "We must make arrangements," assuring me that she had talked severely to persuade people that there was nothing between us. She bid me call upon her next day at three. This was advancing with rapidity. I saw she was no very wise personage, so flattered her finely. "Ah, Madame, I understand you well. This country is not worthy of you. That is true" (like a mere fool). "You are not loved here as you ought to be." Billon came and repeated gross bawdy. This was disgusting. When I got home I was so full of my next day's bliss that I sat up all night.

SUNDAY 13 JANUARY. By want of sleep and agitation of mind, I was quite feverish. At seven I received a letter from Mme.___telling me that people talked of us, and forbidding me to come to her or to think more of the "plus malheureuse de femmes." This tore my very heart. I wrote to her like a madman, conjuring her to pity me. Billon came and went out with me in my coach. He told me I had lost her merely by being an *imprudent* and discovering my attachment to all the world. I had wrought myself up to a passion which I was not master of. I saw he looked upon me as a very simple young man; for amongst the thorough-bred libertines of Turin to have sentiment is to be a child. I changed my lodgings. She wrote to me again. I wrote to her an answer more mad than my former one. I was quite gone. At night I saw her at the opera. We were reserved. But I told her my misery. She said, "C'est impossible." I was distracted.

MONDAY 14 JANUARY. Night before last I plainly proposed matters to Mme. St. Gilles. "I am young, strong, vigorous. I offer my services as a duty, and I think that the Comtesse de St. Gilles will do very well to accept them." "But I am not that kind of woman." "Very well, Madame, I shall believe you." I thought to take her *en passant.* But she was cunning and saw my passion for Mme. B __, so would not hazard with me. I liked the opera much tonight, and my passion was already gone. Honest Billon said, "If you want to make love, I can find you a girl." I agreed to this by way of cooling my raging disposition to fall in love. At night Mme. St. Gilles seemed piqued that I pursued her no longer, and, suspecting that I was enchained by Mme. B __, she said, "Really, you are a little mad. You get notions, and your head turns. I'll tell you: I think you have studied a great deal. You ought to go back to your books. You should not follow the profession of gallant or you will be terribly taken in. Be careful of your health and of your purse. For you don't know the world." Although my former love-adventures are proof enough that it is not impossible for me to succeed with the ladies, yet this abominable woman spoke very true upon the whole. I have too much warmth ever to have the cunning necessary for a general commerce with the corrupted human race.

TUESDAY 15 JANUARY. Wrote all the morning. After dinner saw the King's palace, where are a number of very excellent pictures. I was shown the King's own apartment. I took up his hat and cane, but found them neither lighter than silk nor heavier than gold. In short, they could not be distinguished from the hat and stick of uncrowned mortals.

I then went to Billon's, who had a very pretty girl for me with whom I amused myself. I then went to another ball at the Théâtre de Carignan. I tired much. Billon had promised to have a girl to sleep with me all night at his lodgings. I went there at eleven but did not find her. I was vexed and angry.

FRIDAY 18 JANUARY. I then went to Billon's, where I had a pretty girl. I was disgusted with low pleasure. Billon talked of women in the most indelicate manner. I then went to Mme. Burgaretta's, where I found two more swains. She grumbled and complained of a headache; and she dressed before us, changing even her shirt. We indeed saw no harm; but this scene entirely cured my passion for her.

TUESDAY 22 JANUARY. I set out at eleven. As I went out at one of the ports, I saw a crowd running to the execution of a thief. I jumped out of my chaise and went close to the gallows. The criminal stood on a ladder, and a priest held a crucifix before his face. He was tossed over, and hung with his face uncovered, which was hideous. I stood fixed in attention to this spectacle, thinking that the feelings of horror might destroy those of chagrin. But so thoroughly was my mind possessed by the feverish agitation that I did not feel in the smallest degree from the execution. The hangman put his feet on the criminal's head and neck and had him strangled in a minute. I then went into a church and kneeled with great devotion before an altar splendidly lighted up. Here then I felt three successive scenes: raging love—gloomy horror—grand devotion. The horror indeed I only *should* have felt. I jogged on slowly with my *vetturino,* and had a grievous inn at night.

SATURDAY 26 JANUARY. I walked out a league to where is the famous echo. It is at a palace which was not finished on account of the dampness of the soil. It has three tier of pillars in front, and would have made a noble thing. I fired a pistol from the window of an upper story opposite to a wall; the sound was repeated fifty-eight times.

I then went to the opera. The house was very large; the audience so-so. Rough dogs often roared out "Brava." The singers seemed slovenly. Blackguard boys held the sweeping female trains and often let them go to scratch their head or blow their nose with their finger. I wished to have had gingerbread or liquorice to give them.

TUESDAY 29 JANUARY. After sitting up all night I set out drowsy and slumbered along. I got to Parma at night. I sent to M. Deleyre, *bibliothécaire du jeune prince,* a letter which M. Rousseau had given me for him, in which the illustrious philosopher praised me and at the same time painted my melancholy disposition. M. Deleyre came to me immediately, I found him a genteel amiable Frenchman with a simplicity of manners that charmed me. We were at once acquainted, and talked with unreserved gaiety. He said M. Rousseau was ever the same in private life that he professes himself in his writings. He said he hardly slept any, for he had passed part of a summer with him and heard him almost every hour in the night give signs of being awake. Perhaps I have taken up this anecdote wrong, for Deleyre must have slept as ill as Rousseau to have heard him awake. M. Deleyre said that M. Rousseau had now and then an inclination to reassemble the Jews, and make a flourishing people of them. What a vigorous mind must he have, and how much ambition!

MONDAY 25 MARCH. Mr. Morison, a Scottish antiquary, began to show me the most remarkable sights of Rome. We went out in the morning, as we intended to do every day. We saw the Pope go by in procession through one of the principal streets on his way to the Minerva. It was thus I saw for the first time a dignitary who was so important in former times, and who still remains a prince of extraordinary power. We saw the ceremony at the Minerva, where his Holiness was carried on a magnificent chair decorated with a figure of the Holy Ghost. He made the round of the church and gave his blessing to the whole congregation, who knelt before his Holiness. Then he took his place on a sort of throne, where, after he had performed certain sacred rites of which I understood nothing, people kissed his slipper. After this there was a procession of Roman girls who had received dowries from a public foundation, some to be married and others to become nuns. They marched in separate groups, the nuns coming last and wearing crowns. Only a few of them were pretty, and most of the pretty ones were nuns. It was a curious enough function.

WEDNESDAY 27 MARCH. We walked to where the house of Cicero had stood. A statue there resembles him a great deal. Struck by these famous places, I was seized with enthusiasm. I began to speak Latin. Mr. Morison replied. He laughed a bit at the beginning. But we made a resolution to speak Latin continually during this course of antiquities. We have persisted, and every day we speak with greater facility, so that we have harangued on Roman antiquities in the language of the Romans themselves.

FRIDAY 5 APRIL. Gordon said, though as heretic [he was] sure to be damned, was glad to see so many other people going to heaven. Chapel of Vatican. High mass; quite solemn. Then procession. Then Pope from window, malediction and benediction, &c. The whole atrium filled with people on knees. Then saw ceremony of washing feet of twelve priests of various nations. Did it with great decency. Then table. Pope said grace; served on knee with a dish, and presented it to each priest. Mingled grandeur and modesty: Peter and *Servus Sevorum;* looked [like] jolly landlord, and smiled when he gave to drink. . . .

SATURDAY 6 APRIL. Yesterday far out for antiquities. Morison, ill humoured Scot, disputed *matter.* He near impertinent, but kept him right. Then owned [you were] Catholic once, as Rousseau [had been]. He quite stony.

FRIDAY 12 APRIL. Yesterday walked to Genzano. . . . Morison quite sulky; low to dispute with him. You have seen how vain, how impossible to make others as you. So from hence, never dispute. Be firm.—Night, new girl. Swear no women for week. Labour hard.

THURSDAY 2 MAY. Yesterday much better. Discovered beasts. Shaved; ludicrous distress. . . . Swear conduct. Remember family. See Mountstuart often, as [he is a] good lad.

SATURDAY 4 MAY. Yesterday dined Lord Mountstuart's. He quite man of fashion, fine air; true Stuart. Immense crowd. Confused and tired and hipped. Honest Colonel mighty good. Then had drive with Mallet. . . . Home and better—This day at nine, Willison's, and sit, a plain, bold, serious attitude. . . . Drive off hypochondria, and pray God. . . . See often Lord Mountstuart and M. Mallet.

MONDAY 6 MAY. Yesterday morning called on Colonel Edmondstone. . . . Saw with him Colonna Palace and Falconieri. Was very bad but patient. . . . This day, Murray immediately. Then Willison, or first call Lumisden and talk over scheme, whether head or owl, &c. Have Hamilton to dine, and talk to him of it. Talk to Lumisden of money affairs and get things settled, or speak to Edmondstone. One hundred pounds extraordinary will do all, and stay less in France. . . .

TUESDAY 7 MAY. Yesterday began half-length at Willison's earnest desire. . . . Idle day. Durst not sit up for fear of heating blood. . . .

FRIDAY 10 MAY. Yesterday . . . sat much to Willison all day, and at night wrote, but baddish.—This day finish letters and sit in all morning, and think, and see what you want, and prepare. Have Mr. Lumisden to consult and fix all plans, and correspond with him sensibly for life. Think to stay at Durlach or in French province or Antwerp till spring; then London a little. Then home and at Auchinleck [for] health and law till June. Swear conduct more and more. But remember God gives us different powers. Marry not yet. Swear no risk with women, and drink little wine.

SATURDAY 11 MAY. Yesterday . . . at three with Abbé Winckelmann at Cardinal Alexander Albani's villa. . . . Garden like spread periwig. Night, Lord Mountstuart's, easy. Wild stories. . . .

SUNDAY 12 MAY. Yesterday . . . after dinner went to Corso like one *enragé,* and amused for last time. You're never to go back. . . . Now swear no *libertinage,* except Florentine lady. Ask Lord Mountstuart for commission to Bob Temple. . . . Little exercise for fear of fever. . . .

THURSDAY 16 MAY. Yesterday . . . began Tasso. . . . Talked with Mallet. Told all story of Rousseau and Voltaire. Wrong to be so talkative; make him say he won't mention it. . . . Night, baddish. Supped my Lord's. Saw you fawned a little. 'Tis really better [to be] independent; by merit rise.

FRIDAY 7 JUNE. Yesterday . . . my Lord at night spoke only bawdy, and told story of Colonel at Siena: "My God, I shot my piece," and then cunningly saying, "when I was in the army," &c. "She will never pardon you."

[ITALIAN JOURNAL] All great men who have written histories have begun their works with an introduction giving a brief statement of their intentions. I therefore advise my readers that I plan to write a concise account of the tour I had the honour to make through Italy with his Excellency, my Lord Mountstuart.

We left Rome on the fourteenth day of June 1765. The party consisted of my Lord, who was twenty years old; Colonel Edmonstone, who was more than forty; M. Mallet, sometime professor, who was more than thirty; and Baron Boswell, who was twenty-four. Thus our ages are all given; our characters will be revealed on the road.

FRIDAY 14 JUNE. My Lord and I were in the same carriage; we slept much, but we read some of the *Persian Letters,* and talked about the characters of many men. At dinner, M. Mallet said he felt weak, but he ate a great deal and recovered his vigour; he said we would soon see a Turkish war. The Colonel was a little taciturn. We stayed at night at Terni, and talked to our innkeeper's son, a young tailor. We laughed a great deal.

In the middle of the night my Lord was troubled in his sleep, and he had the most fantastic dreams. He shouted continually at me, "Boswell, what are you upsetting your chamber-pot for? Why are you playing an air on your little bassoon, and why are you holding out your sword?"

SATURDAY 15 JUNE. We arrived by evening at Foligno. The Colonel and I walked a little through the town. He promised me a good bowl of punch at his country-house in Scotland. My Lord was very angry to see us a little late for supper. My Lord told me many bawdy stories and we also talked about superstitions. I was afraid that ghosts might be able to return to earth, and for a time wished to get into bed with my Lord. But I lay quiet.

SUNDAY 16 JUNE [ITALIAN JOURNAL, CONTINUED]. I had taken too much of a medicine, which made me very sick. I was a poor companion, but after dinner I was very well. My Lord was in a childish mood, calling me *Jamie* continually. I told him that the Stuart family had many weaknesses, one of which was to enjoy childish jokes. James I, though a man of learning and of wit, as wit was then understood, caused himself to be despised by his liking for low jokes. My Lord disputed this opinion strongly, and we were really excited. At night every one was tired.

THURSDAY 20 JUNE [ITALIAN JOURNAL, CONTINUED]. All our differences were settled. My Lord laughed as usual and talked freely.

FRIDAY 21 JUNE. It was a very hot day. We stayed all morning at home, and after dinner we left for Ferrara, where we arrived late. We had a violent dispute as to whether it was necessary to stay to look at the city. Every one was in a bad temper. Some days before, the Colonel had offended M. Mallet by calling him insolent, and our Professor was terribly angry at the brave officer. But this evening the two were united in saying that I was the cause of all our confusion. I laughed at this display of human weakness.

SATURDAY 22 JUNE. More human weakness. We were all in a good mood, though nothing had really been changed. The Colonel, the Professor, and I viewed Ferrara as the beautiful remains of a great but ruined city. We had a bad day; at night we reached Rovigo.

SATURDAY 29 JUNE. Dined General's; superb. Evening, Lady Wentworth's a little. Then home. My Lord and you on couch till two. He said you was a most odd character. All the English disliked you. Quite changeable: "Shall I put out that candle? 'No!' In two minutes. 'Yes!'" Pushing. Mallet said Rousseau had laughed at you. Voltaire writes to any young man well-recommended and of fire; then forgets him, "that English bugger." . . . MOUNTSTUART. "You are very honest, very honourable. I would do anything to serve you, and in a case of importance, entrust you. Yet you may be disagreeable. [You will be an] imperious husband and father."

TUESDAY 2 JULY. Yesterday morning went with my Lord, &c. to St. Mark's church. Old mosaic. Luckily, a solemn service. Saw also Doge's palace and in halls some good pictures. In council room roared out, "Cursed be your senate!" &c. Had sad headache. After dinner agreed with Mallet no raillery for a week. He owned he could never be happy; knew its physical causes, which people ridiculously made moral. Madness [is] being stuck with objects out of proportion to their distance of time, place, or connection with us. . . . Found tennis court; played a little. Home; sad distress of headache. Lay down, slept hour; better. Went to Lady Wentworth's; played whist ill. Home and had soup. Comfortable; better.

WEDNESDAY 3 JULY. Yesterday morning Mallet said, "We are four odd men." . . . Mme. Micheli dined; gay, lively, *appétissante*. Marked her. Afternoon, called on her. Long alone; immediate amour. Chevalier and lady came in.—This day, out immediately. See Dominican's friend and Johnson's translator, and at twelve, Mme. Micheli. Be easy and bold, and try fairly, and say you'll stay while you can, at any rate. She'll excuse, &c. See this fairly. . . . Be dressed in brown silk. *Retenu,* and try gondolas and all expedients with Madame.

THURSDAY 4 JULY. Yesterday morning strolled in gondola till twelve. Then Madame's alone. By her on couch. Talked of religion, philosophy. BOSWELL. "[I would wish] to enjoy everything possible without causing harm to others." She said: "Libertines do not even get so much enjoyment out of—well, anything you choose. They are like drunkards who want merely to get brutally drunk. And do you know, Sir, I believe that all the exquisite notions which Aretino has left to us in writing and in pictures were invented by people who restrained their desires." Kissed hand often. She, half coy, said debauchery to yield before long time. Going away, [I] said, "I hope that your long time becomes short." . . . Mallet said, "I will describe your character as the greatest oddity to my children: a man with no system, and with false ideas. You have no attachments, no friends of long standing. They were your toadies not your friends." Shocked with wonder that a wretch could think so of you. Told him: "I have a very bad opinion of you. I have never lived quietly with a man of whom I had so bad an opinion. Perhaps I am wrong." At night, Madame's. Old noble there. Supped, and to bed late.

SUNDAY 7 JULY. Yesterday disputed plan. He changed to Milan by Mallet's advice, who with selfish cunning and impertinence opposed you. You was quite in rage and thought to go away. Evening Mme. Micheli's. She had sat up, &c. At supper my Lord and you told all whoring. Weak; can keep nothing. Resolve *retenu* . . . This morning, up early and to work like Wilkes. Then Mallet and apologies. No more disputes ever. Twelve. Cavaliera. Take her on it fair, and ask to do her with hand. Settle papers or you're gone. Swear new conduct and try, &c.

MONDAY 8 JULY. Yesterday morning came Baretti, Johnson's friend; curious Italian. Copy. At breakfast, disputed with Mallet, [with] Father's grand eloquence. Mallet said: "My valet will write like that. No miracles since the second century." Low joke. BOSWELL. "When you see him, you will get down on your knees. David Hume a child in comparison to him. His *Dictionary* [is] great philosophy: all the axiomatical knowledge of the language; clear ideas." Hot dispute. BOSWELL. "M. Mallet, if you annoy me, I shall have to crush you." . . . Night, Madame; all lengths. MME. MICHELI. "I admit that I'm old-fashioned, but I would be wretched. Never in my life. Once I was in danger, but escaped." Touched with her goodness. All other liberties exquisite. Quite bold.—This day, letter to Father, &c.

TUESDAY 9 JULY. Yesterday . . . Baretti's, who showed you some letters of Johnson's; rich. Gave books. Was quite miserable, and said Devil had created us: "Why not die like dog?" &c., &c. Pitied him. Home with Mallet a little, who said Fontenelle was insensible: "He used to dine twice a week with a friend. One took asparagus with butter, the other with oil and vinegar. One day the friend died. [Fontenelle said] 'Put all the asparagus in oil,'" &c . . .

SATURDAY 13 JULY. Yesterday . . . resolved [to] alter conduct. Home and made speech: "We have lived as enemies, wrangling like children.

From this time, I swear no more so." Quite happy with good resolve. Up late, but quite gone.

SUNDAY 14 JULY. Yesterday morning sick with being late up, but kept out. Told Mallet too resolution: no more jangling. MALLET. "We shall see how long that lasts."

FRIDAY 26 JULY. Yesterday my Lord waked you boldly and showed *erect and tall*. Quite ludicrous this, but diverting. Drove briskly. Dined at Bergamo. . . . Disputes with my Lord. He said, "I shall always esteem you, but you're most disagreeable to live with. Sad temper," &c. Smiled to hear this. Was in strong spirits and afraid of nothing. At night, Milan; curious sensations. Again dispute with Mallet. . . . This morning up immediately. Rinse well. Then wash feet and hands with warm water and soap, and all private parts with milk and water. Then have illustrious barber. . . . Have long conference with my Lord and own being in wrong, not for obstinacy but loose conduct. Say sorry, and you'll be on guard.

[Received 11 August, Rousseau to Boswell. Original in French]

Môtiers, 30 May 1765

THE STORMY CRISIS in which I have found myself since your departure from this has not allowed me any leisure to answer your first letter, and hardly allows me leisure to reply in a few words to your second. To confine myself to what is immediately pressing, the recommendation which you ask for Corsica; since you have a desire to visit those brave islanders, you may inquire at Bastia for M. Buttafoco, Captain of the Royal Italian Regiment; his house is at Vescovato, where he resides pretty often. He is a very worthy man, and has both knowledge and genius; it will be sufficient to show him this letter and I am sure he will receive you well, and will contribute to let you see the island and its inhabitants with satisfaction. If you do not find M. Buttafoco, and will go directly to M. Pascal Paoli, General of the nation, you may in the same manner show him this letter, and as I know the nobleness of his character I am sure you will be very well pleased at your reception. You may even tell him that you are liked by my Lord Marischal of Scotland, and that my Lord Marischal is one of the most zealous partisans of the Corsican nation. You need no other recommendations to these gentlemen but your own merit, the Corsicans being naturally so courteous and hospitable that all strangers who come among them are made welcome and caressed.

I have Mlle. Le Vasseur's thanks to give to you, and my own reproaches; but I will await your return from Italy, when I hope you will come to receive both.

[c. 6 SEPTEMBER. SIENESE REFLECTIONS] It is true that Siena does not have great variety and may appear a little tedious to an active mind. The nobility is very ignorant, or if they have knowledge, they make very little use of it in conversation. I have often wondered how it is possible for human beings to live from day to day without cultivating the mind, without progressing in knowledge, without any increase in intellectual enjoyment. The philosophical systems which assert man to be an animal who is continuously improving are contradicted by this city.

FRIDAY 11 OCTOBER. After a few hours of sleep, was called at six by Signor Giuliano and another Corsican, who beat at my door. Was confused a little, but recollecting grand expedition, blood recovered bold circulation. Wrote Rousseau and Dempster. At eight the little boat carried me to the bark, and we set sail. The good people had waited all night for me when the wind was so good that we should have been in Corsica ere morning. This day there was little wind. I was sick a very short while and threw up a little, but felt firm nerves in comparison of myself on the passage to Holland. A Corsican played a sort of guitar or lute, and I played my flute, and so did Jacob. The bark belonged to a Corsican of Pino. He carried wine to Leghorn. He spoke English. To save himself, he had the Tuscan flag (the Emperor's), and a Leghorn shipmaster, Ignazio Gentili. I lay down in the cabin bed, but was eat up by mosquitoes and other vermin. I eat cold tongue and bread and some of the crew's rice. There were ten aboard: two poor Corsican merchants, six Corsican sailors, the master, and a boy from Leghorn. I tried to read a little the disputes of Corsica, but could give no attention. Thought hardly any, and was content to be so. Jacob was firm and felt no sickness but wished to have a long voyage, and at night was delighted to see nothing but the sky and the sea. They laid a mattress on the provision chest, and hung a sail on the side of the bark and on four chairs, and under this tent you slept. At the Ave Maria they all kneeled, and with great fervency said their evening orisons to the Queen of Heaven. It affected you a good deal.

[Boswell to Rousseau. Original in French]

Leghorn, 11, October 1765

I HAVE RECEIVED YOUR LETTER, ILLUSTRIOUS PHILOSOPHER. I see that you do not forget me. Some time ago I started to write a very long letter to you entirely about myself. At present, I account myself, my petty pleasures and petty anxieties, as nothing. In half an hour I embark for Corsica. I am going directly to the territories of Paoli. The worthy Count

Rivarola has given me recommendations in plenty. I am all vigour, all nobility. If I perish on this expedition, think of your Spanish Scot with affection, and we shall meet in the paradise of imaginative souls. If I return safely, you will have a valuable account. I cannot write. I shall be able to speak. Death is nothing to me.

THE JOURNAL OF A TOUR TO CORSICA

Having resolved to pass some years abroad for my instruction and entertainment, I conceived a design of visiting the island of Corsica. I wished for something more than just the common course of what is called the tour of Europe; and Corsica occurred to me as a place which nobody else had seen, and where I should find what was to be seen nowhere else, a people actually fighting for liberty and forming themselves from a poor, inconsiderable, oppressed nation into a flourishing and independent state.

When I got into Switzerland, I went to see M. Rousseau. He was then living in romantic retirement, from whence, perhaps, it had been better for him never to have descended. While he was at a distance, his singular eloquence filled our minds with high ideas of the wild philosopher. When he came into the walks of men, we know alas! how much these ideas suffered.

He entertained me very courteously, for I was recommended to him by my honoured friend the Earl Marischal, with whom I had the happiness of travelling through a part of Germany. I had heard that M. Rousseau had some correspondence with the Corsicans, and had been desired to assist them in forming their laws. I told him my scheme of going to visit them after I had completed my tour of Italy, and I insisted that he should give me a letter of introduction. He immediately agreed to do so whenever I should acquaint him of my time of going thither, for he saw that my enthusiasm for the brave islanders was as warm as his own.

I accordingly wrote to him from Rome, in April 1765, that I had fixed the month of September for my Corsican expedition, and therefore begged of him to send me the letter of introduction, which if he refused I should certainly go without it and probably be hanged as a spy. So let him answer for the consequences.

I recollect with astonishment how little the real state of Corsica was known, even by those who had good access to know it. An officer of rank in the British navy, who had been in several ports of the island, told me that I run the risk of my life in going among these barbarians; for that his surgeon's mate went ashore to take the diversion of shooting and every moment was alarmed by some of the natives who started from the bushes with loaded guns and, if he had not been protected by Corsican guides, would have certainly blown out his brains.

Nay at Leghorn, which is within a day's sailing of Corsica and has a constant intercourse with it, I found people who dissuaded me from going thither because it might be dangerous.

I was, however, under no apprehension in going to Corsica. I had now been in several foreign countries. I had found that I was able to accommodate myself to my fellow creatures of different languages and sentiments. I did not fear that it would be a difficult task for me to make myself easy with the plain and generous Corsicans.

Before I left Leghorn, I could observe that my tour was looked upon by the Italian politicians in a very serious light, as if truly I had a commission from my Court to negotiate a treaty with the Corsicans. The more I disclaimed any such thing the more they persevered in affirming it, and I was considered as a very close young man. I therefore just allowed them to make a minister of me till time should undeceive them.

Though from Leghorn to Corsica is usually but one day's sailing, there was so dead a calm that it took us two days. The first day was the most tedious. However, there were two or three Corsicans aboard, and one of them played on the *cetra*, which amused me a good deal. At sunset all the people in the ship sung the Ave Maria with great devotion and some melody. It was pleasing to enter into the spirit of their religion, and hear them offering up their evening orisons.

The second day we became better acquainted, and more lively and cheerful. The worthy Corsicans thought it was proper to give a moral lesson to a young traveller just come from Italy. They told me that in their country I should be treated with the greatest hospitality, but if I attempted to debauch any of their women I might expect instant death.

I chose to stop a while at Corte to repose myself after my fatigues, and to see everything about the capital of Corsica. The morning after my arrival here, three French deserters desired to speak with me. The foolish fellows had taken it into their heads that I was come to raise recruits for Scotland, and so they begged to have the honour of going along with me; I suppose with intention to have the honour of running off from me as they had done from their own regiments.

I went up to the Castle of Corte. The Commandant very civilly showed me every part of it. As I wished to see all things in Corsica, I desired to see even the unhappy criminals. There were then three in the Castle: a man for the murder of his wife, a married lady who had hired one of her servants to strangle a woman of whom she was jealous, and the servant who had actually perpetrated this barbarous action. They were brought out from their cells that I might talk with them. The murderer of his wife had a stupid, hardened appearance, and told me he did it at the instigation of the devil. The servant was a poor despicable wretch. He had at first accused his mistress but was afterwards prevailed with to deny his accusation, upon which he was put to the torture by having lighted matches held between his fingers. This made him return to what he had formerly said, so as to be a strong evidence against his mistress. His hands were so miserably scorched that he was a piteous object. I asked him why he had committed such a crime; he said, "Because I was without understanding." The lady seemed of a bold and resolute spirit. She spoke to me with great firmness and denied her guilt, saying with a contemptuous smile as she pointed to her servant, "They can force that creature to say what they please."

The hangman of Corsica was a great curiosity. Being held in the utmost detestation, he durst not live like another inhabitant of the island. He was obliged to take refuge in the Castle, and there he was kept in a little corner turret, where he had just room for a miserable bed and a little bit of fire to dress such victuals for himself as were sufficient to keep him alive; for nobody would have any intercourse with him, but all turned their backs upon him. I went up and looked at him. And a more dirty, rueful spectacle I never beheld. He seemed sensible of his situation and held down his head like an abhorred outcast.

It was a long time before they could get a hangman in Corsica, so that the punishment of the gallows was hardly known, all their criminals being shot. At last this creature whom I saw, who is a Sicilian, came with a message to Paoli. The General, who has a wonderful talent for physiognomy, on seeing the man said immediately to some of the people about him, "Behold our hangman." He gave orders to ask the man if he would accept of the office, and his answer was, "My grandfather was a hangman, my father was a hangman. I have been a hangman myself and am willing to continue so." He was therefore immediately put into office, and the ignominious death dispensed by his hands hath had more effect than twenty executions by firearms.

It is remarkable that no Corsican would upon any account consent to be a hangman. Not the greatest criminals, who might have had their lives upon that condition. Even the wretch who for a paltry hire had strangled a woman would rather submit to death than do the same action as the executioner of the law.

When I had seen everything about Corte, I prepared for my

journey over the mountains, that I might be with Paoli. My Corsican guides appeared so hearty that I often got down and walked along with them, doing just what I saw them do. When we grew hungry, we threw stones among the thick branches of the chestnut trees which overshadowed us, and in that manner we brought down a shower of chestnuts with which we filled our pockets, and went on eating them with great relish; and when this made us thirsty, we lay down by the side of the first brook, put our mouths to the stream and drank sufficiently. It was just being for a little while one of the "prisca gens mortalium," who ran about in the woods eating acorns and drinking water.

While I stopped to refresh my mules at a little village, the inhabitants came crowding about me as an ambassador going to their General. When they were informed of my country, a strong, black fellow among them said, "English! they are barbarians; they don't believe in the great God." I told him, "Excuse me, Sir. We do believe in God, and in Jesus Christ too." "Um." said he, "and in the Pope?" "No." "And why?" This was a puzzling question in these circumstances, for there was a great audience to the controversy. I thought I would try a method of my own, and very gravely replied, "Because we are too far off." A very new argument against the universal infallibility of the Pope. It took, however, for my opponent mused a while, and then said, "Too far off! Why, Sicily is as far off as England. Yet in Sicily they believe in the Pope." "Oh." said I, "we are ten times farther off than Sicily." "Aha!" said he, and seemed quite satisfied. In this manner I got off very well. I question whether any of the learned reasonings of our Protestant divines would have had so good an effect.

When I at last came within sight of Sollacarò, where Paoli was, I could not help being under considerable anxiety. My ideas of him had been greatly heightened by the conversations I had held with all sorts of people in the island, they having represented him to me as something above humanity. I had the strongest desire to see so exalted a character, but I feared that I should be unable to give a proper account why I had presumed to trouble him with a visit, and that I should sink to nothing before him. I almost wished yet to go back without seeing him. These workings of sensibility employed my mind till I rode through the village and came up to the house where he was lodged.

Leaving my servant with my guides, I passed through the guards and was met by some of the General's people, who conducted me into an antechamber where were several gentlemen in waiting. Signor Boccheci-ampe had notified my arrival, and I was shown into Paoli's room. I found him alone, and was struck with his appearance. He is tall, strong, and well made; of a fair complexion, a sensible, free, and open countenance, and a manly and noble carriage. He was then in his fortieth year. He was dressed in green and gold. He used to wear the common Corsican habit, but on the arrival of the French he thought a little external elegance might be of use to make the government appear in a more respectable light.

He asked me what were my commands for him. I presented him a letter from Count Rivarola, and when he had read it I showed him my letter from Rousseau. He was polite but very reserved. I had stood in the presence of many a prince, but I never had such a trial as in the presence of Paoli. I have already said that he is a great physiognomist. In consequence of his being in continual danger from treachery and assassination, he has formed a habit of studiously observing every new face. For ten minutes we walked backwards and forwards through the room hardly saying a word, while he looked at me with a steadfast, keen, and penetrating eye, as if he searched my very soul.

This interview was for a while very severe upon me. I was much relieved when his reserve wore off and he began to speak more. I then ventured to address him with this compliment to the Corsicans: "Sir, I am upon my travels, and have lately visited Rome. I am come from seeing the ruins of one brave and free people; I now see the rise of another."

He received my compliment very graciously, but observed that the Corsicans had no chance of being like the Romans, a great conquering nation who should extend its empire over half the globe. Their situation, and the modern political systems, rendered this impossible. "But," said he, "Corsica may be a very happy country."

Some of the nobles who attended him came into the room, and in a little we were told that dinner was served up. The General did me the honour to place me next him. He had a table of fifteen or sixteen covers, having always a good many of the principal men of the island with him. He had an Italian cook who had been long in France, but he chose to have a few plain substantial dishes, avoiding every kind of luxury and drinking no foreign wine.

I felt myself under some constraint in such a circle of heroes. The General talked a great deal on history and on literature. I soon perceived that he was a fine classical scholar, that his mind was enriched with a variety of knowledge, and that his conversation at meals was instructive and entertaining. Before dinner he had spoken French. He now spoke Italian, in which he is very eloquent.

We retired to another room to drink coffee. My timidity wore off. I no longer anxiously thought of myself; my whole attention was employed in listening to the illustrious commander of a nation.

He recommended me to the care of the Abbé Rostini, who had lived many years in France. Signor Colonna, the lord of the manor here, being from home, his house was assigned for me to live in. I was left by myself till near supper time when I returned to the General, whose conversation improved upon me as did the society of those about him, with whom I gradually formed an acquaintance.

Every day I felt myself happier. Particular marks of attention were shown me as a subject of Great Britain, the report of which went over to Italy and confirmed the conjectures that I was really an envoy. In the morning I had my chocolate served up upon a silver salver adorned with the arms of Corsica. I dined and supped constantly with the General. I was visited by all the nobility, and whenever I chose to make a little tour I was attended by a party of guards. I begged of the General not to treat me with so much ceremony, but he insisted upon it.

Of these particulars, the most valuable to my readers, as well as to myself, must surely be the memoirs and remarkable sayings of Paoli, which I am proud to record.

Talking of the Corsican war, "Sir," said he, "if the event prove happy, we shall be called great defenders of liberty. If the event shall prove unhappy, we shall be called unfortunate rebels."

The French objected to him that the Corsican nation had no regular troops. "We would not have them," said Paoli. "We should then have the bravery of this and the other regiment. At present every single man is a regiment himself. Should the Corsicans be formed into regular troops, we should lose that personal bravery which has produced such actions among us as in another country would have rendered famous even a marshal."

I asked him how he could possibly have a soul so superior to interest. "It is not superior," said he; "my interest is to gain a name. I know well that he who does good to his country will gain that, and I expect it. Yet could I render this people happy, I would be content to be forgotten. I have an unspeakable pride. The approbation of my own heart is enough."

He said he would have great pleasure in seeing the world and enjoying the society of the learned and the accomplished in every country. I asked him how with these dispositions he could bear to be confined to an island yet in a rude uncivilized state, and instead of participating Attic evenings, "noctes coenaeque Deum," be in a continual course of care and of danger. He replied in one line of Virgil: "Vincet amor patriae laudumque immensa cupido." This, uttered with the fine open Italian pronunciation, and the graceful dignity of his manner, was very noble. I wished to have a statue of him taken at that moment.

His notions of morality are high and refined, such as become the father of a nation. Were he a libertine his influence would soon vanish, for men will never trust the important concerns of society to one they know will do what is hurtful to society for his own pleasures. He told me that his father had brought him up with great strictness, and that he had very seldom deviated from the paths of virtue. That this was not from a defect of feeling and passion, but that his mind being filled with important objects, his passions were employed in more noble pursuits than those of licentious pleasure. I saw from Paoli's example the great art of preserving young men of spirit from the contagion of vice, in which there is often a species of sentiment, ingenuity, and enterprise nearly allied to virtuous qualities. Show a young man that there is more real spirit in virtue than in vice, and you have a surer hold of him during his years of impetuosity and passion than by convincing his judgment of all the rectitude of ethics.

He said to me one day when we were alone, "I never will marry, I have not the conjugal virtues. Nothing would tempt me to marry but a woman who should bring me an immense dowry, with which I might assist my country."

But he spoke much in praise of marriage, as an institution which the experience of ages had found to be the best calculated for the happiness of individuals and for the good of society. Had he been a private gentleman, he probably would have married, and I am sure would have made as good a husband and father as he does a supreme magistrate and a general. But his arduous and critical situation would not allow him to enjoy domestic felicity. He is wedded to his country, and the Corsicans are his children.

He often talked to me of marriage, told me licentious pleasures were delusive and transient, that I should never be truly happy till I was married, and that he hoped to have a letter from me soon after my return home, acquainting him that I had followed his advice and was convinced from experience that he was in the right.

His heart grew big when he spoke of his countrymen. His own great qualities appeared to unusual advantage while he described the virtues of those for whose happiness his whole life was employed. "If," said he, "I should lead into the field an army of Corsicans against an army double their number, let me speak a few words to the Corsicans to remind them of the honour of their country and of their brave forefathers—I do not say that they would conquer, but I am sure that not a man of them would give way. The Corsicans," said he, "have a steady resolution that would amaze you. I wish you could see one of them die. It is a proverb among the Genoese, 'The Corsicans deserve the gallows, and they fear not to meet it.' There is a real compliment to us in this saying."

He told me that in Corsica criminals are put to death four and twenty hours after sentence is pronounced against them. "This," said he, "may not be over-catholic, but it is humane."

Although the General was one of the constituent members of the court of sindacato, he seldom took his chair. He remained in his own apartment, and if any of those whose suits were determined by the sindacato were not pleased with the sentence they had an audience of Paoli, who never failed to convince them that justice had been done them. This appeared to me a necessary indulgence in the infancy of government. The Corsicans, having been so long in a state of anarchy, could not all at once submit their minds to the regular authority of justice. They would submit implicitly to Paoli, because they love and venerate him. But such a submission is in reality being governed by their passions. They submit to one for whom they have a personal regard. They cannot be said to be perfectly civilized till they submit to the determinations of their magistrates as officers of the state entrusted with the administration of justice. By convincing them that the magistrates judge with abilities and uprightness, Paoli accustoms the Corsicans to have that salutary confidence in their rulers which is necessary for securing respect and stability to the government.

The *ambasciatore inglese,* as the good peasants and soldiers used to call me, became a great favorite among them. I got a Corsican dress made, in which I walked about with an air of true satisfaction. The General did me the honour to present me with his own pistols, made in the island, all of Corsican wood and iron and of excellent workmanship. I had every other accoutrement. I even got one of the shells which had often sounded the alarm to liberty. I preserve them all with great care.

The Corsican peasants and soldiers were quite free and easy with me. Numbers of them used to come and see me of a morning, and just go out and in as they pleased. I did everything in my power to make them fond of the British, and bid them hope for an alliance with us. They asked me a thousand questions about my country, all which I cheerfully answered as well as I could.

One day they would needs hear me play upon my German flute. To have told my honest natural visitants, "Really, gentlemen, I play very ill," and put on such airs as we do in our genteel companies, would have been highly ridiculous. I therefore immediately complied with their request. I gave them one or two Italian airs, and then some of our beautiful old Scots tunes: *Gilderoy, The Lass of Patie's Mill,* "Corn rigs are bonny." The pathetic simplicity and pastoral gaiety of the Scots music will always please those who have the genuine feelings of nature. The Corsicans were charmed with the specimens I gave them, though I may now say that they were very indifferently performed.

My good friends insisted also to have an English song from me. I endeavoured to please them in this too, and was very lucky in that which occurred to me. I sung them "Hearts of oak are our ships, Hearts of oak are our men." I translated it into Italian for them, and never did I see men so delighted with a song as the Corsicans were with the *Hearts of Oak.* "Cuore di quercia," cried they, "bravo Inglese!" It was quite a joyous riot. I fancied myself to be a recruiting sea officer. I fancied all my chorus of Corsicans aboard the British fleet.

I mentioned to him the scheme of an alliance between Great Britain and Corsica. Paoli with politeness and dignity waived the subject by saying, "The less assistance we have from allies, the greater our glory." He seemed hurt by our treatment of his country. He mentioned the severe proclamation at the last peace, in which the brave islanders were called the rebels of Corsica. He said with a conscious pride and proper feeling, "Rebels! I did not expect that from Great Britain."

I expressed such hopes as a man of sensibility would in my situation naturally form. He saw at least one Briton devoted to his cause. I threw out many flattering ideas of future political events, imaged the British and the Corsicans strictly united both in commerce and in war, and described the blunt kindness and admiration with which the hearty, generous common people of England would treat the brave Corsicans.

I insensibly got the better of his reserve upon this head. My flow of gay ideas relaxed his severity and brightened up his humour. "Do you remember," said he, "the little people in Asia who were in danger of being oppressed by the great king of Assyria, till they addressed themselves to the Romans; and the Romans, with the noble spirit of a great and free nation, stood forth and would not suffer the great king to destroy the little people, but made an alliance with them?" He made no observations upon this beautiful piece of history. It was easy to see his allusion to his own nation and ours.

Paoli said, "If a man would preserve the generous glow of patriotism, he must not reason too much."

Though calm and fully master of himself, Paoli is animated with an extraordinary degree of vivacity. Except when indisposed or greatly fatigued, he never sits down but at meals. He is perpetually in motion, walking briskly backwards and forwards. Mr. Samuel Johnson, whose comprehensive and vigorous understanding has by long observation attained to a perfect knowledge of human nature, when treating of biography has this reflection: "Thus Sallust, the great master of nature, has not forgotten in his account of Catiline to remark that 'his walk was now quick, and again slow,' as an indication of a mind revolving something with violent commotion."

Paoli told me that the vivacity of his mind was such that he could not study above ten minutes at a time. "My head is like to break," said he. "I can never write my lively ideas with my own hand. In writing, they escape from my mind. I call the Abbé Guelfucci. 'Come quickly, take my thoughts,' and he writes them."

Paoli has a memory like that of Themistocles, for I was assured that he knows the names of almost all the people in the island, their characters, and their connections. His memory as a man of learning is no less uncommon. He has the best part of the classics by heart, and he has a happy talent in applying them with propriety, which is rarely to be found. This talent is not always to be reckoned pedantry. The instances in which Paoli is shown to display it are a proof to the contrary.

"As steel sharpeneth steel, so doth a man the countenance of his friend," says the wise monarch. What an idea may we not form of an interview between such a scholar and philosopher as Mr. Johnson and such a legislator and general as Paoli!

I repeated to Paoli several of Mr. Johnson's sayings, so remarkable for strong sense and original humour. I now recollect these two. When I told Mr. Johnson that a certain author affected in conversation to maintain that there was no distinction between virtue and vice, he said, "Why, Sir, if the fellow does not think as he speaks, he is lying; and I see not what honour he can propose to himself from having the character of a liar. But if he does really think that there is no distinction between virtue and vice, why, Sir, when he leaves our houses let us count our spoons." Of modern infidels and innovators, he said, "Sir, these are all vain men, and will gratify themselves at any expense. Truth will not afford sufficient food to their vanity, so they have betaken themselves to error. Truth, Sir, is a cow which will yield such people no more milk, and so they are gone to milk the bull." I felt an elation of mind to see Paoli delighted with the sayings of Mr. Johnson, and to hear him translate them with Italian energy to the Corsican heroes.

I repeated Mr. Johnson's sayings as nearly as I could in his own peculiar forcible language, for which prejudiced or little critics have taken upon them to find fault with him. He is above making any answer to them, but I have found a sufficient answer in a general remark in one of his excellent papers: "Difference of thoughts will produce difference of language. He that thinks with more extent than another will want words of larger meaning."

I hope to be pardoned for this digression.

He said the greatest happiness was not in glory but in goodness, and that Penn in his American colony where he had established a people in quiet and contentment, was happier than Alexander the Great after destroying multitudes at the conquest of Thebes.

The last day which I spent with Paoli appeared of inestimable value. I thought him more than usually great and amiable when I was upon the eve of parting from him. The night before my departure a little incident happened which showed him in a most agreeable light. When the servants were bringing in the dessert after supper, one of them chanced to let fall a plate of walnuts. Instead of flying into a passion at what the man could not help, Paoli said with a smile, "No matter"; and turning to me, "It is a good sign for you, Sir. *Tempus est spargere nuces.* It is a matrimonial omen; you must go home to your own country and marry some fine woman whom you really like. I shall rejoice to hear of it."

This was a pretty allusion to the Roman ceremony at weddings, of scattering walnuts. So Virgil's Damon says,

Mopse, novas incide faces: tibi ducitur uxor.
Sparge, marite, nuces: tibi deserit Hesperus Oetam.

When I again asked Paoli if it was possible for me in any way to show him my great respect and attachment, he replied, "Remember that I am your friend, and write to me." I said I hoped that when he honoured me with a letter, he would write not only as a commander but as a philosopher and a man of letters. He took me by the hand and said, "As a friend." I dare not transcribe from my private notes the feelings which I had at this interview. I should perhaps appear too enthusiastic. I took leave of Paoli with regret and agitation, not without some hopes of seeing him again. From having known intimately so exalted a character, my sentiments of human nature were raised; while by a sort of contagion I felt an honest ardour to distinguish myself, and be useful as far as my situation and abilities would allow; and I was, for the rest of my life, set free from a slavish timidity in the presence of great men, for where shall I find a man greater than Paoli?

The General, out of his great politeness, would not allow me to travel without a couple of chosen guards to attend me in case of any accidents. I made them my companions to relieve the tediousness of my journey. One of them called Ambrosio was a strange iron-coloured, fearless creature. He had been much in war; careless of wounds, he was coolly intent on destroying the enemy. He told me, as a good anecdote, that having been so lucky as to get a view of two Genoese exactly in a line, he took his aim and shot them both through the head at once. He talked of this just as one would talk of shooting a couple of crows. I was sure I needed be under no apprehension; but I don't know how. I desired Ambrosio to march before me that I might see him.

I was upon my guard how I treated him. But as sickness frets one's temper, I sometimes forgot myself and called him "blockhead"; and once when he was at a loss which way to go, at a wild woody part of the country, I fell into a passion and called to him, "I am amazed that so brave a man can be so stupid." However, by afterwards calling him friend and speaking softly to him I soon made him forget my ill humour, and we proceeded as before.

Paoli had also been so good as to make me a present of one of his dogs, a strong and fierce animal. But he was too old to take an attachment to me, and I lost him between Lyons and Paris. The General has promised me a young one to be a guard at Auchinleck.

I walked from the convent to Corte purposely to write a letter to Mr. Samuel Johnson. I told my revered friend that from a kind of superstition agreeable in a certain degree to him as well as to myself, I had during my travels written to him from *loca sollennia,* places in some measure sacred. That as I had written to him from the tomb of Melanchthon, sacred to learning and piety, I now wrote to him from the palace of Pascal Paoli, sacred to wisdom and liberty, knowing that however his political principles may have been represented, he had always a generous zeal for the common rights of humanity. I gave him a sketch of the great things I had seen in Corsica, and promised him a more ample relation.

Mr. Johnson was pleased with what I wrote here, for I received at Paris an answer from him which I keep as a valuable charter. "When you return, you will return to an unaltered, and I hope unalterable, friend. All that you have to fear from me is the vexation of disappointing me. No man loves to frustrate expectations which have been formed in his favour; and the pleasure which I promise myself from your journals and remarks is so great that perhaps no degree of attention or discernment will be sufficient to afford it. Come home, however, and take your chance. I long to see you and to hear you, and hope that we shall not be so long separated again. Come home, and expect such a welcome as is due to him whom a wise and noble curiosity has led where perhaps no native of this country ever was before."

M. de Marbeuf made merry upon the reports which had been circulated that I was no less than a minister from the British Court. The Avignon *Gazette* brought us one day information that the English were going to establish *un bureau de commerce* in Corsica. "O Sir," said he, "the secret is out. I see now the motive of your destination to these parts. It is you who are to establish this *bureau de commerce.*"

Idle as these rumours were, it is a fact that when I was at Genoa, Signor Gherardi, one of their secretaries of state, very seriously told me, "Sir, you have made me tremble, although I never saw you before." And when I smiled and assured him that I was just a simple traveller, he shook his head, but said he had very authentic information concerning me. He then told me with great gravity, "That while I travelled in Corsica, I was dressed in scarlet and gold, but when I paid my respects to the Supreme Council at Corte, I appeared in a full suit of black." These important truths I fairly owned to him, and he seemed to exult over me.

SATURDAY 30 NOVEMBER. Letters: Father, ill, seriously recalling [you]. Hipped with old ideas. [From] Dick, kind; Signora, all love. What variety! Dined with immense pleasure.

[Lord Auchinleck to Boswell]

Edinburgh, 10 August 1765

MY DEAR SON. —I received a letter from you dated from Rome the 4th of June, and your mother received another from the same place dated the 12th of that month; and these are the last letters we have had from you. This is really an inexcusable neglect. For after I had condescended to allow you to travel a little longer in Italy to attend Lord Mountstuart, you must be sensible it was highly proper to inform me of your progress and intended route, not only to give me a reasonable satisfaction, but also to let me know what—and where—credit I should order for you. And what adds to the fault is that I got communicated to me this day a letter from Herries & Cochrane at London, to Coutts & Company here, acquainting that they had got a letter from you dated from Venice, the 17 of July, in which you wrote to them that, besides the £100 from Rome, you had drawn for £60 from Venice, and desired them to send you a credit upon Lyons and upon Paris. And as these gentlemen, you might be sure, would furnish no credit without my ordering it, and have wrote to Coutts & Company here to know what my directions are, by this strange conduct of yours I am not in condition to say anything with judgment for want of information. This much I can say, that you have spent a vast deal of money, for since you left Geneva in January last you have got no less than £460 sterling, which is much beyond what my income can afford, and much beyond what the sons of gentlemen near double my estate have spent on such a tour; and that makes it quite necessary now to put an end to peregrination. You have had full opportunity to be satisfied that pageantry, civil and ecclesiastic, gives no entertainment to thinking men, and that there is no end nor use of strolling through the world to see sights before unseen, whether of men, beasts, birds, or things, and I hope are, with the poet, saying "Utinam remeare liceret ad veteres casas," and will return with a proper taste and relish for your own country. For if that were not to be your disposition, I should most heartily repent that ever I agreed to your going abroad, and shall consider the money spent in the tour you have made as much worse than thrown away. But I choose to banish all such gloomy suspicions, and hope to my infinite satisfaction to see you on your return a man of knowledge, of gravity and modesty, intent upon being useful in life. If this be so, your travelling will be a little embellishment to the more essential talents, and enable you to make a better figure in your own country, which is the scene of action Providence has pointed out for you.

And now to return to what route you are now to follow. There is nothing to be learned by travelling in France. I can say this from my own experience. So what I propose and insist on is that you come directly from Lyons to Paris, which as the metropolis of France is worth while to say you have seen, and which you may see fully in three or four days; and you should see Versailles, Marly, and Trianon—the King's three palaces—all very near Paris, which won't take up above three or four days more. In short, stay at Paris and the environs of it ten days or a fortnight at farthest, and then set out for Calais and so come over to London, from which, after staying eight or ten days, set out for Scotland.

Edinburgh, 14 August 1765

What is above was wrote on Saturday, but delayed to be sent off in expectation yet of a letter from you, but there is none. The trial I mentioned came on Monday at seven in the morning and did not end till this morning at one o'clock. The jury by a great plurality of voices found the panels guilty both of the incest and of the murder by poison, which they returned as their verdict to us this afternoon.

Edinburgh, 15 August

This day we resumed the consideration of this melancholy affair and repelled sundry pleas for arrest of judgment, and thereafter adjudged the Lieutenant to be hanged the 25 of September and his body to be delivered to the surgeons to be anatomized. This we preferred to the hanging in chains, as we wished to have no memorial of such shocking crimes. Mrs. Ogilvy pleaded she is with child, so a jury of midwives is to examine and report tomorrow, and if it is true, we shall delay sentence till November. I have only to add that I hope we shall have the pleasure of meeting soon. I am your affectionate father,

ALEXR. BOSWEL.

[Lord Auchinleck to Boswell]

Glasgow, 16 September 1765

MY DEAR SON,—I have received yours from Parma, which surprised me greatly, for I expected you had got to Paris, and would be home directly; and never imagined that you would have been returning to places where you had formerly been.

Since that letter, I came to Auchinleck, where I was taken dangerously ill and was a' death's door; indeed, for a day or two I expected every hour would have been my last. My distemper was a total suppression or obstruction of urine. At length by the assistance of Mr. Parlane, a surgeon of this place, I got the water drawn off. He stayed with me there about eight days but could not stay longer, and therefore as the operation required to be repeated twice a day, I came in with him here eight days ago. I bless God that I enjoy now a great deal of ease except during the operation; but as the distemper remains, God only knows what may be the event. This my state, I should think, will make you incline to accelerate your return; because I hope you have impressions of filial duty, besides knowing of what consequence it is to you in after life that I, before I die, come to be satisfied, from what I see of your conduct, that you are become a man such as I and your other friends could wish you to be.

Your mother, who is here with me, is troubled with rheumatisms. She remembers you with affection. David is well. I had a letter from him since I came here. He is careful and I hope will do well. As for John, he is still in England, full of pride and ill nature, and disposed to follow no sort of business that he is capable for, so to be an idle load upon the earth and discontented with the station, place, and people that he happens to be in and with; which is the necessary consequence of having no business nor settled way of employing time. I am your affectionate father,

ALEXR. BOSWEL.

[Lord Auchinleck to Boswell]

Edinburgh, 1 October 1765

DEAR SON,—Your conduct astonishes and amazes me. You solicited liberty to go for four months to Italy. I opposed it as altogether useless; but upon your pressing importunity, contrary to my own opinion, I agreed to it, and thereafter allowed you one month more. You went there January last. Upon your writing that Lord Mountstuart was anxious you should stay some time with him in Italy, and upon his Lordship's desiring that I might agree to it, by a letter to Baron Mure, as you noticed the advantages might attend a friendship with that Lord and the benefit of having Colonel Edmondstone and M. Mallet's counsel, I agreed readily to the thing. But when I heard of Lord Mountstuart's coming over, how surprised was I that you had not come along with him, but stayed in a country where you had nothing to do, and where all you could learn could be of no use in after life. I flattered myself, however, you would haste away, take a passing view of France, and be home about this time or before it. I have wrote letters on the back of letters to you, telling you to come home. Whether any of them have reached you I cannot say. It is possible not, for one thing is most extraordinary in your conduct; you give me no notice where you will be when any letter I can write may reach you, but leave me to guess. I have this day got a letter of yours which had the London postmark on it, so that I hoped you had got there. But when I came to open it, I found it was from Siena; and you tell me you were to stay there three weeks or a month, and this in order, as you write, to learn the Italian language. As you don't say where you are to go after this, or what your scheme is, I must suppose you intend fixing in Italy, where that language can only be of use to you; for in this country it is no better than Arabic. If you have any view of returning home, I desire, as I did in my former letters, you may do so speedily; that you don't stop in France, except about ten days or a fortnight about Paris and its environs, that you may say you have been there, which is all the benefit travellers have over others. I wrote in my last I have been, and still am, under great distress with a stoppage of urine, that has forced us to come to Edinburgh for the aid of physicians. Your mother, who is equally astonished at your conduct with me, remembers you. So does your brother David; which is all from your affectionate father,

A.B.

TUESDAY 10 DECEMBER. I found a very tolerable inn at Vado and got some fresh fish. I sent an express to Savona who brought me for answer that my dog had been seen at the butchers' stalls; but it was too late to find him. However, as the gates were shut, he could not be gone out of the town, and therefore I might have him by sending next morning before the gates could be opened. Jacob slept in the same room with me. He told me he had bought malaga at two livres, four sols a bottle. I was in a great passion with him and said, "It makes me angry to have a servant who spends money in such a fashion." Upon this he told me he had bought a capon which cost him two livres, and said, "All the other gentlemen buy provisions. They are right-thinking people."

WEDNESDAY 11 DECEMBER. At eleven came three men from Savona bringing my dog along with them. The principal person among them said he had bought my dog for *six francs* from a butcher. I, overjoyed to have him again, gave the money without considering that the fellow had no right to sell a dog which was not his own. Thus was I cheated by a crafty Ligurian. I considered, however, that if I had made him be sent after me, it would have cost more. I was in rage against the brute for running away and plaguing me, and I resolved to punish him sufficiently, so I took him to the inn, tied him to a bedstead, and beat him without mercy.

Jacob was very rude in talking of my severity to Jachone: "If my brother did a thing like that, I would thrash him." Thus talked with rough manner my Swiss peasant. I made him hold his tongue, but was really fretted. I continued to beat Jachone from time to time, and gave him nothing to eat, so that I humbled him very well.

THURSDAY 12 DECEMBER. We went up three leagues and put in at Noli. I still starved Jachone, and discharged Jacob to give him any victuals. I stepped down on shore (after being drawn to land by the sailors, which I called [the] best manner of going in [a] boat), and when I returned I found Jacob feeding my dog. I called to him, "How dare you give anything to that dog when I forbade it?" He replied, "Yes, I have given him something, *sacré dieu!*" as if he had been speaking to a brother peasant. I said, "Upon my word, you are a fine man!" "Well," said he, "I *am* a man. I am not a fool." You said, "You are the most impertinent rascal I have *ever* known." He said, "Sir, you knew that long ago. You should not have taken me with you." Such changling passed between a master and his servant. Shameful! I could do nothing as I owed the fellow thirty louis, but I resolved if possible to borrow money at Antibes and turn him off from thence.

I determined to go by land, so left Jacob and my baggage in the felucca, and desired the master to call in at Razzi and Monaco and one or two of the other ports, if I should make him a sign from any of them. I took Jachone with me, pulling him along with a good cord, and, whenever he was rebellious, beating him sorely. I even hung him fairly up twice upon trees for half a minute, but he grasped them with his feet and saved his neck. I walked five miles to Finale (the first post, which a punster would say should be the last).

Here I saw a sort of Genoese triumphal arch erected on I don't know what occasion. There was a Latin inscription upon it, as how thunder had set the sand on fire, which did not pass the arch, and this happened during the magistracy of Signor somebody. The same meaning was put into verse below, and the poet took the license of paying a compliment to the magistrate by hinting that it was owing to him that the kindled sand went no farther. I began to copy this inscription, but the Commandant, a suspicious fool, came up and told me that he could not allow me to do it without an order from the Governor, and very gravely did he write to his Excellency desiring to know if it should be permitted to a stranger to copy the inscription on the triumphal arch. When he had done, I told him that as I must wait half an hour for the answer it was not worthwhile, for indeed I would not wait ten minutes for it. I wished to have copied out my inscription by force, or have made a riot. I should have done so in any other state, where I was sure that the government would take to task a foolish commandant, but I considered that the Genoese would hardly do me the justice which I had a right to expect.

I eat a bit and then got a horse and a postilion to run afoot with me to Pietra. Here the post would oblige me to take two horses. I went to a little inn where the people seemed civil and got me a quiet fellow who agreed to go with me cheap, but insisted on taking two horses as there was much water on the road. I set out at ten. It was very dark. I began to ruminate on Italian robberies and assassinations and was vastly uneasy. I took my louis and put them loose in my pocket, leaving two in my purse for the rogues if they should come. I rode in most disagreeable anxiety, but was three or four times comforted by passing snug, smoky towns.

SATURDAY 14 DECEMBER. About a league before I came to San Remo, I saw a curious grotto, a cave just by the side of the road. It is now a chapel dedicated to the Madonna Annunziata. It is fifty foot in length from the great altar (there being three) to the door in front (having also a side door), and thirty-three foot broad. A poor hermit lives on the brow of the declivity which overhangs this chapel, which he shows to such as are curious, though my guide told me I was the first he had seen examine it with attention. The hermit lighted me with a torch up a little stair cut in the rock till we got above the great altar. We advanced along a passage in the rock four or five foot broad, but diminishing as we advanced both in breadth and height. We were above a hundred foot from the front door. The hermit told me the passage had no end, and indeed I saw a vast way beyond where we were, but advanced no farther, as we were obliged to creep upon all four and I began to want fresh air. There is from the roof of this chapel and the passage a continual dropping of water, which it seems is looked upon as a kind of miracle. I inquired of the hermit and of my guide how this curious grotto had been made, supposing that there would certainly be some singular tradition with regard to it; but all the information they could give me was that the Madonna had made it herself. I gave the hermit some money. He very seriously asked me if I intended it for the Madonna or for him, a piece of scrupulous honesty, this, which I am afraid is not to be found in the greatest number of the mendicant religious, nor in those ragged laymen who in white iron boxes collect from passengers their charity for the souls in purgatory. As I considered the hermit to have more need of money than the Virgin has of masses, I told him what I gave was for himself.

At night I arrived at Ventimiglia, an old town situated on a steep hill. They frightened me here so much with robbers being on the frontiers, and assured me besides that the gates of Mentone were never opened in the night-time, that I lay at the post-house, where the landlord and landlady were Spaniards; and vastly courteous was mine host, a fine young fellow. I slept in my clothes with Jachone in my arms.

TUESDAY 17 DECEMBER. Jachone went back to the inn where I dined, for which I beat him till his nose bled, and then letting him loose, he run off from me before the chaise. On my arrival at Fréjus, Jachone was found waiting at the gate of the town. I found a most excellent inn here, a good table d'hôte, and a bedroom as if in a private house in Britain.

WEDNESDAY 18 DECEMBER. Jogged most sluggishly along. Disputed with Jacob, who said he knew me perfectly and that it was impossible for servants to live well with me, as I was not, like other gentlemen, content with external acquiescence, but would always show them clearly that they were wrong. He is very right. I am always studying human nature and making experiments on the lowest characters, so that I am too much in the secret with regard to the weakness of man in reality, and my honest, impetuous disposition cannot take up with that eternal repetition of fictitious minutiae by which unthinking men of fashion preserve a great distinction between master and servant. By having Jacob so free with me, I have felt as servants do, and been convinced that the greatest part of them laugh in their sleeve very heartily at the parade of their lords, knowing well that eating, drinking, sleeping, and other offices of nature are common to all. Jacob said, "I believe, Sir, that you have been badly brought up. You have not the manners of a nobleman. Your heart is too open." I confessed to him that I was two and twenty before I had a servant. Said he, "The son of a gentleman ought to be accustomed early to command a servant, but reasonably, and never to joke with them; because each must live in his state according to his quality. You, Sir, would live just like a peasant. And you force a servant to speak in a way he shouldn't, because you torment him with questions. You want to get to the bottom of things. Sir, I do not think you should marry. At least, if you marry, you should not live in the same house with your wife; otherwise, *ma foi!* there will shortly be disputes, and a quarrel which cannot be made up. Sir, this is what you should do: marry a lady, give her a certain allowance, and let her have her house where you can go when you find it agreeable and not be inconvenienced; and you must never see your children, or otherwise they will be as badly brought up as you. I hope, Sir, you will not take this in bad part."

THURSDAY 19 DECEMBER. The noble highway which leads from the country near Antibes to Toulon is admirable, like what is in the Scots Highlands. This evening I arrived at Toulon.

I put up at the Croix de Malte and was tolerably well. Three posts before I arrived, Jachone was a-missing. I enquired of all passengers before us on the road, but he had not advanced. I was quite uneasy, quite feverish with anxiety about him. Jacob said, "Sir, you are getting yourself in a fever over a wretched cur." I sent an express for him three posts.

FRIDAY 20 DECEMBER. Before I got up, my express returned with Jachone. The voracious brute had returned to where I dined and had eat a whole hare which was hung up before a window. I insisted with Jacob that Jachone had laid a plan for this, and that his inclination was to dine at the tables d'hôte at thirty-five sous *par repas*. The sergeant from Corsica said I should give Jachone so much a week, as I did to my servant. I saw that it was to no purpose to beat the brute as he did not understand what I meant, being very stupid. I therefore resolved to carry him along with me just like a trunk or a packet that could move of itself.

SATURDAY 21 DECEMBER. I arrived at Marseilles about eleven. A little way before you come to it, on the Toulon road, is the best *vin cuit* in France. This is a particular sort of wine, which, after having been boiled is excellent to drink a glass of with a crust of bread, by way of breakfast. At Marseilles I put up at the Nouvelle Rose, a very bad inn; the table d'hôte was dirty, and through the room where it was held were some of us obliged to pass to our rooms. The service was bad and the master impertinent.

The gallant Duncan Drummond had told me at Genoa of a very good girl whom he kept a long time, and had with him eight months at Minorca. Since I arrived at five and twenty, I have determined never again to risk my constitution with women. But Drummond having assured me that Mlle. Susette was honest, safe, and disinterested, and counselled me to put in at that port, I went to her after the comedy. My *valet de place* was a German who spoke French and English, a tall and decent pimp. He showed me her lodgings. I found her a fine little lively girl, with hardly any of the vile cant of prostitutes. After examining me very shrewdly if I was really a friend of Drummond's, she agreed to let me pass the night with her. I went home and supped, and returned to her. She had a handsome bedroom prettily furnished. She was so little that I had an idea as if she was a child, and had not much inclination for her. I recalled my charming Signora at Siena, and was disgusted at all women but her, and angry at myself for being in the arms of another. Susette chatted neatly and diverted me. I sacrificed to the graces. I think I did no harm.

MONDAY 23 DECEMBER. I returned Ross his money. He had been this morning at his banker's and had got more gold to give me. This will do him honour while I live. Birkbeck furnished me twenty louis, which made me easy. I breakfasted with Pennant. I heard that my cousin Willy Cochrane lived in the same stair. I went up to him and found him very bad of a consumption. I am grown hard. I regret the distress of a relation, but do not feel it much. I was sorry not to have heard of him sooner. I used rather to dislike his manner. Sickness had softened and bettered it. I liked him. All is changes, and odd ones too.

Pennant made me dine with him. But first I went and saw the galleys. It was curious to see a row of little booths, with signs, all occupied by slaves, many of whom looked as plump and contented as any decent tradesman whatever. I went into one of the galleys where the slaves were mostly working in different ways in order to gain some little thing. I was told that many of them make rich, as they are allowed a great deal of time for themselves when lying in the harbours. I talked with one who had been in the galleys twenty years. I insisted with him that after so long a time custom must have made even the galleys easy. They came about me, several of 'em, and disputed my proposition. I maintained that custom made all things easy, and that people who had been long in prison did not choose to come out. "Ah," said the slaves, "it is otherwise here. It is two prisons. If we could escape, we should certainly do it. A bird shut up in a cage desires freedom, and so much the more should a man desire it. At first we shed tears, we groaned, but all our tears and groans availed us nothing." I was touched with the misery of these wretches, but appeared firm, which made them not show much grief. Mallet, who used to joke me on being an eternal disputer, might now say, "Baron, you dispute even with galley-slaves." One of them gave me a very full account of their manner of life. When he would tell me of their being out at sea, he said "Quand nous sommes en campagne." This it seems is a galley phrase. I could not but smile at it. They said, "Nous aimerons mieux les campagnes des bois." I was much satisfied with having seen a galley. I gave the slaves something to drink.

TUESDAY 24 DECEMBER. The French officer and I walked about a little and saw Aix. I stopped to get my shoes cleaned. He paid I suppose a denier for me, saying, "As they say in England, I'll pay the little expenses and you'll pay the big ones." So we went to a café, where I paid for breakfast. French easy impudence is amazing. Both the nails of my great toes were now in the flesh and made me suffer sadly.

At night I came to the ferry where you pass over to the territories of Avignon. The man who waited at the *bureau des droits* would not pass me, but would send his son for the *patron du vaisseau*. I asked him if he would pass me if the *patron* was there. He said yes. Upon which I ordered the postilion to mount, and away we went a mile to the next village, where was the *patron*, for so they call the master in Provençal, that detestable corruption of Italian and French. He who takes the bark by the year entertained me well with bread and figs and almonds baked with honey, as is the custom in the country in the Christmas holidays. I carried the master with me; but when I arrived, my friend of the bureau desired a particular order to pass me. I had been informed that he would play that trick, and was prepared for him. I talked with a voice like an Indian chief and beat my staff upon his floor and asked him, "Did you not say that you would pass me if the master were here? Postilion, take note of his words, I will see the end of this affair." Thus did I threaten the rogue, though I knew well I could do him no manner of harm. He was frightened and agreed to pass me, so over I went and paid genteelly. Poor Jachone runs along with me, but is sadly covered with mud and greatly fatigued. The night was very cold.

I arrived at Avignon about eleven. It was comfortable to enter a good warm town. I put up at St. Omer's, the table d'hôte excellent, but my room was cold and smoky and I was ill off. The want of a servant was hard upon me. I however served myself wonderfully well, and by doing duty as a *valet de chambre* learnt to command well as a master, just as young officers learn by doing the duty of common soldiers. I had some warm wine and bread to comfort me, and then went to the Cathedral and heard the midnight mass. This was a most perfect satisfaction to me. I recollected how Dr. Boswell told my mother of the splendid solemnity in Roman Catholic countries on Christmas Eve. I saw this now in France, and in a town under the dominion of the Pope. I was truly devout.

TUESDAY 31 DECEMBER. I had a great dispute with the mistress of the inn because she charged me too much. I was, however, obliged to pay her more than I ought to have done; after which she had the impudence to tell me that she heard there was an order for all the English to leave the country, and that she would be sorry. "Yes," said I, "sorry at not being able to rob them as you have robbed me." The ostler was a true Gaul. He asked *pour boire*. I told him he would hardly rise the night before to let me in. He said, "I did not know that it was you. If I had known that, I should have hastened to serve you." What an impudent rascal, when I am sure he did not know me from any other. He asked me if I would send him back by the postilion *pour boire*. I joked and said, "Perhaps." He thought I refused him, and, from licking the ground beneath my feet, he cried, "I hope to God that your horse falls with you." Notorious villain.

At the first post from Nîmes was a little horse, which, when I passed before, pleased me so much that I thought of buying him, and so riding quietly to Paris; but my toes were so bad that the great postboots hurt me terribly and I suffered severely. Besides, I saw it was an idle scheme to buy a French post-horse which had probably many faults. At__, I found the Marseilles courier arrived. I agreed to go with him to Lyons for three louis, he paying for me at the inns. I paid for our dinner here. One of my feet was now swelled prodigiously, by reason of an inflammation in the toe. The courier was a fine, open, hearty fellow, a *bourgon*. I saw in him what good health can do. His *brouette* was not a bad machine, though it went pretty rough. We drew our curtains and had wrappings enough to keep us warm. The landlord where we dined fell upon an excellent contrivance for my swelled foot. He bought me a hare's skin into which I put it, and so kept it as easy and warm as could be.

WEDNESDAY 1 JANUARY. We rumbled along, never stopping but to devour wild fowl and drink wine. Poor Jachone had sad work of it. The icy road hurt his feet and he used to whine most grievously. I was hard-hearted enough to let him suffer. We drove along still all night. I slept now and then tolerably.

THURSDAY 2 JANUARY. This morning we came to a very steep hill. The horses tried to pull us up, but could not. The courier attempted to put a stone under one of the wheels, but the wheel went back with such rapidity that it cut the point of his forefinger so that he was obliged to have a joint cut off. He bore it with great good humour and we drove along merrily to Lyons. My feet were so bad that I could not walk across my room, so I hopped about as well as my lameness would allow. La Marie, an old maid of the inn, was my *gouvernante,* and I let myself be taken care of by her, and went early to sleep in a soft bed with the curtains drawn, and was as much a lazy old man as if I had been sixty and never had seen Paoli. Poor Jachone had his feet swelled and sore with fatigue. I caused make a bed of hay for him in the corner of my room, where he lay very snugly. Jacob arrived this very day and came to me in the evening. He was just as glad to see me as if he had been with me all his life; but he said he would not go to Paris even if I should insist on it, for he saw that he should spend what money he had gained.

FRIDAY 3 JANUARY. The surgeon of a *charité* here came and dressed my feet. He was a fat and an alarming dog, for he very gravely advised me to pull out my nail altogether, "because," said he, "in so doing, you will have no more risk of ever being troubled with it." As well might he have advised me to cut off my hand, had I hurt it. He gave me a softening plaster for my toe and bid me wait till I got to Paris to have it cured. I sent to a Mme. Boy de la Tour, for whom her sister, Mlle. Roguin at Yverdon, had given me a recommendation a year ago. I knew she was a friend of M. Rousseau and begged she would inform me where he was. She let me know that he was at Paris. This gave me a bounce of joy, for I now saw him just before me, and pleased myself with talking to him fully of the noble affairs of Corsica. I immediately wrote him a most spirited letter. I also wrote to Dr. Pringle begging he would settle my being on an independent and genteel footing on my return to Scotland. I enclosed, open for his perusal, a letter for my father in which I talked strongly of my views and promised to do my best. Jacob came and received all that I owed him, and took leave of me. I told him that I regarded him as a very worthy man, but that I was, however, glad that he left me; for, after having rebelled and been so free, it was impossible he could be a good servant for one of my disposition. He seemed angry a little at this. He made awkward speeches as how he wished to have served me better, and was sorry for having ever offended me, and was much obliged to me for my goodness to him, &c. Thus was I at last separated from my Swiss governor. I wished him sincerely all happiness.

SUNDAY 12 JANUARY. Approached Paris, Invalides appeared as St. Paul's does, coming to London. Was not affected much. Came to bureau, got baggage, and in fiacre to Mme. Duchesne's; Rousseau gone.

TUESDAY 14 JANUARY. Yesterday little surgeon dresses my toes. In all day writing.

FRIDAY 17 JANUARY. Yesterday visited Hon. Alexander Murray;

heard all his story. Quite Lord Elibank. Was pleased to revive such ideas. Surgeon [said cure would be] slow.

SATURDAY 18 JANUARY. Was at burial of Sir William Gordon of Park, on ramparts at Douai, a six and twenty pounder at his head and sentry at his foot. John Bain pronounces oration: "Pretty man of Scotland. [Let] nae mon seek for justice; [he'll] gae awa' wi' sair heart. March!"

TUESDAY 21 JANUARY. Stayed in all day writing. Received a letter from Mr. Johnson, treating you with esteem and kindness. Was nobly elated by it, and resolved to maintain the dignity of yourself.

WEDNESDAY 22 JANUARY. Went and found Horace Walpole, whom you had treated with by cards, lean, genteel man. Talked to him of Corsica. He said you should give something about them, as there are no authentic accounts. You said you intended to do so.

SATURDAY 25 JANUARY. Yesterday taken up all day to get trunk out of *douane,* except with Strange, who told James's death. Was dull a little. Met there a young fellow who gave you names of good bordellos. Went to fiacre [and said] "Do you know any of these?" [He knew] Mme. Hecquet; went. Mlle. Constance, tall, quite French lady. Feigned simplicity. [She said.] "I'll show you all the sights."

MONDAY 27 JANUARY. Heard mass at Théatins. Went to Ambassador's Chapel; old ideas of Church of England, in some measure. Sermon made you gloomy, or rather tired. At Wilke's saw in *St. James's Chronicle,* Mother's death. Quite stunned; tried to dissipate [grief.] Dined Dutch Ambassador's: much of Corsica. At six Mme. Hecquet's as in fever. Constance elegant.

TUESDAY 28 JANUARY. Yesterday morning sent to Foley; got letter from Father, written by David. Too true; Mother gone. Was quite stupefied. In all morning. Wept in bursts; prayed to her like most solemn Catholic to saint. Roused philosophy; sung Italian gently to soothe. But would not have hurt prejudices by doing so before others. Called on Principal Gordon, told him privately sad news. Had company with him who had said mass for requiem to old James. Lord Alford (Sir John Graham) genteel man. Curious feelings; was prudent, but with true philosophy sustained your distress; was decent. Had strong enthusiasm to comfort Father all his life.

[Lord Auchinleck to Boswell]

Edinburgh, 11 January 1766

MY DEAR SON,—In my last I acquainted you that your dear mother was indisposed, and was to get a vomit that evening on which my letter was wrote; I did not then apprehend her to be in any danger, but from that time forward she daily turned worse of a slow and obstinate fever, which at length put a period to her valuable life this morning half an hour after seven. Among her last words, a very little time before her death she audibly though with a faltering tongue said, "I have fought the good fight of faith, I have finished my course, henceforth is prepared for me a crown of glory," and when she had expressed a longing for death and was asked if she did not wish to recover to be a comfort to her family, she answered she wished to be with Christ, which is far better. She left us without any struggle or even a groan, and as it were fell asleep. You have lost a most affectionate and kind mother, and will doubtless be affected deeply with this awful stroke as we and all your friends here are; and as upon the back of this, diversions of any kind cannot have any relish with one of your sensibility, it will occur to you how much I need your assistance, this irreparable breach made upon me besides the having my old bodily trouble still hanging about me; and therefore, it will be needless to tell you that I expect you home with all speed.

WEDNESDAY 29 JANUARY. Yesterday felt more the sad news. Recalled her kind, affectionate concern. Was deeply touched, but thinking of her being in heaven, was easy. Was pious and had manly hope. Had heard Mlle. Le Vasseur was arrived, and had sent to her; went this morning to Hôtel de Luxembourg. She was with Mme. de la Roche, *première dame de la Maréchale*. She was just as at Môtiers. Told her sad news. She told you her anxiety about journey, and [said], "Mon Dieu, Monsieur, if we could go together!" You said you came to propose it to her. She showed you Rousseau's letter from Paris, where he agrees to her coming, and gives directions to wash his new shirts, &c., [adding.] "Do nothing hastily," and another from London, [saying,] "Resign yourself to suffering a great deal."

THURSDAY 30 JANUARY. Went for third time to Mlle. Le Vasseur; tired of her complaints. Ordered matters prudently.

FRIDAY 31 JANUARY. Yesterday morning after having been up all night and written sixteen or seventeen letters, and felt spirits bound in veins, kept post-horses waiting from six till nine, then was still in confusion. Cried, "Is it possible that my mother is dead?" Set out, and at Hôtel de Luxembourg took up Mademoiselle. Was serious and composed. Passed by castle at __, [asked,] "Whose is that château?" Duc de Fitzjames. [You said,] "God be blessed! The blood of the Stuarts has always some distinction. It is the most illustrious blood in the world." Dined__; was mild but gloomy, and now and then thought Mother alive and gave starts. Night was manly, but hurt by Mademoiselle's mean kindness to servants, &c. Talked much of Rousseau always.

[EDITORIAL NOTE: The entries for the first eleven days of February 1766, which are said to have filled some twelve pages of manuscript, are now missing from Boswell's journal, having been destroyed just prior to the transference of the papers to Colonel Isham.* They narrated in detail the progress of an amorous episode with which Boswell and Thérèse Le Vasseur occupied the time of their leisurely crossing from Paris to London. A small slip of paper, bearing the words "Reprehensible Passage" in the hand of Sir William Forbes (one of Boswell's literary executors) and signed with his initials, was found within the wrapper which enclosed this portion of the journal, and must have referred to something in the missing pages. Colonel Isham was fortunate enough to have read the whole passage before it was destroyed, and from him are gleaned the following notes on one of the most extraordinary episodes of Boswell's career.

It does not appear that before leaving Paris Boswell had formed any scheme of seducing Thérèse, and the day of his departure found him tense and harassed by difficulties in getting started, and deeply unhappy over his mother's death. But the intimacy of travel and the proximity in which the pair found themselves at inns at night precipitated an intrigue almost immediately. On the second night out they shared the same bed; Boswell's first attempt, as often with him, was a fiasco. He was deeply humiliated, the grief he was trying to repress came back upon him, and he wept. Thérèse, with a Frenchwoman's tenderness and sympathy, put her arm around him to console him and laid his hand on her shoulder. His grief and embarrassment waned; as he recorded on another occasion, his powers were excited and he felt himself vigorous. Next day he was very proud of himself, and in the coach he congratulated Thérèse (who was almost twenty years his senior) on her good fortune in having at last experienced the ardours of a Scotch lover. Thérèse stunned him by denying that she had great cause for gratitude: "I allow," she said, "that you are a hardy and vigorous lover, but you have no art." Then, with quick perception seeing him cast down, she went on, "I did not mean to hurt you. You are young, you can learn. I myself will give you your first lesson in the art of love."

Since Boswell's success as a lover depended on his maintaining a

---

*The acquisition and preservation of a great portion of the papers of James Boswell was made possible by the philanthropy of Lieut.–Col. Ralph Heyward Isham. This Editorial Note is printed from *Boswell on the Grand Tour*, edited by Frank Brady and Frederick A. Pottle.

feeling of superiority, this announcement filled him with terror. The apartment in which they were lodged that night was in the shape of an L: a private dining-room with the bed in an alcove at one end. As bedtime approached, he grew more frightened. In the earlier period of his life, as the journal printed in the present volume shows, he drank little, but on this occasion he secured from the servant a full bottle of wine and concealed it in the dining-room. Thérèse retired; Boswell remained reading. Thérèse called him; he went in clutching the wine, but instead of joining her, he paced up and down asking questions about Rousseau. At last, when no further diversion would avail, he drained the bottle and reluctantly slipped into bed.

He gave some details of her instruction. He must be gentle though ardent; he must not hurry. She asked him, as a man who had travelled much, if he had not noticed how many things were achieved by men's hands. He made good technical progress, though he was not wholly persuaded of her right to set up for a teacher; he said she rode him "agitated, like a bad rider galloping downhill." After a while her lectures bored him, and he brought up the subject of Rousseau, hoping at least to gather a few *dicta philosophi* for his journal. Thérèse in her turn found that dull. It was a mistake, he finally reflected, to get involved with an old man's mistress.

The first entry of the journal on the other side of the hiatus not only furnishes unequivocal evidence of the liaison, but also vindicates Boswell's claim to vigour.]

WEDNESDAY 12 FEBRUARY [Dover]. Yesterday morning had gone to bed very early, and had done it once: thirteen in all. Was really affectionate to her. At two set out in fly; breakfasted Rochester on beefsteaks. Mrs. Morrice, a woman who had been married to a sergeant, and a bluff, true Englishman sat with you. Mademoiselle was much fatigued. Came to London about six, to Swan at Westminster Bridge. Was now so firm that London made no impression. You was good to her. Sent to Stewart, and then went to his house. You was quite easy. Macpherson was there. You was talked to much of Corsica, but said nothing but calm account of what you saw, and when they said, "Who could send over this intelligence?" you said, "You must ask Gazetteer." Carried her to David Hume. Then went to Temple; embraced most cordially in old style.

THURSDAY 13 FEBRUARY. Then went to Mlle. Le Vasseur, with whom was Hume. You breakfasted, and then carried her out to Chiswick. She said Hume had told her you was "mélancholique," which was in your family. You was too high. You was ready to kill any offender. You gave her word of honour you'd not mention *affaire* till after her death or that of the philosopher. Went to Rousseau; delivered her over. *Quanta oscula, &c.!* He seemed so oldish and weak you had no longer your enthusiam for him. Told him all about Corsica, and he cried, "Pardi! I am sorry not to have gone there." He was incited by what he heard. He was to go to Wales. You asked if Scotland had not a claim to him. He said, "I shall act like the kings; I shall put my body in one place, and my heart in another."

Back to London. Immediately to Johnson; received you with open arms. You kneeled, and asked blessing. Miss Williams glad of your return. When she went out, he hugged you to him like a sack, and grumbled, "I hope we shall pass many years of regard." You for some minutes saw him not so immense as before, but it came back.

PART V

BOSWELL

IN SEARCH OF

A WIFE

28 April 1766 — 25 November 1769

INTRODUCTION

I T IS HARD to think a finer woman lived than Margaret Montgomerie, afterward Mrs. James Boswell. She forbore. The man was no saint. He felt himself diminished by his father and unfulfilled by his profession. His drunkenness increased. He was bad at gambling. His philandering never ceased.

Margaret emerges to our view from the shadows. We have never heard Boswell mention her. We have therefore no reason to believe that she had been much in his thoughts, but I think we might begin to wonder, even before he does—why *not* Margaret for his wife? Oddly, Boswell chose Margaret to accompany him on a visit to a prospective wife, a very young woman very ravishing and very rich, and it was at that point that I began to feel, with Margaret, how well Boswell might do to consider this woman beside him, though she is not so young, perhaps not ravishing, and certainly not rich.

He will choose her finally above the complaint of his father that she brings with her no wealth or useful distinction. Boswell to the end of his father's life would complain of his father's rudeness to her. His wisdom in choosing Margaret may have elevated him in her estimation, as it does in mine: she loved him better for that show of good taste. She was virtuous and self-contained, independent, lit from within. She cared little for the wide world or fame, and not too much for Mr. Johnson, as the great man detected on his visit to Edinburgh. His was a world she never entered, although she was beautifully literate, as her sensitive letters reveal.

We saw Boswell last in February, in Mr. Johnson's embrace, "hugged . . . like a sack." We rejoin him two months later in Edinburgh. He was a man of two cities. In July of this year he was admitted to the bar as "advocate." His first client was John Reid, accused of stealing sheep. Boswell was appointed by the Justiciary Court to conduct Reid's defense, which he apparently did with sufficient skill: against the formidable opposition of the Crown, Boswell obtained the jury's verdict "not proven," and Reid went free. But we will meet John Reid again.

Boswell was now in his twenty-sixth year. His experience of several capital cases exposed him to the powerful realities of life, law, and Man's nature. Often a reader may also suspect in Boswell's defense of forlorn criminals an element of morbidity, an unnatural—or all too natural —fascination with the idea of standing as close as possible to death. He had a penchant for theological cross-examination on the eve of execution. (In 1776 Boswell conducted an interrogation of the Scottish philosopher and historian David Hume, seven weeks before the latter's death. Boswell found Hume at home, "lean, ghastly, and quite of an earthy appearance." Indeed, "just a-dying." Hume was a famous and ardent nonbeliever. "I had a strong curiosity," wrote Boswell, "to be satisfied if he persisted in disbelieving in a future state even when he had death before his eyes. I was persuaded from what he now said, and from his manner of saying it, that he did persist.")

Yet Boswell's conspicuous attentiveness to his doomed clients was humanitarian as well, and his affinity for unfortunate people may explain somewhat his rapport with Mr. Johnson, whose charity was well known. Boswell was by nature a public defender, as his father appeared by nature to be essentially a stern judge. Boswell's language in contemplating his clients was not, indeed, the language of twentieth century social reform, but on questions of crime and punishment he possessed generous sentiments within the severe practice of his own era. The harshness of Scottish justice—"this narrow country," he said—was often agonizing to Boswell and may have precipitated within him the desperate behavior we sometimes associate with despair.

Whatever the reason, his vices were Margaret's trial. Months before his marriage he wrote in his journal, "I was quite drunk. I am sorry for it. I behaved ill to Margaret, my own affectionate friend. . . . I was very sorry, and resolved to make up to her for what she had suffered by my future good behaviour." He will report himself often in this spirit —offense to his wife, followed by remorse and resolution.

When, in March 1768, Boswell goes again to London after twenty months of application to the law in Edinburgh, he will enjoy the young author's delight in meeting a perfect stranger who has read his book: for Boswell is "Corsica Boswell" now. In London, literary capital of the English-speaking world, he has been sufficiently reviewed and is now sufficiently celebrated. "The most direct compliments were paid to me, without the least delicacy. 'Dr. Wayman, this is Mr. Boswell, author of the Account of Corsica.' WAYMAN. 'Mr. Boswell is a very respectable character!' Such broad hints as these were thrown about."

And again, even as in his anonymous unheralded past, "I patrolled the great metropolis. . . ."

I have never wholly understood the spirit of the mock contract drawn between Margaret and Boswell more than a year before their marriage. We know the earnestness of jests. She agreed not to marry him, in view of his "temper so inconstant": a woman fool enough to marry Boswell (so she affirmed) deserved nothing less than "to be banished out of Great Britain during all the days of my life." She must afterward have thought herself at moments fool indeed to have married a man so difficult, so inconstant. She had long been skeptical of the institution of marriage. "I have not yet perceived such charms in the matrimonial state," she once wrote to Boswell, "as to make me enter very deep into any plot to get myself a member of that society. . . ." She knew the unpopularity of her position, for she immediately added, "this I know will gain but small credit, being inconsistent with female dependence."

At last they married. She was two years older than he—"a little older than I am," Boswell recorded in his journal one day at Stratford, happily observing that Shakespeare's wife had been *seven* years older. The inconstancy Margaret had recognized in Boswell during their courtship continued into marriage. Their love was not blind but sufficiently hopeful, and it inspired, among other things, beautiful correspondence. Margaret's letter accepting Boswell's proposal of marriage displays passionate wisdom. Little wonder that Boswell carried it with him to exhibit to the nation's first man of literature on his last bachelor jaunt to London. There he remained for two months until the very eve of his marriage.

[Boswell to William Johnson Temple]

IN SHORT, Sir, the gardener's daughter, who was named for my mother and has for some time been in the family as a chambermaid, is so very pretty that I am entirely captivated by her. Besides my principle of never debauching an innocent girl, my regard for her father, a worthy man of uncommon abilities, restrains me from forming the least licentious thought against her. And therefore, in plain words, I am mad enough to indulge imaginations of marrying her. Only think of the proud Boswell, with all that you know of him, the fervent adorer of a country girl of three and twenty. I rave about her. I was never so much in love as I am now. My fancy is quite inflamed. It riots in extravagance.

I know as well as you can tell me that a month's or perhaps ten days' possession of this angelic creature would probably make her appear to me insipid as does to you Celia "who at Berwick deigns to dwell." I have a clear remembrance of my being tormented with many such passions, all which went off in a little time, and yet, Temple, I am still dreaming of delightful nuptials. She and I were in a manner brought up together. As far back as I can remember, we used to build houses and make gardens, wade in the river and play upon the sunny banks. I cannot consider her as below me. For these six or seven years past I have seen her little. Before I went abroad she had begun to be timid and reserved, for Lord Eglinton admired her extremely and wanted to seduce her. For my part I saw nothing more about her than in many good-looking girls in the neighborhood. But since my return from my travels I have been quite enchanted with her. She has a most amiable face, the prettiest foot and ankle. She is perfectly well made, and has a lively, genteel air that is irresistible.

I take every opportunity of being with her when she is putting on fires or dressing a room. She appears more graceful with her besom than ever shepherdess did with a crook. I pretend great earnestness to have the library in good order and assist her to dust it. I cut my gloves that she may mend them. I kiss her hand. I tell her what a beauty I think her. She has an entire confidence in me and has no fear of any bad design; and she has too much sense to form an idea of having me for a husband. On the contrary, she talks to me of not refusing a good offer if it is made to her. Enchanting creature! must she be enjoyed by some schoolmaster or farmer? Upon my honour, it cuts me to the heart. If she would not marry anybody else, I think I could let her alone. That we may not be too often seen together, she and I write notes to each other, which we lay under the cloth which covers my table. This little curious correspondence, which to her is an innocent amusement, makes my heart beat continually. She has a fine temper. She has read a great deal, for I always supplied her with books. In short, she is better than any lady I know.

What shall I do, Temple? Shall I lay my account with all its consequences and espouse her? Will not the exquisite languish of her eyes charm away repentance? Shall I not pass a life of true natural felicity with the woman I love and have a race of healthy and handsome children? Good heavens! what am I about? It would kill my father. Have I returned safe from London, from Italy, and from France to throw myself away on a servant maid? You might apply to me what was said of St. Paul when the viper fastened upon his hand after the shipwreck: "Whom though he hath escaped the sea, yet vengeance suffereth not to live."

I have got a lock of her hair which I dote upon. She allowed me to cut it off. If I should marry her, I would never suffer her to dress better than she does now. I think I could pass my whole life agreeably with her assistance. I am not fit for marriage in all the forms. A lady would not be compliant enough, and would oblige me to harass myself with an endless repetition of external ceremony and a most woeful maintaining of *proper conduct.* Whereas my dear girl would be grateful for my attachment, would be devoted to me in every respect, would live with me just as a mistress without the disgrace and remorse. After all my feverish joys and pains, I should enjoy calm and permanent bliss in her arms. Was there ever such madness?

[Boswell to Temple]

Moffat, 17 May 1766

MY DEAREST FRIEND,—I have been a week here, and to prevent that rodomontade of which you have frequently accused me, let me tell you at once that my love for the handsome chambermaid is already like a dream that is past. I kept the extravagant epistle which was to inform you of it till I should see if absence would not free me from the delirium. I can now send you with a good grace what would certainly have alarmed you, but will now be truly amusing. Romantic as I am, it was so strange a scene in the play of my life that I myself was quite astonished at it. I give you my word of honour it was literally true. There are few people who could give credit to it. But you, who have traced me since ever I fairly entered upon the stage, will not doubt of it. It is a little humbling, to be sure. It was the effect of great force and great weakness of mind. I am certainly a most various composition.

In the meantime, my friend, I am happy enough to have a *dear infidel,* as you say. But don't think her unfaithful. I could not love her if she was. There is a baseness in all deceit which my soul is virtuous enough ever to abhor, and therefore I look with horror upon adultery. But my amiable mistress is no longer bound to him who was her husband. He has used her shockingly ill. He has deserted her. He lives with another. Is she not then free? She is. It is clear, and no arguments can disguise it. She is now mine, and were she to be unfaithful to me, she ought to be pierced with a Corsican poniard. But I believe she loves me sincerely. She had done everything to please me. She is perfectly generous, and would not hear of any present. She has hitherto been boarded here, which lays us under a restraint. I have found out a sober widow, in whose house is the rendezvous of our amours. But I have now prevailed with my love to let me take a house for her, and as it will be my family I shall provide what is necessary. In this manner I am safe and happy and in no danger either of the perils of Venus or of desperate matrimony.

I am now advancing fast in the law. I am coming into great employment. I have this winter made sixty-four guineas, which is a considerable sum for a young man. I expect that this first year I shall clear, in all, about a hundred pieces.

THURSDAY 5 FEBRUARY . . . In morning went to Mrs. Leith and took house. Mind at ease; determined to be generous and let Miss _____ do as she pleased. Very busy all day. Tea, Lord Hailes. [Was] going to write noble letter to Miss _____ ; sent for by her; went. She tender as ever, quite affectionate. Saw all was easy. You felt too much like married man, but 'twas gay. Then at nine, Clerihue's and Mr. William Wilson and Bryce, [a] client. Saw [that law was a] form of fleecing poor lieges. Hurt *tant soit peu,* [soon] firm again.

SATURDAY 7 FEBRUARY. With honest Doctor [Boswell] and a Doctor Livingston walked out to Sir Alexander's. Fine day. Was powerful like Johnson; very much satisfied. Evening with Miss _____ . She had taken other house, so resolved to give up yours. A little gloom still, a little fever.

MONDAY 9 FEBRUARY. Robert Hay's trial. You opened and strongly protested his innocence; quite calm. Lasted till eight. Jaded a little.

TUESDAY 10 FEBRUARY. Very busy. Poor Hay condemned.

WEDNESDAY 11 FEBRUARY. Visited Robert Hay. Why it is, I know not, but we compassionate less a genteel man [in affliction than a poor man]. He was very quiet. You had a kind of sentiment as if he was utterly insensible to good. But he said if he had got time, he would have been a new man as from his mother's breast, and wept. Had Bible. Spoke to him seriously and calmly; bid him free innocent people, but not impeach a companion if [he held information] in trust. At eight, Miss _____ a little.

SUNDAY 15 FEBRUARY. Morning, Erskine called; told you what applause you got. You was quite firm and gay. Church, forenoon. Home between sermons, then to prison. Such an audience! Young divine preached: "Be not slothful in business" &c.—not at all applicable to his hearers. Great genius required for a jail preacher. You sat in the closet, like an aisle. You did not like to hear the divine in his prayer talk of *a disgraceful death.* 'Twas too shocking to his unhappy hearers. He should have preached on patience, on the necessity of punishment, on the corruption of man's nature, on the mercy of God. [They sang] psalms, with precentor reading [them] line [by line] with a doleful tone. Your mind now so strong [that such a scene produces] no impression. . . .

Went and saw poor Hay. He was bad and all heaving—could not speak. His aged mother there, and his wife (a soldier's wife), very well looked. Then David Hume's, who was next day to set out for London; tea with him. He agreed to manage your Account of Corsica with Millar.

[Sir John Pringle to Boswell]

London, 10 February 1767

DEAR SIR . . . I continue to have the satisfaction of hearing from different hands of your applications to business, and of the figure which you have made and are likely to make at the bar. I believe that I told you in a former letter, but I must repeat it, that my pleasure is the greater, as in this event I have had my vanity gratified in thinking that I judged well when I told you that your genius, however differently it then appeared to you, was most calculated for that profession, which you seem now to have embraced in earnest. I will go further, since you must now give a little credit to my predictions, and tell you that if you continue to give application you will soon get the start of all our young men in the Parliament House, and will give the tone for a new eloquence very different from what prevailed there in my time. You have the advantage of possessing the English language and the accent in a greater degree than any of your rivals, and a turn for expressing yourself in a clear and energetic manner, without those hyperbolical modes of speech that were introduced long ago, and were still kept up during my youth, and which slipped from the bar to the tea tables at Edinburgh.

By letters which I have since my return had from my worthy friend your father (for I have had more than one upon the subject), I have the comfort to find that you have made him very happy; and I have the superstition to believe that whilst you go on in this train (I mean sobriety, diligence in your business, and attentions to the best of parents) God will bless you, not only with conferring upon you his imperceptible favours, but will even condescend to gratify you with reputation and other worldly enjoyments, which we may desire but never set our hearts upon. You may be assured that your father's confidence in you and his affection will daily augment; for, between ourselves be it spoken, could you expect that, after all is passed, he should all at once consider you as arrived at the full maturity of your judgment? Permit me to predict once more. In a year, or two at furthest, if you persevere in this course, my sage friend, so far will he be from seeing you in the light of a boy that he will not only communicate to you all his most secret affairs, but will consult you upon them and show a regard to your judgment.

In order to hasten this confidence, I will presume to suggest what may be the most proper means: that is, I would advise you to look out for a wife, and to make such a match as he and the whole world shall approve of. After examining that affair with some attention, I am much for early nuptials, and indeed so much that if I were in your place I should set immediately about them. I am persuaded that you would have a great deal of satisfaction in following that plan; for your temper is good, you would have joy in children, and I believe I may add that you have had too much experience of the vague and vicious pleasures not to relish the confined and virtuous ones as soon as you will make the comparison.

TUESDAY 17 FEBRUARY. . . . Evening with Miss _____, dressed in the very black she had charmed you with on Sunday. You was delighted with her. . . .

SATURDAY 21 FEBRUARY. You was quite overpowered with papers to draw. Had been accustomed too much to make the law easy, and write papers like essays for a newspaper, without reading much. Saw labour and poring necessary, and reading long papers. Dined Samuel Mitchelson's with Sir Alexander Dick and family. Evening with Miss _____, again in black. Allowed you full sight; enchanted with her. She said, "Next night I'll wear black and let candles burn to keep you longer."

SUNDAY 22 FEBRUARY. . . . You stayed in the afternoon and wrote letters. Evening was with Miss _____, who came instantly on your sending [for her, and was] very kind.

WEDNESDAY 25 FEBRUARY. At five Miss _____ with you; pretty well. At eight, at Mrs. Dunbar's in Gosford's Close, low house but comfortable, with William Taylor and John Stobie consulting on cause of old Barclay, [the] Quaker [of] London. Four bottles [of] good claret drunk, quite style of old consultations. Home and finished paper. Was with Father; was hearty. Asked him, "Am I not doing as well as you would wish?" HE "Yes." Took his hand.

SATURDAY 28 FEBRUARY. . . . At six with Miss _____, in varying humour. She upbraided you; almost would give up *concert*. Talked of expense offending you, [and] parted angry with you. [As you came out] met _____, [and showed] alarm. You supped Lady Betty's with Grange, Dr. Gregory, Arbuthnot and his ladies. Pleasant, but you was a little drowsy.

SUNDAY 1 MARCH. Miss Blair of Adamton in [our] seat [at church], handsome, stately woman; good countenance. Dined Duchess of Douglas, very hearty. . . . Before dinner had been with Miss _____, and settled plan how to explain last night's alarm. You and she were as fine as ever. At six she met you. By having lived luxuriously so much last week, you was confused and debilitate, [and] performed only one—a kind of ludicrous distress.

TUESDAY 3 MARCH. . . . Tea, Grange; Erskine there. Read part of your London Journal; delighted [them]. Talked of your fever for Mrs. Dodds. They showed you weakness; you saw 'twas only sudden resolution to be free. Sat till near three—extraordinary night.

[Boswell to Temple]

In a former part of this letter I have talked a great deal of my sweet little mistress. I am, however, uneasy about her. Furnishing a house and maintaining her with a maid will cost me a great deal of money, and it is too like marriage, or too much a settled plan of licentiousness. But what can I do? I have already taken the house, and the lady has agreed to go into it at Whitsunday. I cannot in honour draw back. Besides, in no other way can I have her. But I have had more intelligence of her former intrigues. I am hurt to think of them. I cry, "Damn her, lewd minx." I am jealous. What shall I do?

Oh, my friend! were you but here; but, alas! that cannot be. Mamhead is not within a call. It ought to be so, for you should always be my pastor; and I might now and then be yours. Friend of my youth, explain to me how we suffer so severely from what no longer exists. How am I tormented because my charmer has formerly loved others! I am disgusted to think of it. My lively imagination often represents her former loves in actual enjoyment of her. My desire fails, I am unfit for love. Besides, she is ill-bred, quite a rompish girl. She debases my dignity. She has no refinement. But she is very handsome, very lively, and admirably formed for amorous dalliance. What is it to me that she has formerly loved? So have I.

What is to be thought of this life, my friend? Hear the story of my last three days. After tormenting myself with reflecting on my charmer's former loves and ruminating on parting with her, I went to her. I could not conceal my being distressed. I told her I was very unhappy, but I would not tell her why. She took this very seriously, and was so much affected that she went next morning and gave up our house. I went in the afternoon and secured the house, and then drank tea with her. She was much agitated. She said she was determined to go and board herself in the north of England, and that I used her very ill. I expostulated with her. I was sometimes resolved to let her go, and sometimes my heart was like to burst within me. I held her dear hand. Her eyes were full of passion. I took her in my arms. I told her what made me miserable. She was pleased to find it was nothing worse. She had imagined that I was suspicious of her fidelity, and she thought that very ungenerous in me, considering her behaviour. She said I should not mind her faults before I knew her, since her conduct was now most circumspect. We renewed our fondness. She owned she loved me more than she had ever done her husband. All was again well. She said she did not reproach me with my former follies, and we should be on an equal footing. My mind all at once felt a spring. I agreed with her. I embraced her with transport.

That very evening I gave a supper to two or three of my acquaintance, having before I left Scotland laid a guinea that I should not catch the venereal disorder for three years, which bet I had most certainly lost and now was paying. We drank a great deal, till I was so much intoxicated that instead of going home I went to a low house in one of the alleys in Edinburgh where I knew a common girl lodged, and like a brute as I was I lay all night with her. I had still so much reason left as not to "dive into the bottom of the deep," but I gratified my coarse desires by tumbling about on the brink of destruction. Next morning I was like a man ordered for ignominious execution. But by noon I was worse, for I discovered that some infection had reached me. Was not this dreadful? I had an assignation in the evening with my charmer. How lucky was it that I knew my misfortune in time. I might have polluted her sweet body. Bless me! what a risk! But how could I tell her my shocking story? I took courage. I told how drunk I had been. I told the consequences. I lay down and kissed her feet. I said I was unworthy of any other favour. But I checked myself. I gloried that I had ever been firmly constant to her while I was myself. I hoped she would consider my being drunk as a fatal accident which I should never again fall into. I called her my friend in whom I had confidence, and entreated she would comfort me.

How like you the eloquence of a young barrister? It was truly the eloquence of love. She bid me rise; she took me by the hand. She said she forgave me. She kissed me. She gently upbraided me for entertaining any unfavourable ideas of her. She bid me take great care of myself and in time coming never drink upon any account. Own to me, Temple, that this was noble—and all the time her beauty enchanted me more than ever. May I not then be hers? In the meantime I must shut up, and honest Thomas must be my guardian.

SATURDAY 14 MARCH. Tea, Miss _____; provoked her with old stories. Grange had been with you in the forenoon, and insisted you had no morals. You was shocked. You saw Miss _____ had no sentiment. You had sore conflict. But you resolved to try one winter, to enjoy fully so strong a passion. You then fancied you could inspire her with finer feelings. You grew fond. Her eyes looked like precious stones. Some delirium seized you. She seemed an angel.

SUNDAY 15 MARCH. Had message from Miss _____; she was to set out next day. Was in, quiet all this day. Captain Erskine and Houston Stewart drank tea with you. Houston was dissipated as ever. You felt calm superiority, but not to shock him you assumed dissipation a little. You had wrote earnestly to Miss _____. She came at eight, and sat a while with you. It was vastly kind.

MONDAY 16 MARCH. You called on Miss _____ and passed a great part of the forenoon, as she was not to go till Tuesday. You again spoke of old stories. She was fretted. You were both very uneasy. You saw her temper such that no eloquence could touch her. But you was her slave. Returned at five to tea. She was young and vivacious. What a temperament! You gave word in honour you'd never again allow her to be ill spoken of by Grange in your presence. You were like man and wife. . . . Went to Lady Betty's. She had been ill; you was so. [She still] appeared invalid. Was restless, having promised to Miss _____ to return. You talked much of Miss _____ , and Lady Betty and the Captain rated you about her. At eleven you went to her. You was let softly in. She was quite kind. But the recollection of her former tricks galled you, for your heart was affected. You had been with Lord Monboddo and talked of your flame. He quoted Ulysses and Circe: "Sub domina meretrice vixisset turpis et excors." You saw how lightly passions appear to those not immediately affected by them, for even to yourself will this afterwards seem light. You was all resigned to sweet Miss _____ . You chased away all reflection. You drank in instant delight. You sat till one, and parted with great fondness in hopes of meeting. Home, Father still up. Lady Betty bore the blame of late hours.

TUESDAY 17 MARCH. [Was] feverish [and felt like] Mark Antony, quite given up to violent love. . . . Then Miss G_____ and gave money for [your] house, &c. Had laboured hard all winter, but now passion made you at once give up the fruits of your labour, which you had carefully collected. . . .

THURSDAY 19 MARCH. Waked in tender anguish: "What, shall I give her up?" Your melting moments rushed on your mind: her generosity —ah! For some seconds a real fit of delirium [seized you], tossing in your distempered mind [the thought of] instant self-destruction. Bless me! is this possible? It was literally true. Got up, roused, grew better. Bad weather had kept you still in town yesterday. However set out today, the same family form. John Bruce, Mr. Stobie, Matthew Dickie, [and] Bob Boswell all down with you to the Back Stairs. This composed your mind. It was, as it were, quilted with good, comfortable, family ideas. Jogged on. Good conversation on law. Dined Livingstone; night, Bedlay's new house. Father gave you account of the Hamilton memorial after supper, [but] left it off. In your room begun letter to Miss _____ . Was gloomy but resolved; considered she had not feeling [enough] to be much affected.

FRIDAY 20 MARCH. Heavy snow. Father resumed the Hamilton memorial. Astonished at his memory, and how all this time he has never said a word, and yet has it so perfectly. [He has a] prodigious strong mind, singular frame. Dined Strathaven; night, Sornbeg, [to which you] walked up from Galston. Comfortable and easy, reflected on the gradual course of things. Was contented. Sat up late and finished letter to Miss _____ . Sent it; was firm as if it had been a year after.

SUNDAY 22 MARCH. Lay abed long and reflected comfortably on being free from Laïs. We did not go to church. I wrote to M. de Sommelsdyck a calm family letter which my father read, I am sure, with satisfaction. We read some of old Mr. Robert Bruce's Scots sermons, and a chapter of the Greek New Testament, and a psalm of Buchanan. We were very happy. We are now friends as much as my father's singular grave and steady temper will allow; for he has not that quick sensibility which animates me. Since the beginning of last winter he has ceased to treat me like a boy. This evening I thought with astonishment, "Is it really true that a man of such variety of genius, who has seen so much, who is in constant friendship with General Paoli, is it possible that he was all last winter the slave of a woman without one elegant quality?"

MONDAY 23 MARCH. Mr. Dun, Hallglenmuir, &c., here. I roused my mind and wrote the Introduction to my Account of Corsica.

FRIDAY 27 MARCH. Began my Account of Corsica, [and found I] could labour well. Father studied Douglas memorials and at intervals [read] *Don Quixote*. [He was] much entertained with him. Joked on my Account; called it quixotism.

[Boswell to Temple]

My life is one of the most romantic that I believe either you or I really know of, and yet I am a very sensible, good sort of man. What is the meaning of this, Temple? You may depend upon it that very soon my follies will be at an end, and I shall turn out an admirable member of society. Now that I have given my mind the turn, I am totally emancipated from my charmer, as much as from the gardener's daughter, who now puts on my fire and empties my chamber-pot like any other wench; and yet just this time twelvemonth I was so madly in love as to think of marrying her.

What say you to my marrying? I intend next autumn to visit Miss Bosville in Yorkshire. But I fear, my lot being cast in Scotland, that beauty would not be content. She is, however, grave. I shall see. There is a young lady in the neighbourhood here who has an estate of her own between two and three hundred a year, just eighteen, a genteel person, an agreeable face, of a good family, sensible, good-tempered, cheerful, pious. You know my grand object is the ancient family of Auchinleck, a venerable and noble principle. How would it do to conclude an alliance with this neighbouring princess, and add her lands to our dominions? I should at once have a very pretty little estate, a good house, and a sweet place. My father is very fond of her. It would make him perfectly happy.

He give me hints in his way: "I wish you had her." No bad scheme this. I think a very good one. But I will not be in a hurry. There is plenty of time. I will take to myself the advice I wrote you from Naples, and go to London a while before I marry.

I am not yet quite well, but am in as good a way as can be expected. My fair neighbour was a ward of my father's. She sits in our seat at church in Edinburgh. She would take possession here most naturally. This is a superb place: we have the noblest natural beauties, and my father has made most extensive improvements. We look ten miles out upon our own dominions. We have an excellent new house. I am now writing in a library forty foot long. Come to us, my dearest friend. We will live like the most privileged spirits of antiquity. I am now seriously engaged in my Account of Corsica. It elevates my soul, and makes me *spernere humum*. I shall have it finished by June.

THURSDAY 2 APRIL. You was still bad. At night had fear of ghosts, [thinking of] poor Robert Hay.

FRIDAY 3 APRIL. . . . You laboured hard and with spirit.

SATURDAY 4 APRIL. Accounts came of the Corsicans having made a descent on Capraja, with a letter from Mr. Dick confirming it and informing you that all your correspondence was safe. You was roused. You had not felt your blood in fermentation of a long time before. You only regretted that you don't feel *yourself* more manly. This your own fault. Resolved more guarded conduct.

FRIDAY 10 APRIL. Your toe was pretty well, and you walked in the Broomholm with Matthew. You talked of Miss Blair. I felt my openness too great. I might soon acquire a habit of telling everything. By doing so a man becomes quite easy, but loses delicacy and dignity. You thought it best to own a libertine misfortune and regret your fault. The same company continued all night, with honest Hallglenmuir. You found time, however, to advance a little in Corsica.

MONDAY 13 APRIL. Corsica advanced. Treesbank and Polquhairn dined. The latter told you gross scandal of Mrs. _____ . It hardly hurt you, so well are you grown.

THURSDAY 16 APRIL. Waterhead breakfasted. You and he agreed that venereal disorders do not hurt the constitution. Only severe cures do. There may be a good deal in this. But Waterhead and I have both been wild, so are not impartial judges, for no doubt such disorders do harm.

SATURDAY 18 APRIL. Corsica advanced. Mr. Brown went home. Sent Dorando to Foulis. Imagined he might perhaps scruple to publish so strong an allusion to the Douglas cause; left him to himself.

MONDAY 20 APRIL. Corsica advanced. At night I began to write an account of the Boswells from my father's dictating.

TUESDAY 21 APRIL. Corsica still understood to advance.

WEDNESDAY 22 APRIL. Corsica still.

THURSDAY 23 APRIL. Corsica advanced.

Mr. Smeaton was struck with my subtle philosophy. He defended himself by some abstract doctrines of the schoolmen, and I let him off. I found he had afterwards said to James Bruce that he had conversed with many, but he had never found a gentleman who had such a foundation, and if I lived I must be a very great man.

MONDAY 1 JUNE. The ladies agreed to stay one day longer. But it was a wet day. My mind had been relaxed by elegant dissipation. I called myself to my post and wrote Corsica as well as ever. At night Bruce Campbell with us. [I was] too free and rampageneous. Time must cure all.

[Boswell to Temple]

Edinburgh, 12 June 1767

MY DEAR TEMPLE, The lady in my neighbourhood is the finest woman I have ever seen. I went and visited her, and she was so good as to prevail with her mother to come to Auchinleck, where they stayed four days, and in our romantic groves I adored her like a divinity. I have already given you her character. My father is very desirous I should marry her. All my relations, all my neighbours approve of it. She looked quite at home in the house of Auchinleck. Her picture would be an ornament to the gallery. Her children would be all Boswells and Temples, and as fine women as these are excellent men. And now, my friend, my best adviser comes to hear me talk of her and to fix my wavering mind.

I must tell you my Italian angel is constant. I had a letter from her but a few days ago, which made me cry. And what shall I tell you? My late Circe, Mrs. _____ , is with child. What a fellow am I!

You will also have my Account of Corsica. How happy am I that my Temple comes to give it his friendly revisal. My Lord Hailes has given me seven folio pages of remarks upon it. He says, "I am much entertained and instructed." Is not this noble? You may have very good lodgings in the same stair with us. When I get your answer fixing a particular day, I shall secure them for you. We shall live entirely in the luxury of philosophy and friendship. We shall have the society of Dr. Blair, Dr. Gregory, Dr. Ferguson, and our other *literati*. But we shall keep the best portion of our time sacred to our intimate affection.

My dearest friend! Is it not a distinguished felicity to participate of the highest friendship as much as the greatest and best of other ages have done? This is literally the case with you and me. We are divine madmen to the dull and interested many. Will you come on Saturday or on Monday? Why, O why, is it session time! Temple, you must be at Auchinleck. You must see my charming bride.

In the meantime, I must tell you that on Tuesday last, drinking Miss Blair's health (for that is the name of my angelic princess), I got myself quite intoxicated, went to a bawdy-house, and passed a whole night in the arms of a whore. She indeed was a fine, strong, spirited girl, a whore worthy of Boswell if Boswell must have a whore, and I apprehend no bad consequences. But I am abashed, and determined to keep the strictest watch over my passions.

Give Miss Blair my letter. Salute her and her mother; ask to walk. See the place fully; think what improvement should be made. Talk of my mare, the purse, the chocolate. Tell you are my very old and intimate friend. Praise me for my good qualities—you know them; but talk also how odd, how inconstant, how impetuous, how much accustomed to women of intrigue. Ask gravely, "Pray, don't you imagine there is something of madness in that family?" Talk of my various travels —German princes—Voltaire and Rousseau. Talk of my father; my strong desire to have my own house. Observe her well. See how amiable. Judge if she would be happy with your friend. Think of me as the great man at Adamton—quite classical too! Study the mother. Remember well what passes. Stay tea. At six, order horses and go to Newmilns, two miles from Loudoun; but if they press you to stay all night, do it. Be a man of as much ease as possible. Consider what a romantic expedition you are on; take notes; perhaps you now fix me for life.

I am an unhappy man. The consequences of my debauch are now fatal, for I have got a disease from which I suffer severely. It has been long of appearing and is a heavy one. I shall stay a month here after the Session rises, and be cured. I am patient under it, as a just retribution for my licentiousness. But I greatly fear that Mrs. _____ is infected, for I have been with her several times since my debauch, and once within less than a week of the full appearance of mischief. In her present situation the consequences will be dreadful; for, besides the pain that she must endure, an innocent being cannot fail to be injured. Will you forgive me, Temple, for exclaiming that all this evil is too much for the offence of my getting drunk because I would drink Miss Blair's health every round in a large bumper? But general laws often seem hard in particular cases. I am not, however, certain that Mrs. _____ will be ill. I would fain hope that she may have escaped. I have told her the risk she runs. Her good temper is astonishing. She does not upbraid me in the least degree.

[Received ? 2 October, Margaret Montgomerie to Boswell]

Lainshaw, Thursday [1 October 1767]

DEAR JAMIE,—I beg the favour of you to take the trouble to bring out a gown of mine with you. I shall write the mantua-maker to bring it to you, but, if she neglect to do it, she is a Miss Tait who lives in Milne's Square; so I'll be obliged to you if you'll send to her.

I am glad you propose being here so soon. I hope you intend being at the October meeting at Ayr, as I dare say your favourite Miss Blair will be there; and as the Duke of Gordon has convinced you he is in earnest, I hope you will continue fixed in resolutions of following his example. I was at Pollok this week and left Mrs. Montgomerie in perfect health.

I fancy you have seen Lord Eglinton, as I met him on his way to Edinburgh. I beg my compliments to Davy. All here join in best wishes to you and him. Adieu, dear James, and believe me, your affectionate cousin and obliged

M. Montgomerie.

Will expect you and David the beginning of the week.

[Boswell to Temple]

Edinburgh, 24 December 1767

My dearest Friend,—On Monday forenoon I waited on Miss Blair; I found her alone, and she did not seem distant. I told her that I was most sincerely in love with her, and that I only dreaded those faults which I had acknowledged to her. I asked her seriously if she now believed me in earnest. She said she did. I then asked her to be candid and fair as I had been with her, and to tell me if she had any particular liking for me. What think you, Temple, was her answer? *No.* "I really," said she, "have no particular liking for you. I like many people as well as you."

(Temple, you must have it in the genuine dialogue.) boswell. "Do you indeed? Well, I cannot help it. I am obliged to you for telling me so in time. I am sorry for it." princess. "I like Jeanie Maxwell (Duchess of Gordon) better than you." boswell. "Very well. But do you like no man better than me?" princess. "No." boswell. "Is it possible that you may like me better than other men?" princess. "I don't know what is possible." (By this time I had risen and placed myself by her, and was in real agitation.) boswell. "I'll tell you what, my dear Miss Blair, I love you so much that I am very unhappy. If you cannot love me, I must if possible endeavour to forget you. What would you have me do?" princess. "I don't really know what you should do." boswell. "It is certainly possible that you *may* love me, and if you shall ever do so I shall be the happiest man in the world. Will you make a fair bargain with me? If you should happen to love me, will you own it?" princess. "Yes." boswell. "And if you should happen to love another, will you tell me immediately, and help me to make myself easy?" princess "Yes, I will." boswell. "Well, you are very good" (often squeezing and kissing her fine hand, while she looked at me with those beautiful black eyes).

PRINCESS. "I may tell you as a cousin what I would not tell to another man." BOSWELL. "You may indeed. You are very fond of Auchinleck; that is one good circumstance." PRINCESS. "I confess I am. I wish I liked you as well as I do Auchinleck." BOSWELL. "I have told you how fond I am of you. But unless you like me sincerely, I have too much spirit to ask you to live with me, as I know that you do not like me. If I could have you this moment for my wife I would not." PRINCESS. "I should not like to put myself in your offer, though." BOSWELL. "Remember, you are both my cousin and my mistress. You must make me suffer as little as possible. As it may happen that I may engage your affections, I should think myself a most dishonourable man if I were not now in earnest, and remember I depend upon your sincerity; and whatever happens you and I shall never again have any quarrel." PRINCESS. "Never." BOSWELL. "And I may come and see you as much as I please?" PRINCESS. "Yes."

Amidst all this love I have been wild as ever. I have catched another memorandum of vice, but a very slight one. Trust me in time coming. I give you my word in honour, Temple. I have nothing else to save me.

My black friend has brought me the finest little girl I ever saw. I have named it Sally. It is healthy and strong. I take the greatest care of the mother, but shall have her no more in keeping.

I have this day received a large packet from Paoli, with a letter in elegant Latin from the University of Corte, and also an extract of an oration pronounced this year at the opening of the University, in which oration I am celebrated in a manner which does me the greatest honour. I think, Temple, I have had my full share of fame. Yet my book is still to come, and I cannot doubt its doing me credit.

SATURDAY 2 JANUARY. About nine my father was taken ill with his old complaint. Thomas went express to Edinburgh. The President showed a friendly concern which will ever make him be regarded by me. For some hours my father was in agony. In the view of death he gave me the best and most affectionate advice. He spoke of Miss Blair as the woman whom he wished I would marry. How strong was this. I was in terrible concern. He said if business did not succeed with me after his death I should retire to the country. He charged me to take care of my brothers, to be a worthy man, and keep up the character of the family. I firmly resolved to be as he wished, though in somewhat a different taste of life. I looked my watch a hundred times. A quarter before one Thomas arrived with the catheter. In five minutes my father was easy. What a happy change! Went calmly to bed. It was an intense frost and the ground was covered with snow.

SUNDAY 3 JANUARY. My father was quite easy. I went out for an hour with the President in his chariot. Talked freely on the Douglas cause.

Heard how it struck him in its various points. Saw how foolish the suspicions against him were. Resolved to take men as I find them. Was assured by the President that I should do well as a lawyer. Saw no difficulties in life. Saw that all depends on our frame of mind. Lord and Lady Hyndford were here. The day passed well. In the evening I adored my God; I had now no doubt of the Christian revelation. I was quite satisfied with my being. I hoped to be happy with Miss Blair.

MONDAY 4 JANUARY. After breakfast, set off. My father remarked how foolish and wicked evil-speaking was. The President afforded a good instance, as so many false reports had been raised against him as to the Douglas cause. We dined at Newbattle. I experienced that calm tranquillity in presence of great people for which I have often wished and have now acquired. Much attention was paid me. Returned to town. Supped Sir George Preston's.

TUESDAY 5 JANUARY. I was at home all day except calling half an hour for Sally's mother. Felt all inclinations gone and that I now acted from principle alone.

WEDNESDAY 6 JANUARY. In all day. Matthew Dickie dined with us. The terrible cold weather made me consider keeping warm as almost business enough.

THURSDAY 7 JANUARY. Breakfast Mr. Webster's. Old ideas revived in an agreeable manner. When my mind was weak, ideas were too powerful for me. I am now strong; I can discern all their qualities but am master of them. I was formerly, in many articles of thought, like a boy who fires a gun. He startles at the noise, and, being unable to wield it, he can direct it to no steady point. I am now master of my gun, and can manage it with ease. I called for Lord Leven, visited Mr. George Frazer, called for Lord Dalhousie, visited Lady Crawford. Miss Montgomerie, John and George Frazers dined.

FRIDAY 8 JANUARY. In all day. Felt myself now quite free of fancies. Was amazed to find how much happiness and misery is ideal. Passed the evening at Mr. Moncrieffe's with the Chief Baron, Miss Ords, &c. Felt myself now quite indifferent about making a figure in company. Am I grown dull? Or is it a calm confidence in a fixed reputation?

SATURDAY 9 JANUARY. Busy with election law. John Chalmer showed me an old opinion of Duncan Forbes, and reflected how curious it was that the opinion remained while the man was no more. A hint such as this brings to my mind all that passed, though it would be barren to anybody but myself. At home all day consulting and writing law papers till six. Went and saw *The Suspicious Husband* and *Citizen;* had my London ideas revived. Went home with Mr. Ross and supped and drank a cheerful glass. He gave me all the history of his marriage. He put me into my old romantic frame. I wished again for adventures, for proofs of my own address and of the generosity of charming women. I was for breaking loose from Scots marriage. But my elegant heiress and the old family of Auchinleck brought me back again.

SUNDAY 10 JANUARY. In forenoon, writing to Zéihde, &c. Church afternoon. Heard Heiress was to have a knight. Was not so much shocked as before. I did not indeed fully believe it. Visited Sally's mother. Was tired of her.

SATURDAY 16 JANUARY. Had a consultation on the Forfar politics. In the forenoon, as we went along in the coach, the Earl of Eglinton was at the Cross. I jumped out and he and I embraced most cordially. I had a strange pleasure in showing my intimacy with his Lordship before the citizens of Edinburgh. It is fine to be sensible of all one's various sentiments and to analyse them.

I told him I loved Miss Blair much and wished to marry her if she liked me, and I gave him all our history. He said I was right to be honest with her; that her answers were very clever, and that it was probable she liked me. But he said I did not show her attention enough; that a woman had a right to be courted as much as a husband after marriage had a right to command. That if I insisted on a woman showing much love for me, I was certain of being taken in by any artful girl who wanted to have a man with a good estate. That I should tell Miss Blair, "if I have any chance, I'll do all in my power to be agreeable. If not, I'll make myself easy as soon as possible." He said my Yorkshire beauty would not do so well, that she would be miserable in this country; and he quoted a blunt saying of the Highlanders that "a cow fed in fine Lowland parks was unco bonny, but turned lean and scabbed when she was turned out to the wild hills". Up came Matthew Henderson and swore he believed Sir Alexander Gilmour was to have the Heiress. My Lord advised me to write to her and know as to this. Such admirable advice did I get from a man of great genius who knows the world perfectly. He talked to me of my neutrality in the Ayrshire elections. I felt I was wrong. I was now quite free of hypochondria. Walking home after convoying my Lord to the Bow, I met a girl. Like a madman I would try the experiment of cooling myself when ill. What more mischief may it not bring!

SUNDAY 17 JANUARY. In all forenoon. At dinner my father was out of humour because I had been so late abroad. I bore with him quite calmly. At five met at Mr. Macqueen's with Messieurs Rae, Alexander Murray, and Armstrong, as counsel for Raybould, the forger, as I allow myself to consult on criminal business on Sundays.

TUESDAY 19 JANUARY. Was at the anniversary meeting of the Faculty of Advocates. Had the true old sensations, and felt myself *Mr. James Boswell,* comfortable and secure. Recollected how formerly I should have been wretched with a life so void of vivid enjoyment, but now had force of mind enough to be content. At Clerihue's we were very merry. The Dean after many ladies had been drank called out, "Here is a toast: a young lady just in her teens—Miss Corsica. Give her a gentleman!" All called out, "Paoli!" I drank too much. I went to a close in the Luckenbooths to seek a girl whom I had once seen in the street. I found a natural daughter of the late Lord [Kinnaird], a fine lass. I stayed an hour and a half with her and drank malaga and was most amorous, being so well that no infection remained. I felt now that the indifference of the Heiress had cured me, and I was indifferent as to her. I was so happy with Jeanie Kinnaird that I very philosophically reasoned that there was to me so much virtue mixed with licentious love that perhaps I might be privileged. For it made me humane, polite, generous. But then lawful love with a woman I really like would make me still better. I forgot the risk I run with girl. She looked so healthy and so honest I had no fears.

FRIDAY 22 JANUARY. My father and I dined at Lord Coalston's. I had written to Miss Blair to tell me if she was going to be married to Sir Alexander Gilmour, and if she was disengaged and did not write me so I should *upon honour* consider it to be the same thing as if she was engaged. No answer had come yet, so I began to exert all my spirit to be free.

MONDAY 25 JANUARY. In all day. M. Dupont drank tea with me; had two consultations. Supped Mrs. Hamilton of Bangour's, an Edinburgh evening. Found I was fit for any company. Before My Account of Corsica came out, I was desirous to have all my visit paid, as I thenceforward intended if possible to maintain a propriety and strictness of manners.

TUESDAY 26 JANUARY. All the evening was employed in writing to Paoli, Mr. Burnaby, &c. before the great era of the publication of my book. I sat up till past two.

WEDNESDAY 27 JANUARY. My father and Claud and I dined at Lord Barjag's. It was just a family dinner. I felt myself palled with insipidity, so high is my taste of society grown. I drank tea at Mrs. Hunter's of Polmood, and revived Sommelsdyck and Auchinleck ideas. I then came home and wrote papers busily till seven. Then had a consultation at the Hon. Alexander Gordon's. Then supped Mrs. Cockburn's. A great company there. Felt myself quite easy, but still subject to fall in love with the woman next me at table.

THURSDAY 28 JANUARY. My father was confined with a severe cold. I saw his great worth and value to me, when I was reminded of the danger of losing him. I resolved to act towards him in such a way as to make his life comfortable, and give me the consolation after he is gone that I have done my duty, and may hope for the same attention from my son.

SUNDAY 31 JANUARY. Forenoon at church. Dined Mr. Moncrieffe's with Prebendary Douglas and lady, Lady and Miss Eden, all from Durham, who wished much to see the author of *The Essence of the Douglas Cause*. Lord John Murray was there. All was elegant and really agreeable. At night went to Sally's mother and renewed gallantry.

TUESDAY 2 FEBRUARY. At seven met Mr. Alexander Orme and Holmains, George Frazer, William Hay, and Jamie Baillie at Clerihue's at a treat given by the heritors of Lochmaben. Mr. Ross had come up to me and asked me to sup with him; so I went and found Sir Johns Cathcart and Whitefoord. We were very merry and pleasant. I drank a great deal, though I was not well yet. Between two and three I went to Sally's mother's and renewed again. What a life do I lead!

FRIDAY 5 FEBRUARY. I supped at Lord Monboddo's with Lords Coalston and Kneet, Mrs. Murray of Stormont, &c. I was quite easy. I saw lords of session in a quite different light from what I have done by looking only at awful judges. Claret fevered me, and I again went to Sally's mother and renewed.

SATURDAY 6 FEBRUARY. Breakfasted at the President's. Was too late for a cause before Lord Monboddo. Determined to confine myself to the Parliament House all the forenoon. Considered the law is my profession, my occupation in life. Saw it not to be such a mystery as I apprehended.

SUNDAY 7 FEBRUARY. Church forenoon. Heard Mr. Butter in St. Paul's Chapel, afternoon. Drank tea with Mrs. Montgomerie-Cuninghame. Then visited Lady Maxwell. Was quite cheerful and well. Mr. Fullarton (the Nabob) came in. Miss Blair was now arrived. He proposed we should go and visit her. We went. She was reserved and distant. I saw plainly all was over. Yet I could not be quite certain. Fullarton and I came away together. I liked the man. I asked him freely how he was. We owned candidly to each other that we were both for Miss Blair. I insisted that he and I should not part that night. I carried him to sup at Mrs. Montgomerie-Cuninghame's and then we adjourned to Clerihue's. I opened the Nabob's mind, and he and I gave each other a fair recital of all that we hoped from the Heiress. It was agreed I had her heart once, and perhaps still, if she was not engaged to Sir Alexander Gilmour. "Come," said I, "we shall be at our wits' end. If you'll ask her tomorrow, upon honour I'll ask her." We shook hands and wished all happiness to him who should succeed. Never was there a more curious scene. At two in the morning I went to Sally's mother, and, being flushed with claret, renewed my love.

MONDAY 8 FEBRUARY. Between nine and ten went to Miss Blair. "Come, before they come in, are you engaged or no?" She seemed reserved. I said, "You know I am much in love with you, and, if you are not engaged, I would take a good deal of trouble to make myself agreeable to you." She said, "You need not take the trouble. Now you must not be angry with me." "Indeed no," said I. "But is it really so? Say upon your word, upon honour." She did so. I therefore was satisfied. My spirit was such that, though I felt some regret, I appeared quite easy and gay. I made her give me breakfast, and with true philosophy I put my mind in a proper frame. It was agreed that we were not to ask her if she was engaged. She gave me a lecture on my conduct towards her, in talking without reserve. At twelve the Nabob was with her, and she treated him with the greatest coldness.He and I met at the Cross at two and joked and laughed with all our acquaintance. I did the Nabob much good, for I relieved him from serious love by my vivacity. I have one of the most singular minds ever was formed.

11 FEBRUARY. I have allowed my letter to lie by till this day. The Heiress is a good Scots lass. But I must have an Englishwoman. My mind is now twice as enlarged as it has been for some months. You cannot say how fine a woman I may marry; perhaps a Howard or some other of the noblest in the kingdom.

SATURDAY 13 FEBRUARY. I dined at Lord Justice-Clerk's with my father. Lords Kinnoul, Coalston, Kames, Baron Winn, &c., were there. I drank pretty freely, and after five went to Sally's mother and renewed. She told me she was again, she believed, as before. I was a little embarrassed, but just submitted my mind to it. I then went to Crosbie and had some tea. Then he and I went Mr. James Hay's and had a consultation with Mrs. Smith of Forret. It was quite in old style, and when it was over honest Mr. Hay gave us a couple of bottles of claret. This inflamed me again and I went back to Sally's mother. She really looked pretty.

SUNDAY 14 FEBRUARY. I sat in all forenoon. Afternoon, went to church. Tea at home, then went to the good Doctor's.

MONDAY 15 FEBRUARY. This day I heard from Mr. Dilly that my Account of Corsica was ready for publication, so I ordered Mr. Neill to give out copies in Scotland.

THURSDAY 18 FEBRUARY. My book was published this day, and felt my own importance. I danced with the Countess of Crawford, so opened the ball. I was quite as I wished to be; only I am positive I had not so high an opinion of myself as other people had. I look back with wonder on the mysterious and respectful notions I used to have of authors. I felt that I was still subject to attacks of feverish love, but I also knew that my mind is now firm enough soon to recover its tone.

SUNDAY 21 FEBRUARY. In all forenoon. I had dreamt of Raybould under sentence of death. I was gloomy. Afternoon, church. Tea home, then visited Raybould, that my gloomy imagination might be cured by seeing the reality. I was shown up to him by Archibald, the soldier who was to be tried for murder. The clanking of the iron-room door was terrible. I found him very composed. I sat by him an hour and a half by the light of a dim farthing candle. He spoke very properly on religion. I read him the 4 Chapter of the 1 Epistle of John and lectured upon it. On verse 18 I discoursed on *fear* very appositely, by an illustration taken from Robert Hay, the soldier who was hanged last year. "There, John," said I, "did he lie quite sunk, quite desperate, and neither would eat nor drink, and all for *fear*, just terror for dying. But the comfortable doctrine of Christianity prevents this." I was quite firm, and I was astonished to compare myself now with myself when a boy, remarkably timorous. Raybould seemed wonderfully easy. I therefore talked quite freely to him. "But, John, have you no fear for the immediate pain of dying?" "No," said he, "I have had none as yet. I know not how it may be at the very moment. But I do think I shall be quite composed." I looked steadfastly at him during this and saw he was speaking truly. One certain sign of his being much at ease was the readiness with which his attention was diverted to any other subject than his own melancholy situation; for when a man is much distressed he is still fixed in brooding over his calamity. But Raybould talked of his wife's journey down in all its particulars, just as if he had been an indifferent, ordinary man.

He told me when he came first to Scotland he did not know the difference between an agent and an advocate. I saw him beginning to smile at his own ignorance. I considered how amazing it would be if a man under sentence of death should really laugh, and, with the nicest care of a diligent student of human nature, I as decently as possible first smiled as he did, and gradually cherished the risible exertion, till he and I together fairly laughed. How strange! He very calmly examined whether a man dying of sickness or one in his situation was worst. He said one in his situation. I argued that one dying of sickness was worst, because he is weakened and unable to support the fear of death, whereas one in his situation was quite well but for the prospect before him.

Raybould, however, maintained his proposition, because, he said, the man weakened by sickness was brought to a state of indifference. I bid him farewell. It was truly a curious scene. I went and sat a while at the worthy Doctor's.

WEDNESDAY 24 FEBRUARY. I went to see Raybould's execution. I was invited up to the window of one _____, a merchant, by _____, who knew me. I tried to be quite firm and philosophical, and imagined Raybould in some future period telling what he felt at his execution. The most dreadful event seems light when past, and I made it past by imagination. I felt very little; but when he stood long on the ladder I grew impatient, and was beginning to have uneasy sensations. I came home. Mr. William Wilson, S., Mr. Walter Scott, &c. dined. At night I was with Lady Crawford at *The Beggar's Opera,* which quite relieved any gloom. The songs revived London ideas, and my old intrigues with actresses who used to play in this opera. I was happy in being free of Miss Blair. The farce was *The Vintner Tricked.* It was curious that after seeing a real hanging I should meet with two mock ones on the stage. I went with Houston Stewart and renewed our old acquaintance at Caddie Miller's with oysters and claret. We sat till two, very agreeably. When I came home I was a little dreary, but it went off and I slept well.

WEDNESDAY 16 MARCH. It is very odd that it is hardly possible to set out upon a journey without being in confusion. I was so not a little this morning. My worthy friend Johnston came and stayed by me while I packed my trunk, the sign of a real friend. He who can stand by a man while he packs his trunk would attend him to the place of execution were he going to be hanged; for really one packing his trunk and one going to be hanged are pretty much the same company to a friend. My travelling companion was Mr. Robertson near Alloway, one of the contractors for paving the streets of London, but who was going thither for the first time. Mr. John Small, one of the macers of the Court of Session, was to ride by us into the chaise to Haddington, where we had a beefsteak, having set out at two o'clock. We seemed hearty and easy. Only I, whose combustible, or rather inflammable, soul is always taking fire, was uneasy at having left *Mary,* a pretty, lively little girl whom accident had thrown in my way a few days before. She was one of those females who either from wickedness or misfortune are the slaves of profligate men. She was very young, and I resolved to try if there was virtue in her; so I left her as many guineas as she said she could live upon till my return. I got two of my friends to promise to go to her and offer her a high bribe to break her engagement to me, and to write me what she did. I find I am still somewhat of a Don Quixote, for now am I in love with perhaps an abandoned, worthless being; but we shall see. We went to Dunbar at night, where we drank the finest small beer I ever tasted in my life, and had a good supper and warm punch.

SUNDAY 20 MARCH. After a long sleep and a copious breakfast, we went and saw the cathedral. It is prodigiously noble Gothic edifice. Small and Robertson stayed all the time of service. But I slipped away to a coffee-house where I fell into conversation with a Sir George (I believe, Armytage) about Corsica. He talked very warmly for them and seemed to know a good deal about them. I began to think he must have learnt his knowledge of me. So I asked him if the Corsicans had any seaports. "Oh, yes, Sir," said he, "very good ones. Why, Boswell's *Account of Corsica* tells you all that." "Sir?" said I, "what is that?" "Why, Sir," said he, "a book just now published." "By an officer in that service, Sir?" said I. "No," said he. "I have not the pleasure of being acquainted with the gentleman, but Mr. Boswell is a gentleman who was abroad and who thought he would pay a visit to Corsica, and accordingly went thither and had many conversations wih Paoli" (Pioli he pronounced it), "and he has given its history and a full account of everything about the island, and has shown that Britain should make an alliance with Corsica." "But, Sir," said I, "can we believe what he says?" "Yes, Sir," said Sir George, "the book is authentic and very accurate." I was highly pleased.

We went at night to the inn on Barnby Moor. We were now jumbled into old acquaintance. I felt myself quite strong, and exulted when I compared my present mind with my mind some years ago. Formerly my mind was quite a lodging-house for all ideas who chose to put up there, so that it was at the mercy of accident, for I had no fixed mind of my own. Now my mind is a house where, though the street rooms and the upper floors are open to strangers, yet there is always a settled family in the back parlour and sleeping-closet behind it; and this family can judge of the ideas which come to lodge. This family! this landlord, let me say, or this landlady, as the mind and the soul are both she. I shall confuse myself with metaphor. Let me then have done with it. Only this more. The ideas—my lodgers—are of all sorts. Some, gentlemen of the law, who pay me a great deal more than others. Divines of all sorts have been with me, and have ever disturbed me. When I first took up house, Presbyterian ministers used to make me melancholy with dreary tones. Methodists next shook my passions. Romish clergy filled me with solemn ideas, and, although their statues and many movable ornaments are gone, yet they drew some pictures upon my walls with such deep strokes that they still remain. They are, indeed, only agreeable ones. I had Deists for a very short while. But they, being sceptics, were perpetually alarming me with thoughts that my walls were made of clay and could not last, so I was glad to get rid of them. I am forced to own that my rooms have been occupied by women of the town, and by some ladies of abandoned manners. But I am resolved that by degrees there shall be only decent people and innocent, gay lodgers.

MONDAY 21 MARCH. I was now become quite composed, and never spoke for speaking's sake, or was uneasy because I was silent. The truth is I am now conscious of having attained to a superior character, and so rest satisfied. Robertson had read my *Corsica* and could tell a good deal about it. He sung pretty well, and in the chaise, when he thought I was not minding him, he hummed an amazing number of tunes.

TUESDAY 22 MARCH. About two we arrived at London and put up at the Star and Garter in Bond Street. The streets and squares of the metropolis with all the hurry and variety struck me to a certain degree, but by no means as they had once done, and I contentedly felt myself an Edinburgh advocate. Our Lord President, who had made us live with economy upon the road, finding that of twenty-nine guineas set apart for our expenses there remained two, would needs conclude the session with a jovial repast. Accordingly, we had a cod with oyster and shrimp sauce, some other dishes, and three bottles of the best claret I ever drank. Prentice and Rowden, the two landlords, were called in to take a glass, and in short we were great men. Upon the whole, it was as good a journey as ever was made; and, as in all other scenes, though words do but imperfectly preserve the ideas, yet such notes as I write are sufficient to make the impressions revive, with many associated ones. What should there be in this house but a club every Tuesday called the Roman Club, consisting of gentlemen who were at Rome the same year I was; and who should be upstairs alone but my friend Consul Dick? I sent to him, and he came down immediately. We embraced and in a few words renewed our covenant of cordiality. I then got into a hackney-coach and drove to Mr. Russel's, upholsterer, Half Moon Street, Piccadilly, where I had admirable lodgings. After unpacking my trunk, I sallied forth like a roaring lion after girls, blending philosophy and raking. I had a neat little lass *in armour,* at a tavern in the Strand. I then went to the Consul's and supped, and was quite hearty.

WEDNESDAY 23 MARCH. The Consul had provided me not only good lodgings, but a good servant. His name was Anthony Mudford, a Somersetshire lad who had served his time to a hairdresser. I gave him a guinea a week for everything. I called on Lord Mountstuart. But he was out of town. I waited on the Duke of Queensberry for ten minutes, as he had to dress to go to Court. He received me well, and assured me that Mr. Douglas would run no risk.

I had this morning been at Tyburn seeing the execution of Mr. Gibson, the attorney, for forgery, and of Benjamin Payne for highway robbery. It is a curious turn, but I never can resist seeing executions. The Abbé du Bos ingeniously shows that we have all a strong desire of having our passions moved, and the interesting scene of a man with death before his eyes cannot but move us greatly. One of weak nerves is overpowered by such spectacles. But by thinking and accustoming myself to them, I can see them quite firmly, though I feel compassion. I was on a scaffold close by. Payne was a poor young man of nineteen. He was pale as death, and half a corpse before the rope was put round his neck. Mr. Gibson came in a coach with some of his friends, and I declare I cannot conceive a more perfect calmness and manly resolution than his behaviour. He was dressed in a full suit of black, wore his own hair cut round and a hat, was a man about fifty, and as he drove along it was impossible to perceive the least sign of dejection or gloom about him. He was helped up on the cart. The rope was put round his neck, and he stood with the most perfect composure, eat a sweet orange, and seemed rationally devout during prayers by Mr. Moore, the ordinary of Newgate, who is really a good man and most earnest in the duties of his sad office, which I think a very important one. Stephen Roe, the last ordinary, was but a rough-spun blade. Never did I see death without some horror but in the case of Mr. Gibson. It seemed a very easy matter. I always use to compare the conduct of malefactors with what I suppose my conduct might be. I believe I confounded the people about me by my many reflections. I affected being shocked that punishment might have an effect on their minds, though it had none upon my own. I never saw a man hanged but I thought I could behave better than he did, except Mr. Gibson, who, I confess, exceeded all that I could ever hope to show of easy and steady resolution.

I run about all the forenoon, and got to Mr. Dilly's about three. It was comfortable to find myself in the shop where my book was published, and, from the great connection between author and bookseller, I was very kindly received.

We went to Guildhall to see the poll for members. It was really grand. Harley (Lord Mayor), Beckford, Trecothick, Sir Richard Glyn, Mr. Deputy Paterson, and Mr. Wilkes all stood upon the hustings, that is to say, a place raised by some steps at one end of the room. They had true London countenances. I cannot describe them. It was curious for me to look at Wilkes here and recollect my scenes with him at Rome, Naples, and Paris. The confusion and the noise of the mob roaring "Wilkes and Liberty" were prodigious. I met here Mr. Herries and Sir William Forbes, and, after having had enough of the confusion, I went to them and drank a glass of claret. They showed me my Corsican gun and pistols. But the dog had broken loose and was running about town. Thomas, Mr. Herries's servant, and Will, the butcher's man, and I went and patrolled an hour in the Borough, but did not see him. I returned by Dilly's and drank tea. Doctors Saunders and Smith were there. I found it to be a very hospitable house. In the Strand I enquired at the girls for a Miss Simson whom I had known formerly. One of them very obligingly went with me to a Miss Simson's. But she was not the same. However, they both seemed good-natured, and I sat and drank some port with them, and then tossed up which I should make my sultana. Luckily the lot fell on my obliging conductress. I however was *armed*.

THURSDAY 24 MARCH. I patrolled the great metropolis the whole morning. I dined at the worthy Consul's; a lady and a gentleman were there. We were easy enough. At night I still patrolled, I cannot tell where. But about ten I came to Sir John Pringle's. He received me with his usual grave, steady kindness. General Clerk was with him. The conversation turned on the wars of Venus. The General assured me that oil was an infallible shield. Sir John nodded assent; I resolved to try it fairly.

FRIDAY 25 MARCH. I dined at my good kinsman Godfrey Bosville, Esquire's. Nobody was there, but just the family that I left. He received me with true kindness. I then went to Covent Garden and in one of the courts called for a young lady whom I had seen when formerly in London. I did not find her but I found Kitty Brookes, as pretty a lively lass as youth need see. The oil was called and I played my part well. I never saw a girl more expert at it. I gave her only four shillings, to try her generosity, She never made the least sign of discontent, but was quite gay and obliging. Just as I was going away I turned back and again we loved. Then was the time for her to ask something. Yet she made not the smallest advance. I fell on my knees and kissed her hand: "My dear Kitty, you are a virtuous girl. I could marry you this moment."

I then came home, and Maconochie and I went to Percy Coffee-house, Rathbone Place, to meet Mr. Guthrie, the historian and Critical Reviewer, who had fought the battle of Douglas in the *Review*, and had praised my *Account of Corsica*. He was an old gentleman about sixty, had on a white coat and a crimson satin waistcoat with broad gold lace, and a bag-wig. We had port and madeira and a hearty supper. He had a great deal of the London author. He praised my book much, and drank a bumper to Pascal Paoli, *omni titulo major*. He told me he and my father had been at the same class in the College.

He praised my *Account of Corsica* much, though he found some faults with it. "You will see my opinion of it," said he. It was curious to sit with the very person whom in a little I should look upon as an awful reviewer. He took me by the hand and said my conversation exceeded my writing. "Well," said he, "you are a genius. A thousand people might have thought of making themselves famous before one would have thought of Corsica." He asked Maconochie and me to dine with him on the Sunday sennight. When the old man praised my book, I paid him a very genteel compliment. "Sir," said I, "amidst such historic oaks as yours, it is well if a little praise can be given to such a shrub as mine, growing on the rocky surface of Corsica."

SATURDAY 26 MARCH. On my coming to London I had called on Mr. Samuel Johnson, but found he was gone to Oxford and was living at New Inn Hall. I was very anxious to see again my revered friend. I had written him many letters and had received none from him of a long time. I had published my *Account of Corsica,* in which I had spoken very highly of him, yet he had taken no notice of it. I had heard he was displeased at my having put into my book a part of one of his letters to me. In short, I was quite in the dark concerning him. But, be it as it would, I was determined to find him out, and if possible be well with him as usual. I therefore set out early this morning in the Oxford fly.

I immediately had some coffee and then got a guide to show me New Inn Hall. Mr. Johnson lived in the house of Mr. Chambers, the head of that hall and Vinerian Professor at Oxford. I supposed the professor would be very formal, and I apprehended but an awkward reception. However, I rung and was shown into the parlour. In a little, down came Mr. Chambers, a lively, easy, agreeable Newcastle man. I had sent up my name, "Mr. Boswell". After receiving me very politely, "Sir," said he, "you are Mr. Boswell of Auchinleck?" "Yes, Sir." "Mr. Johnson wrote to you yesterday. He dined abroad, but I expect him in every minute." "Oho!" thought I, "this is excellent." I was quite relieved. Mr. Chambers gave me tea, and by and by arrived the great man. He took me all in his arms and kissed me on both sides of the head, and was as cordial as ever I saw him. I told him all my perplexity on his account, and how I had come determined to fight him, or to do anything he pleased. "What," said he, "did you come here on purpose?" "Yes, indeed," said I. This gave him high satisfaction. I told him how I was settled as a lawyer and how I had made two hundred pounds by the law this year. He grumbled and laughed and was wonderfully pleased. "What, Bozzy? Two hundred pounds! A great deal."

I had longed much to see him as my great preceptor, to state to him some difficulties as a moralist with regard to the profession of the law, as it appeared to me that in some respects it hurt the principles of honesty; and I asked him if it did not. "Why, no, Sir," said he, "if you act properly. You are not to deceive your clients with false representations of your opinion. You are not to tell lies to a judge." "But," said I, "what do you think of pleading a cause which you know to be bad?" "Sir, you don't know it to be bad till the judge determines it. I have said that you are to state your facts fairly; so that your thinking, or what you call knowing, a cause to be bad must be from reasoning, must be from thinking your arguments weak and inconclusive. But, Sir, that is not enough. An argument which does not convince you yourself may convince the judge before whom you plead it; and if it does convince him, why, then, Sir, you are wrong and he is right. It is his business to judge, and you are not to be confident in your opinion, but to say all you can for your client and then hear the judge's opinion." "But, Sir," said I, "does not the putting on a warmth when you have no warmth, and appearing to be clearly of one opinion when you are in reality of another, does not such dissimulation hurt one's honesty? Is there not some danger that one may put on the same mask in common life, in the intercourse with one's friends?" "Why, no, Sir. Everybody knows you are paid for putting on a warmth for your client, and it is properly no dissimulation. The moment you come from the bar you resume your usual behaviour. Sir, a man will no more carry the artifice of the bar into the common intercourse of society than a man who is paid for tumbling upon his hands will continue tumbling upon his hands when he ought to be walking on his feet." Wonderful force and fancy. At once he satisfied me as to a thing which had often and often perplexed me.

I told Mr. Johnson a story which I should have recorded before this time. The day before I left London, coming through Bloomsbury Square and being dressed in green and gold, I was actually taken for Wilkes by a Middlesex voter who came up to me. "Sir, I beg pardon, is not your name Wilkes?" "Yes, Sir." "I thought so. I saw you upon the hustings and I thought I knew you again. Sir, I'm your very good friend; I've got you five and twenty votes today." I bowed and grinned and thanked him, and talked of liberty and general warrants and I don't know what all. I told him too, between ourselves, that the King had a very good opinion of me. I ventured to ask how he could be sure that I was a right man and acted from public spirit. He was a little puzzled. So I helped him out. "As to my private character, it would take a long time to explain it. But, Sir, if I were the devil, I have done good to the people of England, and they ought to support me." "Ay," said he. I am vexed I did not make more of this curious incident. After carrying my voter half-way down Long Acre, I stopped and looked him gravely in the face. "Sir, I must tell you a secret. I'm not Mr. Wilkes, and what's more, I'm a Scotsman." He stared not a little, and said, "Sir, I beg pardon for having given you so much trouble." "No, Sir," said I, "you have been very good company to me." I wonder he did not beat me. I said to Mr. Johnson that I never before knew that I was so ugly a fellow. He was angry at me that I did not borrow money from the voter. Indeed, it would have made a fine scene at Brentford when he demanded payment of the real Wilkes, and called him a rogue for denying the debt.

I spoke of Guthrie. "Sir," said Mr. Johnson, "he has parts. He has no great regular fund of knowledge, but by reading so long and writing so long he no doubt has picked up a good deal." The great man still retained his prejudice against Scotland. The night before, he told us he had lately been a long while at Lichfield, but had wearied sadly. "I wonder at that," said I; "it is your native place." "Why," said he, "so is Scotland your native place." This night I talked of our advances in literature. "Sir," said he, "you have learnt a little from us, and you think yourselves very great men." Hume I knew he would abuse. "Sir," said he, "Hume would never have written history had not Voltaire written it before him. He is an echo of Voltaire." "But Sir," said I, "we have lord Kames." "You have Lord Kames," said he; "keep him, ha! ha! ha! We don't envy you him. Do you ever see Dr. Robertson?" BOSWELL. "Yes." JOHNSON. "Does the dog ever talk of me?" BOSWELL. "Indeed he does, and loves you." He said the severest thing of Robertson without intending it, for I pushed him to say what he thought of Robertson's *History*. "Sir," said he, "I love Robertson, and I won't talk of his book." He was very hard on poor Dr. Blair, whom he holds wonderfully cheap for having written *A Dissertation on Ossian*. Talking of the future life of brutes, "Sir," said he, "if you allow Blair's soul to be immortal, why not allow a dog to be immortal?" I wanted much to defend the pleasing system of brutes existing in the other world. Mr. Johnson, who does not like to hear any ideas of futurity but what are in the Thirty-nine Articles, was out of humour with me, and watched his time to give me a blow. So when I, with a serious, metaphysical, pensive face, ventured to say, "But really, Sir, when we see a very sensible dog, we know not what to think of him," he turned about, and growling with joy replied, "No, Sir; and when we see a very foolish fellow, we don't know what to think of him." Then up he got, bounced along, and stood by the fire, laughing and exulting over me, while I took it to myself and had only to say, "Well, but you do not know what to think of a very sensible dog." About twelve they left me.

MONDAY 28 MARCH. I breakfasted with Mr. Stewart. Then he and I went to Mr. Chambers's and found him and Mr. Johnson drinking tea. I talked of the scorpion killing itself when encircled with hot coals. Mr. Johnson said that Maupertuis is of opinion that it does not kill itself, but dies of the heat, and that its clapping its tail to its head is merely a convulsion from the excessive pain, and it does not sting itself. I told him I had often tried the experiment, that it ran round and round, and finding no outlet retired to the centre, and, like a true Stoic philosopher, gave itself the fatal sting to free itself from its woes. "This will end 'em." I said it was a curious fact, as it showed suicide in an insect. Mr. Johnson would not admit the fact. I said I would write to the great Morgagni, the anatomist, and get him to examine the head of one after the experiment, and to tell whether it was stung or not. Mr. Johnson said the report of Morgagni would convince him. I shall certainly try to get it. Mr. Johnson said that the woodcocks fly over to the northern countries, which is proved because they have been observed at sea. He said swallows certainly sleep all the winter; many of them conglobulate themselves by flying round and round, and then all in a heap throw themselves under water, and lie in the bed of a river. This appeared strange to me. I know not if Mr. Johnson was well founded in it. Our conversation was quite on natural philosophy. Mr. Johnson told us one of his first essays was a Latin poem on the glow-worm.

I then talked of law and of our courts of justice in Scotland, of which I gave them a very good account. I found that having been two years a lawyer in real business had given me great force. I could not be sensible of it, while living always with the same people. But I felt it when I was with Mr. Johnson.

Mr. Stewart went home with me. Riall, an honest Irishman who had studied civil law with me at Glasgow, came and saw me. He was now become a divine. We all three went to dine at Dr. Smith's. He had several more company; among the rest, Dr. Wilmot of Trinity, a pleasant, jovial parson who loves hunting and a glass dearly. He was well acquainted with Mr. Johnson, and said he submitted patiently to be bruised by him in order to enjoy his conversation. I had drank tea with Mr. Stewart in an Oxford coffee-house, while he listened to a wonderful variety of anecdotes which I gave him. Said he: "You are an extraordinary man, and have had extraordinary good fortune in meeting with such a singular variety. It has been said that Mr. Johnson is a walking library. You are a walking collection of men." Mr. Chambers was not come in when we came to his house. Mr. Johnson came and entertained us, bowed and said, "Your servant, gentlemen," and was really courteous.

The house is a good one, and genteelly furnished. We talked of the Chinese and Russians. Mr. Johnson advised me to read Bell's *Travels*. I asked him if I should read Du Halde's *China*. "Why, yes," said he, "as one reads such a book; that is to say, consult it." When Mr. Chambers came we had a good supper. Mr. Johnson was excellent company. He laughed a good deal. I really found him more cheerful and gay. His mixing more in society had dissipated much of that gloom which hung upon his mind when he lived much alone, when he brooded in the Temple.

We talked of adultery. Mr. Johnson showed how highly criminal it was, because it broke the peace of families and introduced confusion of progeny. "These constitute the essence of the crime, and therefore a woman who breaks her marriage vows is so much more criminal than a man. A man, to be sure, is criminal in the sight of God, but he does not do his wife a very material injury if he does not insult her; if, for instance, from mere wantonness of appetite, he steals privately to her chamber-maid. Sir, a wife ought not greatly to resent this. I should not receive home a daughter who had run away from her husband on that account. A wife should study to reclaim her husband by more attention to please him. Sir, a man will not once in a hundred instances leave his wife and go to a harlot, if his wife has not been negligent of pleasing." "Upon my word," said I, "he is grown liberal upon our hand." "But," said Mr. Chambers, "suppose a husband goes a-whoring, and then poxes his wife." "Why Sir, if he poxes her, it is a bodily injury, and she may resent it as she pleases."

I asked him if it was not hard that one deviation from chastity should so absolutely ruin a woman. JOHNSON. "Why, no, Sir; the great principle which every woman is taught is to keep her legs together. When she has given up that principle, she has given up every notion of female honour and virtue, which are all included in chastity." I argued that virtue might be found even in a common street-walker. He laughed, and as I had told him of my Dutch lady, "Why," said he "I shall have the Dutch lady; you can get a wife in the streets." I told him my objections to the Dutch lady were her superior talents. "O Sir," said he, "you need not be afraid, marry her; before a year goes about you'll find that reason much weaker, and that wit not near so bright." O admirable master of human nature!

At Henley we came out and went and looked at the machine with which they are levelling a very steep hill on the London side, by digging it down and throwing the earth into the hollow at the bottom. This is done without horses, by two carts which are contrived to work as buckets in a well. There is a road cut down the hill, they having begun at the foot of it, and cut upwards as they removed the earth. A number of men dig the earth and throw it into the cart, to which a strong rope is fixed, which is wound upon a horizontal wheel above the face of the hill yet entire. The moment the cart is full, a bell is rung to warn the man at the bottom of the hill, who then lets go the cart which he has emptied into the hollow. Then two men go, one on each side of the loaded cart (or but one for each cart, I forget which. I now recollect the two men on each side of the loaded cart only set it a-going), for a little way and push it along; then one returns to his companions, and one goes along with the cart, guiding it till he gets to the brink of the deep bottom; then he has a long piece of wood fixed to the cart, but so as to be twisted about. This he twists till he fixes the end of it between two spokes of the left wheel, and so stops the cart.

In the meantime the weight of the loaded cart going down the hill pulls up the empty cart, which is filled, and then pulls up the other. The wheel to which the rope is fixed is so made as not to turn too quickly; so it lets down the cart at a moderate pace. At three or four different places there are across the road double horizontal trees, or long pieces of wood, which are fixed by swinging ligatures or insertions in notches to a post. Upon these trees the rope is put to preserve it from trailing and being rubbed on the hill. The man who guides each cart runs now and then a little before it. He who goes down runs to draw out the tree on one side to receive the rope. He who goes up runs to draw out the tree to receive the rope on the other side; and as the one side is drawn out, the other falls in, and it is so contrived that by these means the ropes are always kept at a proper elevation. This method was invented lately by a Dissenting clergyman at Henley. It is exceedingly useful, by making that be done by two men which would require a great number of horses and oxen.

Brentford, [then] home. Sallied [out in search of] Kitty. Borrowed [money] from Matthew; raged. Then Dun's, left watch and purse, and had [only a] crown. Wanted two [whores] like Bolingbroke. Got red-haired hussy; went to Bob Derry's, had brandy and water. She went for companion; found her not. Then once. Then home with her. Watchman lighted us, and she paid penny. Horrid room; no fire, no curtains, dirty sheets, &c. All night; three here.

WEDNESDAY 30 MARCH. About six in the morning I decamped. I was despicable in my own opinion for having been in the very sink of vice. I walked about a while and looked at the windows.

I called this morning on Mrs. Macaulay. She was denied, but her servant came running after me: "Sir, my mistress is at home to Mr. Boswell." I was shown into her study, where she was sitting in a kind of

Spanish dress. Two gentlemen were with her, who went away. She was very complimentative to me, but formal and affected, and she whined about liberty as an old Puritan would whine about grace. In short, I was rather disgusted with her.

[received c. 26 April]

Oxford, 23 March 1768

MY DEAR BOSWELL,—I have omitted a long time to write to you, without knowing very well why. I could now tell why I should not write; for who would write to men who publish letters of their friends without their leave? Yet I write to you in spite of my caution to tell you that I shall be glad to see you, and that I wish you would empty your head of Corsica, which I think has filled it rather too long. But, at all events, I shall be glad, very glad, to see you. I am, Sir, yours affectionately,

SAM JOHNSON.

[Boswell to Johnson]

London, 26 April 1768

MY DEAR SIR,—I have received your last letter, which, though very short and by no means complimentary, yet gave me real pleasure, because it contains these words, "I shall be glad, very glad, to see you." Surely you have no reason to complain of my publishing a single paragraph of one of your letters; the temptation to it was so strong. An irrevocable grant of your friendship, and your dignifying my desire of visiting Corsica with the epithet of "a wise and noble curiosity", are to me more valuable than many of the grants of kings.

But how can you bid me "empty my head of Corsica"? My noble-minded friend, do you not feel for an oppressed nation bravely struggling to be free? Consider fairly what is the case. The Corsicans never received any kindness from the Genoese. They never agreed to be subject to them. They owe them nothing; and when reduced to an abject state of slavery by force, shall they not rise in the great cause of liberty and break the galling yoke? And shall not every liberal soul be warm for them? Empty my head of Corsica! Empty it of honour, empty it of humanity, empty it of friendship, empty it of piety. No! while I live, Corsica and the cause of the brave Islanders shall ever employ much of my attention, shall ever interest me in the sincerest manner. . . . I am, &c.

JAMES BOSWELL.

SUNDAY 1 MAY. I talked of not writing till the very day a paper was needed; "because then," said I, "one runs downhill. Till then, one is labouring up the hill, but one is at the top the moment the point of necessity is reached. To write before that is double fatigue; but I must do so for my clients, lest running too quick downhill I miss something. Slowly going up, I take all." . . .

MONDAY 2 MAY. Morning, letter from Zélide; termagant! . . . Sent note to David Hume. He came, was most placid. Said it required great goodness of disposition to withstand baleful effects of Christianity. . . . Just then entered Mr. Johnson. I jumped [up] and embraced [him, crying] "Thou great man!" JOHNSON. "Don't call names." He would not dine; had bad spirits. I run on about the praise of my book. JOHNSON. "Sir, your book is very well. The *Account* may be had more from other books. But the *Tour* is extremely well. It entertains everybody. Sir, everybody who wishes you well [is] pleased." Asked him to review. JOHNSON. "No, one ass [should not] scratch [another]." . . . [Talk of] liberty. JOHNSON. "Sir, they mistake [in ranting about] universal liberty without [considering] private. Political liberty is only as many private [persons] as can be happy. Liberty of press not much. Suppose you and I and two hundred more restrained: what then? What proportion?" BOSWELL. "Ay, but [suppose] ten thousand [restrained] from reading us?" JOHNSON. "Yes, they are the wretches [to be pitied.] . . .

SATURDAY 14 MAY. Mr. Kennedy, then Sir John Dick and Captain Medows. I talked of some things though [they are] in my book. I have observed Mr. Johnson do so. Almost every man you meet is, either from not having read or [from] having forgotten, just as if he had never seen a book. Sir John Pringle, Dr. Franklin, Mr. Rose, [and] Mr. Burgh dined. All was elegant. You maintained [author should] never correct [his] book. Sir John opposed. "But," said I, "Lord Kames has made [his] *Elements of Criticism* so 'tis not the same book." SIR JOHN. "Then it's another book"—very well. Burgh [was] always saying, "Ah, that came off so fine and dry!" and Sir John [sat] with leg crossed and [talked with] shrewd gravity and satisfaction. You was quite happy and pleased *as a man*.

SUNDAY 15 MAY. Baretti talked strongly against our liberty. BARETTI. "Had you been content like other nations to have just jogged on, with sometimes a good king, sometimes a worse, you'd have done very well, as other nations. But to please your mad notions of claims of right, you did an unjust and barbarous thing to turn away your king, and sacrificed four hundred of the best families, and by restraining the king's power so much you force him and his ministers to load you with taxes to purchase power which they ought to have."

He argued for the Italian ceremonies. "They are innocent," said he, "and our people are better so than yours, who get into taverns with whores and bottles and pots of beer." "But," said I, "the mind is hurt by that kind of idolatry, and drawn from just notions of God." "Nay," said he, "has any common people just notions of God?" "Yes," said I, "the people here." "No," said he, "they never think of God but with 'damn' joined it." He was really well tonight.

FRIDAY 20 MAY. Called at Mansfield's. I was received. My Lord came forward and took [me] by the hand very courteously: "Mr. Boswell, your servant. I am glad I was at home. I should have been very sorry not to have seen you." I said, "My Lord, your Lordship never took any man by the hand who is more truly proud to have the honour of waiting upon your Lordship than I am." After talking of my having been ill, thus went the dialogue. MANSFIELD. "You have travelled a great deal, Sir." BOSWELL. "Why, yes, my Lord, I was very fond of seeing as much as I could, and travelled as much as my father would allow me." MANSFIELD. "Pray, Sir, how did you leave your father?" BOSWELL. "Very well, my Lord."

SUNDAY 22 MAY. Between eight and nine at night went to Lord Mansfield's, being his levée. Found him alone; drank a dish of tea with him. He was quite easy with me.

In a little, my Lord Oxford came. Then Lord Mansfield assumed all the state of a chief justice. Went to the opposite side of the room and sat by my Lord, and kept me down as I tried to speak. I was *étourdi* enough to talk of Wilkes, which Lord Mansfield did *not* relish. When Lord Oxford went, Lord Mansfield became quite easy again. Came close to me and resumed his urbanity.

[In June Boswell returned to his home country, Edinburgh and Auchinleck, where he remained until leaving for Ireland in the spring of 1769.]

[Agreement between James Boswell and Margaret Montgomerie]

AT EDINBURGH, the eighth day of August one thousand seven hundred and sixty-eight years, I, Margaret Montgomerie, sister of the late James Montgomerie of Lainshaw, Esquire, considering that Mr. James Boswell, advocate, my cousin, is at present so much in love with me that I might certainly have him for my lawful husband if I choose it, and the said James being of a temper so inconstant that there is reason to fear that he would repent of his choice in a very short time, on which account he is unwilling to trust himself in my company; therefore, I, the said Margaret Montgomerie, hereby agree that in case I am married to the said James Boswell any time this year, or insist upon his promise thereto within the said time to take place any time thereafter, I shall submit to be banished out of Great Britain during all the days of my life. In witness whereof I have subscribed this paper written by the said James Boswell.

MARGT. MONTGOMERIE.

[Boswell to Temple, 24 August 1768]

I am exceedingly lucky in having escaped the insensible Miss Blair and the furious Zélide, for I have now seen the finest creature that ever was formed: *la belle Irlandaise*. Figure to yourself, Temple, a young lady just sixteen, formed like a Grecian nymph with the sweetest countenance, full of sensibility, accomplished, with a Dublin education, always half the year in the north of Ireland, her father a counsellor-at-law with an estate of £1,000 a year and above £10,000 in ready money. Her mother a sensible, well-bred woman. She the darling of her parents, and no other child but her sister. She is cousin to some cousins of mine in this county. I was at their house while she and her father, mother, and aunt were over upon a visit just last week. The Counsellor is as worthy a gentleman as ever I saw. Your friend was a favourite with all of them. From morning to night I admired the charming Mary Ann. Upon my honour, I never was so much in love. I never was before in a situation to which there was not some objection. But "here every flower is united", and not a thorn to be found. But how shall I manage it?

In the meantime both the father and the aunt write to me. What a fortunate fellow am I! What variety of adventures in all countries! I was allowed to walk a great deal with Miss. I repeated my fervent passion to her, again and again. She was pleased, and I could swear that her little heart beat. I carved the first letter of her name on a tree. I cut off a lock of her hair, *male pertinaci*. She promised not to forget me, not to marry a lord before March. Her aunt said to me, "Mr. Boswell, I tell you seriously there will be no fear of this succeeding, but from your own inconstancy. Stay till March." All the Scotch cousins too think I may be the happy man. Ah! my friend, I am now as I ought to be. No reserved, prudent, cautious conduct as with Miss Blair. No, all youthful, warm, natural; love. Pray tell me what you think. I have a great confidence in your judgment. I mean not to ask what you think of my angelic girl. I am fixed beyond a possibility of doubt as to her. Believe me, she is like a part of my very soul. But will not the fond parents insist on having quality for their daughter, who is to have so large a fortune? Or do you think that the Baron of Auchinleck is great enough? Both father, mother, and aunt assured me of my high character in Ireland, where my book is printed, the "third" edition. That is no bad circumstance. I shall see in what style the Counsellor writes, and shall send some elegant present to my lovely mistress.

This is the most agreeable passion I ever felt. Sixteen, innocence, and gaiety make me quite a Sicilian swain. Before I left London, I made a vow in St. Paul's Church that I would not allow myself in licentious connections of any kind for six months. I am hitherto firm to my vow, and already feel myself a superior being. I have given up my criminal intercourse with Mrs. ———. In short, Maria has me without any rival. I do hope the period of my perfect felicity as far as this state of being can afford is now in view.

The affairs of the brave Corsicans interest me exceedingly. Is it not shocking in France to send a great armament against such a noble little people? I have had four letters from the General this summer. He and his countrymen are resolved to stand to the last. I have hopes that our Government will interfere. In the meantime by a private subscription in Scotland I am this week sending £700 worth of ordnance. The Carron Company has furnished me them very cheap. There are two 32 pounders, four 24's, four 18's, and twenty 9 pounders, with one hundred fifty ball to each. It is really a tolerable train of artillery. . . .

And now, my dear friend, I trust that you will forgive my long silence and will be assured that I ever am, with the warmest regard, your affectionate and faithful

JAMES BOSWELL.

[Boswell to Temple, 9 December 1768]

And now as to myself. What think you, my friend, Miss Blair is Miss Blair still. Her marriage with the Knight is not to be. I understand that when terms came to be considered, neither answered the expectations which they had formed of each other's circumstances, and so the match was broken off. After the departure of my *belle Irlandaise,* I was two or three times at Adamton and, upon my word, the old flame was kindled. The *wary mother,* as you called her, told me that it was my own fault that her daughter was not long ago my wife. But that after the young lady had shown me very particular marks of regard, corresponded with me, &c., I had made such a joke of *my love for the Heiress* in every company that she was piqued and did not believe that I had any serious intentions. That in the meantime the Knight offered, and what could she do? Temple, to a man again in love this was engaging. I walked whole hours with the Princess. I kneeled; I became truly amorous. But she told me that really she had a very great regard for me, but did not like me so as to marry me. You never saw such coldness. Yet the Nabob told me upon his honour and salvation that he had it from one who had it from Miss Blair's own mouth last year that she was truly in love with me, and reckoned upon having me for her husband.

My relapse into this fever lasted some weeks. I wrote to her as usual the most passionate letters. I said, "I shall not again have the galling reflection that my misery is owing to my own fault." Only think of this, Temple. She might have had me. But luckily for me she still affected the same coldness, and not a line would she write. Then came a kind letter from my amiable Aunt Boyd in Ireland, and all the charms of sweet Marianne revived. Since that time I have been quite constant to her, and as indifferent towards Kate as if I never had thought of her. She is still in the country. Should I write to her and tell her that I am cured as she wished? Or is there more dignity in just letting the affair sleep? After her behaviour, do I, the candid, generous Boswell, owe her anything? Am I anyhow bound by passionate exclamations to which she did not even answer? Write to me immediately, my dear friend. She will be here soon. I am quite easy with her. What should I do? By all that's enchanting I go to Ireland in March. What should I say to Kate? You see I am still the old man. I have still need of your advice. Write me without delay. I shall soon give you a more general epistle.

Adieu, my dearest friend. My kind compliments to Mrs. Temple. Ever yours,

JAMES BOSWELL.

P.S. I am just now a good deal in debt. If you want any credit from me, let me know some weeks before. Excuse this. Whatever I can do you may always depend on.

TUESDAY 25 APRIL. Miss Montgomerie and I set out from Auchinleck. My father was so averse to my Irish expedition that she had not resolution to agree to accompany me. Dr. Johnston took leave of me, and seemed most anxious for my safe return. My father walked out, and I did not take leave of him. It was a delightful day. We were calm and social. We came to Treesbank at four. Mr. Campbell had been at a burial, so dinner was not begun. We were cordially entertained, and very merry here.

WEDNESDAY 26 APRIL. I gave up my place in the Lainshaw chaise to Lady Treesbank, and rode my mare. Miss Annie Cuninghame was with us. We came to Lainshaw to dinner. The Captain said he would fulfil his promise of going to Portpatrick with me. This left no objection to Miss Montgomerie's going, especially as both her sisters were clear for it. This was a great point gained to me. I felt myself quite at home at Lainshaw.

THURSDAY 27 APRIL. Drink makes men appear numerous. We feel double as well as see double. Mrs. Montgomerie-Cuninghame and Mrs. Campbell came out to us and brought us home. I was quite drunk. I am sorry for it. I behaved ill to Margaret, my own affectionate friend. Such terrible effects may intoxication have.

FRIDAY 28 APRIL. I rose with a headache and the disagreeable reflection that I had offended Margaret. When she came down I found her so much hurt that she would not have set out on our Irish jaunt, had she not been so kind that she would not assign the cause of her staying. I was very sorry, and resolved to make up to her for what she had suffered by my future good behaviour. We took some breakfast at Lainshaw; and then we and the Captain, Mrs. Montgomerie-Cuninghame, and Lady Treesbank all drove to Irvine, where Mr. Graham had breakfast ready for us at his house. On the road it was curious for me to think how different things in reality may be from what they appear. Margaret and I on bad terms were yet driving in one chaise, and going on a jaunt of pleasure all the way to Dublin. But the quarrels of friends never last.

SATURDAY 29 APRIL. I felt myself in love with another woman than Marianne. I spoke of it to Margaret. She is always my friend and comforter. She and I were now admirable company. I observed that there were few people but were mixed characters, like a candle: half wax, half tallow. But Sir Adam Fergusson was all wax, a pure taper, whom you may light and set upon any lady's table. I observed that she and I had more enlarged views, as we had fancy to look beyond what really is ours—like one whose house has a prospect not only of his own lands, but of many beautiful objects at a distance. When I talked that Corsica was a very hilly country, Margaret observed that the French would have *uphill* work there.

We came at night to Ardmillan. Mr. Craufurd we had met going to Ayr, and he could not be home; but we found his mother, a fine old lady full of life, an Episcopal and a Jacobite, and his three sisters. We were most hospitably entertained, but my serious passion hung heavily on my mind. I feared that the lady was engaged, and I was in great uneasiness all night.

SUNDAY 30 APRIL. I was restless and rose at six, and walked to the top of the highest mountain, from whence I saw a great way. The sea and Aisla pleased me. Ardmillan stands at the foot of a hill. There is little planting about it. But a good garden, some fields in excellent culture, and pretty green hills with a prospect as far as Ireland. The old lady and I were great friends. I read part of the service of the day to her, and took her prayer-book with me that I might get silver clasps put upon it at Dublin. No man ever understood the little arts of obliging better than I do, and the peculiar beauty in my case is that what others have done from designing views, I do from an amiable disposition to make people happy. No doubt, I have sometimes had my designs, too. But, in general, I have none.

The Captain found himself fatigued, so Miss Montgomerie and I agreed that he should go no farther. We dined here, and at four we set out and took a Sabbath day's journey to Ballantrae. By the way, my serious passion came into my mind with more force than ever. I imagined that Miss Montgomerie knew the lady's mind, and from some things she said I concluded that the lady was engaged. I was amazingly affected. I cried bitterly, and would not speak to my companion. I, who was on an expedition to court a pretty young lady at Dublin, and had with me a most agreeable companion, was miserable from love of another woman, and would not speak to my companion. Such a mind! I never was in greater torment, nor indulged gloomier schemes. We had a good inn at Ballantrae. For ten minutes I continued as bad as in the chaise, till Miss Montgomerie by chance discovered the cause of all my misery, and with her usual kindness assured me that I was mistaken. I then enjoyed the most delightful calm after a dismal storm. We drank tea comfortably after our journey, read part of the evening service, had some agreeable religious conversation, and then supped cheerfully. I was so much rejoiced that, after she went to bed, I got Mactaggart the landlord to drink with me till I staggered. Such wild transitions! A punster would say the landlord might be called *Macstaggered*.

MONDAY 1 MAY. My last night's riot hurt me a little. I begged my companion's pardon, we breakfasted, and set out in good humour. I entertained my companion with stories of Mr. Samuel Johnson, and we walked up the monstrous hill of Glen App very cleverly. We stopped at _____, a place now Sir Thomas Wallace's, formerly a Colonel Agnew's. It is just a piece of low ground gradually descending from the bottom of a range of hills. There is a neat house, and the most is made of the space that ever I saw, there being a fine garden with variety of flowers and fruit both on standards and walls, fish-ponds, and a few pretty enclosures. The sea is just before it, and the avenue is in the old style. I had a great desire to buy this place. It was such a one as I had often fancied in a romantic mood, and I thought I and my companion could live at it most happily.

We drank tea, and then they walked down with us to the port, where we engaged a boat, the *James and* _____, Captain Cosh, commander, to carry us to the other side of the water. As we knew we would be sick, we determined to sail that night and try to sleep, as there was a good cabin. We had our company to sup with us, and were very well. Mr. Campbell of Airies, the collector of the customs here, arrived at home about eleven, and came to us. I had not seen him for seventeen years. We were very cordial. At twelve my companion and I went aboard. I tried to brave it out for a while, but grew very sick. She was better than I. Only I got some sleep, which she did not. Nothing can be severer than to be sick at sea, for one has no hope that immediate relief may come, as in other sicknesses. One grows quite weak. I thought my Irish jaunt madness, and that I would not try another. Such are our minds at times. It was a very moderate breeze. We got over in about five hours.

TUESDAY 2 MAY. It was pleasant to see the Irish shore. . . .

WEDNESDAY 3 MAY. Mrs. Boyd carried Miss Montgomerie and me to wait of the Countess Dowager Mount Alexander, a French lady, who was first married to a peer of France, and afterwards to Lord Mount Alexander, by whom she has a great estate about Donaghadee. She is a fine, lively old lady, has been much in the gay world, but lives now quite retired and dresses like a common farmer's wife. But as she has read a great deal, she is very good company. I should have mentioned that Mrs. Boyd and Miss Montgomerie had last night resolved not to go with me to Dublin. This vexed me much; and, although I said nothing, they saw me in such an humour that they this morning agreed to attend me. Our day passed very comfortably. We had with us at tea and supper a Mr. Sempill and his two daughters. I was really pleased to hear the Irish tone. But, being still sincerely in love with one whom I do not name, I was vastly uneasy in being distracted between that passion and my Irish schemes.

Donaghadee, 3 May 1769

MY DEAR TEMPLE,— I am fairly landed in the kingdom of Ireland, and am tomorrow to proceed for Dublin to see my sweet Mary Ann. But, my worthy friend, to whom my heart is ever open and to whom I must apply for advice at all times, I must tell you that I am accompanied by my cousin Miss Montgomerie, whom I believe you saw at Edinburgh, and she perhaps may and perhaps ought to prevent my Hibernian nuptials. You must know that she and I have always been in the greatest intimacy. I have proved her on a thousand occasions, and found her sensible, agreeable, and generous. When I was not in love with some one or other of my numerous flames, I have been in love with her; and during the intervals of all my passions Margaret has been constantly my mistress as well as my friend. Allow me to add that her person is to me the most desirable that I ever saw. Often have I thought of marrying her, and often told her so. But we talked of my wonderful inconstancy, were merry, and perhaps in two days after the most ardent professions to her I came and told her that I was desperately in love with another woman. Then she smiled, was my confidante, and in time I returned to herself.

She is with all this, Temple, the most honest, undesigning creature that ever existed.

Well, Sir, being my cousin german, she accompanies me on my Irish expedition. I found her both by sea and land the best companion I ever saw. I am exceedingly in love with her. I highly value her. If ever a man had his full choice of a wife, I would have it in her. But the objections are she is two years older than I. She has only a thousand pounds. My father would be violent against my marrying her, as she would bring neither money nor interest. I, from a desire to aggrandise my family, think somewhat in the same manner. And all my gay projects of bringing home some blooming young lady and making an *éclat* with her brilliant fortune would be gone.

And yet my charming seraph, my Marianne, melts my heart. Her little bosom beats at the thoughts of seeing me—forgive my vanity—you know, strange as it may be, that women of all tempers and ages have been fond of me. Temple, you never failed me yet. What shall I do? This is the most delicate case of the many that I have laid before you. I must, however, tell you that my father is quite averse to Marianne, and declares he never will agree to it. But if *her* father gives me a round sum, I do not fear *mine*. But if I am certain that my cousin sincerely loves me, wishes to have me, and would be unhappy without me, what should I do?

FRIDAY 5 MAY. I showed Miss Montgomerie a letter I had written to Temple to have his advice how to proceed in my distracted war of passions. She would not allow me to send it. But convinced me that the other lady was of so generous a temper that I might marry anyone I liked best, or found most for my interest, and she would even help me to do so. I admired the other lady from the bottom of my heart, and all that Miss Montgomerie told me of her with intention to make me easy only served to distract me more, as it showed me more of her excellent character.

SATURDAY 6 MAY. Lisburn is one of the prettiest towns I ever saw. The High Street is a good breadth, and consists of admirable brick houses, all inhabited by substantial people. We dined there. A Counsellor Smyth, formerly their Member, said to Miss Macbride that if I was come over to raise contributions for the Corsicans a considerable sum might be raised in Lisburn. I saw here a very odd sign: "Groceries, liquors, and coffins sold here." I made Miss Montgomerie look at it, lest my telling it should appear the report of a traveller.

At Lisburn I visited my old acquaintance, Dr. Traill, Bishop of Down and Connor. I was a very little while with him. He told me that, when he read in my *Tour to Corsica* that I had played to the brave Islanders on my flute, he thought how he had made me a present of it.

[Boswell has now returned to Edinburgh.]

SATURDAY 17 JUNE. The reports concerning the Corsicans were various. I was uneasy. Grange brought me Mr. Macdonald, an obliging and clever surgeon, to take care of me. I passed part of the forenoon at Lord Mountstuart's, but was both ill and low-spirited. So sent an apology to Mr. David Ross, where I was engaged to dine, and stayed quietly at home. Was very gloomy. Wrote to *my lady*.

SUNDAY 18 JUNE. Lay quiet abed all day. Was calm. Sir George Preston, Dr. Webster, and Grange visited me.

MONDAY 19 JUNE. The Commissioner dined. I had mentioned *my lady* by the by to many as a supposable case, if I had spirit to overcome my mercenary views. All approved. Even the Commissioner and Mr. Stobie were not against it. The Lieutenant indeed was. I stayed at home all day and was rather better. Sir Alexander Dick drank tea, and _____ .

TUESDAY 20 JUNE. The Dean of Faculty showed me a letter from Colonel Lockhart of Carnwath, from Florence, confirming the defeat and destruction of the Corsicans. I was quite sunk. I thought of retiring to the country. I felt myself unable for the law. I saw I had parts to make a figure at times. But could not stand a constant trial. I received a most comforting letter from M. I just worshipped her. I was at home all day, except paying a short visit to Lord Mountstuart, and being at the Parliament House. The Doctor was with me a while. He commended M. highly as a sensible woman, a fine woman.

[Margaret Montgomerie to Boswell]

How sorry I am for the poor Corsicans. I'm afraid the accounts of their defeat is but too true. I doubt not but you will see the General, as it's said he is on his way to England. I am much distressed with a headache tonight, but could not think of missing this post, as I have not another opportunity till Tuesday.

May I once more entreat you to keep up your spirits, and do not keep the house too close. Exercise is absolutely necessary for your body, and society is a great relaxation to the mind. I approve much of your sober plan and hope you will continue it, and I am certain you will find it will make a great change on your sentiments; but is it necessary to be shut up to live sober? I hope not. Keep company with those who are so, and you will soon have a relish for that way of life.

[Boswell to Dempster]

Edinburgh, [?21] June [1769]

I WAS RECEIVED AT Dublin with open arms by a numerous and creditable set of relations. But I give you my word, I found myself under no engagements. The young lady seemed the sweetest, loveliest little creature that ever was born. But so young, so childish, so much *yes* and *no*, that (between ourselves) I was ashamed of having raved so much about her. I candidly told my situation: that I had come quite contrary to my father's inclination. That was enough for the present, and a genteel distance was the proper conduct. At the same time I found myself like a foreign prince to them, so much did I take; and I was assured of her having for certain £500 a year. You know me, Dempster. I was often carried by *fancy*, like a man on the finest race-horse; and, at all events, I would have her. But my cousin hung on my *heart*. Her most desirable person, like a heathen goddess painted alfresco on the ceiling of a palace at Rome, was compared with the delicate little Miss. Her admirable sense and vivacity were compared with the reserved quietness of the Heiress. I was tossed by waves and drawn by horses. I resolved to fix nothing. My cousin gave me that advice herself, for I had assurance enough to consult her deliberately. My journey to Scotland with her, during which I was a little indisposed and had occasion to see a new proof of her affectionate attention, has inclined me to her more and more.

Here then I am, my friend, at no loss to determine whom I really love and value of all women I have ever seen, but at a great loss to determine whom I should marry. No man knows the scene of human life better than you do. At least, no man gives me such clear views of it. Therefore, pray assist me.

SATURDAY 24 JUNE. Auchline and two daughters, a Mr. McIntosh, and Miss Betty Boswell dined and drank tea. I was obtuse at night. My father talked to me of marriage. I avoided the subject. M. had my heart.

SUNDAY 25 JUNE. I lay quietly abed all day and read Tissot *On the Health of Literary Persons* and Strange's *Catalogue of Pictures*. The former gave me some curious thoughts. The latter cheered me with fine ideas of painting and the lives of painters. I felt the pleasures of taste to be exquisite. I thought of Margaret. But then, money would enable me to buy pictures, and my Irish connection make a pretty anecdote in my life. So I wavered. But then again, Margaret was like Raphael's mistress; and what real happiness all my life should I have with her! I was just calm. Sir George Preston and Dr. Webster visited me. At night I rose and read a good deal of the Bible. I was a Christian, but regretted my not being more devout, more regularly pious. This would make me happier.

TUESDAY 27 JUNE. The Reverend Mr. Foord, our housekeeper's brother, and Matthew Dickie dined with us. At seven I went to the Goldsmiths' Hall to the first night of a new society for speaking on different subjects. I was quite flat and had no ambition, yet I spoke with force and spirit on Britain's right to tax her colonies.

THURSDAY 29 JUNE. I dined at Lord Monboddo's. We were alone before dinner a while, and I talked to him of my marrying. He was first for the child, as a man may form such a one as he pleases. But when I assured him I had a bad temper, and he observed that it requires great patience to breed a wife, as it does to breed a horse, he was clear for one already formed, and for Margaret, saying, "How it will tell is nothing."

FRIDAY 30 JUNE. I had a most interesting letter from Margaret. I was much affected by it, and wrote a long letter to her. At night I was at Mr. Moncrieffe's, but finding brag run high, I calmly gave it up and looked on. I was quite dull, thinking that I had given up all gay and brilliant schemes of marriage. At supper they talked of the Duke of Kingston marrying Miss Chudleigh from principles of honour and gratitude. I thought if he acted so towards a woman of her character, what ought I to do for a woman of real worth? I was resolved; and, what is really curious, as I considered that I was to make up for the want of £10,000 by frugality, my mind took the strongest bend that way, and I looked with aversion on a fine table and every piece of elegance then around me, wishing just for absolute plainness. I had, however, some suspicions that my father intended to *prendre encore une femme,* and that soured me totally. But I had no certainty for this.*

SATURDAY 1 JULY. At night my father hinted to me something of what I had suspected. I was amazed and hurt. It threw me quite into wild melancholy. It is many years since I, as it were, pulled myself up by the roots from the place where nature placed me; and though I have allowed myself to be brought back I have never taken firm root, but am like a tree sunk in a flowerpot that may be lifted at any time very easily. I must now endeavour to get matters settled so as to determine either on remaining where I am, or going somewhere else.

TUESDAY 4 JULY. Whenever I do not mention my breakfasting, dining, drinking tea, or supping somewhere abroad, it is to be understood that I was at home. Business now began to look better. I walked in the Meadow with Lord Monboddo and talked of M. He said there was no question she was the woman for me, thought her being a little older nothing, and said she'd bring me children worth rearing, which is

*Boswell will soon be certain enough. His father plans to remarry, an event which will trouble Boswell for some time ahead.

seldom the case nowadays. I mentioned to him my apprehensions concerning my father. He said it would be very foolish at his time of life—a terrible thing—a burthen on a family, &c. Bid me not delay getting a settlement made, which my marriage only would do. I saw Lord Monboddo's regard for me, and I was really happy with the scheme of *my lady*. I wrote to her at night and was in fine spirits. I drank tea at Mr. Thomas Boswall's.

FRIDAY 7 JULY. Messieurs Baillie, Colquhoun, George Fergusson, Blair, and Law, advocates, and William Macdonald and James Frazer, writers, dined with us. I was dull enough, but contented to be so. I had this day an answer from Temple, finely written, but preferring interest and ambition to the heart. I hoped easily to bring him into my opinion. Yet I considered what I owed to my family. But then again, insuring health, sense, and genius to my successor would be better than great riches. A man too rich is like a man too fat. Besides, I could save more than £10,000 portion by the manner in which I would live with M. So I continued firm, but was uneasy at not hearing from her for some days. At seven I was at Clerihue's at a consultation for Douglas against Duke Hamilton and Lord Selkirk. I felt myself weak and without much memory or application.

SATURDAY 8 JULY. About noon Mr. Maconochie and I set out in a post-chaise for Bothwell Castle, to be present at the celebration of Douglas's birthday on Monday the 10 of July. We had a great deal of conversation. I wavered somewhat as to my plan of life still: whether to remain here, or go to the English bar. Maconochie showed himself a little man of admirable common sense, observation, activity, and really a good share of neat taste from having seen so much of the world. We dined at Whitburn, and got to Bothwell Castle to tea. I rejoiced to see the Duchess, now that all was well. Douglas and the Duke of Queensberry were there before us, as also Captain William Douglas of Kelhead and a Mr. Douglas of Fechil, somewhere in the North, a young gentleman just come from Vienna, having travelled several years. He had much the foreign air, and brought my travels fresh into my mind. I then for a little disliked the thoughts of marriage. But then again, I thought it was time to settle and be comfortable; and my valuable M. had me all to herself.

SUNDAY 9 JULY. We sauntered about very agreeably. There is a fine bank of wood here. Douglas and I got by ourselves a while. We seemed great intimates. I told him I did not like to trust him abroad till he had a wife and a child. "Then," said he, "go along with me"; and described our travelling together, very agreeably. I told him it would take me quite out of the line of the Scotch law which I had taken, and I would not easily settle to it again. He argued that it might be made up to me. I was, for a while, very fond of the thought, which pleased my roving fancy and would furnish a good chapter in my life. But I thought warmly of Margaret. Douglas said a very good thing. "Boswell," said he, "you should now be just a worthy country gentleman, and not seek any more fame. You never can make yourself better known than you have done by your *Account of Corsica*. It is better known than Sir James Steuart's book. Be satisfied with it. You have just fallen upon a lucky thought." I was struck with this. We were very comfortable. The worthy Duke was very good company. I was deeply in love with M., and often wished to slip away to see her.

MONDAY 10 JULY. This was indeed a joyful day. The Duke assured me that he would be ready to do me any service in his power. We were busy in the morning concerting toasts and seeing that all was in good order. A numerous company came. We were about seventy at table. The Duke, Mr. Douglas, and I had each a copy of sixteen excellent toasts. Two engineers attended and took charge of a cannon and mortar. Whenever they were charged they made a sign with a handkerchief to a servant who was placed at the door, and who gave notice to me. I then rose up and called with an audible voice, "Charged, all charged." Then a toast was given and I called "Fire!" to the servant, who made a sign to the engineers, and the artillery went off. I was quite in my element, and had much satisfaction in philosophising upon the Douglas cause and the grand period then before my eyes. I could not but drink pretty freely, but I was not drunk. We had fireworks, bonfires, and a ball, and a crowd of country people huzzaing. During the whole, I was constant to M. Mr. Maconochie and I set out half an hour after eleven and drove all night. It was very light, and I had a curious, agreeable, drowsy satisfaction.

TUESDAY 11 JULY. We came to Livingstone about three in the morning, and got some fried chicken and a bottle of madeira with Mr. Mackellar, the landlord, for company. I know not how it is, but I am very fond of the road between Edinburgh and Auchinleck. It brings a crowd of agreeable, family, sober ideas into my mind. However, travelling it as I now did seemed odd. It was like dancing in a church. I got to town just in time to throw off my laced coat and waistcoat, get on black clothes, and be ready at nine o'clock to attend some causes in the Parliament House. A thousand questions were put to me. I was sleepy all day, but stood it well very.

WEDNESDAY 12 JULY. I had received a letter from Sir John Dick informing me that Paoli was safe at Leghorn. This was great comfort to me. I was anxious and uneasy at having no letter from M. this week. I was apprehensive she was offended with me. Dempster was now in town. He came and saw me, and heard my anxious, irresolute situation with patience and complacency. He bid me treat it lightly. He said I was yet far from matrimony, and could easier return than advance. That supposing Glasgow to be marriage and Edinburgh the state of a bachelor, I was no farther on my road than Fountainbridge.

THURSDAY 13 JULY. I received a letter from M. in a style that made me think she was angry and had given up all love for me. She appeared to me so cool and indifferent that I was absolutely shocked. I thought with a kind of distraction of the world in which one whom I thought I knew so intimately could be so changeable. My head turned giddy, and I am positive no man was ever more severely tortured by love. Worthy Grange represented to me that it was all my own fault, for I had acknowledged to him that I had written to her with such censure that no woman of spirit could bear; and that I ought rather to be grateful to her for writing at all, and should make an apology for what I had written. He pacified me a little. But I have a wretched satisfaction in being surly. I, however, was much affected, and could for gleams of thought have almost cried; and, had she been near me, would have fallen at her feet. Yet my obstinate, unreasonable pride still rose again. I determined not to write till I was more moderate. Dempster was gone home, which I regretted.

After the House I had a walk with Lord Monboddo. He said I might be sure my father had thoughts *de se remarier,* and pushed me to think of marrying directly. He was clear and irrestible for M. I thought, "How curious is this compared with her last letter and its effects on me." Mr. Claud, Miss Betty, and Grange dined with us. I was quite thoughtful and vexed on a complication of accounts: my father, Margaret, and a very bad symptom of illness. I drank tea at Grange's along with Mr. Macdonald, the surgeon. But was really low. My heart was softened. I was all gratitude to M. But alas! what could I do for her? I was ready to give her myself, but was persuaded it would make her miserable.

At night I had a serious conversation with my father. He talked of my not minding affairs at home. That gave me a good opportunity to say that I really had no encouragement as I was in so incertain a way, and that he even talked *de se remarier.* He in a manner acknowledged his having such views. I spoke in the strongest terms, and fairly told him he should be no more troubled with me. I was really calm and determined. It is wonderful to think how he and I have differed to such a degree for so many years. I was somewhat hurt to find myself again thrown loose on the world. But my love of adventure and hope made me surprisingly easy. My great unhappiness was thinking of M. And yet in any way she could not but suffer, for I could not think of marriage when he exposed himself at his years and forgot my valuable mother. O unfeeling world! I declare I am not, nor ever could be, so much so. And yet, honest man! he talked of his affection for me and what he had suffered on my account with a tone that moved me, though I was quite irritated against him now. I am truly a composition of many opposite qualities.

[Received 13 July, Margaret Montgomerie to Boswell]

[Lainshaw] Saturday [8 July 1769]

I AM MUCH OBLIGED TO YOU for both your letters, and would have taken the very first opportunity of telling you so had I not recollected your intended visit to Bothwell Castle.

I heard of both the marriages. You ask me if I feel any regret when I hear of a good match going off. I answer, not the smallest when I have no attachment, notwithstanding the opinion a certain friend of mine entertains of me. I have not yet perceived such charms in the matrimonial state as to make me enter very deep into any plot to get myself a member of that society; however, this I know will gain but small credit, being inconsistent with female dependence. I must therefore be satisfied to lie under the general aspersion. I could not help being a little nettled at that part of your letter where you tax me with a too great degree of frankness to gentlemen. Without any regard to character, most men are more industrious to hide their faults than a friend of mine has ever shown himself to be; and, as I only meant civility, I see no reason why I should give myself the trouble to pry into the real worth of a common acquaintance.

FRIDAY 14 JULY. I continued most unhappy. Having sat up till four in the morning, I was very feverish. I love M. from my soul, but saw myself to be incapable of any lasting connection. Grange and I walked down to Leith Links and saw a review of Cary's, the Forty-third Regiment. It entertained me somewhat. One of the Scots Greys, who stood as a sentinel to keep off the mob, did his duty so faithfully and yet with so much good nature that I gave him a shilling to drink. A little after this, I wanted to buy a bit of gingerbread. So, to make a trial of human nature, I came to my Grey and asked if he would give some halfpence to buy some gingerbread. This was a pretty severe trial, for many fellows would have damned me and denied they had ever seen me. But my honest Grey said, 'O yes, Sir," and immediately pulled out a leathern purse. He had indeed but one halfpenny, but he gave me it very cheerfully; and, instead of buying gingerbread with it, I keep it with a piece of paper wrapped round it, on which I have written the anecdote.

I came home for a little. My father came into my room and spoke to me a little on indifferent subjects. But I shunned him. Grange and I dined comfortably at Purves's. He advised me strongly against any desperate scheme. But I was quite determined. Mr. Macdonald blooded me today to begin the cure of a severe symptom. It is hard for one night of Irish extravagance to suffer so much. I wrote a law paper this afternoon. But could hardly fix my attention. I then went to Mr. Moncrieffe's and played three rubbers at whist with him and Lord Galloway and David Kennedy, and then supped. I was observed to be very dull. It passed all to be on account of the fate of Corsica.

SATURDAY 15 JULY. I took a walk on the Castle Hill with Mr. Maconochie, and told him my dilemma. He was vexed, but advised me to be prudent. I became quite outrageous, and was mad enough to ask him if it would not be allowable to cut off _____ , before he ruined his family. But this I certainly did not seriously mean for a moment. I went in the stage to Pinkie, to have talked with Commissioner Cochrane. But he was from home. My father and Miss Betty drove past in a chaise. I was quite chagrined. I hired a chaise and went to Sir Alexander Dick's. Amidst all my gloom the sweet place and amiable people soothed me. I told him my dilemma. He was vexed, and bid me do anything to prevent it. I was at home all the evening. My father sent for me to him. But I would not sit down. I just spoke a few sullen words. I was quite gone.

SUNDAY 16 JULY. After a wretched, feverish night I awaked in a dreadful state. I have no doubt that evil spirits, enemies to mankind, are permitted to tempt and torment them. "Damn him. Curse him," sounded somehow involuntarily in my ears perpetually. I was absolutely mad. I sent for worthy Grange and was so furious and black-minded and uttered such horrid ideas that he could not help shedding tears, and even went so far as to say that if I talked so he would never see me again. I looked on my father's marrying again as the most ungrateful return to me for my having submitted so much to please him. I thought it an insult on the memory of my valuable mother. I thought it would totally estrange him from his children by her. In short, my wild imagination made it appear as terrible as can be conceived. I rose and took a little broth, and, in order to try if what I liked most could have any effect on me when in such a frame, I went to the chapel in Carrubber's Close, which has always made me fancy myself in heaven. I was really relieved. I thought of M., and loved her fervently. But I was still obstinate. A clergyman from Leith preached on these words, "I have learned, in whatever state I am, therewith to be content." He said many good things on contentment, and that the text informed us it was to be *learnt*. I was averse to learn any good.

I then went and drank tea at the Miss Mackenzies'. M. again here in fancy. I am really constant. I wanted to be gloomy and like a man of such resolutions as I then had. But the agreeable company around me and my own gaiety insensibly made me otherwise. I then sat a while with Lady Crawford, with whom I have always a great deal of sentimental conversation. She made me love M. still more. I should have mentioned that in the forenoon my father wanted to speak to me, and I absolutely refused it by running away from him. I was very gloomy at night.

[Boswell to Margaret Montgomerie]

Edinburgh, 17 July 1769

MY DEAREST PEGGIE,—The enclosed will account to you for my long silence. It has been long in comparison of our frequent correspondence. Though your last letter but one made me imagine you had given me up, and I was for a while piqued and enraged, you see how humble I became, and how a true passion tears the heart. But my pride has made me keep the enclosed by me, and since I wrote it I have thought seriously that I am not fit for marriage with any woman. If I could behave so to such a valuable and affectionate woman as you, what a shocking temper must I have! The frankness for which I blamed you is really a perfection, for I never saw you improperly free.

My present situation is dreadful. What an infamous woman must she be who can impose on an old man worn out with business, and ruin the peace of a family! I am employing all prudent methods to prevent the ruinous scheme.

EDITORIAL NOTE: This is to my knowledge Boswell's only effort at story-writing. The characters of the story are drawn obviously enough from Boswell's own life and family: so obviously that the story has far more merit as autobiography than as fiction. M. H.

ON SECOND MARRIAGES: A TRUE STORY
IN QUEEN ANNE'S REIGN

The duties which become essential to a man from the relation of family in the present state of society are most important and serious, and a neglect or transgression of them is often attended with such fatal consequences as I am now about to relate. A gentleman of distinction in

Berkshire was at a proper age married to one of the best women that ever lived. He was one of those men of strong sense, prudence, and application to business, whose usefulness to society makes them generally respected. His lady brought him several children, all of whom she lived to see in a fair way of succeeding in the world, and then was carried off by a sudden illness. The gentleman's eldest son was then abroad upon his travels, but, being deeply affected with the loss of his valuable mother, and the distress into which his father was thrown, he returned home immediately. Though he had a distinguished genius, and a fire and impetuosity which could hardly brook the least control and disposed him to enjoy all the variety of life, regard for his father and for the family from which he was descended made him resolve to give up all the gay schemes of happiness which he had formed, and submit himself to a plan of living which he considered to be a perpetual succession of disgust. In order to this, he deadened his mind gradually, till he brought himself to a kind of state of indifference, forced himself to take a share in the dull employments and insipid society around him, and at length brought himself to be perfectly content. While the truly dutiful son conducted himself in this manner, the father, who had appeared almost inconsolable for the death of his wife and had been warned of mortality by a severe distemper, gave all the reason in the world to believe that he could have no other intention than to pass the rest of his days with a becoming gravity and abstraction, and would wish to see his heir assume in some measure the place which, in the course of nature, he was destined one day to fill. But instead of this, in little more than two years after the death of his wife, the father began to think of a second marriage. He communicated his design to his son with that awkward hesitation which generally shows itself when we are about to do anything of which we are ashamed. The young gentleman was shocked at the idea. He could hardly allow himself to believe such a thing of his father. Being of a melancholy temper, he began to doubt the reality of all apparent worth when he saw so shameful an instance of selfishness. His heart grew big, and he with difficulty could restrain himself from breaking out into sallies of indignation. He employed a prudent person to talk to the lady whom his father had in view, and to represent to her that if she complied with his proposals she would not only have the meanness to become the legal prostitute of libidinous old age, but would be the cause of destroying the peace of a family and ruining a young man of merit. He at the same time remonstrated to his father in the strongest terms, conjured him to remember his deceased spouse and told him plainly that the keenness of his feelings were such that if his father put his scheme in execution, he would from that moment renounce him for ever. But vile interest in the one and wretched appetite in the other of these parties prevailed over every proper sentiment, and produced a second marriage. The son, who was equally determined as he was warm, quitted his ungrateful father and retired to a distant country, where he indulged his gloomy reflections without restraint, and would upon no account listen to any terms of reconciliation. The father soon perceived that age and distemper are miserably suited for conjugal society, and for all the art of his new wife he saw her disgusted with his nauseous fondness. The respectable character which he had maintained was now sunk in folly and dotage. He became the subject of drunken jests, and *turpe senilis amor—peccet ad extremum ridendus* were every day applied to him. None of his children would see a man who, for the selfish gratification of at most but a few years, had exposed himself, affronted the memory of their mother, driven from his country a son who did honour to it, and ruined a family which had supported itself for ages. He died in great agony both in body and mind, and may serve to teach decorum and generosity of conduct to those who come after him.

TUESDAY 18 JULY. I continued as bad as ever. I appeared before my father in some causes, and had a strange satisfaction in pleading calmly to a man with whom I could not have any intercourse in private. I felt a kind of regret to leave the Parliament House, to which I have a kind of family attachment. But I considered all attachments to be now at an end. I was really in a terrible state. Lord Monboddo desired to speak with me after the House. I accordingly took a walk with him, when he told me that he had just had a long and serious conversation with my father, who had complained to him of my behaviour, told him that it was my choosing to live in the irregular state of a bachelor which made him think of marrying again, and my Lord said if I would not alter my plan he was right. "But," said he, "will you let me negotiate between you? Yours is an estate and a family worth preserving." I said I could marry no other woman but Margaret. "Well," said he, "be serious and firm, and I hope to settle matters." This gave me quite a new set of thoughts.

I had told Douglas my uneasiness, and he promised to be my firm friend in all events. I went in the coach with the Duchess to Lord Chief Baron's, where we dined along with the Duke of Queensberry and Douglas. I was in perfect spirits. The sight of grandeur made me for a second or two consider if I was not wrong to give up all schemes of marrying for ambition and wealth. But M. soon brought me back. I soon saw that my real happiness is not in such objects. That I only love sometimes to contemplate them, and that I would do it with double satisfaction when I have Margaret for my companion. Every different attempt to make me waver makes my love steadier. The Duchess and I paid a visit to Lady Alva and the young Countess of Sutherland, and then returned to town, the mob huzzaing and crying, "Douglas for ever!" I supped with my father. But Mr. Brown was with us, as I wished to avoid particular conversation. We were, however, tolerably well.

WEDNESDAY 19 JULY. Mr. Walter Campbell and his wife, Mrs. Ritchie, Lord Monboddo, and Tilquhilly dined with us. I was persuaded to go to the assembly. There was a fine company, and I felt myself wonderfully calm and constant. I renewed my acquaintance with my old friend, Lady Colville. I was mad enough to dance one country dance. Mrs. Walter Campbell was my partner, which made me dance with violence. It did me much ill.

THURSDAY 20 JULY. I was hurt by having danced. David Armstrong, Grange, and I took a chaise and saw a race at Leith. At night I resolved to put M.'s affection to the strictest trial. I wrote to her, taking no notice of any hopes of a compromise, but told her plainly that if she would go off with me and live on my £100 a year, with the interest of her £1,000, I was ready to marry her. I bid her think fully, and give me no reasoning but a direct answer. I wrote to Temple of this, while I told him of the prospect of a compromise. This was truly romantic, and perhaps too severe a trial of a woman of so much good sense and so high a character.

MY DEAR COUSIN,—I know I shall have a friendly and affectionate answer to the last letter which I wrote to you. But in the meantime, I am going to write you a calm and determined epistle, in few words but of infinite importance to us both.

You never knew till we were in Ireland that I had at different periods of my life been deeply in love with you. That has, however, been the case; and had not vanity or some other artificial motive made me, from time to time, encourage my fancy in other schemes, the genuine inclinations of my heart would ever have been constant to my dear Peggy Montgomerie. As it was, you know how fond I have been of you, and how I have at different times convinced you that my love for you was truly sincere. While wavering in my resolutions, I was always determined that if your happiness depended upon having me, I would not hesitate a moment to make my best friend happy. And I accordingly begged in a late letter that you would tell me freely if that was the case.

I was at the assembly last night, and saw a variety of beauties. I was not inconstant to you for a moment. Indeed, after standing the trial you did in Ireland, there could be little fear. Any other person than you would be apt to disregard what I say in my present situation. But I think I may trust to the generosity of a *noble-minded woman*, as Dempster calls you. I therefore make you this proposal. You know my unhappy temper. You know all my faults. It is painful to repeat them. Will you, then, knowing me fully, accept of me for your husband as I now am—not the heir of Auchinleck, but one who has had his time of the world, and is henceforth to expect no more than £100 a year? With that and the interest of your £1,000, we can live in an agreeable retirement in any part of Europe that you please. But we are to bid adieu for ever to this country. All our happiness is to be our society with each other, and our hopes of a better world. I confess this scheme is so romantic that nothing but such love as you showed at Donaghadee could make you listen to it. Nor ought I to be surprised if a woman of your admirable sense and high character with all who know you should refuse to comply with it, should refuse to sacrifice every prudent consideration to me. But as I love you more than I can express, you will excuse me for making this proposal. I am ready upon these terms to marry you directly. And, upon my honour, I would not propose it now, were I not fully persuaded that I would share a kingdom with you if I had it. I also solemnly promise to do everything in my power to show my gratitude and make you happy. Think seriously of this. Give me any positive answer you honestly can. But I insist on no mediocrity, no reasoning, no hesitation. Think fully, and one way or other tell me your resolution. I am much yours,

JAMES BOSWELL

SATURDAY 22 JULY. I breakfasted at Queensberry House with all the excellent friends there. Then Douglas carried me in his phaeton to the race at Leith. It was a handsome carriage with pretty mares, and he drove with great spirit among the crowd of company, always coming to pay his attentive duty to the worthy Duke. I was exceedingly happy.

I dined quietly at home with my brother. Grange drank tea with me. At night my father, having dined abroad and drank, cheerfully spoke to me of Lord Monboddo's telling him of my scheme as to M. I endeavored to be as reserved as possible, but insensibly he and I fell into our usual bad humour. It is hard.

SUNDAY 23 JULY. I went to Mr. Erskine's church and heard Dr. Gibbons preach. This was an English clergyman recommended to me by Mr. Dilly. In the morning I had been at the burial of John Mair, an extractor and the best formalist about the House, and then I breakfasted with Professor Wallace, who showed me a genealogy of the family of Fullarton vouched by papers for above five hundred years. It is curious how pleasing variety is. Mr. Wallace's style of conversation amused me much, and when I saw his law papers neatly bound up, with accurate indexes, and amongst them some of my own writing, the business of Scotch lawyer acquired value in my mind, and I thought of continuing at it even in the worst event. But while I was in church, I thought that if M. gave me a prudent, cold, evasive answer, I would set sail for America and become a wild Indian. I had great thoughts of my acquiring strength and fortitude, and could not regret much leaving all I had known, as I should adore God and be happy hereafter. Between sermons, I called on Lady Preston and told her my dilemma. She was vastly hurt, and joined with me in rage. I then went to Queensberry House, I told my cousin, Willy Douglas, my dilemma. He was struck and said, "I sincerely commiserate you."

TUESDAY 25 JULY. The important answer from M. was brought to me in the Parliament House: "I accept of your terms." For a minute or two my habits of terror for marriage returned. I found myself at last fixed for ever; my heart beat and my head was giddy. But I soon recovered and felt the highest admiration and gratitude on a conduct so generous. Her letter was finely written, and did me more real honour than anything I have ever met with in life. I determined to make it my study to do all in my power to show my sense of her goodness. And I became calm and easy, thinking that as I was now fixed in the most important concern, everything else was but secondary. The Commissioner dined with us. At night I was at the Society, and spoke against repealing the Marriage Act.

[Received 25 July, Margaret Montgomerie to Boswell]

[Enclosed in a wrapper endorsed by Boswell] The most valuable letter of my valuable friend, which does honour to both her and me. *Vraye Foi.*

[Lainshaw] Saturday [22 July 1769]
I HAVE THOUGHT FULLY as you desired, and in answer to your letter I accept of your terms, and shall do everything in my power to make myself worthy of you. J.B. with £100 a year is every bit as valuable to me as if possessed of the estate of Auchinleck. I only regret the want of wealth on your account, not being certain if you can be happy without a proper share of it. Free of ambition, I prefer real happiness to the splendid appearance of it. I wish you could meet me at Glasgow on Saturday. Could you not come that length in the fly and return on Monday? Let me know and I'll be there any day you will appoint.

My heart determines my choice. May the Almighty grant His blessing and protection, and we need not be afraid; His providence extends over all the earth, so that wherever you go I shall willingly accompany you and hope to be happy. Had you been, as you mention, in your former prosperity, I should perhaps have indulged myself in female prudence, &c., but I think this is not now the time for dissimulation. I am therefore ready to meet you when you please and to join my fate to yours. Is not this as full an answer as you could wish? Say nothing of the affair to your father, as you are sure he will never consent; and to disobey after consulting is worse than doing it without saying a word.

My heart is more at ease than it has been of a long time, though still I feel for what I'm afraid you suffer. Be assured, my dear Jamie, you have a friend that would sacrifice everything for you, who never had a wish for wealth till now, to bestow it on the man of her heart.

I wrote two letters, one on Friday and one on Tuesday. I hope the contents of neither have offended you. My anxiety about your happiness made me use every argument in my power to prevail on you to stay at home. In hopes of meeting with you soon, I shall only add that I most sincerely am, my dear Jamie, your faithful and affectionate

M.M.

Sunday. I did not get this sent off yesterday, so have had one other night to think of it, and am still determined in my resolution to go with you where you please. Write me soon and let me know if you can meet me.

WEDNESDAY 26 JULY. I was in great uneasiness on account of my illness, but Macdonald and Dr. Cairnie, whom I also consulted, made me give over terrible apprehensions. I was this afternoon at a meeting of the late Mr. Adie's trustees. At night I wrote to M. She had proposed to meet me on Saturday at Glasgow. But I could not get so far, as the Duke was to dine with us. I begged to know if she could come to Whitburn. I was very desirous to see her.

SATURDAY 29 JULY. This has been a good week for me in the way of business. I have cleared twenty guineas, and have really been able to do very well. I am ready for whatever may happen. My dearest Margaret is my great object.

I find it is impossible to put upon paper an exact journal of the life of a man. External circumstances may be marked. But the variations within, the workings of reason and passion, and, what perhaps influence happiness most, the colourings of fancy, are too fleeting to be recorded.

In short, so it is that I defy any man to write down anything like a perfect account of what he has been conscious during one day of his life, if in any degree of spirits. However, what I put down has so far an effect that I can, by reading my Journal, recall a good deal of my life.

SUNDAY 30 JULY. I was at church all day. I fancied M. sitting beside me as she used to do. Sir George and George Webster dined with us. It was curious to observe how my father's manner awed and checked the freedom of conversation. This is really hard to bear. I was in very good humour today. I recollected my former follies; I saw that my father had indulged and forgiven me more than I could a son of mine if I had one. I therefore would have no resentment against him, let him do as he pleased. I would just consider his marrying again as a fatality by which he was killed and his estate overwhelmed, and, without farther connection either with the one or the other, I would go and live as easily and agreeably as possible with my dearest M. I wished to tell him something like this at night. But I found myself kept back as usual.

TUESDAY 1 AUGUST. Mr. John Chalmer, Mr. James Neill from Ayr, and Grange dined with us. At five I drank tea along with Maclaurin at Mr. John Swinton's, at a consultation. I really, for the most part, like the business of the law. There is a kind of entertainment in observing the progression of causes, and a great variety of ideas are made to work.

WEDNESDAY 2 AUGUST. Dempster was in town in his way to London. I had written him a letter while he was sick, which I said just came on its tiptoes to enquire how he was. I went now and found him at Peter Ramsay's, and observing him thin, "Dempster," said I, "your belly has been imitating the India stock of late—falling"; a very proper similitude for a director of the East India Company. I told him I was fixed to M. He said he was much pleased; that his only surprise was how I could do so rational a thing. He said it was just as if either he or I could be transformed into a female, and the one marry the other. He was quite against my outrage, supposing my father to marry again. He said I had a title to remonstrate, and try to prevent it; but if my father insisted for it, it was my duty to submit. He said it was not an insult to the memory of a first wife to marry a second. "I suppose," said I, "you will say it is no more so than it is an insult upon boiled beef to eat afterwards of roast mutton." "Just so," said he, "when the first course is gone, why not take a second?" This lively argument would have some truth if a wife were looked upon with as little sentiment as a dish at one's table.

Dempster said that all schemes of flying one's country were bad, because the moment there is a variation in the sentiments of a person who does so he is miserable, because it is very difficult for him to return.

Said I, "Would it not be noble for me to get among the wild Indians in America?" "What," said he, "would you give up for ever with me, with Miss Montgomerie?" I was sorry to part with him. I dined at Lord Monboddo's with the Duke of Queensberry and Douglas, and we were so well and cheerful that it was agreed we should all meet again at supper too. I was in admirable spirits, with perfect sobriety.

THURSDAY 3 AUGUST. I do not recollect this day.

FRIDAY 4 AUGUST. My father came into my room this morning and told me that although he thought my scheme of marriage improper and that Margaret and I would part in half a year, yet as I insisted for it he would agree. I was really very grateful to him, and hoped to be able to behave to his satisfaction.

SATURDAY 5 AUGUST. I had agreed to go to Lainshaw to see Margaret. I accordingly set out this morning in the fly. There was a very good company, and I was calm and just as I could wish. I was taking a glass of madeira at Graham's when Sir James Steuart sent to me that he was in the house and would be glad to see me. I went to him. I told him I had a companion whom I would wish to introduce. "Oh," said he, "bring him in by all means." "There he is," said I, pointing to my bottle of madeira, which I had made the waiter set upon the table. Sir James made it very welcome, and he and I were very social. He argued for prudent, interested marriages. I told him of mine. He opposed my scheme, "For," said he, "whenever you have enjoyed a woman you are in love with, love goes off." "No fear," said I, "my mistress and I are old friends; and surely our friendship will not be lessened because we enjoy happiness together? Do you think two friends will become less so by drinking a bottle of champagne together? I grant you that if the champagne is the only connection that brings two people together, their love will not last; but my situation is quite different." I really thought I had the better of Sir James when I argued for love. I received here a kind letter from Margaret. I was in the best frame imaginable.

I took a post-chaise and set out for Lainshaw. It pleased me to drive through Glasgow, and recall a variety of ideas. I got to Lainshaw before ten. The poor Captain was very ill. When I saw my valuable Margaret, I was in more agitation than I could have believed. Mrs. Cuninghame and I had a serious conversation, and all was now certainly fixed. It is impossible to write down all that M. and I said.

SUNDAY 6 AUGUST. We did not go to church, but stayed quietly at home. I felt myself serene and happy, and I had infinite satisfaction in seeing my dear M. as happy as I was. As I was to set out next morning at three to be in time for the fly I did not go to bed, but kept Mr. Grahames and Dr. Dean with me over a bowl of punch. M. went to bed early, as she was to go with me. During the night I became anxious and frightened that still I should not have her.

MONDAY 7 AUGUST. When she came down in the morning, I told her my uneasiness and insisted that we should take each other's hands and solemnly engage ourselves. We did so, and I was easy. We had an agreeable drive to Glasgow, where we breakfasted. I was happier than I can describe. It was curious to look back, and then to consider my present situation. It vexed me that I could not immediately marry. But I pleased myself that the scheme's being known for some time before would be more creditable, as it would show it to be no sudden flight.

TUESDAY 8 AUGUST. My father and Balmuto and I dined along with him and the two Mr. Riddels and William Macdonald at Mr. Campbell of Ashnish's. I drank freely and then I went to Fortune's, where Mr. Moncrieffe's guests were entertaining him, and there I became outrageously jovial and intoxicated myself terribly, and was absurd and played at brag and was quarrelsome. How unhappy is this!

WEDNESDAY 9 AUGUST. I was quite gloomy and dejected. I wrote a long letter to Margaret. That valuable woman will make me the man I wish to be.

[Received ? 11 August, Margaret Montgomerie to Boswell]

[Lainshaw] Thursday [10 August 1769]

WITH THE UTMOST IMPATIENCE I wait the arrival of the post in hopes he will bring me a letter from my dear friend. What an anxious, uneasy time I have spent since I received your last letter! I am fearful you are not well—your fatigue, hard drinking, and going to the opera all join to make me unhappy. I imagine you perhaps met some companion there who prevailed you to sup abroad, and by that means finished the irregularities of the day. Oh, what would I give to be certain this was not the case, and to hear you had not suffered in the least by your journey! I can write no more till I see what accounts the post brings. I am just going to set off for Stewarton, so adieu for a little and God bless you, my best friend.

I am happy to think your father treats you with so much kindness. It shall be my constant endeavour to behave so to him as that he shall have no cause to regret your choice. I am sensible of my faults, and very desirous to amend them. He shall ever find me dutiful to him, and extremely ready to follow his directions, as far as lies in my power.

As to your going to London, I cannot, will not, object if it's your interest to be there, but how will your father relish such an expedition?

I'm afraid he will be greatly offended. In that case, I should be extremely uneasy. If your health is not in question, you could see Mr. Johnson some other time, but you are surely the best judge yourself. I pretend not to dictate; I only wish you to act so as not to disoblige my uncle when he is so very good to you.

You are quite right as to my anxiety. I suffer as much from that as you can possibly imagine. I must surely see you before you set out for London. If you are determined to go, I'll endeavour to be in Edinburgh before you leave it. There's a great odds betwixt the distance of the two places to me; in the one I can see you in a day, but I would have no sort of excuse for setting out to London without the ceremony had been put over. I really think it should; it would have been much more satisfactory to me to think I had it in my power to see you without giving real cause for censure; and, when once people are determined, the sooner they put it over the better. I must have many promises of sobriety before I give my consent to your going to London.

Consider, my dear Jamie, that my happiness is entirely in your power, and I'm sure your generosity will make you deny yourself an indulgence that may be hurtful to you as well as your friend. Lord Eglinton sent his compliments to me by Mr. Grahames today, and bid him tell me he heard for certain I was to be married to Mr. Boswell. How in the world does everybody know so well? It must surely be from you, for I declare it is not from me they know anything of the matter.

SATURDAY 12 AUGUST. The session rose today. Lord Monboddo took leave of me, hoping to meet me next as a married man. My father was to have set out for Auchinleck today. But some business detained him. John went, and my father and I were easy and well. After dinner he talked of Margaret and me. Said we had both very good sense, but were thoughtless, and must become just different beings. I told him I was under necessity to go to London for a little to clear my constitution. He acquiesced. The evening passed well.

SUNDAY 13 AUGUST. My illness was visibly decreasing, so I resolved to stay in and take care of it for a week or a fortnight, and be pretty well before I set out for London. My father and I had a warm dispute at night on male and female succession. I argued that a male alone could support a family, could represent his forefathers. That females, in a feudal light, were only vehicles for carrying down men to posterity, and that a man might as well entail his estate on his post-chaise, and put one into it who should bear his name, as entail it upon his daughter and make her husband take his name. I told him that the principle of family, of supporting the race of Thomas Boswell of Auchinleck, was what supported my mind, and that, were it not for that, I would not submit to the burthen of life here, but would go and pass my days in a warm climate, easy and gay. I bid him consider that he had the estate of Auchinleck, at least the old stamen of it, in prejudice of no less than four females. That excluding females might at a time hurt a fond father who had daughters and no sons. "But what," said I, "is a sorry individual to the preservation of a family? Is there any comparison? Besides, in that view, why will you make the son whom you see miserable on account of some woman who may appear nobody know when?" I saw he was quite positive in the strange, delusive notion of *heirs whatsoever,* and I had the mortification to be sensible that my dissipated and profligate conduct had made him at all think of an entail, and made any arguments from me of little force. I, however, hoped to get him prevented from ruining his family. I was quite in a fever, for I declare that the family of Auchinleck is my only constant object in this world. I should say, *has been* so. For my dearest M. is now as firmly established. I determined to leave the country if he made the settlement which shocked me. I told him so, and I knew M. would not complain. Indeed I was too hot for a son to a father. But I could not help it. I was like an old Roman when his country was at stake.

I fell upon a most curious argument which diverted my own fancy so much that it was with difficulty I could preserve my gravity when uttering it. "If," said I, "you believe the Bible, you must allow male succession. Turn to the first chapter of Matthew: 'Abraham begat Isaac, Isaac begat Jacob,' &c. If you are not an infidel, you do not renounce Christianity, you must be for males." Worthy man! he had patience with me. I am quite firm in my opinion on this point. It will not do to say a grandson by a daughter is as near as a grandson by a son. It leads into a nice disquisition in natural philosophy. I say the *stamen* is derived from the *man.* The woman is only like the ground where a tree is planted. A grandson by a daughter has no connection with my original stock. A new race is begun by a father of another name. It is true a child partakes of the constitution of his mother, gets some of his mother's blood in his veins. But so does he as to his nurse, so does he as to the ox whose beef he eats. The most of the particles of the human frame are changed in a few years' rotation. The stamen only continues the same. Let females be well portioned. Let them enjoy liberally what is naturally intended for them: dowries as virgins, a share of what their husbands have while wives, jointures when widows. But for goodness' sake let us not make feudal lords, let us not make barons, of them. As well might we equip them with breeches, swords, and gold-laced hats.

In every age some instances of folly have occurred to humble the pride of human nature. Of these, the idea of female succession is one of the most striking. A foolish fondness for daughters has introduced it, when fathers thought they could not do enough for them. Like the ancient Scottish clergy, who became so very fond of the Virgin Mary that, not satisfied with *Aves* and other acknowledgments, they gravely disputed in a synod at St. Andrews whether they should not say *Pater Noster*, "Our Father which art in Heaven", to her. Spottiswood relates this as a most monstrous absurdity. To make a woman a feudal lord is much such another. If it be said that remote heirs male may be in the lowest ranks, surely remote heirs female may be so too. I love the late Earl of Cassillis, who, when settling his estate, being told by his man of business that he had called all the heirs male, "Then," said he, "give it to the devil." This was the true spirit and dignity of the ancient peer.

[Boswell to Margaret Montgomerie, 21 August 1769]

I do not wonder at your panic and reluctance to go to Auchinleck. Nobody but such as know my father's way perfectly can imagine how hard it must be upon you. For the truth is that his manner of keeping people in awe, joined with his peculiar talent of putting what he pleases in a contemptible light, is galling beyond expression to a feeling mind. The best remedy which I have found against the effects of this has been to prepare myself calmly for it, as for a piece of *caricatura* which I am certain is unjust but which may entertain me. A great part of the happiness of lovers and friends consists in the high opinion which they entertain of each other. In what particular way you think of me, I cannot know; but am convinced that you have a value for me, as I have for you, as much as ever man had for woman, and for which I have often given the best reasons. Now how terrible must it be for any one of us to have the other represented as a very inconsiderable being. However, allowance must be made. No other person can think equally high of us as we do of each other, and my father less so perhaps than anybody else. Let us bear it patiently, and hope to make him by degrees think better of us. I approve of your not being in too great a hurry to go to Auchinleck. I have written to my father telling him that, as I now look upon you as my *wife*, it will be very obliging to me if he will send his chaise for you, or at least write to you, and behave to you with kindness as his daughter-in-law. My letter will be with him this afternoon. You may wait a day or two, and see what effect it produces. As this is our sacrament week at Auchinleck, he may put off sending for you till next week. But if you do not hear from him by Friday, I would have you send your letter to him. You will observe that I have shortened it considerably and have struck out the paragraph justifying yourself as to our marriage. I think you have no need of a justification. Are not you my equal? Are not you his own niece? Keep in mind your own value, my dearest. Keep in mind that you are my spouse, the woman whom I have preferred to all others for her real merit. Will you forgive me for rejoicing in my reformation? and let me add the woman whom I have preferred to the temptations of fortune? for so you know to be true. On my account, as well as your own, I will not suffer you to write to my father as if you were a milliner or a tenant's daughter whom his son had married in a foolish fit of love. Remember you are *my lady*. I have also thought it best to keep out the paragraph as to some of your relations having contributed to prejudice him against you. Let all these things be forgotten. My life for it, we shall hear no more of them now. I have taken the same liberty with the expression, "If you admit me into your family," because I wish if possible that he should invite us rather than that we should propose it. With the alterations I have made, I am of opinion your letter will be of service to prepare him for receiving you.

I do really believe that the reason of his asking you to come to him is to talk with you calmly, and judge how far it will be proper for him to have us to live in family with him. Do not suspect him of attempting to make you give up your marriage with me. Let us not, amidst many unhappy differences, forget his real worth. It was from him that I derived that strict regard to truth and to honour which I have ever preserved. He has already plainly given his consent to the match. He has said so to myself; and he knows that I went to Lainshaw the day after, and that I am positively engaged to you. No, no, my dearest life, you wrong him when you carry your apprehensions so far. All you have to fear is a kind of chilling and dispiriting method in which he may talk to you.

I should not imagine he will, like the Doctor, be inquisitive as to when I made my proposals, and all the circumstances of our attachment. If it should so happen, you must tell him that, in the very time of my schemes for heiresses, I used often to make strong professions of love to you, to tell you that I would marry you rather than any other woman, were if not that I was resolved to have £10,000 with a wife.

That, at the same time, I bid you not mind me; and that accordingly you considered all I said to be words of course. That when you was at Auchinleck last spring, I paid you more than ordinary attention. That before you was aware, this made some impression on you. That you concealed your sentiments, as you knew I was upon another scheme, and besides imagined that he would not approve of a match for me by which I got neither money nor any new connections that could be of use to me. That you wished much to avoid going to Ireland, but that I insisted on it, and got your sister and the Captain to join their influence.

That on the journey to Ireland I became unusually thoughtful and uneasy, told you that you was the woman on earth whom I really loved, that I had been in love with you in my earliest years and twenty times since, that you was my friend whom I valued, and that I was miserable to think that I was going to marry another, which was at the same time not honourable, considering my love for you. That you then began to think me serious, but still resolved to keep your mind to yourself, and, though you should be unhappy, let me do what was most for my interest. That at Donaghadee I put myself in such a passion with you at your declining to go to Dublin that you was so much affected as to let me know the impression I had made upon your mind, though you at the same time continued your resolution to keep both our secrets. That in Dublin I saw everything fair for me; but confessed to you that although I was distracted between gay views of fortune and real attachment, the latter would prevent me at that time from making any advances to the Heiress.

That my passion continued in the same way till we returned to Lainshaw. But you did not allow yourself to reckon on me as yours, though we corresponded very frequently this summer. That you received a letter from me, telling you that my father was going to marry again, which hurt me so much that I was to leave Scotland for ever, and that I then owed to you that I durst not see you, because I had been indulging hopes of getting his consent to marry you, and that to see you in view of parting for ever would almost turn me mad. That you was shocked with this letter, wrote to me in the most earnest terms and used every argument to reconcile me to my father's scheme; but in vain. That your affection for me was such that you wished to let me know that you would go with me. That while you was in that situation, you received a letter from me, telling you that if I were not conscious I would share a crown with you if I had it, I would not make the proposal I was going to make: which was that if you chose to joint the interest of your £1,000 to my £100 a year, and would go with me to some agreeable retirement, I was ready to marry you directly. That you readily accepted my proposal, trusting to God's providence which extends over all the earth. That I was most grateful for this; I informed you that I had hopes of a mediation by means of Lord Monboddo. That this having accordingly taken place, and my father having kindly told me that he would give his consent to our marriage, I came to you at Lainshaw, and then we solemnly engaged ourselves *as we should answer to God.*

This, my dear Peggie, is, I think, a just and true abstract of our story. It does you great honour, and I appear a better man than people have imagined. Take courage, and tell this slowly to my father, and I am almost sure it will please him. Take care, at the same time, to let him know that as you have always been my confidante, and are therefore the best judge of me, you can assure him I never was before in the style in which you now know me to be. Do as I direct you, and there will be no room for dissimulation. Be rather silent and reserved, and let him take the lead. What a comfort would it be if you and I could make him happy, and prevent his doing a very improper thing which would lessen his character and estrange him from me. The Commissioner was with me this forenoon. He again repeated what I formerly wrote to you, and said he was persuaded that if you and I humour my father, and behave properly, he never will marry again. So let us be much in earnest. I give you full liberty to come under all engagements for me as to sobriety, application, and every part of my behaviour. Be not hurt by what my father may throw out either against you or me. Just let it blow over and by your gravity and cheerful composure of manners conciliate his affection. I cannot help indulging hopes that before two years are over he may be perfectly satisfied with us, and that we may be living together in the greatest harmony. Assure him of my sincere wishes for this. How comfortable, how respectable would it be for all of us!

Mr. David Hume was with me this morning, and gave a philosophical opinion that our marriage must be a happy one. Were it not for his infidel writings, everybody would love him. He is a plain, obliging, kind-hearted man. By the by, as a tax for the privilege of keeping Mr. Temple's letter, I must put you on to the trouble of sending me a copy of that part of it where he desires me to put some questions to Mr. Hume on the study of history. You must know my friend Temple is a man of much reading, especially since he was married. He says to me in a late letter, "You will be surprised and vexed to find how much knowledge I have acquired." This is a delicate reproof to me for my idleness and dissipation.

I have now fixed Monday next for setting out on my London journey.

SUNDAY 27 AUGUST. I was at home, calm and comfortable, having fixed next day for setting out. Miss Webster said of my marriage, "It's in every drawing-room in town." "Ay," said George, "but it is not in a bedroom yet." A real *bon mot,* upon honour—by an Edinburgh cloth merchant. I supped at worthy Dr. Boswell's. Talking of Johnson, he said he was a Herculean genius, just born to grapple with whole libraries. The Hon. James Cochrane was there. My marriage was talked of, and I was quite easy and cheerful.

MONDAY 28 AUGUST. As I had full time to prepare for setting out on this jaunt, I thought for once to have everything quite ready a day before. But I find leaving a place where one has been for some time is like dying and so leaving the world, in this respect: that something is always forgotten. Last night I recollected owing a number of letters. So in order to get them dispatched, I was obliged to sit up till five this morning. I was called before seven, so was a little feverish and uneasy. However, my constitution is now so much changed for the better that this did not disconcert me, and I rose in good spirits.

It was a fine day. My companion was a man between forty and fifty, dressed in black, with buckskin breeches and boots and a queuewig. He had been many years a merchant in London, and was acquainted with various branches of trade. I made our conversation turn upon it, and learned a good deal from him as to some mercantile causes in which I am concerned. I have heard my father say that the old Earl of Aberdeen was continually asking questions at everybody he met, by which he was always picking up knowledge of one kind or other. This is sometimes a good rule. But if too often applied I should think it would be ridiculous. A great deal of the knowledge to be casually picked up from those we meet is hardly worth having.

We eat an egg at Norton, and drank a dish of tea at Cornhill, and got at night to Wooler Haugh Head. Mr. Kinloch proved a knowing man in his profession, spoke very slow but very distinctly, and was extremely obliging and really careful of me, as he knew I had not been well.

WEDNESDAY 30 AUGUST. There came up to us this morning about seven in the fly, Mr. Dodds, a little, fat woollen-draper in Newcastle, a cheerful old gentlewoman, and her daughter Mrs. Topham, wife to one of Sir Francis Delaval's tenants. We all breakfasted together, and then set out. We were exceedingly chatty, and well entertained with that kind of broken conversation that leaves no trace behind it. I told them I was to be married so soon as I returned from London. Being free with absolute strangers is really and truly no freedom. For when you say, "I am to do so and so," to people who know nothing about you, it is the same thing as if you said A or B are to do it, and you are amused with their remarks and sometimes even helped by their advice. I said my great study at present was to get a proper posy or motto for my spouse's wedding-ring: "With this ring I thee wed." Mrs. Topham had none on hers. But her mother had a very good one. "Love and live happily." I took a memorandum of it in my pocket-book, and said I questioned if I should find a better.

THURSDAY 31 AUGUST. We breakfasted at Ferrybridge. The joy of an English breakfast in a clean, handsome inn, after having travelled a couple of stages, is great. We took up here another good old woman, a Yorkshire farmer's wife. I was in a droll humour, and, seeing rich clover fields, I started a scheme of feeding the human race upon them. I was for bringing up a young child with a calf, giving it a little milk for so long, keeping it in a cowhouse at night, and, in the daytime, making the calf and it feed in a clover field. There is no describing the rage of the worthy farmer's wife at this doctrine. "You are little better than an atheist!" said she. "I don't believe you fears either God or man." I persisted with great composure and gravity to enforce my system, and I thought my other companions would have died of laughing. Mr. Dodds was quite overcome. It is, however, really a bad thing to joke in that manner. How are people to be sure that a man is in earnest, when they have seen him, with the earnest and serious appearance of truth, maintaining what is farthest from his mind?

We dined very well at Barnby Moor, and instead of waiting near an hour, as we did yesterday at Northallerton, we had dinner immediately. The farmer's wife left us at Tuxford, not a little regretted by Mr. Howell, to whom she very cordially communicated a brandy bottle which she had in her pocket.

We got into Grantham before eight. I went and called on my acquaintance, the Reverend Mr. Palmer, chaplain to Sir John Cust, the Speaker of the House of Commons, a sensible, knowing man who improves much on acquaintance. He insisted I should sup with him, and he entertained me in a plain, friendly manner. His lady was indisposed; but he introduced to me his children, a daughter and two sons, saying before his eldest son that he was glad he would have it to say that he had taken by the hand the friend of the great Paoli. It is amazing how much and how universally I have made myself admired. This is an absolute fact. I am certain of it, and with an honest pride I will rejoice in it. Mr. Heron, another clergyman here, supped with us. We talked of Johnson, and particularly of his wonderful knowledge of the world, which I observed was most extraordinary, as he had lived so much in the retirement of Oxford and the Temple. Mr. Palmer remarked very justly that to know the world really well one must not be too much in it. One will see better what is going on and be able to trace the springs of action better by standing sometimes at a side. I pursued the thought. "One," said I, "should not be too early in the world, otherwise he will never know it fully; that is to say, in a philosophical sense. If he goes into it early, he becomes so insensibly accustomed to everything that he never enquires into its causes. Let him first study human nature in speculation, and form to himself a habit of examining it as exerted in active life, and then every scene he sees will be an experiment, and he will in time acquire much knowledge of the world. Though perhaps being late of entering upon it may make one's manners somewhat awkward. But that is but of inferior consequence." I went to my inn and had a few hours' sleep.

FRIDAY 1 SEPTEMBER. We set out at three o'clock, breakfasted at Stilton, dined at Biggleswade, and got to London between eight and nine. The sights of London again put me in high spirits. I cannot well account how it has had so strong an effect upon me since I can remember anything. Both before I saw it and since, my ideas of it have been very high. Messrs Howell and Dodds were set down in Gray's Inn Lane. Mr. Kinloch and I took a hackney-coach in Holborn and drove to Mr. Dilly's. There was nobody in the house at this time but the two brothers, who received me with a most lively joy. I introduced Mr. Kinloch to them, and he stayed and supped with us. I was quite at home. I liked to see the effects of being an author. Upon the strength of that, here were two booksellers who thought they could not do enough for me.

At eleven I walked down to my revered friend Mr. Samuel Johnson's to see if he was in town. But Miss Williams, the blind old lady who lives with him, told me he was down at Brighton. I sat some little time with her, and was rejoiced just to sit in Mr. Johnson's parlour, and see his inkhorn standing on the table. Miss Williams advised me to go to the Jubilee in honor of Shakespeare, at Stratford upon Avon. Indeed, when I left Scotland I was resolved not to go. But as I approached the capital I felt my inclination increase, and when arrived in London I found myself within the whirlpool of curiosity, which could not fail to carry me down.

Mr. Dilly insisted that I should live at his house, where I should be quite at home. I accepted of his kind invitation; and was pleased to be lodged in the house of my bookseller in the Poultry, in one of the most frequented streets of the city of London, where coaches pass at all hours. I was calm and well.

SATURDAY 2 SEPTEMBER. I went immediately and waited on Sir John Pringle. My principal intention in coming to London now was to put myself under the care of the famous Dr. Kennedy, to purify my blood from every remain of vicious poison. Sir John received me with his usual reserved kindness. He was not for my applying to Kennedy, but just taking Mr. Forbes, a regular surgeon, as the phrase is. However, he allowed me to please myself. It is amazing to see a man of Sir John's character so impregnated with partiality as to refuse its just credit to a medicine which has undoubtedly done wonders. I tried him formerly as to Keyser's pills, and found him equally prejudiced. As Sir John has witnessed many of my weaknesses and follies, and been always like a parent to me, I cannot help standing much in awe of him. He would insist that I was not yet in earnest to marry. I told him that I could not show him the inside of my mind as one does a watch, but that I was certainly conscious that my wheels now went calmly and constantly. He said, "Vous avez encore un peu de vertige." I was slightly angry and a good deal diverted, as I was sure of my being quite a different man from what he had formerly known me.

I went to Lincoln's Inn Fields and called on Dr. Kennedy. I had a letter for him from my uncle the Doctor, but would not deliver it till I saw how I liked him. He was a very old gentleman, large and formal and tedious, but seemingly worthy. After talking over my case with him, I told him who I was and gave him my uncle's letter. He allowed me to go to Shakespeare's Jubilee before I began my course of his medicine. I then went to a Mr. Dalemaine, an embroiderer in Bow Street, Covent Garden; gave him, cut out in paper as well as I could, the form of a Corsican cap, and ordered *Viva la Libertà* to be embroidered on the front of it in letters of gold.

SUNDAY 3 SEPTEMBER. I thought much on my dearest Peggie. She and I were very happy together in Dublin at different places of worship; I wished to have had her here with me. After this I shall not mention my dearest in my Journal, unless when something extraordinary occurs. To say that I love her and wish to have her with me is like saying my pulse beats and my blood circulates. It is to be always understood.   .

MONDAY 4 SEPTEMBER. I breakfasted with Mr. Dempster. He had company with him, so nothing material passed. In one of the streets of Soho I met Mr. Sheridan, whom I had not seen for many years. I lie under many obligations to him, as he took a great concern about me when I was a very idle, impetuous young fellow, and had me often in his house in the kindest manner. So I was happy to meet with him, and promised to come and dine with him without ceremony, when I was not engaged. I then called on Mr. Thomas Davies, bookseller, whom I must always remember as the man who made me acquainted with Mr. Samuel Johnson. He is a very good kind of man himself, and has been long my acquaintance. He told me that Mr. Berenger, the Master of Horse, who it seems is mighty delicate and polite, said that Mr. Johnson was, in a genteel company, like an ox in a china-shop. He overturns everything. I dined at home, and after dinner Mr. Dilly and I walked about searching all over the town for my necessary accoutrements as a Corsican for the Stratford Jubilee. Some I had made on purpose. Others I borrowed. But at last I got everything in order, and everything that I wanted went into such small bounds that I could carry the whole in my travelling bag, except my musket and staff.

TUESDAY 5 SEPTEMBER. I set out at seven in the Oxford fly, having for my companions a tradesman of Oxford, brother to Fletcher the bookseller in St. Paul's Churchyard, a cook-maid going home to Lord Harcourt, and the nurse of some nobleman's child, carrying it in her lap. We were all quiet, obliging, good-humoured people. We breakfasted at Slough. At Maidenhead the nurse left us. We jogged along. But I cannot say anything either instructive or entertaining passed. We dined at Henley, where we were joined as messmate by a brisk lawyer's clerk. We got to Oxford about six. I put up at the Angel Inn.

The grandeur and solemnity of Oxford as a literary retreat always fills me with agreeable reverence. But it makes my heart sore, too, for it recalls the memory of Sir James Macdonald. I may add, too, the memory of Frank Stewart. Last time I was at Oxford he supped with me, along with Mr. Samuel Johnson and Mr. Chambers, the Vinerian Professor, in the very room where I now sat.

I had a fine thought in a letter to Miss Montgomerie tonight. "Let us not," said I, "have much concern about settlements. In contracting and binding two lovers, the elegant passion is often destroyed; just as we have seen a bunch of flowers, of roses, jessamine, and honeysuckle, lose their flavour in being tied together." The thought is pretty, and is better expressed in my letter, if I could recollect it. It is amazing how much of sentiment consists in expression. Nothing but hard science remains the same when put in different words.

Mr. Mickle supped with me, and a little before twelve I set out in a post-chaise alone for Stratford, not having been able to find an idle scholar in all the university to accompany me. They were all gone already. It was very dark, and I was afraid both of being robbed and being overturned, so could not sleep.

. . . for, after having given her genteelly for some amorous interviews, I pretended that I had spent all my money. "My dear," said I, "such is my situation. I gave you when I had money. Now, when I have none, will you favour me with your company? I can hardly ask such a [thing, much as] I [wish] to try." She. . . .*

. . . tints of delight, I allowed myself no other liberty than once drawing my hand gently along her yellow locks. I had my valuable spouse ever present before me, and not only my reason but my heart and every feeling were even at that moment sensible of her superiority. I was wholly hers. I told Miss Reynolds with a most engaging address, "You are not made for this way of life. You have not the qualifications for it, except, indeed, being very pretty and very agreeable. You have not

---

*Here and above about three pages of Boswell's manuscript have been torn away, whether by himself or by a shocked reader at a later time we do not know.

the avarice, the falseness, which is requisite. I wish to have you out of it."
She promised to me that she would go into the millinery business and
behave properly.

Oxford, 5 September 1769

MY DEAREST LIFE,—My last was not half an answer to yours. You
quite overpower me with goodness. What return can I make for the
beautiful sentiments of sincere regard which your last contains? Indeed,
my dear friend, my only uneasiness now proceeds from melancholy
fears, at times, that this happiness is too great to last long in human life,
and an anxiety lest you should *really* imagine that I am not sufficiently
sensible of what I owe to you. There is the most refined delicacy in your
manner of expressing a doubt that my affection is not so strong as yours,
because I can go at such a distance from you with so much ease. This
would strike most people. But be assured, my dear Peggie, it is not a just
conclusion. Consider that it was absolutely necessary for me to go to
London, and a journey which appears long to you cannot affect in the
same manner one who has travelled so much as I have done. And, since
I am upon this subject, believe me, my going to Shakespeare's Jubilee,
and wishing to see many friends and enjoy many amusements, ought not
to be interpreted as marks of indifference. I am forwarding the recovery
of my health; I am acquiring an additional stock of ideas with which to
entertain you. I am dissipating melancholy clouds, and filling my mind
with fine, cheerful spirits.

You are, however, my constant object. What we read in the old
romances is realised in me. Upon honour, my dearest life, I just adore
you. I took the liberty to show my friend Dempster your noble, generous
letter *accepting of my terms*. He said it was the finest letter he had ever
read, and with the greatest warmth he rejoices at our being to be united.
He gives me franks for you, and he says very pleasantly that, next to
seeing my face, you will be happy to see his hand.

I left London this morning and came in the post-coach to this
venerable seat of learning, on my road to Stratford. The Jubilee begins
tomorrow. I have forty miles yet to go. So I take a post-chaise at every
stage, and well wrapped up in a greatcoat I travel all night asleep; and
shall be at Shakespeare's birth-place tomorrow morning early, and put
myself under the tuition of Mr. Garrick, who is steward of the Jubilee. I
assure you my Corsican dress will make a fine, striking appearance. My
gun slung across my shoulder, my pistol at one side and stiletto at
another, with my bonnet or kind of short grenadier cap, black, with *Viva
la Libertà* (that is, "Long live liberty", or, as the English say, "Liberty for
ever") embroidered upon its front in letters of gold, will attract much
notice. I have that kind of weakness that, when I looked at myself in the
glass last night in my Corsican dress, I could not help thinking your

opinion of yourself might be still more raised: "She has secured the constant affection and admiration of so fine a fellow." Do you know, I cannot think there is any harm in such a kind of weakness or vanity, when a man is sensible of it and it has no great effect upon him. It enlivens me and increases my good humour.

WEDNESDAY 6 SEPTEMBER. The first view of the Avon and of the town where Shakespeare was born gave me those feelings which men of enthusiasm have on seeing remarkable places. Cicero had them when he walked at Athens.

I was exceedingly dirty; my hair hung wet about my ears; my black suit and the postilion's grey duffle above it, several inches too short every way, made a very strange appearance. I could observe people getting together and whispering about me, for the church was full of well-dressed people. At last Mr. Garrick observed me. We first made an attitude to each other and then cordially shook hands. I gave him a line I had written to let him know I was incognito, as I wished to appear in the Corsican dress for the first time they should know me. Many of those who had stared, seeing that I was intimate with the steward of the Jubilee, came up to him and asked who I was. He answered, "A clergyman in disguise."

At dinner in the amphitheatre, I found my old brother soaper, Dr Berkeley, who introduced me into a party where he was. It consisted of several ladies and gentlemen. A Mrs. Sheldon, an Irish lady, wife of Captain Sheldon, a most agreeable little woman, pleased me most. I got into great spirits. I paid her particular attention. I began to imagine that she was stealing me from my valuable spouse, I was most unhappy from this imagination. I rose and went near the orchestra, and looked steadfastly at that beautiful, insinuating creature, Mrs. Baddeley of Drury Lane, and in an instant Mrs. Sheldon was effaced. I then saw that what I feared was love was in reality nothing more than transient liking. It had no interference with my noble attachment. It was such a momentary diversion from it as the sound of a flageolet in my ear, a gay colour glancing from a prism before my eye, or any other pleasing sensation. However, the fear I had put myself in made me melancholy. I had been like a timorous man in a post-chaise, who, when a wagon is passing near it, imagines that it is to crush it; and I did not soon recover the shock. My having had no sleep all night, travelled in the rain, and suffered anxiety on account of my pocket-book, no doubt contributed to my uneasiness. I recollected my former inconstancy, my vicious profligacy, my feverish gallantry, and I was terrified that I might lose my divine passion for Margaret, in which case I am sure I would suffer more than she. I prayed devoutly to heaven to preserve me from such a misfortune, and became easier.

FRIDAY 8 SEPTEMBER. After the joy of the Jubilee came the uneasy reflection that I was in a little village in wet weather and knew not how to get away, for all the post-chaises were bespoke, I don't know how many times over, by different companies. We were like a crowd in a theatre. It was impossible we could all go at a time.

I sauntered about till about two, when I went into Payton's public room to have some dinner. At a table by themselves sat two gentlemen who seemed to know me. I asked them if I could have anything to eat. They asked me to sit down with them; I did so. They were both Lichfield men. The one, Mr. Bailye, a middle-aged gentleman who had been at school with Garrick and knew Mr. Samuel Johnson well. The other, Lieutenant Vyse of Sir Joseph Yorke's Dragoons, who also knew Mr. Johnson, being the son of a clergyman in Lichfield in whose family my revered friend is intimate. They both named me, and we dined very agreeably together. It is fine to have such a character as I have. I enjoy it much.

I then took the parish clerk and went into the great church, and viewed calmly and solemnly the tomb of Shakespeare. His wife lies buried beside him. I observed with pleasure that she was seven years older than he, for it has been objected that my valuable spouse is a little older than I am.

I went to Mr. Garrick and gave him a parcel of my *Verses*. He read them to me in such a manner that I was quite elated. They seemed admirable. My money had run short. So I asked him to let me have five guineas. He told me his brother George had taken almost all he had from him. "Come, come," said I, "that won't do. Five guineas I must have, and you must find them for me." I saw very well that he was not making any serious difficulty. "Well," said he, "you are right, you are a stranger. I must get you them." So he run to Mrs. Garrick, and brought me them. I went to bed in good time.

SUNDAY 10 SEPTEMBER. We stopped at Hounslow and had coffee and tea. Captain Johnston was born at Dumfries, but had not been in Scotland for a vast many years, and had acquired the true English oddity. He said he should find nobody in London on a Sunday, and therefore he would stay a couple of hours at Hounslow, and take a chaise and drive in at night. A true John Bull scheme. Surely he would tire as much at Hounslow, one should think, as in London. We persuaded him off his project, and came all to town together. I found at Mr. Dilly's two

French translations of my *Account of Corsica*. One of them had come consigned to Mr. Wilkes, who sent me many compliments. I had a desire to visit the pleasant fellow, but thought it might hurt me essentially. The translation of my book flattered my vanity. It is a curious sensation one has from reading one's own composition when put in a foreign dress.

MONDAY 11 SEPTEMBER. I called on Dr. Kennedy, and this night I began to take the Lisbon Diet Drink.

[Received 11 September, Johnson to Boswell]

Brighton, 9 September 1769

DEAR SIR,—Why do you charge me with unkindness? I have omitted nothing that could do you good or give you pleasure, unless it be that I have forborne to tell you my opinion of your *Account of Corsica*. I believe my opinion, if you think well of my judgment, might have given you pleasure; but when it is considered how much vanity is excited by praise, I am not sure that it would have done you good. Your *History* is like other histories, but your *Journal* is in a very high degree curious and delightful. There is between the *History* and the *Journal* that difference which there will always be found between notions borrowed from without and notions generated within. Your *History* was copied from books; your *Journal* rose out of your own experience and observations. You express images which operated strongly upon yourself, and you have impressed them with great force upon your readers. I know not whether I could name any narrative by which curiosity is better excited or better gratified.

I am glad that you are going to be married; and as I wish you well in things of less importance, wish you well with proportionate ardour in this crisis of your life. What I can contribute to your happiness I should be very unwilling to withhold; for I have always loved and valued you, and shall love you and value you still more as you become more regular and useful: effects which a happy marriage will hardly fail to produce.

I do not find that I am likely to come back very soon from this place. I shall, perhaps, stay a fortnight longer; and a fortnight is a long time to a lover absent from his mistress. Would a fortnight ever have an end? I am, dear Sir, your most affectionate, humble servant,

SAM JOHNSON.

TUESDAY 12 SEPTEMBER. Between five and six I came home and stood to have a drawing of me, as the armed Corsican chief at Stratford, taken by Mr. Wale. It was pleasing to think that I was at that moment getting my figure done in London, to be engraved for four thousand *London Magazines*.

SATURDAY 16 SEPTEMBER. I walked out betimes to visit my cousin Charles. I was impatient, curious, and agitated to think of meeting for the first time with him. He received me in the passage, and I at once saw him to be a son of Thomas Boswell of Auchinleck. Each of us could perceive a family likeness in the other. He proved to be a sensible, plain, well-bred gentleman, very cordial, and very good company. I cannot describe what satisfaction I had from seeing a descendant of our ancient family. We were just like brothers. I told him a great deal about Scotland, and he entertained me with telling me a great deal about Jamaica. "Come," said he, "will you take pot luck with us?" And turning to his mistress, "We are not," said he, "in order yet, as we are just got into this house. But I see he's an easy man." I was engaged to dinner, but promised to come back and drink tea.

I observe continually how imperfectly, upon most occasions, words preserve our ideas. This interview is but faintly seen in my Journal. And all I have said of the Stratford Jubilee is very dim in comparison to the scene itself. In description we omit insensibly many little touches which give life to objects. With how small a speck does a painter give life to an eye! The vivid glances of Garrick's features, which cannot be copied in words, will illuminate an extent of sensation, if that term may be used, as a spark from a flint will throw a lustre in a dark night for a considerable space around it. Certain looks of my dearest life and certain tones of her voice, which I defy all the masters of language to show upon paper, have engaged my soul in an angelic manner. I find myself ready to write unintelligibly when I attempt to give any kind of idea of such subjects.

I dined with Mr. Sheridan. He had nobody with him but his two daughters and two sons, who were surprisingly grown since I saw them in 1763, and seemed to be a fine family. I observed to Mr. Sheridan that although my father and I differed a good deal, yet upon the whole our system was much the same. That we were like two men on horseback who set out from a post at one part of a circle in order to reach a post at

an opposite part. My father |o| takes the northern and rugged side. I

again take the southern, gay side. He is very angry to see me taking what is seemingly the direct contrary road to his. But if he will have patience, he will find us both at the same ending place. In the meantime, however, he cries, "It is a strange thing you will not come with me," and is very ill pleased. While I cry, "Never mind. Let me take my own way. I shall do well enough."

SUNDAY 17 SEPTEMBER. I made an experiment to see if I could go home without asking the way at all. So I walked from street to street a long time. At last I found myself in the field near to the Foundling Hospital. This was not so safe. So I just turned back, was happy to get again into a crowded street, and then asked my way and got to my quarters in good time.

MONDAY 18 SEPTEMBER. I had promised to pay a visit to my old friend Mr. Love, and see him in his greatness as manager of the Theatre Royal on Richmond Green. So I this morning set out in the Richmond stage. Among the passengers was one who, I believe, was a German old lady. She spoke broken English. But, knowing the antipathy of the people of this country to foreigners, she thought to persuade us that her manner of speaking was owing only to loss of teeth.

It was a most delightful day. Richmond seemed delicious. Mr. Love's theatre is a very handsome one, having everything in miniature. He and I, after seeing it, took a walk on the banks of the Thames, and recalled our having walked together on Arthur's Seat. Mrs. Love looked very well, though verging on fifty.

THURSDAY 21 SEPTEMBER. I then called at Mr. Thomas Davie's, the bookseller. Dr. Goldsmith was there. I had not seen him for near three years. We met quite frankly. He pleased me by telling me that he had supped the night before in a company where I was highly spoken of, and that Mr. Colman had very justly observed that my character was simplicity: not in a sense of weakness, but of being plain and unaffected.

I called at Dempster's, and finding no letter from my dearest was uneasy. It was not a post day from Scotland. So Dempster cheered me with hopes for next day. He and I had a dissertation on my plan of life. We agreed that I might be happy with a seven years' seat in Parliament, if it could be had easily. But, in the meantime, I was very well with the law in Scotland.

FRIDAY 22 SEPTEMBER. I breakfasted with Mr. Forbes, who has the best breakfast in London, having marmalade made him by his nieces in Scotland. I then went to Old Bond Street and called on Paoli. A footman who opened the door said he was not well and could not see company and made a great many difficulties. "Stay," said I. "Get me a bit of paper and pen and ink, and I'll write a note to him." His *valet de chambre* came down. Seeing something about him like what I had been used to see in Corsica, I asked him in Italian if he was a Corsican. He answered, "Yes, Sir." "Oh, then," said I, "there is no occasion to write. My name is Boswell." No sooner had I said this than Giuseppe (for that was his name) gave a jump, catched hold of my hand and kissed it, and clapped his hand several times upon my shoulders with such a natural joy and fondness as flattered me exceedingly. Then he ran upstairs before me like an Italian harlequin, being a very little fellow, and, opening the door of the General's bedchamber, called out, "Mr. Boswell". I heard the General give a shout before I saw him. When I entered he was in his night-gown and nightcap. He ran to me, took me all in his arms, and held me there for some time. I cannot describe my feelings on meeting him again. We sat down and instantly were just as when we parted. I found myself much rusted in my Italian. The General made a fine observation upon a man's being in want of language. "When," said he, "I came over to Italy, and was obliged there and in Germany to speak French, in which I had not a fluency from want of practice, *je trouvais mon âme renfermée comme dans un cachot.*" An admirable metaphor. The more it is considered, the better it appears. How well does it show the soul up, and ideas struggling to get out! He had a number of newspapers on his table. He was struck with the daring style of the political writings in them. Said he: "I am come here to a northern country, and I find the newspapers all on fire."

I left him a little to go and look at the company going to and coming from Court, to please my monarchical genius. I met the worthy Duke of Queensberry in his chair in St. James's Street. He made his chairmen set him down, and shook hands with me cordially. I told him of Paoli's arrival, and asked him if he would not go and see him. He said he should be very happy. "But where," said he, "and how shall I find him?" "Just now," said I, "my Lord. Follow me, chairmen." So I just walked back to his lodgings, and introduced the Duke. His Grace seemed much struck. He said, "Je rencontrais mon ami, Monsieur Boswell. Il vous dira combien j'ai été intéressé pour vous." The General behaved with the utmost ease and politeness. I sat by with joy in my heart and a cheerful smile on my countenance to see my illustrious friend and the worthy Duke together.

Paoli's lodings were in the house where the Duchess of Douglas had lived. They were the most magnificent, I suppose, to be hired in all London. I dined with Paoli; Count Gentili and Abbé Guelfucci were with us. I felt myself just as when at Sollacarò. As I hardly hoped to meet Paoli in this world again, I had a curious imagination as if I had passed through death and was really in Elysium. This idea made me not afraid of actual death, of which I think so often, just as my grandfather Mr. James Boswell did. I was filled with admiration whenever the General spoke. I said that after every sentence spoken by him I felt an inclination to sing *Te Deum*. Indeed, when he speaks it is a triumph to human nature and to my friendship. He said he believed that, in a course of years, perhaps moral events would be calculated just as physical ones are. That, as there is a gradual progress in states, it might be calculated such a year will be a war, just as we see in the almanac that there will be an eclipse. I fear this is too curious.

I then went to Dempster's, and, finding no letter from my dearest Peggie, I was really uneasy. I sat down and wrote to her, which did me good. The General's arrival obliged me to alter my retired, frugal system. It was my duty to attend upon him, and be genteelly dressed accordingly. So I ordered a genteel, plain, slate-blue frock suit, and a full suit of a kind of purple cloth with rich gold buttons, and Mr. Dilly supplied me with a silver-hilted sword. Paoli said he was sorry he had not room for me in the house with himself. I could have wished it. But I did my best, and immediately took very handsome lodgings within a few doors of his, at a M. Renaud's, an old Swiss, whose wife kept a milliner's shop. She was a well-behaved, obliging woman. The Bishop of Peterborough had been her lodger many years. Indeed the apartments were excellent. I had a large dining-room with three windows to Old Bond Street, a bedchamber, and a dressing-room, both looking into Burlington Gardens. So that I saw a pretty large extent of green ground and stately trees in the very centre of the court end of the town.

I took a coach to Carey Street about eleven. Mrs. Careless was in bed with her husband, whom I had never seen. Phoebe called her up. She seemed amazed when she heard that I was to leave my lodgings in her house after sleeping there only one night. And I dare say she had a shrewd suspicion that I was about no good, when I shifted so suddenly. It looked somewhat like a highwayman. However, I told her the reason of it, paid her five and twenty shillings, the whole week's money, and left my new address. And thus did I quit *Sans Souci,* though it sounded like the seat of the King of Prussia, and the maid Phoebe, though a song in *The Spectator* says:

> My time, O ye Muses, was happily spent,
> When *Phoebe* went with me wherever I went.

Such nonsense. But I may now and then play myself with ideas. I paid for my apartments in Old Bond Street a guinea and a half a week, only the half of what they bring in winter. I found there a pretty little Yorkshire maid called Mary. I determined however to get a servant who could speak Italian. It seemed pleasant thus to move from lodging to lodging.

SATURDAY 23 SEPTEMBER. I went this morning and sat for above an hour to Mr. Miller, who was engraving a print of me in the Corsican dress.

SUNDAY 24 SEPTEMBER. Last time I was with Dr. Campbell, he told me that he was beginning to agree with Mr. Johnson about the colonists. "Sir," said Johnson, "they are a parcel of convicts, and if they get anything short of hanging they ought to be content."

MONDAY 25 SEPTEMBER. I sat with the General and gave him a lesson on the English language by reading newspapers with him. He and I reclined upon a couch, and his vivacity, nobleness of thought, and engaging manners raised my ideas and made me truly happy. I then told him how the thoughts of my father's marrying again had agitated me, and from that I introduced an account of my dearest spouse's generous behaviour. In a cursory way, he seemed to approve my warm resentment of my father's conduct. But we soon passed from it to the beautiful subject of Miss Montgomerie. I took out her *most valuable letter*. Paoli read it, and translated it with elegant spirit into Italian. "Free of ambition, I prefer real happiness to the splendid appearance of it" struck him much. He read it over again and again, and repeated it, saying, "Questo è sublime" (This is sublime). He with much cordiality wished me all happiness. This was a rich evening.

[Boswell to Margaret Montgomerie]

Mr. Johnson settled my mind fully this afternoon as to my father. "Sir," said he, "the disputes between you and him are matters of sensation, not of judgment. So it is in vain to reason with him. He grumbles because you come to London. He cannot understand why it is very right you should from time to time enjoy London. There is no help for it. Let him grumble."

Mr. Johnson is of opinion that when a man marries and becomes the head of a family, he ought to have his own house, and cannot possibly be happy under his father's roof, more especially if circumstances are such, from temper or anything else, that a man and his father cannot live well together even while the son is unmarried. He advises me strongly to have my own house. He says my father will treat you and me much better when we have our own home and leave him at night. As to my father's marrying again, he thinks it had much better not happen. Mr. Johnson says that if you and I live near my father and are often with him, it will be as effectual in preventing his marrying again as living with him would be. Be not uneasy. I shall do nothing rashly, nor take any hasty resolutions. I again beg you may just think of me as your friend and lover. Leave everything else to time.

[Manuscript of *The Life of Johnson*]

When I found fault with a gentleman of my acquaintance for entering into a second marriage, as it showed a disregard of his first wife, he said, "Not at all, Sir. On the contrary, were he never to marry again, it might be concluded that his first wife had made him heartily sick of marriage; but by taking a second wife he pays the highest compliment to the first, by proving that she made him so happy as a married man that he has a mind to be so a second time." . . .

On the evening of the 10 October, I presented Dr. Johnson to General Paoli. I had greatly wished that two men for whom I had the highest value should meet. They met with a manly ease, mutually conscious of their own abilities and of the abilities one of each other. The General spoke Italian and Dr. Johnson English, and understood one another very well with a little aid of interpretation from me, in which I compared myself to an isthmus which joins two great continents. Upon Johnson's entering the room the General said, "From what I have read of your works, Sir, and from what Mr. Boswell has told me of you, I have long had you in great esteem and veneration." The General talked of language being formed on the particular ideas and manners of a country, without knowing which we cannot know the language. We may know the direct signification of single words, but by these no beauty of expression, no sally of genius, no wit is conveyed to the mind. All this must be by allusion to other ideas. "Sir," said Johnson, "You talk of language as if you had never done anything else but study it, instead of governing a nation." The General said, "Questo è un troppo gran complemento" (This is too great a compliment). Johnson answered, "I should have thought so, Sir, if I had not heard you talk." The General asked him what he thought of the spirit of infidelity which was so prevalent. JOHNSON. "Sir, this gloom of infidelity, I hope, is only a transient cloud passing through the hemisphere which will soon be dissipated and the sun break forth with his usual splendour." "You think then," said the General, "that they will change their principles like their clothes." JOHNSON. "Why, Sir, if they bestow no more thought on principles than on dress, it must be so." The General said that "a great part of the fashionable infidelity was owing to a desire of showing courage. Men who have no opportunities of showing it in real life take death and futurity as objects on which to display it." JOHNSON. "That is mighty foolish affectation. Fear is one of the passions of human nature, of which it is impossible to divest it. You remember that the Emperor Charles V, when he read upon the tombstone of a Spanish nobleman,

'Here lies one who never knew fear,' wittily said, 'Then he has never snuffed a candle with his fingers.' "

On Thursday 19 October I had a long evening with him at his house by ourselves. He advised me to complete a Dictionary of words peculiar to Scotland, of which I showed him a specimen. "Sir," said he, "Ray has made a collection of North Country words. By collecting those of your country you will do a useful thing towards the history of the language." He bade me also go on with collections which I was making upon the antiquities of Scotland. "Make a large book, a folio." BOSWELL. "But of what use will it be, Sir?" JOHNSON. "Never mind the use; do it."

I mentioned to him that I had seen the execution of several convicts at Tyburn two days before, and that none of them seemed to be under any concern. JOHNSON. "Most of them, Sir, have never thought at all." BOSWELL. "But is not the fear of death natural to us all?" JOHNSON. "So much so, Sir, that the whole of life is but keeping away the thoughts of it." He then, in a low and earnest tone, talked of his meditating upon the awful hour of his own dissolution, and in what manner he should behave upon that occasion: "I am uncertain," said he, "whether I should wish to have a friend by me, or have it all between God and myself."

Talking of our feeling for the distresses of others:—JOHNSON. "Why, Sir, there is much noise made about it, but it is not true. No, Sir, you have a decent feeling to prompt you to do good: more than that Providence does not intend. It would be misery to no purpose." BOSWELL. "But now if I were in danger of being hanged?" JOHNSON. "I should do what I could to bail you, but when you were once fairly hanged I should not suffer for you." BOSWELL. "Would you eat your dinner that day, Sir?" JOHNSON. "Yes, Sir, and eat it as if you were eating it with me. Why, there's Baretti who is to be tried for his life tomorrow; friends have risen up for him on every side, but if he should be hanged, none of those friends will eat a slice of plum pudding the less. Sir, that sympathetic feeling goes a very little way in depressing the mind."

THURSDAY 26 OCTOBER. When we were alone I introduced the subject of death, and endeavoured to maintain that the fear of it might be got over. To my question, if we might not calm our minds for the approach of death, he answered in passion, "No, Sir, let it alone. It matters not how a man dies, but how he lives. The act of dying is not of importance, it lasts so short a time." He added, with an earnest look, "A man knows it must be, and submits. It will do him no good to whine."

I attempted to continue the conversation. He was so provoked that he said, "Give us no more of this," and was thrown into such a state of tumult that he expressed himself in a way that alarmed and distressed me; showed an impatience to have me leave him, and, when I was going away, said, "Don't let us meet tomorrow."

I went home exceedingly uneasy. All the harsh observations which I had ever heard made upon his character crowded into my mind; and I seemed to myself like the man who had put his head into a lion's mouth a great many times with perfect safety, but at last had it bit off.

Next morning I sent him a note acknowledging that I might have been in the wrong, but it was not intentionally; he was therefore, I could not help thinking, too severe upon me. That notwithstanding our agreement not to meet today, I would call in my way to the City, and stay five minutes by my watch. "You are," said I, "in my mind since last night surrounded with cloud and storm. Let me have a glimpse of sunshine, and go about my affairs in serenity and cheerfulness."

Upon entering his study I was glad that he was not alone, which would have made our meeting more awkward. There were with him Mr. Steevens and Mr. Tyers, both of whom I now saw for the first time. My note had, or his own reflection, softened his ferocity, for he received me very complacently; so that I unexpectedly found myself at ease, and joined in the conversation.

He said the critics had done too much honour to Sir Richard Blackmore in writing so much against him. That his *Creation* had been helped by various wits, a line by Philips and a line by Tickell; so that by their aid and that of others the poem had been made out.

I defended Blackmore's lines, which have been celebrated for absolute nonsense:

> A painted vest Prince Voltiger had on,
> Which from a naked Pict his grandsire won.

I maintained it to be a poetical conceit. A Pict being painted, if he is slain in battle and a vest is made of his skin, it is a painted vest won from him, though he was naked.

Johnson spoke unfavourably of a certain pretty voluminous author, saying, "He used to write anonymous books and then other books commending those books, in which there was something of rascality."

I whispered him, "Well, Sir, you are now in good humour." JOHNSON. "Yes, Sir." I was going to leave him, and had got as far as the staircase. He stopped me, and smiling said, "Get you gone—*in*"; a curious mode of inviting me to stay, which I accordingly did for some time longer. . . .

[Received ? 30 October, Margaret Montgomerie to Boswell]

Lainshaw, 24 October 1769

I AM JUST RETURNED FROM THE POST OFFICE quite disappointed at not receiving a letter from my dear friend. I was not well and very low-spirited, and therefore stood in need of comfort, but your former goodness to me puts it out of my power to complain. I have just now had very melancholy accounts of poor Lord Eglinton. He was on his way to Lord Glasgow's and met an excise officer amongst his enclosure at Ardrossan; as he is a notorious poacher, my Lord ordered him to deliver his gun, which he positively refused, adding he would part with it and life together. My Lord upon this jumped out of his coach, and the fellow presented his piece to him, warning him to keep off; in the meantime Campbell's foot struck a stone and he fell back into a furrow; when, seeing Lord Eglinton advancing towards him, he fired and shot him through the body. Expresses are gone every way for assistance, but, by the accounts I have received, I'm afraid all is over with him. I have sent off to get the particulars from Charles Crookshanks, and shall be able to give you distinct information about this unhappy affair as soon as the express returns.

The man has just arrived and has brought me a letter from one of the surgeons, which I enclose to you. Oh, what a melancholy thing it is to lose one's friend in such a shocking, barbarous manner! The fellow is put in jail, and was examined before the magistrates of Irvine. He confessed he shot my Lord, but insists that he was in the way of his duty and therefore not culpable. He had information of smugglers coming that way, if one can credit his method of telling the story. But surely the law was open to him; if my Lord did an unwarrantable thing, he therefore ought to have sought his redress in that way.

What an afflicted family! Poor Lady Eglinton parted with him in great health and spirits, and in a few hours after had him brought back a woeful, bloody spectacle.

How vain, how transitory, is every earthly enjoyment! O that such a striking instance of mortality may teach us to keep in mind our latter end, and so to number our days as to apply our hearts unto wisdom.

I cannot write anything else, I am so distressed with this sad accident. I really hardly know what I am doing. Write me soon, my dear Jamie, and tell me how you do. I am more and more anxious about you. When I feel so much for the danger an old and intimate acquaintance is in, what must I not suffer for the man I prefer to every earthly being, when I consider that he is not well, and, for aught I know, may at present be under the greatest distress?

I suppose next letter I write will inform you that your old friend is now no more. I was told so this moment, but as it was not from certain authority I do not assert it for a truth, though Mr. Fleming's account makes it extremely probable.

Adieu, my dearest friend. May the Almighty bless and preserve you to your ever faithful and affectionate

M.M.

[Received ? 8 November, Margaret Montgomerie to Boswell]

Lainshaw, 31 October 1769

Though you may believe I wished and likewise expected to have seen you sooner than I now can, yet, as you tell me your absence is necessary, I submit. I cannot help being uneasy at the thoughts of General Paoli's being witness to the ceremony. It's at any rate an awful affair, and would be doubly so in the presence of so great a man. To be sure, I ought to carry my views much higher and consider myself before the Supreme Being, but sensible objects have too great an effect on our minds, and are apt to draw them off from things of greater importance. I sincerely wish he may not come, but if he does, and you signify to me your desire to have him, you may believe I shall agree, whatever it should cost me. Do not again take a disgust at me and think me a weak, awkward, spiritless being. Remember, with advantages vastly superior to mine, you yourself was uneasy in the presence of the illustrious Chief. You bid me tell you every thought of my heart and have no other confidant but you. I really have none, and do fairly acknowledge to you that I wish you could steal out of Edinburgh when nobody can suspect where you are going, and let the ceremony be put over as privately as possible, as I would like to remain in the country till you thought it necessary for me to come to town; however, determine on whatever is most agreeable and convenient for yourself, and be assured I shall willingly comply with whatever you judge right.

You would be greatly shocked with the accounts of poor Lord Eglinton's death. His murderer is nephew to Netherplace. I doubt not but they will apply to you to be his counsel, but I am likewise certain their application will be in vain. It was put in the newspapers that it was accidental, but my Lord expressed himself in a very different manner, and his servants were witnesses to its being designed. I forgot if I told you Lord Eglinton settled £100 a year on Charles Crookshanks and two hundred a year on Mrs. Brown.

[Manuscript of *The Life of Johnson*]

I was detained in town till it was too late on the 9th, so went out to him early in the morning of the 10th November. "Now," said he, "that you are going to marry, do not expect more from life than life will afford. You may often find yourself out of humour, and you may often think your wife not studious enough to please you, and yet you may have reason enough to consider yourself as upon the whole very happily married."

Talking of marriage in general he observed, "Our marriage service is too refined. It is calculated only for the best kind of marriages, whereas we should have a form for matches of convenience, of which there are many." He agreed with me that there was no absolute necessity for having the marriage ceremony performed by a regular clergyman, for this was not commanded in Scripture.

I was volatile enough to repeat to him a little epigrammatic song of mine on matrimony, which Mr. Garrick had a few days before procured to be set to music.

A Matrimonial Thought

In the blithe days of honeymoon,
With Kate's allurements smitten,
I loved her late, I loved her soon,
And called her dearest kitten.

But now my kitten's grown a cat,
And cross like other wives,
Oh! by my soul, my honest Mat,
I fear she has nine lives.

My illustrious friend said, "Mighty well, Sir, but don't swear." Upon which I altered, "Oh! by my soul" to "Alas, alas!"

He was good enough to accompany me to London, and see me into the post-chaise which was to carry me on my road to Scotland.

[*Scots Magazine*]

25 [NOVEMBER]. At Edinburgh, Alexander Boswell, Esquire, of Auchinleck, one of the Lords of Session and Justiciary, to Miss Betty Boswell, second daughter of John Boswell, Esquire, of Balmuto, deceased.

25 [NOVEMBER]. At Lainshaw, in the shire of Ayr, James Boswell, Esquire, of Auchinleck, advocate, to Miss Peggie Montgomerie, daughter of the late David Montgomerie of Lainshaw, Esquire.

This is the marriage contract between James Boswell, Esquire, eldest son to the Right Honourable Alexander Boswell, Esquire, of

Auchinleck, one of the Lords of Session and Justiciary in Scotland, and
Miss Peggie Montgomerie, daughter to the late David Montgomerie of
Lainshaw, Esquire.

The said parties do hereby agree that, in consideration of the
sincerest mutual love and regard, they will, on or before the holy festival
of Christmas next to come, be united to each other by marriage.

They solemnly engage to be faithful spouses, to bear with one
another's faults, and to contribute as much as possible to each other's
happiness in this world; hoping through the merits of their blessed
Saviour, Jesus Christ, for eternal happiness in the world which is to
come.

In faith of which, this paper, written by the said James Boswell,
Esquire, is subscribed by him at London on the thirty-first day of
October in the year of our Lord one thousand seven hundred and
sixty-nine, before these witnesses: Pascal Paoli, General of the Corsicans,
and Samuel Johnson, Doctor of Laws, and author of *The Rambler* and
other works.

JAMES BOSWELL.

*Io sottoscritto ho veduto, e sono stato presente quando il Signore Giacomo
Boswell ha sottoscritto questo foglio.*

PASQUALE DE PAOLI.

SAM: JOHNSON, Witness.

BOSWELL
FOR THE DEFENCE

14 March 1772 – 21 September 1774

INTRODUCTION

O N SEVERAL OCCASIONS in his journal, Boswell compares departure to death. His jaunts to London began in dread. His departure for London on March 14, 1772, was different from previous departures: his responsibility has enlarged, for he is now "a domestic man" parting from his wife for a distant destination for a necessarily long period: four hundred miles, for two months.

Part of his business in London in this year was his conduct of an appeal before the House of Lords in the case of a Scottish schoolmaster named Hastie, who had been relieved of his duties because of an excess of severity in punishing his students. Boswell's reasoning in this case would be strengthened by his consultation with Mr. Johnson, from whom, in the same motion, Boswell was collecting material to enrich his journal. Indeed, Johnson's disquisition on the efficacy of punishment in general, and on the probable virtue of Hastie in particular, while providing a glorious passage for the journal and the *Life,* was of no assistance to the schoolmaster himself, whose appeal was denied.

Boswell also discussed with Mr. Johnson the problem of his father; elsewhere in London, Boswell sounded out prospects for political preference, as he had sought the Foot Guards nine years before, failing again as he had failed before. He dined well and drank well and felt himself to be more than ever a literary man—Corsica behind, he was thinking forward: "I have a constant plan to write the life of Mr. Johnson," Boswell recorded on March 31.

On March 15, 1773, one year later, his first child, Veronica, was born in Edinburgh. On the same date, in London, Goldsmith's comedy, *She Stoops to Conquer,* played the first performance of its long life. Boswell wrote to him two weeks later expressing "joy" in Goldsmith's "success," and continuing: "The English nation was just falling into lethargy. Their blood was thickened and their minds *creamed and mantled like a standing pool.* . . . You must know my wife was safely delivered of a daughter, the very evening that *She Stoops to Conquer* first appeared. I am fond of the coincidence."

This year Boswell went again to London, once more beset by the anxiety of departure. "I walked down the High Street of Edinburgh, which has a grand appearance in the silence and dusky light of three in the morning, and felt myself like an officer in a campaign. When the fly had rumbled me a mile or two, rational and manly sensations took the place of tender and timid feebleness. I considered that I had left my wife and little daughter well. That I was going to London, whither so many Members of Parliament, lawyers, merchants, and others go and return in safety to their families."

The triumph of this trip was his election to the Literary Club, for which he was sponsored by Mr. Johnson, and whose members included Goldsmith, Garrick, Joshua Reynolds, and Edmund Burke, among other illustrious men.

Later in the same year Boswell and Johnson shared a setting unique to their friendship, which had now been ten years in force. Far from the comfort and sophistication of London, they journeyed by foot, by horse, and by vessels small and large from August to November through the Hebrides, islands of northern Scotland. This was their longest period of uninterrupted companionship.

Of course, Boswell kept his journal, from which was formed his *Journal of a Tour to the Hebrides,* in 1785. Returning, Johnson at last met Lord Auchinleck, of whom he had heard a great deal for a decade. This, Boswell wrote, was a "contest" of "intellectual gladiators." The meeting occurred during Johnson's six-day visit to Boswell's ancestral home near Edinburgh and was marked by occasional moments of tension and by at least one moment of "collision." Over a question of politics Lord Auchinleck and Dr. Johnson "became exceedingly warm and violent, and I was very much distressed by being present at such an altercation between two men, both of whom I reverenced; yet I durst not interfere."

Two days afterward Lord Auchinleck in a "very civil" manner saw Boswell and Johnson off to Edinburgh, where, for ten days, Johnson was the honored guest of the educated community of the city. One imagines Boswell's elevated pride in having arranged such a notable event. Here Johnson met Margaret, whose marriage contract he had witnessed four years earlier, and here he detected in her, in spite of her vast courtesy to him, that disapproval of him which Boswell attributed to Johnson's undue "influence" over her husband.

Johnson departed for London late in November 1773. Boswell "had exhausted all my powers to entertain him. While he was with me, his noble exuberance of genius excited my spirits to a high degree, so that I did not feel at the same time how much I was weakened. I was like a man who drinks hard and is kept in high glee by what is wasting his constitution, but perceives its enfeebling effects as soon as he lives without it."

We approach now the second trial of John Reid.

During the Court of Session, Winter, 1773–74, Boswell was engaged for the defense in several criminal trials. Of each of these we know a little, usually the charge, the disputed circumstances, and the outcome. He conducted a successful appeal for a man who was to have been publicly whipped for having ordered tavern meals for which he could not pay; he unsuccessfully defended two very young women who appear to have killed a woman during the course of a robbery: one of his clients was hanged; her sister, age sixteen, apparently received a lesser sentence; he defended a horse thief who was sentenced to be hanged, but whose sentence was afterward reduced to transportation; he assisted at the defense of five accused arsonists, three of whom won verdicts of "not proven," two of whom were banished.

During most of this period, perhaps from the time of Mr. Johnson's return to London, but for exactly what reason we cannot be certain, Boswell suffered acute melancholy. So protracted a commitment to clients in bleak circumstances cannot have brightened his spirits.

With the beginning of Summer Session, 1774, he resumed his journal, which for some months had lapsed. Perhaps he thought to reclaim his spirits by documenting his grim legal encounters, enclosing them within the pages of his journal, thereby objectifying them, reducing their limits and their chaos to familiar form.

In the past each session had seemed different from every other. The new Session seemed to him at first undifferentiated from the others, promising boredom or continued misery, or both. His journal might then add interest to his occupation. The Session "came on quite simple," he wrote. "It was just the Summer Session 1774 without any other perceptible mark."

Ah, but when Boswell made journal of it, it became as memorable a Session as ever occurred. On the last day of July he arrived "in a fine state of preparation" at the particular business of John Reid. Reid, we remember, had been Boswell's first client and was now again his client, charged, as before, with the theft of sheep. In sheep-raising country the crime was capital.

From that day forward Boswell recorded his business with Reid with attention to the minutest detail, furnishing posterity, as we shall see, with a close account of one man's trial remarkable for its power to convey us to a humble, insignificant scene like hundreds of others, forgotten, but revived by Boswell in all its hues. It is a drama played by remarkable actors: one more engagement between Boswell, advocate for the defense, and Lord Auchinleck, judge; friends of the Crown, friends of the accused; memorable men, women, and children once more enacting the relentless tale of John Reid, flesher in Hillend, near Avonbridge.

SATURDAY 14 MARCH. I was in a flutter to a certain degree at the thoughts of setting out for London, for which I have always had an enthusiastic fondness. I was at the same time seriously concerned at parting with my wife. Everything depends upon our ideas; and I could with truth describe what passed in my mind this day in such a manner as to furnish out a narrative like that of the Londoner in the *Idler* who gives a dreadful detail of the disasters which befell him on a jaunt into the country, such as rain falling upon him from the heavens and many other circumstances. My parting with my wife this day would make just such a figure should I describe it as I really felt it; for to part with a valuable friend and constant companion and go four hundred miles from her, though but for two months, is something considerable to a domestic man who has any turn to anxiety of mind.

I set out about four o'clock in the afternoon. We got to Dunbar at night. The house was dirty and confused. We were served by a *lass* who was both ugly and stupid. When Mr. Wilson asked if she could get him some oatmeal porridge, she answered, "Some oatmeal punch?" Had one of your Englishmen, well prepared to form strange notions of Scotland, heard this, it would have been enough for him to represent us as so devoted to oatmeal that we make our very punch with it.

SUNDAY 15 MARCH. We went on very well, considering the deep roads. We resolved never to dine but only to take some cold meat at midday, which we did very heartily. We got at night to Alnwick.

TUESDAY 17 MARCH. I this day paid a visit at Grantham to the Reverend Mr. Palmer, a clergyman who has a good living there. He was chaplain to Sir John Cust when Speaker of the House of Commons. He carried me upstairs to an elegant room ornamented with some fine prints, and as it was a beautiful forenoon, the sun shone brightly upon them. But I saw what I had never seen before: his spouse, a comely Vandyck figure, and his daughter, one of the loveliest figures I ever beheld. I cannot help being instantaneously affected by the sight of beauty. Mr. Palmer is a man of learning and worth, hospitable and decently social. He has a jolly appearance, not plump and sleek, but a fair well-kept skin, easy and happy. My being accustomed to the bar has made me callous to the most attentive looks of the ablest men. But a glance from a fine eye can yet affect my assurance. I felt this today. I compared myself to one of those animals who by their strong scales or tough skins are invulnerable by a bullet but may be wounded by the sharp points of a sword, which can pierce between the scales or hit some weak point of the skin.

THURSDAY 19 MARCH. The snow was now very thin and we found ourselves in a milder and more benign climate. I looked back on former parts of my life, and my present firmness and cheerfulness of mind had full value by comparison with the weakness and gloominess which I recollected. The very driving in the post-chaise was a considerable pleasure. We arrived in London about five o'clock, having just taken about five days to the journey, and indeed it cannot be performed in less with comfort; that is to say, taking a moderate degree of the refreshments of eating, drinking, and sleeping, which one ought surely to do unless when some necessity obliges to hurry. There was a thick fog over London today, so that I did not get the view of it from Highgate Hill which used to elate me so highly.

General Paoli had invited me to come and lodge at his house, and I indeed reckoned upon being there. I immediately went to his house in Albermarle Street. I asked a chairman which was General Paoli's. "What," said he, "the General who is married to Lady _____ ?" (I did not hear what.) "No," said his companion, "the foreign gentleman." So little is the great Paoli known by some.

When I made a motion to go away and told the General that I had not fixed my lodgings, he asked me to take a room in his house; but I could see that he did not think he had one sufficiently good, and besides that, as Count Gentili was now lodged with him, it would not be convenient that I should be with him too. I considered also that my being lodged there might give the Grub-street writers an opportunity of throwing out low abuse, and saying that he was pensioned by British generosity and kept a Scotsman gratis in his house. I therefore begged leave to decline accepting his invitation but said I should take lodgings near him. I then took my leave for that night and got into the street in a disagreeable uncertainty where I should sleep. I did not know but Mr. Dilly's house might be full; and it was at a great distance from me now. I had no small repugnance at the thought of sleeping at the Lemon-tree, but imagined I might be obliged to land there. As I walked up the Strand and passed through a variety of fine girls, genteelly dressed, all wearing Venus's girdle, all inviting me to amorous intercourse, I confess I was a good deal uneasy. My ideas naturally run into their old channels, which were pretty deeply worn, and I was indulging speculations about polygamy and the concubines of the patriarchs and the harmlessness of temporary likings unconnected with mental attachment. I was really in a disagreeable state and yet would not free myself from it by taking a coach. I resolved never again to come to London without bringing my wife along with me.

FRIDAY 20 MARCH. I find it would be very tedious and idle to put down every visit which I made, so I shall mark only what is of some consequence and not tell that I called at doors and did not find people at home. My views in coming to London this spring were: to refresh my mind by the variety and spirit of the metropolis, the conversation of my revered friend Mr. Samuel Johnson and that of other men of genius and learning; to try if I could get something for myself, or be of service to any of my friends by means of the Duke of Queensberry, Lord Mountstuart, or Douglas, all of whom had given me reason to expect their assistance; to be employed in Scotch appeals in the House of Lords, and also see how the land might lie for me at the English bar; and to endeavour to get my brother David well settled as a merchant in London. There is business enough.

Sir Alexander Macdonald and I are always merry when we meet and always get into the humour of punning and playing upon words, which I cannot help thinking very good amusement. Lady Macdonald said she was just going abroad to visit a lady who was lying in, and who was a great wit. "Ay," said I, "it seems she is a lady of a *pregnant* genius." The Knight and I went in his coach and called for my kinsman Mr. Bosville and for Mr. Dempster, but found neither. He went to a rout; and I strolled about awhile and then went home.

The maid of the house was a pretty little black-eyed girl, and I was informed (as a secret) by Hoggan that Captain Boothby had found her to be very complaisant. This was rather a bad circumstance for me. Before I went to bed the gipsy came, and with a sweet English voice asked, "Do you want anything more tonight, Sir?"

SATURDAY 21 MARCH. I went to Johnson's Court, Fleet Street, and was happy enough to find Mr. Johnson at home. Frank, his black, who had left him for some years, was returned to him, and showed me up to his study. Frank and I were pleased to renew our old acquaintance. I waited a little and then heard the great man coming upstairs. The sound of his feet upon the timber steps was weighty and well announced his approach. He had on an old purple cloth suit and a large whitish wig. He embraced me with a robust sincerity of friendship, saying, "I am glad to see thee, I am glad to see thee. Come sit you down. You have not had my letter?" "No, Sir." (I shall give what passed, as much as I can, in the way of dialogue.) "Well, I am glad you are come, and glad you are come upon such an errand" (meaning to support the schoolmaster of Campbeltown in the House of Lords). "I hope, Sir, there will be no fear of him. It is a very delicate matter to interfere between a master and his scholars; nor do I see how you can fix the degree of severity that a master may use." JOHNSON. "No, Sir. Till you fix the degree of negligence and obstinacy of the scholars, you cannot fix the degree of severity of the master. Severity must be continued until obstinacy be subdued and negligence cured," BOSWELL. "To speak candidly, Sir, this man was rather too severe." JOHNSON. "Has he broke any bones?" BOSWELL. "No." JOHNSON. "Has he fractured any skulls?" BOSWELL. "No." JOHNSON. "Then, Sir, he is safe enough. My master at Lichfield, Hunter, used to beat us unmercifully. He erred in not making a distinction between mistake and negligence; for he would beat a boy equally for not knowing a thing as for neglecting to know it. He would have asked a boy a question, and if he did not answer it, he beat him, without considering whether he had an opportunity of knowing how to answer it. Now, Sir, if a boy could answer every question, there would be no need of a master to teach him."

Then came in a Mr. _____ who was to go out mate in the ship along with Mr. Banks and Dr. Solander. Mr. Johnson asked what were the names of the ships which were to go upon the expedition. Mr. _____ said they were once to be called the *Drake* and the *Raleigh,* but now they were to be called the *Resolution* and the *Adventure.* JOHNSON. "Much better; for had the *Raleigh* returned without going round the world, it would have been ridiculous. To give them the names of the *Drake* and the *Raleigh* was laying a trap for satire." BOSWELL. "Had not you some desire to go upon this expedition, Sir?" JOHNSON. "Why yes; but I soon laid it aside. Sir, there is very little intellectual in the course. Besides, I see but at a little distance. So it was not worth my while to go to see birds fly which I should not have seen fly, and fishes swim which I should not have seen swim."

I told him of the renunciation which I granted to my father of my right to the family estate by my mother's contract of marriage, which I did about the time I became major from a generous principle of preserving the family, as my father threatened, while I was very dissipated and licentious, that he would sell Auchinleck. JOHNSON. "Why, Sir, you did a very foolish thing." BOSWELL. "Last winter, Sir, I had the paper in my hand, my father having left open the bookcase in which it was lying; and I once thought of putting it into the fire, as it was a thing to which he had no right. However, as I had once granted it to him, I had a scruple, and so laid it back again into its place." JOHNSON. "You did right, Sir. To take it and burn it would have been destroying a deed. We should have had you hanged, ha! ha! ha! No. You would not have been hanged, but you might have been whipped, or transported, ha! ha! ha! However, Sir, your father did wrong to take it from you and he ought to give it up to you. If you do not tease him, he will make no use of it and it can do you no harm; for a renunciation granted to him can avail no one else." BOSWELL. "He talks, Sir, of entailing his estate; but he carries on the representation of a family but by males. Don't you think it true representation, Sir?" JOHNSON. "Why, yes, Sir." BOSWELL. "What makes me more anxious with regard to it in our family is a principle of good faith to one of my ancestors who gave the estate to his nephew, passing by his own daughters; and I therefore think that as we received it in trust as a male fee we are bound to continue it as a male fee. I am therefore determined to sign no more papers or give any consent to female succession." JOHNSON. "Why, Sir, from what you have stated, your case is stronger than usual, and since you think it wrong to consent to such an entail as your father talks of making, you should not do it. But let him alone and he'll die without making any."

Thus have I collected this day's conversation, excepting only that I now recollect he advised me to go and see Cox's Museum, which he said for power of mechanism and splendor of show was a very fine exhibition. He seemed happier to me than ever. He said, "I do love thee. I do love thee"; and when I left him he said, "Good-night, dear Sir. I am glad to see you again, very glad to see you again."

SUNDAY 22 MARCH. The increase of London is prodigious. It is really become too large. The consequence is that people live at such a distance from each other that it is very inconvenient for them to meet, and are so crowded that they confuse one another; and it is easier for people who live ten or twelve miles from each other in the country to meet than it is for people who live a few streets from each other in London.

MONDAY 23 MARCH. I breakfasted with Captain Hoggan, and then went to Mr. Johnson's, with whom I had an appointment to spend this day and consider the cause of the Campbeltown schoolmaster. When I came into his study, he was busy preparing a new edition of his folio Dictionary, and had one Mr. Peyton writing to him and picking out words from Ainsworth. I gave him a meaning of the word *side* which he had omitted; viz., father's or mother's side. He said he would put it in. I asked if *civilization* was a word; he said no, but *civility* was. I suggested *humiliating*. He said he had seen it frequently used but he did not know if it could be allowed to be English. With great deference to him, I should think *civilization,* from to *civilize,* a good word and better than *civility* in that sense, as it is better to have a distinct word for each sense than one word with two senses, which *civility* is, in his way of using it.

A Mr. _____ , a tall gentleman like a clergyman, just went out as I came in. He seemed busy about some sort of chemical operations. I was entertained to see how he sent Mr. Peyton an errand. "Mr. Peyton, Mr. Peyton, will you be so good as take a walk to Temple Bar? You will there see a chemist's shop; buy for me an ounce of oil of vitriol; not spirit of vitriol but oil of vitriol. It will cost you three half-pence." Away went Peyton and returned with it, and told it cost but a penny.

I then took out the Session papers in the schoolmaster's cause. I asked if I should read. "No, Sir," said he. "I can read quicker than I can hear." So he read to himself.

The Swede went away, and Mr. Johnson continued his reading of the Session papers. It was curious to see Mr. Samuel Johnson reading his papers like a Lord of Session. As he read Ilay Campbell's Information, he said, "This is a bloody charge against us," and really took a strong interest for the schoolmaster. He laboured very patiently. I said, "I am afraid, Sir, it is troublesome to you." "Why, Sir," said he, "I do not take much delight in it; but I'll go through with it." He read Crosbie's and Ilay Campbell's Informations, and my Reclaiming Petition.

We went over to the Mitre and dined in the room where he and I first supped together, about ten years ago. He ordered some cod and some smelts and some roasted lamb. He eat heartily but drank only negus. He gave me great hopes of my schoolmaster. "Sir," said he, "the government of a schoolmaster is somewhat of the nature of military government; that is to say, it must be arbitrary according to particular circumstances. You must show that a schoolmaster has a prescriptive right to beat, and that an action of assault and battery cannot be admitted against him unless there is some great excess, some barbarity. This man has maimed none of his boys. They are all left the full exercise of their corporeal faculties. In our schools in England many boys have been maimed. Yet I never heard of an action against a schoolmaster. Pufendorf, I think, maintains the right of a schoolmaster to beat his scholars. Besides, Sir, we know not how ill the boys have behaved in this case, so cannot judge whether the degree of severity was proper or not." He promised to assist me by putting down some thoughts upon the subject.

I then went to Lord Mountstuart, who was living at his mother-in-law Lady Windsor's, his own house not being yet ready for him. He received me as if we had not been a day separated, showed me his eldest son, a fine boy, and told me he was always at home in the evening when Parliament was not sitting, and would be happy to see me. John Ross Mackye came in. I told my Lord about my schoolmaster. I said I was keen for him because I was sensible how much the better I myself had been of being heartily licked. My Lord, who has a talent for saying sly things, by the by answered, "I wish you had got a little more of it."

WEDNESDAY 25 MARCH. At night I went to Lord Mountstuart's. Lord Denbigh and John Ross Mackye were with him. Lord Denbigh is a droll genius. He had in his pocket a petition to bring in my schoolmaster's cause on an early day. "Come," said he, "tell me about this schoolmaster's cause; for curse me if I judge of it." I gave him some account of it, and he swore and raved, but I do not remember in what terms. After he and Ross Mackye went away, my Lord and I chatted admirably. But I found that as when he knew me first in Italy I was very odd and extravagant, he could not yet have an idea of my being altered; so was playing foolishly as we used to do. This was a little troublesome. But I considered it would wear off. He said it was impossible to get any survivancy. But he promised he would get me a gown in the Court of Session.

THURSDAY 26 MARCH. I must now remark that since I came last to London I have indulged myself with several interviews with women of the town, from a kind of inclination to entertain my curiosity, without deviating from my fidelity to my valuable spouse. This night completing a week in London, I solemnly resolved to indulge myself so no more; because I could learn nothing but what I had formerly heard over and over again, their stories being mostly the same; and because there was a degree of depravity in associating with them, and, as the idea of the distance between me and them was lessened by my seeing them familiarly, I might fall into an infidelity which would make me very miserable. The heat of the theatre, eating and drinking a variety of things some of which had not suited my constitution, and the cold of the streets had made me ill, and when I got home I was very uneasy.

FRIDAY 27 MARCH. I awaked exceedingly distressed.

SATURDAY 28 MARCH. Mr. John Wright came to me in the morning by appointment to settle his father's case in the appeal, Wright against Ure. After so much variety, though I can hardly call it dissipation, I felt the force of Shakespeare's observation that "if all the year were holidays, to work would be to play." Working at this case solaced me. As we were going on, in came Sir Alexander Macdonald and Major Craufurd of Craufurdland, and they all breakfasted with me, I sitting in my nightcap, and they observing that I was like my father. I indeed felt myself very steady and very composed. Mr. Johnson had said to me, "I should wish to be acquainted with Sir Alexander Macdonald." Every wish of Mr. Johnson's is watched by me, and my friend Sir Alexander was happy to be introduced to him. So away we went.

Mr. Johnson received him very courteously. Sir Alexander, eager to show himself, began. SIR ALEXANDER. "I think, Sir, our chancellors in England are chosen from views much inferior to the office. They are chosen from temporary political views." JOHNSON. "Why, Sir, in such a government as ours no man is appointed to an office because he is the fittest for it. Nor hardly in any other government; because there are so many connexions and dependencies to be studied. A despotic prince may choose a man to an office because he is the fittest for it. The King of Prussia may do it." SIR ALEXANDER. "I have been correcting several Scotch accents in my friend Boswell. I doubt, Sir, if any Scotchman ever attains to a perfect English pronunciation." JOHNSON. "Why, Sir, few of 'em do; because they do not persevere after attaining to a certain degree of perfection. But, Sir, there can be no doubt that they may attain to a perfect English pronunciation if they will. We find how far they attain to it; and there can be no doubt that a man who conquers nineteen parts of the Scottish accent may conquer the twentieth. But, Sir, when a man has got the better of nine tenths, he grows weary, he relaxes his diligence, he finds he has corrected his accent so far as not to be disagreeable, and he no longer desires his friends to tell him when he goes wrong; nor does he choose to be told. Sir, when people watch me narrowly, and I do not watch myself, they will find me out to be of a particular county. In the same manner Dunning may be found out to be a Devonshire man. So most Scotchmen may be found out. But, Sir, little defalcations do not hurt. I never catched Mallet in a Scotch accent; and yet Mallet, I suppose, was past five-and-twenty before he came to London."

BOSWELL. "It may be of use, Sir, to have a dictionary to ascertain the pronunciation." JOHNSON. "Why, Sir, my dictionary shows you the accents of words if you can but remember them." BOSWELL. "But, Sir, we want marks to ascertain the pronunciation of the vowels. Sheridan, I believe, has finished such a work." JOHNSON. "Why, Sir, will you consider how much easier it is to learn a language by the ear than by any marks. Sheridan's dictionary may do very well. But you cannot always carry it about with you; and when you want the word, you have not the dictionary. It is like a man who has a sword that will not draw. It is an admirable sword, to be sure. But while your enemy is cutting your throat, you cannot draw this sword. Besides, Sir, what entitles Sheridan to fix the pronunciation of English? He has in the first place the disadvantage of being an Irishman; and if he says he will fix it after the example of the best company, why, they differ among themselves. I remember an instance. When I published the Plan for my dictionary, Lord Chesterfield told me the word *great* should be pronounced so as to rhyme to *state*, and Sir William Yonge sent me word that it should be pronounced so as to rhyme to *seat* and that none but an Irishman would pronounce it *grait*. Now here were two men of the highest rank, the one the best speaker in the House of Lords, the other the best speaker in the House of Commons, differing so widely."

I went home with Sir Alexander to dinner. He observed that a man should never interrupt another in conversation; because the man who is interrupted will only wait with eagerness to get in again, and while the other is talking will be thinking of what he himself is to say, and consequently the interrupter will be talking to no purpose. This is a just and good practical remark. There was nobody at dinner but my Lady and he and I.

SUNDAY 29 MARCH. Having received a kind invitation to breakfast with the Honourable Mrs. Stuart, an old and intimate friend of my wife's, I accepted it with pleasure. She lived in Queen's Street, Mayfair. Before she appeared, I looked out at the window and saw almost opposite the late Lord Eglinton's house in this street, where he lived when I came first to London, where I lived with him, and where I first learnt the knowledge of life in this metropolis. The many happy days which I have passed there and the recollection of his unhappy death affected me much as I mused by myself. Mr. Stuart was in the country. Mrs. Stuart was in bad health but had a pleasing look, revived agreeable ideas of her as Peggie Cunynghame, and was very entertaining. She had two fine little girls for her children, who were brought into the room, I really believe more from real affection for them than to avoid any scandal by sitting alone with a gentleman. I don't remember how we introduced the subject of matrimonial infidelity. She candidly declared that from what she had seen of life in this great town she would not be uneasy at an occasional infidelity in her husband, as she did not think it at all connected with affection. That if he kept a particular woman, it would be a sure sign that he had no affection for his wife; or if his infidelities were very frequent, it would also be a sign. But that a transient fancy for a girl, or being led by one's companions after drinking to an improper place, was not to be considered as inconsistent with true affection. I wish this doctrine may not have been only consolatary and adapted to facts.

TUESDAY 31 MARCH. I called on Mr. Garrick at his house in the Adelphi. I found him like a little minister of state, standing in the middle of a room, hurried and surrounded with several people, and among them old Cleland, in his youth the author of the *Woman of Pleasure*, that most licentious and inflaming book, and now the grave and prolix *Parliamentarian* in the newspapers. He is the son of Major Cleland, the Will Honeycomb of the *Spectator*. He is a fine sly malcontent. Garrick was talking vainly of his being appointed the executor of a clergyman by "that great man, Lord Camden." "Not a very great man," grumbled Cleland. I saw Mr. Garrick was not at leisure, so I went and breakfasted at the Mount Coffee-house.

I went and called on Mr. Johnson, and he and I came to General Paoli's in a hackneycoach.

We disputed if marriage was natural. The General maintained it was. "My dear Sir," said Mr. Johnson, "it is so far from being easy and natural for a man and woman to live in a state of marriage that we find all the restraints and motives in civilized society are hardly sufficient to keep them together."

This led into a disquisition on the dispute whether there is any beauty independent of utility. The General maintained there was not. Mr. Johnson maintained that there was; and he instanced a coffee-cup which he held in his hand, the painting of which was of no real use, as the cup would hold the coffee equally well if plain: yet the painting was beautiful. The General spoke English much better than I imagined he could do. "Sir," said Mr. Johnson, "you must speak it before your friends, with whom you need not care though you spoil a thought."

We talked of the practice of swearing. The General said that all barbarous nations swore from a kind of violence of temper that could not be confined to earth but was always reaching at the powers above. He said too that there was a greater variety of swearing in proportion as there were among a people greater variety of religious ceremonies.

Mr. Johnson went home with me and drank tea, as no message had come from General Oglethorpe. He said he thought General Paoli had lost somewhat of that grandeur in his air and manner which he had when he came first to England. The observation is just, and the fact is easily accounted for. When he came first here, he was just arrived from being at the head of a nation. Wherever he had passed, and even here, he was addressed in that high character. But after having been near three years just in the style of a private gentleman, much of the majesty of his deportment must insensibly be lost.

I have a constant plan to write the life of Mr. Johnson. I have not told him of it yet, nor do I know if I should tell him. I said that if it was not troublesome and presuming too much, I would beg of him to tell me all the little circumstances of his life, what schools he attended, when he came to Oxford, when he came to London, etc., etc. He did not disapprove of my curiosity as to these particulars, but said, "They'll come out by degrees."

FRIDAY 3 APRIL. I breakfasted at home. Then was awhile at the House of Peers, hearing the appeal, Bruce Kinross against Miss Bruce. I am now quite at home in the House, and take the Usher of the Black Rod's chair very regularly. I went up by water to Paul's Wharf and then walked on to my friend Mr. Dilly's, with whom I had engaged to pass all this day and take a bed in his house at night. He and I and his brother dined comfortably. Then he and I went to the _____ Jews' synagogue, and heard Leoni, a fine singer; _____ , a good strong one, and _____ , a most admirable bass. It was curious to see the Jews talking and laughing together, and no kind of solemnity in their countenances. It was just a plain religion. They executed so much, like a task, and like boys at a task looked off and intermixed other things.

SATURDAY 4 APRIL. Mr. Charles Dilly and I went to the _____ Jews' and the _____ Jews' (where I was last night—the Dutch Jews') Synagogues. I could not help feeling a kind of regret to see the certain descendants of venerable Abraham in an outcast state and sneered at and abused by every fool, at least to a certain degree. We came back to breakfast.

TUESDAY 7 APRIL. I breakfasted with Lord Eglinton, who keeps the best breakfast of any man in London, a complete Union of the good things of Scotland and England: bread and butter and honey and marmalade of oranges and currant jelly and muffins, well buttered and comfortably toasted. The Earl is pleasant, but his conversation does not furnish my Journal as his brother's used to do. I went to the House of Lords and heard out the appeal, Bruce-Carstairs against Miss Bruce. Lord Mansfield had been shaken in his opinion during the hearing; and therefore, though he affirmed, he gave his reasons, and indeed spoke in a most masterly manner. I dined at Mr. Bosville's. There was nobody there but Miss Wentworth. We were plain and comfortable.

In the evening I met at the Queen's Arms in St. Paul's Churchyard with the rest of the partners of *The London Magazine*. It was truly satisfactory to me to find myself the only Scotsman among a company of English, and at the same time the distinction quite forgotten from our union of interest and from my perfect art of melting myself into the general mass. Most individuals when they find themselves with people of a different country cannot get free of their own particular national distinction. The individual, instead of being melted down, as I have remarked of myself, remains as hard as a piece of iron in a crucible filled with lead or silver. I should not wish to be melted so as not to be again separated from the mass. But when the heat is over, I gather myself up as firm as ever, with perhaps only a small plate or thin leaf of the other metal upon me sufficient to make me glitter, and even that I can rub off if I choose it.

FRIDAY 10 APRIL. I dined at General Oglethorpe's, at his house in Lower Grosvenor Street. His lady, whose fortune is his support while our court shamefully neglects him, was a good civil old lady, with some affectation of wit, with which, however, she troubled us but little. Mr. Johnson and Dr. Goldsmith and nobody else were the company. I felt a completion of happiness. I just sat and hugged myself in my own mind. Here I am in London, at the house of General Oglethorpe, who introduced himself to me just because I had distinguished myself; and here is Mr. Johnson, whose character is so vast; here is Dr. Goldsmith, so distinguished in literature. Words cannot describe our feelings. The finer parts are lost, as the down upon a plum; the radiance of light cannot be painted.

SATURDAY 11 APRIL. I then hasted away, took a coach at Fleet Ditch, called at Mr. Johnson in passing and told him I should soon be back with the appellants' case, drove to Spottiswoode's and got it, and then returned and got it fairly tabled before the great man. I got him to read the *Reasons,* and then said I hoped he would write down his thoughts upon the subject. Said he: "There's no occasion for my writing. I'll talk to you." I then proposed he should dictate and I would write. To this he agreed. I therefore sat with most assiduous care and eagerness, and he dictated to me a noble defence, which I preserve. This lasted till after one in the morning. It was the only time that I ever did anything in a cause upon Sunday, except a criminal cause. This indeed might be considered as one, as the schoolmaster was standing trial for his all and for his character. Besides, writing down Mr. Johnson's observations was not properly *working* at my business. I could perceive that what he threw out upon the subject in conversation was stronger and had more fire than what he dictated.*

I forgot to put down that last Sunday, when I was with him, the barber came in to shave him, when he said, "Come away, barber; you

---

*Mr. Johnson's "noble defence" may be read in full in Boswell's *Life of Johnson* at 11 April 1772.

know I seldom give you this trouble on a Sunday." I said I had no scruple to be shaved on a Sunday. "Why no, Sir," said he, "if you shave yourself or your servant does it. But if you employ a barber, and every one else employs him, the barber will have as much work to do on Sundays as on any other day." He said he approved of the custom some people had of having baked meat, a pie, on Sunday, as it could be baked on Saturday and might be eat cold or needed only to be warmed on Sunday, so that a servant was not kept from church.

MONDAY 13 APRIL. I dined at Claxton's. His sister was a plain, easy, cheerful girl. She will be of use to my wife when I bring her to London. I am resolved to bring my wife with me next year, and I am constantly considering and looking out in that view. A Mr. Haistwell dined with us and Mrs. Browne, the widow of Isaac Hawkins Browne, best known by his imitations of different poets in his *Pipe of Tobacco* in Dodsley's *Collection*. She seemed to be a genteel well-bred woman; but I could perceive no impregnation of genius, and I was not well enough acquainted with her to ask her as to minute particulars concerning her husband, which I wished to do. I have really genius for particular history, for biography.

WEDNESDAY 15 APRIL. I breakfasted by appointment with Mr. Garrick. He had there Mrs. _____, a fat sensible woman, and Mr. Pingo, the medal and bust maker. He and Mrs. Garrick were as agreeable as ever. By and by came in Mr. Smith, a _____, and Mr. O'Brien, formerly the player, who since his marriage with Lady Susan Strangeways is quite *the fine man about town*. I thought him agreeable. His foppishness appeared to be only vivacity and neatness. He told us that Fitzherbert was at Mr. Thrale's in Southwark, where Mr. Johnson lives so much, and being shown the brewery, particularly the great *tub*, he asked, "But where's *Diogenes?*" (Meaning Mr. Johnson.) Mr. Garrick complained of a passage in Mr. Johnson's preface to his Shakespeare, in which he insinuates that Mr. Garrick (for *he chiefly* has the old editions of Shakespeare) was not very ready to communicate them. "Now," said he, "not only did his black get any old plays that he sent for, but the key of them was left with the maid, with orders to have a fire and every convenience for Mr. Johnson." I was sorry to find any coldness between Mr. Johnson and Mr. Garrick. They had misunderstood one another. Mr. Garrick had imagined that showing his old plays was a favour. I have since learnt from Mr. Johnson that his idea was that Garrick wanted to be courted for them, and that on the contrary he ought rather to have courted him and sent him the plays of his own accord. He denied that his black ever got any of the them. Mr. Johnson may perhaps be insensibly fretted a little that *Davy Garrick,* who was his pupil and who came up to London at the same time with him to try the chance of life, should be so very general a favourite and should have fourscore thousand pounds, an immense sum, when *he* has so little. He accordingly will allow no great merit in acting. Garrick cannot but be hurt at this, and so unhappily there is not the harmony that one would wish.

I entertained them with an anecdote which I have omitted to put down in its proper place. Some evenings ago when I was at Mr. Johnson's, I took up *The London Chronicle,* in which was an extract from a new book called *Theatrical Biography.* I read some of Mr. Garrick's Life aloud. At last I came to a sentence where the author says that so much having appeared about Mr. Garrick already, he could say nothing new, but would only give some *original retouches.* I stopped at this strange expression, and asked, "Pray, Sir, what does he mean by *original retouches?*" Mr. Johnson, who was heartily weary of my reading aloud what he did not care for, answered, "What does he mean? Why, Sir, how can you ask what such a fellow means? Sir, if you were to ask himself, he can't tell what he means."

In a little came Mr. Johnson. They were all afraid to venture forth. I as usual risked boldly in order to get him to speak. I observed that although he had been confident of my schoolmaster's success and done him all the service he could and still thought he should not have been turned out, he would nevertheless have a joke against him. It was indeed pretty clear that the schoolmaster did not open his school so many hours as he ought to have done. So when I again talked this night of his severity, "Why, Sir," said Mr. Johnson, "he had time for nothing more." Dr. Nowell was mentioned; and I spoke of him with applause for preaching his high Tory sermon on the 30th of January last. But I tried to say something against his expulsion of the six students from Oxford some years ago because they were Methodists, and would not desist from praying and exhorting. JOHNSON. "Sir, that expulsion was extremely just and proper. What had people to do in an university who were not willing to be taught, but who would insist to teach? Where is religion to be learned but in an university? Sir, they were examined and found to be mighty ignorant fellows." BOSWELL. "But, Sir, was it not hard to expel them, for I believe they were good beings?" JOHNSON. "Yes, Sir. I believe they might be good beings. But they were not fit to be in the University of Oxford. A cow is a very good animal in the field. But we turn her out of a garden."

I would needs defend drinking, although Mr. Johnson looked very awful and cloudy upon me for doing so. "Sir," said I, "you know the

maxim *in vino veritas:* a man who is warmed with wine will speak truth."
JOHNSON. "Why, Sir, that may be an argument for drinking if you
suppose men liars; but, Sir, I would not keep company with a fellow who
lies as long as he is sober and whom you must fill drunk before you can
get a word of truth out of him." BOSWELL. "But, Sir, you know all
mankind have agreed in esteeming wine as a thing that can cheer the
heart, can drive away care; in short, the common phrases used with
regard to it prove it to be a good thing. Would not you, Sir, now, allow a
man oppressed with care to drink and make himself merry?" JOHNSON.
"Yes; if he sat next you." This was one of his great broadsides. Langton,
who is a timorous man, said, "I saw that you would bring something
upon yourself." I never was disturbed. I know Mr. Johnson so well and
delight in his grand explosions, even when directed against myself, so
much that I am not at all hurt.

FRIDAY 17 APRIL. I drank tea at Mr. Dilly's; then drank tea a second
time at Mr. Henry Baldwin's, our printer of *The London Magazine.* His
wife was a pretty little genteel woman and his house in very good order.
I then called for Mr. William Wilson. He carried me into his landlord
Mr. Murray's, where was a company sitting after dinner, Sir John
Dalrymple and others. I took a glass or two of wine, and then went
home. As I had promised something for *The London Magazine* next day
and had fallen behind in my Journal, I resolved to sit up all night and
write. I accordingly did so. The time was when I have sitten up four
nights in one week in London. But I found this night very hard upon
me.

SATURDAY 18 APRIL. I called on Mr. Johnson, and found him in
solemn mood, with the great New Testament open again. I have had a
fondness for Sir Francis Osborne's works, and was thinking to publish
an edition of him with his life. I asked Mr. Johnson what he thought of
Osborne. He answered, "A conceited fellow. Were a man to write so
now, the boys would throw stones at him." I consulted him as to my
applying for the Sheriffship of Ayrshire, and securing it by undertaking
the office just now and engaging to let Mr. Duff have the salary for life.
He said, "I would take it if I could get it when the old man dies. But not
now on the terms you mention. That would be confining yourself the
best years of your life for nothing. Your vacation of three months at a
time is a good thing. You can come here; you can go to France; you can
go to Italy." I have omitted to mention that one day since I came last to
London, I spoke to Mr. Johnson of the good that following the law had
done me by filling up my time and preventing me from being listless and
unhappy. But that I thought a country gentleman might contrive to pass

his life very agreeably. "Why, Sir," said he, "you cannot give me an instance of any man who is left to lay out his own time contriving not to have tedious hours."

EDITORIAL NOTE: Later this month Boswell's journal broke off, in May he returned to Scotland, and during the months ahead he was busy at the law. We rejoin him in March of the year after, as he prepares once again to visit London.

TUESDAY 30 MARCH. Being to set out very early for London in the Newcastle fly, my clerk, Mr. Lawrie, had sat up all night in the dining-room to be ready to call me at three in the morning, which he did, and made tea for me. He is a sober, diligent, attentive lad, very serviceable to me and I believe very sensible of my kindness to him. He goes to church regularly, which is rare in this loose age amongst young men of his profession. I had felt a kind of dreary reluctance the night before when I looked forward to the fatigues of my journey, especially the little sleep which one is allowed when travelling by the fly. But the agreeable prospect of being in London, which includes so many interesting and favourite objects, prevailed over the mists of apprehension; though I had still the awful thought that I might never return to Scotland and meet my dearest wife. Either of us might die during our separation. This thought, when it presses strongly upon the mind, is terrible. It is enough to make one never separate from a valuable spouse. Yet how weak would it be to be so influenced. I cannot explain how the mind takes different degrees of firmness and vigour at different times. I walked down the High Street of Edinburgh, which has a grand appearance in the silence and dusky light of three in the morning, and felt myself like an officer in a campaign. When the fly had rumbled me a mile or two, rational and manly sensations took the place of tender and timid feebleness. I considered that I had left my wife and little daughter well. That I was going to London, whither so many members of Parliament, lawyers, merchants, and others go and return in safety to their families. I saw nothing dangerous, nothing melancholy. I had taken leave of my wife last night, which had affected my spirits a good deal. She is of an anxious temper at all times; but being not yet fully recovered from childbirth, she was more anxious than usual. Luckily she did not wake when I set out this morning, so that we had not a second farewell interview.

The company with me in the coach were my brother John, who was going to Newcastle, an English buck who I suppose was a rider, and a Scotchwoman who I suppose was a servant-maid. The buck said, "I have to go on horseback to *Duns*; and I am a *Dunce* for my pains"; upon which the Scotchwoman observed, "*The Lads o' Duns* is a bonny spring." He and she went no farther than Kelso. John and I dined at Wooler. We had the coach to ourselves till we had passed that stage a good way, and then were joined by Mr. _____, steward to Lord Tankerville. At Newcastle we had Dr. Wilson to sup with us; and after supper Mr. _____, who was to go on so far in the London fly next day, drank a glass with us. John and I had not exchanged many words. He is of a most unlucky frame.

WEDNESDAY 31 MARCH. I left John sound asleep in another bed in the room where I lay. He had not so much as bid me farewell. He has bad health, which, I take it, produces that sullen pride and unsocial obstinacy which he has. I find it in vain to try to have the comfort of a brother or a companion from him. I shall study to make him easy, but will not submit to take the load of him upon myself. It is difficult to describe how very heavy his disagreeable behaviour is to those with whom he lives. He is incapable of being pleased by them. Never was there a greater difference between human beings than between him and my brother David and me.

THURSDAY 1 APRIL. I travelled alone all this day, except for about half a stage when I had for my companion the chambermaid of the inn at Tuxford, who was returning home from a visit to her relations, and about the third of a stage when I had a good gentlewoman who was going to Newark. I remember the time when my mind was in such a state of fermentation that whenever the lid put upon it by the restraint of company was removed, it was like to boil over, or rather, to use a better metaphor, when not stirred by company but left to stagnate in solitude, it soon turned upon the fret. But now it has wrought itself into such a sound state that it will *keep* for a long time. The satisfaction which I feel from the comparison of my present with my former self is immense; though I must own that during my fermentation there were grand ebullitions and bright sparkles which I can no longer perceive. I came at night to Grantham.

FRIDAY 2 APRIL. There came into the fly this morning Mr. _____, who had been a strolling player, and Master _____, a young gentleman at Grantham School, who was going to London to see his father and mother during the holidays. The former soon opened, told me he had been bred a coach-painter in Long Acre, London. But having always a violent inclination for the stage, he went upon it, as he said, with design to be cured of his fondness for it. He had now given it up, and was to settle in business as a grocer.

SATURDAY 3 APRIL. I shall make a transition to Mr. Samuel

Johnson's, where I went between ten and eleven at night. He was not come home. I found Frank, his black, my old acquaintance, who showed me into Mrs. Williams's room. I am a favourite with Mrs. Williams. I read to her from *The London Chronicle* Dr. Goldsmith's apology for beating Evans the publisher. I thought when I saw the story in the newspapers that it had been an invention, like Pope's stories of Curll, but on my coming to town I found it to be very true; and I was diverted to find my friend Dilly so keen on the side of the publisher, not only maintaining that Goldsmith had been guilty of a great outrage and ought to be punished by criminal justice, but believing that Evans had beat him black and blue. Goldsmith's apology was written so much in Mr. Johnson's manner that both Mrs. Williams and I supposed it to be his. When Mr. Johnson came home he embraced me with sincere cordiality, saying, "I'm glad you're come." He said to Mrs. Williams, "Dr. Goldsmith's manifesto has got into your paper," meaning *The London Chronicle*. I asked him if Goldsmith writ it, with an air that made him see I suspected he had done it. "Sir," said he, "Dr. Goldsmith would no more have asked me to write such a thing as that for him than he'd have asked me to feed him with a spoon, or to do anything else that argued his imbecility. I as much believe that he wrote that as if I had seen him do it. Sir, had he shown it to any one friend, he would not have been allowed to publish it. He has indeed done it well; but 'tis a foolish thing well done. I suppose he has been so much elated with the success of his new comedy that he has thought everything that concerned him of importance to the public." I said, "I suppose, Sir, this is the first time that he has been engaged in such an adventure." JOHNSON. "Why, Sir, I believe it is the first time he has beat. He may have been beaten before. No, Sir, 'tis a new plume to him."

MONDAY 5 APRIL. I know not how it is, but I am less anxious in being absent from my valuable spouse this year than I was last. Perhaps her having a little daughter to amuse her makes the scene more lively to my imagination; but then ought I not to feel a double anxiety this year, when I am absent both from a wife and a child? In whatever way it is to be explained, I have mentioned the fact. Yet I am certain that I am as fond of my wife as I was last year; nor do I know that my mind is become more rational so as to throw off any vain fears that may arise, as sparks of water are thrown from a grindstone. I wish I may continue as I am while absent from my family.

Kennedy took me into the House of Commons. I heard Dowdeswell, Jenkinson, Stanley, Dyson, Thurlow, Pulteney, Governor Johnstone, and my friend Dempster speak. But I was also fortunate enough to hear Mr. Edmund Burke speak twice. It was a great feast to me who had never heard him before. It was astonishing how all kinds of figures of speech crowded upon him. He was like a man in an orchard where boughs loaded with fruit hung around him, and he pulled apples as fast as he pleased and pelted the Ministry. It seemed to me, however, that his oratory rather tended to distinguish himself than to assist his cause. There was amusement instead of persuasion. It was like an exhibition of a favourite actor. But I would have been exceedingly happy to be him.

SUNDAY 11 APRIL. When I came to Mr. Johnson's, he was not yet come home. By and by he arrived. I had gratified my curiosity much in dining with Rousseau, and I thought it as curious to dine with Mr. Johnson. I supposed we should hardly see knives and forks, and only have the pie which he mentioned. But to my surprise I found everything in very good order. He and I and Mrs. Williams and a Miss _____ were the company. We had a very good soup, a boiled leg of lamb and spinach, a veal pie, an excellent rice pudding, pickled walnuts and onions, porter and port wine. I dined as well as ever I wish to do. The lamb made him tell me a joke. He said Mr. Thrale's sister, Lady Lade, when she saw Sir George Colebrooke in a white waistcoat and green coat, said he was like a leg of lamb and spinach.

He told me he had twelve or fourteen times attempted to keep a Journal, but never could persevere. "The great thing," said he, "is the state of your mind; and you ought to write down everything that you can, for you cannot judge at first what is good or bad; and write immediately while the impression is fresh, for it will not be the same a week after." I told him how uneasy I was at having lost eight hundred pages of my Journal, which were sent from Utrecht where I had left them, and that I was chiefly uneasy for fear that somebody had them, as they really contained a full state of my mind when in a deep melancholy. He comforted me by saying that probably they had fallen into the hands of somebody who could not understand them, and would be destroyed as waste-paper. I am, however, much vexed at this loss, and at the apprehension that they may be lying concealed.

I asked him if he could tell when he was born, when he came to London and such things. Said he, "You shall have them" (or "I'll give you them") "all for twopence. I hope you shall know a great deal more of me before you write my Life."

I ran home, dressed, and went to Lord Mansfield's. Jenkinson was with him, but went away just as I came. My Lord and I were then left tête-à-tête. His cold reserve and sharpness, too, were still too much for me. It was like being cut with a very, very cold instrument. I have not for a long time experienced that weakness of mind which I had formerly in a woeful degree in the company of the great or the clever. But Lord Mansfield has uncommon power. He chills the most generous blood.

I had plucked up enough of resolution by this time, and perhaps had probed his Lordship more than was proper. He is all artificial. He affected to know little of Scotch appeals when over. I catched him, though! I spoke of the one, Parkhill against Chalmers, in a way that showed him I did not think the judgement a good one. Said he, "Were there not particular circumstances there?" I bowed without answering and let him take his own way; upon which he went on, "Ay, there were so and so"—and showed that he well remembered what he affected not to remember. It is unpleasant to see so high an administrator of justice such a man.

MONDAY 12 APRIL. The celebrated female historian, Mrs. Catharine Macaulay, her brother the Rev. Mr. Sawbridge, and another gentleman, had £10,000 lent on the estate of the Laird of MacLeod, and for two years had received no interest. My good friend Dilly had directed them to me for advice; so their attorney, Mr. Heaton of Lincoln's Inn, was to retain me. In the mean time I engaged to breakfast with Mrs. Macaulay this morning and look at her securities. I first drank a dish of tea with Dempster, who I regretted was so busy that I could see little of him. Mrs. Macaulay and I had a very cordial, polite meeting, and she gave me a good breakfast, like any other woman. I looked at her securities and found them good. I dined at Mr. Bosville's. At night I went to Covent Garden and saw *She Stoops to Conquer,* the author's second night. I laughed most heartily, and was highly pleased at once with the excellent comedy and with the fame and profit which my friend Goldsmith was receiving. It was really a rich evening to me. I would not stay to see the farce. I would not put the taste of Goldsmith's fruit out of my mouth.

TUESDAY 13 APRIL. Goldsmith took up the common topic that the race of our people was degenerated and that this was owing to luxury. "Sir," says Mr. Johnson, "in the first place, I doubt the fact. I believe there are as many tall men in England now as ever there were. But, secondly, supposing them grown less, that is not owing to luxury; for, Sir, consider to how very small a proportion of our people luxury can reach. Our soldiery surely are not luxurious, who live on sixpence a day; and so you may take other classes. Luxury so far as it reaches the poor will do good to the race of people. It will increase them. Sir, no nation was ever hurt by luxury; for, as I said before, it can reach but to a very few. Sir, I admit that the great increase of commerce and manufactures hurts the military spirit of a people; because it gives them a competition for something else than martial honours, a competition for riches. It also hurts the bodies of the people; for you will observe there is no man who works at any particular trade but whom you may know from his appearance to do so. One part or other of his body by being more used than the rest deforms in some degree his body. But, Sir, that is not luxury. A tailor sits cross-legged, but that is not luxury." GOLDSMITH. "Come, you're just going to the same place by another road." JOHNSON. "Nay, Sir. I say that is not *luxury*. Let us take a walk from Charing Cross to Whitechapel, through I suppose the greatest series of shops in the world. What is there in any of these shops (if you except gin-shops) that can do any person any harm?" GOLDSMITH. "Well, I'll take you. The very next shop to Northumberland House is a pickle-shop." JOHNSON. "Well, Sir. Do we not know that a maid can in one afternoon make pickles sufficient to serve a whole family for a year? Nay, that five pickle-shops can serve all the kingdom? Besides, there is no harm done to anybody by the making of pickles or the eating of pickles."

Mr. Johnson and Dr. Goldsmith walked home with me. I have forgotten much of this day's conversations. Goldsmith went away. Mr. Johnson drank some tea with me. I told him that Mrs. Macaulay said she wondered how he could reconcile his political principles with his moral, his notions of inequality and subordination with wishing well to the happiness of all mankind, who might live so agreeably had they all their portions of land, and none to domineer over another. "Why, Sir," said he, "I reconcile my principles very well, because mankind are happier in a state of subordination. Were they to be in this pretty state of equality, they'd soon degenerate into brutes, they'd become Monboddo's nation. Their tails would grow. Sir, all would be losers were all to work to all. They'd have no intellectual improvement. All intellectual improvement arises from leisure. All leisure arises from one working for another."

EDITORIAL NOTE: Now Boswell has returned to Edinburgh.

WEDNESDAY 15 JUNE. We dined at my father's. George Frazer, George Webster, and Claud were there. At five I was at the Solicitor's for my first consultation this session. I have at the beginning of several sessions felt a peculiar cast of ideas by which I could distinguish, in my own mind, one session from the rest. This came on quite simple. It was just the Summer Session 1774 without any other perceptible mark. I began to receive my fees this session, as I begin to eat my two eggs on any night, with a pure sameness. I called on Maclaurin as I returned and drank tea with him. I should have observed that as I was walking out to the Solicitor's with Taylor, Sandy Mackenzie's clerk—the consultation being on the cause, Ross of Auchnacloich against Mackenzie of Ardross —Taylor said we would not be the worse of the President's being present; that both he and Gardenstone were good friends to Ardross. I said there was now very little to be expected on the bench from private regard. It is true. For in the first place, the nation is more civilized and judges have better notions of justice. But, secondly, there is actually not such strong friendships or family attachments as were long ago. I do not blame our judges of the last age so much as many people do, because at that time there were many of them plain country gentlemen, not lawyers at all, and because the warmth of their hearts gave them considerable imperceptible bias to one side. And it must be owned that of the many causes that come before the Court of Session there is a good proportion such as the judges will differ upon merely in cool opinion. No wonder then that regard casts the balance without their knowing it.

MONDAY 20 JUNE. It was wet. I was at home all day writing law papers, except being at a consultation from four to six at Mr. Rae's on Earl Fife's politics, where we had a tedious reading of papers, which is really an irksome operation. I observed Rae pretty sound asleep at one time; and I myself was once or twice in that drowsy nodding state which is very disagreeable. How much attention a lawyer ought to give to the causes in which he is employed is not easy to say. But it is certain that when there are many lawyers in the same cause not one of them gives as much attention as he would do were he single.

TUESDAY 21 JUNE. Still wet. Mrs. Montgomerie and I went in a chaise to Bob Chalmers's country house on the seaside, near Musselburgh, to eat a fish dinner. My wife would not venture out, the day was so bad and she was but a month and a day brought to bed. I know not how it has happened that we have had no intercourse since our marriage with Bob Chalmers's family; though, before that, both of us used to visit and be well entertained there. We had refused several invitations from them and never asked them again. These cessations of acquaintance will happen unaccountably. Mrs. Montgomerie's being with us renewed the intercourse, and it was this day renewed as to me very effectually; for I eat of nine kinds of fish and drank various drams and a great deal of port, and was really much intoxicated. Mr. Baron Mure, his lady, and Miss Annie were there. With them, too, I have had no intercourse, though invited, and though he is so much connected with Lord Mountstuart, my *carus Mæcenas,* and is a friendly, sensible, agreeable man. However, things are put to rights at once by some happy occasion. I engaged him, his lady, and daughter to dine with us on Friday, and at the same time Mr. and Mrs. Chalmers; and I engaged that we should dine at the Baron's the week after. I was talkative and vociferous from the liquor which I had drank.

I supped at Sir George Preston's with my wife and Mrs. Montgomerie. Dr. Webster was there with his son Jamie, now Colonel Webster, just arrived from Ireland. I was by this time outrageously intoxicated and *would* drink a great deal of strong port negus, which made me worse. After I got home, I was very ill; not sick, but like to suffocate—a dangerous state—and my valuable spouse was much alarmed.

WEDNESDAY 22 JUNE. I had a miserable headache and in pleading a short cause before Lord Elliock I felt myself incapable of any distinctness. I was vexed at my conduct.

SATURDAY 25 JUNE. Mr. Samuel Johnson has often recommended to me to keep a Journal, of which he is so sensible of the utility that he has several times tried it, but never could persist. I have at different periods of my life persisted a good time, and I am now hopeful that I may continue longer than ever. I shall only put down hints of what I have thought, seen, or heard every day, that I may not have too much labour; and I shall from these, at certain periods, make up masses or larger views of my existence. Mr. Johnson said that the great thing was to register the state of my mind.

I observed to Captain Andrew that we never have a long continuation of agreeable life. It is frequently interrupted. A company who have been very happy together must have the pain of parting. After every enjoyment comes weariness or disgust. We never have a large lawn of agreeable life. It is cut to pieces with sunk fences, ha-has, even where it is smoothest.

FRIDAY 1 JULY. I dined at Lord Monboddo's, where we had Miss Fletcher, Baron Winn, Crosbie, Maclaurin, Sandy Gordon, etc., and Bob Adam. We were sufficiently jovial. To go home to business seemed dull. However, after drinking tea (the only man except my Lord himself), I did go home and had a short consultation; and was pleased that Mr. Lawrie was out of the way, so that it was not my fault that I was idle. I supped at the Horse Wynd Tavern and drank my bottle of old hock, which did me no harm. There was but eight of us. Lord Monboddo was one.

SATURDAY 2 JULY. Dined at Craighouse, and had a party at bowls both before and after dinner. It was wonderful to see Mr. Lockhart, who has now stood fifty-two years at the bar, playing with all the keenness of a young man. Maclaurin and I led one another on to bet and I lost thirteen shillings. To play for a crown, as we did, is incongruous with the healthful field-sport of the bowls. It poisons it with a certain degree of avaricious anxiety. I resolved never to play for more than a shilling.

SATURDAY 9 JULY. The state of my mind must be gathered from the little circumstances inserted in my Journal. The life of every man, take it day by day, is pretty much a series of uniformity; at least a series of repeated alternations. It is like a journal of the weather; rainy—fair —fair—rainy, etc. It is seldom that a great storm or an abundant harvest occurs in the life of man or in the progress of years. Of this week I can observe that my mind has been more lively than usual, more fertile in images, more agreeably sensible of enjoying existence.

Dr. Webster was with us as chaplain; and we had an excellent dinner in No. 9 and abundance of drinking. While Webster sat, we had several good stories and songs. He left us between seven and eight, and then we grew very noisy and drunk, but very cordial as old friends. In short we had a complete riot, which lasted until near twelve at night. We had eleven Scotch pints of claret, two bottles of old hock, and two of port, and drams of brandy and gin; and the bill was 6. 18. 5. So my five-guinea bet turned into a seven-guinea one; for I gave the waiter the balance of that sum over the bill. In our great warmth we signed an agreement to meet annually on the second Saturday of July, as we had "now met, after an interval of six years, in the same good humour and with the same cordial regard for each other that we then did, and considering that such things were rare and valuable in human life." I sat after the rest were gone and took a large bowl of admirable soup, which did me much good, for I was not sick; though after I was in bed my dear wife was apprehensive that I might die, I breathed so ill.

SUNDAY 10 JULY. Though I was neither sick nor had hardly any headache, I was, as it were, half boiled with last night's debauch, and I was vexed to think of having given my valuable spouse so much uneasiness; for she had scarcely slept any the whole night watching me. The reflection, too, of my having this summer so frequently been intoxicated, galled me. A circumstance occurred this morning which I hope will have a lasting impression upon me. There had come a letter to me from Mr. Samuel Johnson last night. My wife improved it well. She said she would not give me it, as I did not deserve it, since I had put myself into a state of incapacity to receive it when it came, and that it would not have been written to me had the writer of it known how I was to be. She would therefore send it back. She thus made me think how shocking it was that a letter from Mr. Samuel Johnson should find me drunk. She then delivered it, and it was a more than ordinary good one. It put me in the best frame, and I determined vigorously to resist temptation for the future.

I was soberly at the New Church in the forenoon. Mr. Logan,

minister at Leith, preached. I then walked down to Lord Dundonald's and dined. He was in great spirits. Colonel Webster and Major Pitcairn, Charles Cochrane's father-in-law, were there. We three drank a bottle of claret each, which just cheered me. We drank tea there, and at night we all met at Dr. Webster's Sunday's supper. The Major was a sensible, good-looking, well-bred man, and my second cousin through the family of Wishaw. We were merry rather to excess.

MONDAY 11 JULY. My Saturday's debauch had relaxed me so as that business seemed irksome; and yet I had a number of papers which I was absolutely obliged to write in a short time, and some of the agents were complaining of delay. In the forenoon Captain Erskine called and gave me a special invitation from Lady Colville to dine with her. To accept of it seemed incompatible with my present state of business. Yet I could not resist. I considered that it would only throw me an hour or two more behind, and that I should be so refreshed with the agreeable interview with quality friends in the country air that I should be able to labour twice as well. I accordingly went. We had only the two Captains, Lady Dalrymple, and her grandchild, Lady Anne Lindsay.

THURSDAY 14 JULY. My father and Lady Auchinleck, Commissioner Cochrane, the Laird of Fullarton and his mother, Mr. Nairne, Dr. Boswell, and Messieurs Alexander Mackenzie and Andrew Stewart, Junior, dined with us. The company went away gradually till I was left with Fullarton, who drank nothing at all hardly, and the two writers, who were both very social. In such circumstances my strong attraction from within requires little aid from any external impulse and easily makes me think that it is a kind of duty or necessity for me to drink. I took rather too much and was to a certain degree feverish with it. I must steadily keep in mind that no man is more easily hurt with wine than I am, and that there is no real advantage gained by being a good bottle-companion. It was unpleasing today to see my father not at all frank or cordial with me or my wife.

FRIDAY 15 JULY. This was a day of complete sobriety and diligence; and I extricated myself from a very difficult cause by persevering till I was master of it. I went in the afternoon to the prison and conferred with my old client John Reid.

MONDAY 18 JULY. Mrs. Mongomerie, my wife and I dined at Lady Colville's, where we had Sir George Preston, his lady, and daughter. Captain Andrew was not there. I was in a disagreeable humour, domineering and ill-bred, insisting to have Sir George's punch made stronger, and in short being really rude. A fit of impatience and coarse violence of temper had come upon me. I was angry at myself and yet so proud that when I saw it was observed with dissatisfaction, I persisted. We drank tea, and I grew calmer. Lady Ann walked in with my wife and me.

FRIDAY 22 JULY. I dined at Lord Dundonald's with my wife and Mrs. Montgomerie. Old General Colville, Captain Blair, Mr. Nairne, and George Webster were there. The Earl was in great spirits; but it was not quite agreeable to hear a man of eighty-three swearing and talking bawdy. One regretted that such admirable vivacity had taken such habits. He however showed a sense of piety; for he said "he never rose in the morning nor lay down at night without thanking GOD for his goodness to him." Then being unquiet after I got home, so that I could not work, went to Mr. Stewart Moncrieffe's, betted at the whist table, and lost a crown, which I grudged. We were ten at supper, Colonel Seton and Castle Stewart for the first time. I indulged in old hock and became very drunk. Colonel Murray, the Duke of Atholl's brother, joined me in supporting male succession. Seton and I were warm friends. Matthew Henderson was very profane. Somebody said he would be made answer for his sins. He said, "I wish I was impanelled in a future state. I would agree to take two hundred years of hell to be ensured of a future state." "Well," said I, "*there* is something spirited. A noble wish for the immortality of the soul. I tell you, Matthew, I shall meet you in a future state, and though, to be sure, you must do penance for such time, yet I am persuaded you will be forgiven." Drinking never fails to make me ill-bred. I insisted to know Moncrieffe's age. He parried me well. How I appeared this night to others, I know not. But I recollect having felt much warmth of heart, fertility of fancy, and joyous complacency mingled in a sort of delirium. Such a state is at least equal to a pleasing dream. I drank near three bottles of hock, and then staggered away. I got home about three in the morning. Mr. Nairne had supped at my house, expecting me home. Mrs. Montgomerie had sat up till two waiting to see me as she was to set out next morning. I was incapable of knowing anything; and my wife was waiting all the time, drowsy and anxious. What a price does such an evening's, or rather night's riot cost me!

SUNDAY 24 JULY. I was very well, and was at the New Church all day and at my father's between sermons. Dr. Blair preached well in the forenoon on, "Who art thou that judgest another man's servant?" He recommended calmness in judging of others to man, who has so much need of indulgence from his Maker. The sermon was very applicable to me. I took it home and resolved to check violence of temper and make allowance even for the President.

I omitted to mention that I called this evening on Sir William Forbes and had a long comfortable tête-à-tête with him upon literary subjects and religious principles, and on the conduct of life. He told me that he kept an accurate account of his expenses, which he was resolved to do to the day of his death; that from his being so much used to figures, it was quite easy to him; that it served as a kind of Journal of his life; that perhaps once a quarter he classed his expenses under different articles, and so saw where to retrench, where to extend.

This day in church while I thought of Mr. Samuel Johnson's death happening some time hence, my mind was damped. I had then a very pretty lively thought that worthy Langton and others, who were touched by that noble loadstone and whose souls would point to heaven like needles to the pole, would remain to console me. It is very wrong that I do not write oftener to Langton.

FRIDAY 29 JULY. Between one and two in the forenoon Mr. William Wilson and I went to a consultation at Mr. Lockhart's on a perplexed question between Fairholm's trustee—Johnston—and Mitchell and Buchanan of Mountvernon. It vexed me that I could not understand it upon reading the papers. It was astonishing to see Mr. Lockhart, who had only read them over as I had done, much master of the cause. He is certainly a prodigy in his profession. My wife and I dined at Lord Alemoor's.

We had an elegant dinner, but I do not recollect much conversation that passed. Lord Alemoor observed that story-telling was the fashion of the last age, but that our wits now entertained with their own sayings. He asked me if I ever studied beforehand the good things which I said in company. I told him I did not. Crosbie agreed that it was so, but said I spoke enough about them *afterwards;* a very just remark. My wife and I stayed to tea. I was well warmed with wine here, and as Lord Gardenstone and Macqueen spoke jovially of supping at Moncrieffe's, this being the last night of meeting for the season and a neck of venison being promised, I determined to go. I did so, and flashed away. Castle Stewart talked of several voters who were against him having died. "If this goes on," said I, "you'll have a *dead* majority." I was really excellent company. I never saw any man more pleased with another than Seton seemed to be with me. There was very hard drinking. I however did not exceed a bottle and a half of old hock. But, with what I had taken at dinner, I was far gone.

SATURDAY 30 JULY. John Reid's trial was to come on next Monday. Michael Nasmith, who at my desire was agent for him, seemed anxious. I promised to him what I had resolved in my own mind: that I should taste no wine till the trial was over. In the afternoon I went with my wife and

Veronica to Heriot's Gardens, which soothed and refreshed me. Veronica walked briskly, with a little help, pulled flowers, and I held her up till she pulled a cherry for the first time. I played a party at bowls with Adam Bell and so many more, drank tea at home calmly, as I had dined, and made up for yesterday's excess. In the evening when it was dusky I visited John Reid. I felt a sort of dreary tremor as he and I walked together in the dark in the iron room. He would own nothing to me.

SUNDAY 31 JULY. I was in a fine state of preparation for John Reid's trial, which was to come on next day. Michael Nasmith, who at my desire had agreed to be agent, called on me between one and two, when I got up and talked with him. Crosbie positively refused to appear for John Reid, as he had warned him after his last trial, but he was willing to give his aid privately. I went in a chair to his house at two, and consulted with him as to my plan of conducting the trial. He instructed me as to the subject of a charge of being habit and repute a thief. He asked me to dine with him, but as he had a company who I knew would drink, I declined his invitation, being resolved to keep myself perfectly cool. I went to the New Church in the afternoon and heard Dr. Blair preach. Sir George and Lady Preston and Miss Preston drank tea with us. In the evening I finished what remained of Walton from the morning. Looked into Sir George Mackenzie's *Criminals,* meditated on the various circumstances of John Reid's trial, and examined separately two exculpatory witnesses as to his getting the sheep (with the theft of which he was charged) from one Gardner. One of them seemed so positive, notwithstanding my earnest request to tell me nothing but truth, that I began to give some credit to John's tale; but it afterwards appeared that great endeavours had been used to procure false evidence. Notwithstanding all my care to be cool, anxiety made me restless and hot after I went to bed.

MONDAY 1 AUGUST. Having passed an uneasy night from anxiety as to the defence of John Reid, who was my first client in criminal business, I rose between six and seven and dictated to Mr. Lawrie my pleading on the indictment. My dear wife, who always takes good care of me, had a bowl of soup ready for my breakfast, which was an excellent morning cordial.

[EDITORIAL NOTE: At eight o'clock on the morning of 1 August, before the High Court of Justiciary, consisting for the moment of four judges: Thomas Miller of Barskimming (The Lord Justice-Clerk), Alexander Boswell Lord Auchinleck, Henry Home Lord Kames, and George Brown Lord Coalston, the trial of John Reid began with the reading of the Lord Advocate's indictment.]

JOHN REID, flesher, lately residing at Hillend, near to the west bridge of Avon, in the parish of Muiravonside and shire of Stirling, at present prisoner in the Tolbooth of Edinburgh, you are indicted and accused, at the instance of James Montgomery of Stanhope, Esquire, His Majesty's Advocate, for His Majesty's interest: THAT WHEREAS, by the laws of this and of every other well-governed realm, *theft,* especially *sheep-stealing,* and *reset of theft,* or the being art and part of both or either of said crimes, by stealing, receiving, or feloniously keeping, or having in one's possession a number of sheep, knowing them to have been stolen, for the purpose of selling, consuming or making gain of them, or by feloniously disposing of the carcasses or skins of part of such sheep, knowing them to have been stolen, are crimes of a heinous nature, and severely punishable, especially when committed by a person of bad fame, habit and repute to be a thief, or sheep-stealer: YET TRUE IT IS, that you, the said John Reid, are guilty actor, or art and part, of said crimes of theft, or sheep-stealing and reset of theft, or of one or other of said crimes, aggravated as aforesaid; IN SO FAR AS you did, upon the sixth day of October last, or upon one or other of the days or nights of the said month of October or of the month of September immediately preceding, or of November immediately following, steal, or feloniously away take from the farm of Medwenhead, in the county of Peebles, the property of William Lawson of Cairnmuir, and rented by Alexander Gray tenant in Lyne, in the said county of Peebles, nineteen sheep, or some other number of sheep, the property of the said Alexander Gray; and, having stolen the same, you did by yourself, or with the assistance of others, your associates, drive said sheep to your said house at Hillend, near to the west bridge of Avon, in the parish of Muiravonside and county of Stirling; and having kept them there and in the neighbourhood thereof, did there kill a certain number of said sheep, and did sell or dispose of the same, or part of the carcasses and skins thereof, to different persons at Falkirk, and in the neighbourhood of your said house, or in the town of Linlithgow; and Robert Paterson, herd to the said Alexander Gray, suspecting that you had stolen said sheep, having gone from said farm of Medwenhead, after the said sheep had been a-missing from thence, to your said house of Hillend, upon the eleventh, or one or other of the days of the month of October aforesaid, he did there discover three of said sheep in a park near to your house, which had been put there by you to graze; and having thereafter gone into your flesh-house or booth, where you was in use to kill sheep, he there found two of said sheep, which had been killed, hanging up without the body-skin, but which, by the marks on their heads, which were not separated from their bodies, he knew to be part of said sheep which had been stolen from the farm of Medwenhead as aforesaid; and you, being conscious of guilt, did immediately, or soon after the arrival of said

Robert Paterson at your said house, abscond and fly therefrom; and thereafter, the property of said three living sheep, and the heads of said killed sheep, having been proved to belong to said Alexander Gray, before the deceased Michael Ramsay of Mungall, Esq., one of the Justices of the Peace for the shire of Stirling, the same were, by his order, delivered to said Alexander Gray. From all which it is evident, that you the said John Reid are guilty actor, or art and part, of the said theft and reset of theft. AT LEAST, time and place aforesaid, a parcel of sheep, amounting to nineteen, or some other number, the property of said Alexander Gray, were stolen from said farm of Medwenhead; and you did feloniously receive a part of said sheep, knowing them to have been stolen, or did feloniously keep the same in your possession, with a view to dispose thereof, and did actually dispose of part thereof, or of part of the carcasses or skins thereof, knowing said sheep to have been stolen; or was otherways guilty actor, or art and part, of said theft and reset of theft, or of one or other of said crimes; and you are a person of bad fame, habit and repute a sheep-stealer. AND you the said John Reid, having been brought before Archibald Cockburn of Cockpen, Esq., His Majesty's Sheriff-Depute of the county of Edinburgh, did, upon the twenty-third day of March last, emit a declaration, tending to show your guilt in the premises; which declaration, signed by you and said Archibald Cockburn, being to be used in evidence against you, will, in due time, be lodged with the clerk of the High Court of Justiciary, before which you are to be tried, that you may see the same. ALL WHICH, or part thereof, or that you the said John Reid are guilty actor, or art and part, of the said theft, and reset of theft, or of one or other of said crimes, aggravated as aforesaid, being found proven by the verdict of an assize before the Lord Justice General, Lord Justice-Clerk, and Lords Commissioners of Justiciary, you ought to be punished with the pains of law, to deter others from committing the like in time coming.

(signed) JAMES MONTGOMERY.

On one side of the bar were arrayed four "procurators" for the prosecution: James Montgomery of Stanhope, Esquire, His Majesty's Advocate; Mr. Henry Dundas, His Majesty's Solicitor; and two other advocates, Mr. William Nairne and Mr. Robert Sinclair. Opposed to this formidable team stood: "Procurator in Defence, Mr. James Boswell, Advocate."

The first phase of the trial was a "pleading on the relevancy" of the "libel." "Boswell for the panel [for the word "panel" we may always read the modern equivalent "defendent."] represented that":

[He] does in general deny the libel as laid. . . . If he has been so unlucky as to have sheep found in his possession which were stolen, he solemnly avers that he did not know them to be so, but although that had been the case, he humbly contends that this libel is irrelevant in so far as it concludes for the pains of law, the import of which he understands to be a capital punishment, upon the second alternative charged; for he is advised that reset of theft is not punishable with death. . . . As to the charge of his being a person of bad fame, habit and repute a sheep-stealer . . . he was tried for that very charge in December 1766, and a verdict of his country was returned finding it not proved, and nothing is better established than that a man cannot be again tried for the same charge of which he has been acquitted; and supposing this charge to be restricted to the time since his former trial, it is well known that when a man has had the misfortune to be tried for any crime, a prejudice is thereby created against his character which is seldom entirely removed from vulgar minds, though he obtains a verdict in his favour.

Boswell concluded with a compliment to the candor and humanity of the Lord Advocate.

ADVOCATUS. I do not wish it should be understood that in this stage of the cause or any after stage I am to insist for any particular kind of punishment. I understand theft to be the subject of arbitrary punishment, and it is in your Lordships' breasts to determine. I am obliged to my learned friend for his compliment to my humanity. But I should not think it a proof of it were I to bring any of His Majesty's subjects to trial for a crime of which he was formerly acquitted. But the solid answer to the argument as to habit and repute is that it is only a circumstance. I should be sorry if the witnesses mix what is ancient. They will speak to his character, as to his complexion. It respects only the punishment, and your Lordships will not carry it farther than it ought to go. . . .

AUCHINLECK. As to habit and repute, it is not a crime in our law. It is a misfortunate thing when a man has it, but a man cannot be punished for having a bad character. It is pretty fair if we get them punished when there is both habit and repute and a proof of the crime. Then habit and repute [is] not only a aggravation but a strong circumstance of guilt.

Court all agreed.

I moved that the time should be restricted to since 1766. . . .

KAMES. If he is habit and repute when the theft was committed or now, that is enough; not that he was habit and repute forty years ago.

The Court had sent summonses in the name of the Crown to forty-five Edinburgh tradesmen and craftsmen, and from these they now chose fifteen to serve as "assize" or jury: seven merchants, two engravers, two jewellers, two booksellers, one printer, one watch-maker.

The first witness called for the prosecution was Robert Paterson, aged fifty and upwards, herdsman. He deponed at great length and most circumstantially about the matters narrated in the indictment:

namely his missing nineteen of his master's sheep and finding three of them feeding in a park near John Reid's house and three of them slaughtered in Reid's flesh-house, all three skinned but two with the heads still on, and his being absolutely sure, both from the natural marks and faces of the sheep and from certain "lug marks," burns, and tar marks, that these were his master's sheep (he "would have known them among a thousand"). And:

"That the distance from Medwenhead to the panel's house may be sixteen or eighteen computed miles, and that it is easy to drive a parcel of sheep from said farm to the panel's house from sun-setting of one day to sun-rising of another in the month of October.

"That soon after he had challenged the three living sheep, William Black sent off the panel's daughter to go in quest of her father and bring him to see what he had to say; that the girl returned soon after without her father and spoke something to William Black by themselves which the deponent did not hear, and depones that he never saw the panel while he was about his house on the above search, except at the time . . . when he first came there and when he did not know him, but now knows the panel to be the same person whom he then saw and conversed with."

A second shepherd was called as witness (as he finished his testimony "Lords Pitfour and Kennet came into Court"), and then a boy, the son of Paterson, the first witness.

BOSWELL for the panel objected that this witness is clearly inadmissible he being not yet thirteen years of age, and having been but a little past twelve at the time when the facts charged are said to have happened. The law is expressly laid down by Sir George Mackenzie in his *Criminals:* Title: Probation by Witnesses, §5. And the same learned author, §12 of the same title, says that if a witness was not *habilis* at the time, he cannot be admitted though he be *habilis* and *major* at the time of his deposition.

SINCLAIR for the prosecutor answered that it was proposed to examine the boy only in the way of declaration, and whatever may have been the opinion of Sir George Mackenzie upon abstract principles, nothing is now better established in practice than to receive the declarations of this kind. . . .

AUCHINLECK. I remember in the first trial I was on, which was for a murder, a little girl swore to having seen the panel mix a powder, which clenched the evidence of poison.

COALSTON. There is a great difference between civil and criminal questions. In the first, people have the choice of their witnesses. In the other, they have not.

He was called.

> JUSTICE-CLERK. Boy, do you go to the Church?—to the Kirk?
> BOY. No. I gang to the meeting-house.
> AUCHINLECK. You know that God made you?
> BOY. (Stupid).
> AUCHINLECK. Wha made you?
> BOY. (with shrill voice). God!
> AUCHINLECK. You ken it's a sin to lie?
> BOY. Ay.
> PITFOUR. You know you are always in the presence of God, and that an over-ruling Providence superintends us all, and that you will be severely punished both in this world and the next if you say what is not true?

(Pitfour Examinator—Age and childhood—strange work! Justice-Clerk and Lord Advocate tried him. But all in vain except as to some trifles. *Dismissed.* Afterwards, Justice-Clerk having said it was no evidence unless taken down, boy called back.)

The testimony of the boy was followed by that of Alexander Gray, the tenant farmer who had owned the sheep; and then the prosecution adduced William Black of Hillend ("aged forty years and upwards, unmarried"). "Solemnly sworn, purged of malice and partial counsel, and interrogate," he deponed:

"That he is acquainted with the panel, who stays in his neighbourhood at Hillend and lives in a house belonging to the deponent and deals in killing of sheep and cattle sometimes, though not to any extent. . . . That the panel went from home upon a Wednesday or Thursday morning early; for the sheep were come before the deponent arose and were not there when he went to bed. That the deponent, said morning, saw part of the sheep going below the panel's house, and the panel was employed in killing some of them. That the deponent at the time had some suspicions that the panel had not come honestly by the sheep, though he had no conversation with him on the subject so far as he remembers, and the reasons of his suspicions were that he had brought home these sheep in the night-time and was in use to bring sheep in the night and did not commonly take the sheep to the markets to be sold but disposed of them privately in the town of Falkirk and the neighbouring towns and not in the public marketplace, and that the panel is a person suspected of sheep-stealing by report of the country. . . . That the deponent said [to Robert Paterson] he ought to get a constable and to claim the sheep before some honest neighbours and consign them in some person's hand until he proved the property. The deponent accordingly got William Marshall, a constable, and James Inglis, and in their presence Robert Paterson claimed the sheep as belonging to his master, Mr. Gray, and showed his master's marks upon them. . . . That when Robert Paterson came in search of the sheep on said Monday the deponent went with him into the panel's house, but was told he was not at home, but at Bridgehill, which is not a quarter of a mile distant. That the deponent sent one of the panel's daughters to tell her father that a man had come to the town claiming the sheep and desired he might come and speak with him, that soon after the girl returned and was crying or *greeting*, said her father would not come back, but desired the deponent would put it up with the man the best way he could. Depones that after that he never saw the panel at his own house, though he was told he had been at it afterwards; but if it was, it must have been in a concealed manner, as the deponent never saw him. That in about two months thereafter the deponent was informed that the panel had been apprehended in his own house about twelve o'clock at night, but the deponent did not see him, as the party had carried him away before he got up.

"And being interrogated for the prisoner, depones that he purchased from the panel a leg of one of the sheep or a side, that is, of those which he brought home in October as aforesaid, but does not remember having purchased mutton from him at any other time. And being interrogated if when he bought the said leg or side he suspected that the sheep had been stolen, depones that there was a general suspicion against the panel, and the deponent was not in use to buy mutton from him, but as nothing had been proved against him and the deponent knew nothing as to that particular parcel, and that others were buying mutton from him at the time, he also bought as said is. That about three years ago or thereby, one William Gardner, who as the deponent believes is now in Stirling Jail, purchased some cows or stots at Falkirk Muir which the panel slaughtered, that the deponent heard that the panel and Gardner had afterwards some disputes together and left off dealing with each other, so far as he has heard, and the deponent never heard that said cattle had been improperly come by. And depones that as he was in bed when the panel came home in October last, he cannot say whether the panel drove home the sheep himself or if they were brought to the panel by some other person. And being interrogated if it does not consist with his knowledge that the panel was in bed in his own house all the night preceding the sheep's coming there in October last, depones that it does not consist with his knowledge whether the panel was in his bed or not that night; all he knows is that the panel went away in the morning, as already deponed to, and was not come home so far as the deponent knows when the deponent went to bed, but was at home next morning when he arose. And depones that there is not six yards between the panel's house and his, and that the panel has a wife and three children."

The prosecution adduced also Robert Shaw of Bridgehill, aged fifty, married, who deponed:

"That he lives within half a mile of the panel's house, that he has known him for many years, that he has a bad character in the neighbourhood and has for several years past been suspected of sheep-stealing. That upon a Monday in the month of October last . . . the panel came over to the deponent's house in order to settle some accounts betwixt them, that when they were so employed the panel's daughter came and said, 'Father, come home as fast as you can,' or words to that purpose, upon which he rose, went to the door with his daughter, and did not again return to the deponent's house. That in a little time after, Jean Neilson came to the deponent's house and told him that the sheep which were in the panel's possession had been challenged as stolen sheep, upon which he went to the door and saw the panel upon the south side of the Water of Avon going westwards and away from his house, which is upon the north side of the Water of Avon; that he was sometimes running and sometimes walking hard, and that he observed him two different times look back. That at this time he saw some men driving three live sheep towards the bridge of Avon, which he afterwards understood were three of the stolen sheep that were challenged that day. Depones that the panel some time ago used to butcher both cattle and sheep, but for some time past only some sheep, and that he has sometimes bought mutton from him. And being interrogated for the panel, depones that the panel never wronged him in any dealings which the deponent had with him."

Two other witnesses for the prosecution, interrogated by Lord Auchinleck, deponed that John Reid had the general reputation of a sheep-stealer. And then, without opposition from Boswell or the need of bringing witnesses, the prosecutor introduced, to be read before the court as promised in the indictment, Reid's "declaration":

At Edinburgh, the twenty-third day
of March, 1774 years

The which day in presence of Archibald Cockburn, Esquire, of Cockpen, advocate, Sheriff-Depute of the Sheriffdom of Edinburgh, compeared John Reid, flesher, lately residing at Hillend, near to the west bridge of Avon, in the parish of Muiravonside and shire of Stirling, presently prisoner in the Tolbooth of Edinburgh, who being examined and interrogate declares that the week before last Michaelmas market at Crieff the declarant was the whole week at home at his own house at Hillend, where he slept every night that week, and that he possesses his house from one William Black, who is his next neighbour. Declares that he killed several sheep that week and sold some of them at Falkirk Market and likewise at home. Declares that he is acquainted with James Inglis, farmer at Haining Miln, and that Inglis was in the declarant's slaughter-house said week, when there were some dead sheep hanging there, but whether tups or ewes the declarant does not remember. And declares that at the same time the declarant had some sheep belonging to him going upon Black's pasture near the house, and being interrogate where he got or bought the sheep that he killed that week and sold either at home or Falkirk Market and also where he got or bought the sheep that were going on Black's pasture, declares that he got them all from one William Gardner in Parkhead of Hillend, who brought them to the declarant's house on the Thursday morning, on which day the declarant began to kill them. Declares that the number of sheep brought by Gardner to the declarant was nineteen, and that he told the declarant he got the said sheep from some horse-copers about Carnwath with whom he had dealings. And being interrogate when he left his own house after Gardner had delivered the said sheep to him, declares that it is very likely he left it on the Monday after, but he will not say that he left it that day. And being interrogate what was his reason for leaving his own house so suddenly, declares that he will not answer that question or any more questions this day, having answered enough already. This he declares to be truth.

Boswell and Reid had formally summoned (on 31 July) no fewer than thirty-three of Reid's neighbours and acquaintances as exculpatory witnesses (eight of these, including William Black, appearing also on the prosecution's list of thirty witnesses). On the same day, as we have seen, Boswell had examined two such witnesses with disconcerting results. He now attempted to adduce only a single witness.

I offered to prove by Andrew Auld what Gardner said as to a bargain between him and Reid as to these sheep.

SOLICITOR. Gardner himself was kept in the prison of Stirling, where he now lies, on purpose that the panel might bring him as an evidence if he thought proper. Instead of doing which, we are to have a proof of a *hearsay* from him.

BOSWELL. I understood that a man convicted by the verdict of his country of housebreaking is infamous and intestable. Besides, though Gardner had been admitted, I should not have chosen to trust the panel's life to the testimony of one in his circumstances.

ADVOCATUS. I agree that the witness shall be examined as to what he has heard from Gardner.

KAMES. I am not for yielding to the King's Advocate to wound the law—to go out of rule to take a hearsay, instead of adducing Gardner.

ADVOCATUS. I am sure I want to do nothing to wound the law. I hold it to be clear law that if Gardner had been transported, what he said as to a bargain between him and the panel might have been proved, as that was the best evidence the nature of the thing would admit. But Gardner stands not transported, though convicted. Mr. Boswell says he thought him intestable and did not adduce him. *There* I put my concession.

KAMES. I never understood that the mistake of a lawyer was to make law. I submit, but I give my testimony against it.

JUSTICE-CLERK. If the prosecutor passes from an objection to a witness, it has been usual for the Court to admit. Had the opinion of the Court been called upon, we probably should all have been unanimous.

I stated that if Gardner had been called and the Lord Advocate had admitted him, the same objection might have come from the Court: that the King's Counsel could not make, by their consent, illegal evidence be received:—so that in either case I should have been deprived of evidence.

Andrew Auld, "indweller in Westcraig," was called. "Could only say that Gardner told him of a bargain between the panel and him above a year ago." "Depones nothing material and dismissed."

"No more witnesses called for the panel."

Boswell himself, however, introduced at this point a reminiscence:

BOSWELL for the panel represented that as there was here a charge against the panel of being habit and repute a common thief, notwithstanding of his being acquitted of that charge by a verdict of his country in the year of 1766, it was of great importance to the panel to show cause for such bad report having prevailed, and he offered to prove by two of the jury upon his last trial that after a verdict of his country was returned acquitting him, the five judges present strongly expressed their disapprobation of the verdict and in such terms as to convey to the minds of a numerous audience that notwithstanding that verdict he was still a guilty man.

His Majesty's Advocate answered that in order to save the time of the Court he had no objection to admit the fact as above stated.

The trial now concluded with speeches of summation by the Lord Advocate and Boswell.

Boswell seems to have been calculating that if he could to some extent discredit the aspersion of "habit and repute a thief," then Reid's own declaration concerning Gardner's role, along with the cross-examination of William Black and perhaps some further intimations from Auld, might persuade the jury that it was at least possible Reid had received the sheep from Gardner innocently. At the same time Boswell was careful not to adduce Gardner himself at the trial, fearing no doubt that his testimony would clearly convict Reid of the crime of "reset of theft" (that is, receiving stolen sheep knowing them to be stolen). We shall see that a few days after the trial Boswell made strenuous efforts to bring Gardner forward, when through Crown action it was no longer possible. Whether a verdict finding Reid guilty only of "reset" would have elicited from this Court the less severe sentence of transportation, we can scarcely now be sure, though Boswell may have had clear enough intimations to the contrary. The allusions to the alternative of reset, in the imperfectly reported speech by the Lord Advocate which follows, are apparently to be read, in the light of legal logic, as meaning that since this alternative has not been advanced by the defence, then the possibility of it should not be allowed to complicate the jury's judgement that Reid's possession of the sheep was guilty: that is, guilt of some kind is obvious, and only one kind is now admissible. Boswell's response will try, on the contrary, to suggest that at least one kind of guilt, the partial guilt of reset, has been abandoned by the prosecution, and that, given the simple alternatives of full guilt and innocence, it is more just to decide for the latter.

LORD ADVOCATE'S CHARGE. . . . As it is impossible for the Public Prosecutor, whoever he may be, to know whether a person accused may not, where there are only circumstances, prove that he bought them, reset is libelled. If there is evidence brought to satisfy the minds of a jury that he did not steal, then there is reset. Here there is no occasion for it; for if this man is not guilty of the actual theft, he is an innocent man. My learned friend has mentioned his former trial. Surely he cannot mean that the respectable judges' (whom I have in my eye) having declared their opinions that it was a bad verdict will do him good. I therefore cannot imagine what use he is to make of it. . . .

Let us consider corroborating circumstances. What is the conduct of this panel? Does he appear like an honest man?—Black, his next neighbour, does not see him for two months, till the law, too cunning for him, overtakes him, and the officers catch him sleeping in his bed. These circumstances speak strongly to the mind. Had he been innocent, had he bought these sheep from Gardner, would he not have come and told the officers so and said, "This man must be a rascal"? . . . Now consider how improbable it is in calculation that on the same day the same number of sheep stolen were sold to the panel. It may perhaps be said Gardner stole the sheep, and therefore the number must be nineteen. But of this the panel has brought no evidence. He has not adduced Gardner. . . . My learned friend, who always does great justice to his clients, especially in this Court, but is sometimes righteous over much (it is excusable when pleading for a panel), set out with a distinction between theft and reset. But he must have greater abilities than he really has (and he has great abilities) if he can persuade you that there was here not a theft but a reset. I do not think that in every case reset should be punished as theft. Here though proof had been brought that the panel had received the sheep from Gardner, the presumption would have been that it was reset. But it appears to me that the proof of actual theft is abundantly strong. Perhaps it may appear stronger to me as I am connected with a sheep country. You gentlemen will judge and will bring in your verdict accordingly.

MY CHARGE. Gentlemen of the jury, you are now to deliberate concerning the life of [a] fellow citizen who stands at this bar charged with the crime of sheep-stealing. My Lord Advocate has summed up the evidence upon the part of the Crown with his usual ability, but with a warmth unusual for his Lordship on such occasions. He has indeed fairly explained the reason for this—his being connected with a sheep country. But you and I, gentlemen, who have no such connexion, will consider the matter calmly and coolly. You at least will, whose duty it is to form a judgement upon it. The indictment charges the panel with three several accusations: theft, reset of theft, and being a person of bad fame, habit and repute a thief. The reset of theft my Lord Advocate has given up, for he has admitted that unless the panel shall be found guilty of the theft in this case, he is to be held as an innocent man. I have therefore to speak only of two accusations, his being guilty of theft and his being habit and repute a thief. I shall begin with the last, as I had occasion to state to the Court when pleading upon the relevancy of this indictment, I again state. . . .

Mr. James Boswell "summed up the evidence . . . in a very masterly and pathetic manner, which did him great honour both as a lawyer and as one who wished for a free and impartial trial by jury" (*Edinburgh Advertiser*, 2 August 1774).

At about five o'clock that afternoon, the Court ordered the jury to be enclosed. They chose the bookseller William Gordon to be their chancellor and the printer John Robertson to be their clerk. They reached a verdict and signed it that evening before supper, and it was known about town, though not to be delivered until the next afternoon.

MONDAY 1 AUGUST [continued]. Michael Nasmith came home with me between five and six, when we dined, drank some porter and port and a bottle of claret. I was in a kind of agitation, which is not without something agreeable, in an odd way of feeling. Having heard that a verdict was found against John Reid, I went at eight to Walker's Tavern, where the jury was met (I having first visited my client and intimated his fate to him), and being elated with the admirable appearance which I had made in the court, I was in such a frame as to think myself as Edmund Burke—and a man who united pleasantry in conversation with abilities in business and powers as an orator. I enjoyed the applause which several individuals of the jury now gave me and the general attention with which I was treated. The Crown entertains the jury on an occasion of this kind, and the bill is authenticated by the initials of the chancellor. We drank a great deal, and by imposing a fine of a pint of claret on any man who mentioned the trial, bets, etc., we had six pints of claret secured for a future meeting; and we appointed to dine together in the same place that day sennight. There was a strange mixture of characters. I was not much pleased at being fixed for another meeting. However, I considered it as unavoidable, and as the buck in one of our farces says, 'twas *life*. We parted about twelve. I was much in liquor, and strolled in the streets a good while—a very bad habit which I have when intoxicated. I got home before one. My dear wife had been very anxious.

[Michael Nasmith to Boswell]

[Edinburgh] 1 August [1774], 7 o'clock

DEAR SIR,—This is truly miserable. The Most unjudicious verdict that can be. But what is still more miserable, it is just: a verdict in general "finding the theft proved" against him. The gentleman who informs me is a stranger to judicial style, thinks these are the capital words. Capital enough! I wish it had been otherwise, for the sake of that respect which *belongs* to a jury and of the dignity that the panel's charge merits. Could we get an innocent panel! But what can be done for guilt? I am in low spirits notwithstanding the good cheer within me. Alwise, my dear Sir, yours most sincerely,

M. NASMITH

TUESDAY 2 AUGUST. My bad rest during the night between Sunday and yesterday, the anxiety of the trial, and the debauch of last night made me in a woeful plight and very unwilling to rise. Worthy John Hall called between seven and eight. I got up, and though hurt by the comparison between his decent sobriety and my riotous conduct, I was comforted to find myself entrusted by him, and the friendship of the family of Stichell continued to one of our family in his connexion.

In the court in the forenoon I received great applause for my spirited behaviour yesterday; and I could also see Scottish envy showing itself. John Reid received his sentence at two o'clock, or rather a little before three.

EDITORIAL NOTE: When the jury had at two o'clock delivered its verdict—"all in one voice" finding "John Reid the panel guilty of the theft libelled"—"Mr. Boswell moved the Court to delay pronouncing sentence for a few days, as he would endeavour to show that a capital punishment should not be inflicted." We have Boswell's hastily scribbled record of the words that followed:

AUCHINLECK. I'll own I think theft by our law a capital crime, more especially as here, where 'tis a *grex*; were it not so, farmers would be in [a] miserable situation. If nineteen not capital, a hundred not, and there would be an end of that useful business. I have therefore no sort of difficulty. If there was anything special, I should be for indulging [the] panel's counsel. But as we have often had this before us, [it] would be indecent.

KAMES. I have no doubt that theft of nineteen, nay of nine, [is] capital. If not, as my brother said, [it] would be dismal, as we could not repress it. And there would be no remedy. 'Tis done by low people. They cannot make reparation. I should like that better. At [the] same time, as we have no act making it capital, though we have had long practice, I'm for indulging [the] young man.

PITFOUR. I will confirm doctrine.

COALSTON. If I thought there was any difficulty or any of your Lordships thought [there was any] difficulty, [I] would delay. But as 'tis clear, [it] would be wrong to delay. This case [is] not new to me. I had occasion to consider it not only by reading all on the subject but by searching [the] records. And so [I] formed [my] opinion. [I have] always followed [this procedure] since I had the honour to sit. I came to [a] clear conclusion. One act of theft [is] not always capital, as of a small thing, as one sheep. But [it is] also clear [that] one theft [can be] capital, as *abigeatus*. And so far as I know, [there is] no instance where when sheep [were] stolen [it has] not [been] capital.

KENNET. I'm willing to grant all indulgence to [the] panel or panel's counsel. I applaud Mr. Boswell's zeal on this occasion and which he has shown on many others. I think delay here improper, as much as if [in a case of] murther.

JUSTICE-CLERK. Your Lordships have a point of law fixed since the Monarchy, that theft [is] capital. It would then be improper and even indecent for the Court to delay upon the relevancy. All your Lordships agreed that theft [is] capital, and indeed [it] would hurt my mind to think that a *grex* should not be capital. So judgement [should be given].

AUCHINLECK. 'Tis a disagreeable part of our office to pass sentence of death on any man. But so are mankind made that it must be. This man [was] before us before, and all of us [were] called on in [the] course of our duty to declare that the verdict was contrary to evidence. Now we have from a most respectable jury a verdict finding [him] guilty of [the theft of a] *grex*. Were he to get off, [he] would go on. His former escape emboldened [him]. We have no choice. I propose that on Wednesday, etc.

JUSTICE-CLERK. John Reid, nothing remains to me now but to pronounce that judgement we the Court unanimously agreed should be pronounced. I am very sorry it is necessary. Your former trial should not have been mentioned, had it not been forced on [the] Court by your counsel, who has exerted all talents and abilities in your defence. But the facts coming out in evidence put it out of his power to do you any service. I do not desire to revive the memory of what is past. God and your own conscience know [as to that.] But, Sir, you are now convicted by verdict of your country of the theft of nineteen sheep. You could not commit that without other crimes. But it can do you no harm to join with my brothers in giving you . . .

[Sentence of Death Against John Reid]

The said Lords . . . decern and adjudge the said John Reid to be carried from the bar back to the Tolbooth of Edinburgh, therein to be detained until Wednesday the seventh day of September next, and upon that day to be taken forth of the said Tolbooth and carried to the common place of execution in the Grassmarket of Edinburgh, and then and there betwixt the hours of two and four o'clock in the afternoon of the said day to be hanged by the neck by the hands of the common executioner upon a gibbet until he be dead, and ordain all his moveable goods and gear to be escheat and inbrought to His Majesty's use, which is pronounced for doom.

THOMAS MILLER
ALEXANDER BOSWELL
HENRY HOME
JAMES FERGUSON
GEORGE BROWN
ROBERT BRUCE

THURSDAY 4 AUGUST. Sir John Dalrymple told me, either yesterday or today, that my behaviour in John Reid's trial would have made my fortune in England. This increased my desire to go; and, either yesterday or today while I walked in the Meadow with Maclaurin, he seemed to think I would do well to try. He said very handsomely, *"I decus, i, nostrum! melioribus utere fatis."* He and I had some conversation on the effect of tunes, and we agreed that there is a *ludicrous* in music independent of the association of ideas. He tried Pope's "Universal Prayer" to the tune of "Our Polly she's a sad slut" and it was quite ridiculous.

SUNDAY 7 AUGUST. My wife and I dined at my father's between sermons. Dr. Boswell, Sir George Preston, and Mr. Webster were there. Veronica always visits there at that time and gets raisins from her grandfather. In the afternoon I went and walked in St. Anne's Yards and the Abbey of Holyrood House. I was like Isaac meditating in the fields. My wife and I drank tea at home by ourselves, then went with our children and walked pleasantly in Mr. Webster's garden. We supped there. He himself sent that he was not to be home to supper. We were uneasy a little; but it turned out that he had gone to baptize a child, and I suppose had found good wine.

WEDNESDAY 10 AUGUST. In the forenoon I had visited John Reid, whom I found very composed. He persisted in averring that he got the sheep from Gardner. I really believed him after I had adjured him, as he should answer to GOD, to tell me the truth. I told him that I was of opinion that a petition to the King would have no effect, but that his wife had applied to me, and I should draw one which he should sign; but that he must not expect anything but death. He very calmly assured me he would expect nothing else. I wondered at my own firmness of mind while I talked with a man under sentence of death, without much emotion, but with solemnity and humanity. I desired John to write his life very fully, which he promised to do. I bid him say nothing as to the *facts* with which he was formerly charged. He had been acquitted by his country. That was enough. His acknowledging that he had been guilty might hurt some unhappy panel who was innocent by making a jury condemn on imperfect circumstantial evidence. It will be a curious thing if he gives a narrative of his life.

At night I gave John Reid's wife a letter to Lord Erroll, from whom she hoped for some assistance, her father having been his tenant these forty years.

[Boswell to the Earl of Erroll]

Edinburgh, 10 August 1774

MY LORD,—This will come to your Lordship's hands along with an application from Clarke, an old tenant of your Lordship's, in favour of John Reid, a client of mine who lies under sentence of death here for sheep-stealing. Reid it seems is son-in-law to Clarke. I may perhaps have been prejudiced, but I really did not think the evidence against Reid sufficient to convict him; and I am afraid his suspicious character determined the jury, which I take to be a dangerous principle. The stolen sheep were found in his possession; but he has uniformly averred that he had them from one Gardner, who has been since sentenced to transportation. He indeed could not *prove* this; but this story is by no means improbable. I am to draw a petition for him to the King in hopes of obtaining a transportation pardon, the evidence being defective and the crime of stealing nineteen sheep being at any rate too small for a capital punishment. If your Lordship will take the trouble to write to Lord Suffolk, it may have great influence, and as the unhappy man's petition will be much better read if a letter from Lord Erroll comes along with it, I shall delay transmitting it for some time till I know your Lordship's determination.

I beg to offer my most respectful compliments to Lady Erroll, and with a very grateful sense of your Lordship's civilities to me, I have the honour to be, my Lord, your Lordship's most obedient, humble servant,

[JAMES BOSWELL].

THURSDAY 1 AUGUST. The confusion and hurry of the last day of the session were much the same as usual. I philosophized, thinking that in all probability all the members of Court would not be alive against another session, though indeed it is remarkable that the members of our College of Justice live long. Death makes as little impression upon the minds of those who are occupied in the profession of the law as it does in an army. The survivors are busy, and share the employment of the deceased. Archibald of McHarg, writer, died this session, and though he had a great deal of business, he was never missed. His death was only occasionally mentioned as an apology for delay in giving in a paper. The succession in business is so quick that there is not time to perceive a blank.

FRIDAY 12 AUGUST. I went home, and till Nicholls joins me, I shall take a short review of this summer session. I never was so busy, having written fifty law papers, nor made so much money, having got 120 guineas. I had been up almost every morning at seven, and sometimes earlier. I had been in the Court of Session almost every morning precisely at nine, Charles Hay and I having agreed that whichever of us was later of coming than the other, after the nine o'clock bell was rung out, should lose a shilling; and I think I was a few mornings a little late, and he a few, so that upon the whole we were equal. I had advanced in practice and kept clear of the President. I had distinguished myself nobly in a capital trial. I had been a good deal in company, and in the best company of the place, both in my own house and in their houses. I had therefore great reason to be satisfied, having enjoyed, withal, good health and spirits. BUT I had been much intoxicated—I may say *drunk*—six times, and still oftener heated with liquor to feverishness. I had read hardly anything but mere law; I had paid very little attention to the duties of piety, though I had almost every day, morning and evening, addressed a short prayer to GOD. Old Izaak Walton had done me good; and frequently in the course of the day, I had meditated on death and a future state. Let me endeavour every session and every year to improve.

MONDAY 15 AUGUST. The day that Lord Pembroke dined with me, I should have mentioned a dispute among the military gentlemen whether experienced soldiers or young ones were best. Colonel Webster was for experienced ones, if they had not been wounded. Colonel Stopford and also General Lockhart, for young ones, saying that there was an ardour in men advancing to action for the first time, under officers of whom they had a good opinion, which soldiers who had seen service had not. The question does not seem clear. I think it has been held that veterans are most effectual troops. Yet I observe in Hentzner's travels that on the tomb of Henry III in Westminster Abbey there was this motto: *War is delightful to the unexperienced.* Whether it is there still, I know not.

THURSDAY 18 AUGUST. I called on Michael Nasmith and he engaged to get my petition for John Reid well copied. I settled my account with the Bank of Scotland; sat awhile with Ilay Campbell about Bedlay. Went to Heriot's Garden with my wife and Veronica, who is really a charming child. She began to walk by herself on Friday the 12th current. She could now cry "Papa" very distinctly.

SATURDAY 20 AUGUST. I have omitted a very pleasing incident. On Thursday forenoon Lord Pembroke called. I met him at the door. He said, "I set out tonight, and am come to ask Mrs. Boswell's commands for London." Mr. Graham of Balgowan was with him. We went up to the dining-room. My bass fiddle was standing in a corner, I having begun again to play a little on it, remembering my father having told me that Lord Newhall resumed it and had one standing in his study. "What!" said Lord Pembroke, "are we brother bassers, as well as brother Corsicans?" His Lordship it seems plays upon it. My wife came and sat awhile, and we were easy and well. There was a polite attention in this visit which did honour to the Earl's disposition.

This morning I drew a petition to His Majesty for John Reid. I could think of nothing else; so Mr. Charles Hay and I read no law, but went with it to Michael Nasmith's, who was very much pleased with it, and undertook to have two fair copies on large paper ready to go by the post at night. Charles went with me to see John. His wife was with him. I adjured him not to say that he was innocent of the theft found proved against him if he was not so; that I had put into the petition what he said, but he would have as good, if not a better, chance by fairly confessing to His Majesty. Charles very properly said to him, "Take care and do not fill up the measure of your iniquity by telling a lie to your Sovereign." I in the strongest manner assured him that I thought the petition would have no effect—that I wrote it only because I had promised to do it; but that I really thought it would be better not to send it, as it might make him entertain vain hopes and prevent him from thinking seriously of death. John professed his conviction that the chance was hardly anything, but was for using the means. I could not therefore refuse him. Charles again addressed him as to his telling a lie, and said, "I may say, you are putting your salvation against one to ten thousand; nay, against nothing." John expressed his willingness to submit to what was *foreordained* for him. "John," said I, "this would not have been *foreordained* for you if you had not stolen sheep, and that was not *foreordained*. GOD does not foreordain wickedness. Your Bible tells you that." I then took it up and read from the Epistle of James, Chap. I, v. 13 and 14: "Let no man say when he is tempted, I am tempted of GOD; for GOD cannot be tempted with evil, neither tempteth he any man. But every man is tempted, when he is drawn away of his own lust, and enticed." This seemed to satisfy him. But people in his situation are very apt to become predestinarians. Dr. Daniel Macqueen, one of the ministers of Edinburgh, told me that when he was minister at Stirling, there was a man under sentence of death there whom some Cameronian or seceding minister had tutored deeply upon predestination till the man was positive that the crime which he had committed was decreed by his Maker; nor could Mr. Macqueen argue him out of this notion. When he came to the place of execution, the man was beginning to harangue the people upon this subject. Upon which, Mr. Macqueen, with his forcible and hurried manner, insisted with the magistrate to order the executioner to do his duty directly; and accordingly the man was thrown off, which prevented his mystical discourse. "He might have put more nonsense into their heads," said Macqueen, "than I could have driven out again in half a year." There was good sense in Mr. Macqueen's conduct; though his acquaintances do not fail in keeping up as a joke upon him his mode of opposing an argument.

Messrs. Charles Hay, Michael Nasmith, Alexander Innes (for the first time), George Webster, Dr. Boswell, and Grange dined with me. We did not drink much. I took port and water. I had played at bowls before dinner with Charles Hay, etc.

Between five and six Mr. Nasmith and George Webster accompanied me to the prison, when I read over the petition to John Reid, and he signed two copies of it. I again adjured him not to sign it if he was not innocent, and again pressed home upon him my conviction that his chance for life was hardly anything. I was wonderfully firm. I told him that I really thought it was happy for him that he was to die by a sentence of the law, as he had so much time to think seriously and prepare for death; whereas, if he was not stopped in that manner, his unhappy disposition to steal was such that it was to be feared he would have been cut off in the midst of his wickedness. I enclosed one copy of the petition to Lord Suffolk, Secretary of State for the Northern Department, and one to Lord Pembroke, and wrote a letter with each copy. I could not help entertaining some faint hope. John Reid's petition was business enough to me for one day.

[Boswell to the Earl of Pembroke]

MY LORD,—Presuming on your Lordship's goodness, I trouble you with the enclosed petition to His Majesty from John Reid, an unfortunate man under sentence of death. I have also transmitted a copy to my Lord Suffolk, Secretary of State for the Northern Department.

John Reid was my first client in criminal business when he was tried in 1766. I have therefore a particular concern in his fate and wish much that he should not be hanged.

May I beg that your Lordship may make me certain that the petition reaches His Majesty. There is a prejudice against the man in this country. It would therefore be happy of a transportation pardon could be obtained for him at once, his crime at any rate not being atrocious. I have the honour to be with very great regard, my Lord, your most obliged and obedient humble servant,

[JAMES BOSWELL].

SUNDAY 21 AUGUST. There came an invitation to Mr. Nairne to sup at Dr. Webster's with my wife and me, which he did. Sandy Webster was returned from a voyage to Russia. Dr. Webster had no mercy on John Reid, because he had attempted to get witnesses to perjure themselves to bring him off. Said George: "This is what every man would do in his place. To preserve my life I would perjure all mankind. Nay, supposing all the stars in the firmament to be inhabited, I would perjure all their inhabitants." This was a sort of grand thought. But, to be sure, no thinking man of good principles would make even one person commit the crime of perjury, to save a short and uncertain life at the risk of salvation.

WEDNESDAY 24 AUGUST. I dined at Nairne's, who had ten guests assembled without any kind of assortment, so that drinking only made the cement of the company. Nothing worth mentioning passed, except a fancy of my own upon Lochée's Military Academy at Chelsea, in which boys are made encamp, etc., to prepare them for war. I observed that it was absurd to make them suffer the hardships of a campaign without necessity. That they might as well be wounded and carried to an hospital, or even some of them be killed; and that the Master of the Academy would approve of their being distressed for want of provisions. I shall work up this into an essay for *Rampager*.

THURSDAY 25 AUGUST. I was very sick and had a severe headache, and lay till between ten and eleven, when I grew better. There was no Law College today. Crosbie called on me in the forenoon, in great indignation at the Bailies of Edinburgh for having sentenced Henry McGraugh, an Irishman, to be imprisoned, whipped, and banished because he had called for victuals and drink in public houses and then told that he had not money to pay for them. Crosbie begged that I would inquire into the affair.

I communicated to Crosbie a scheme which I had of making an experiment on John Reid, in case he was hanged, to try to recover him. I had mentioned it in secrecy to Charles Hay and Mr. Wood the surgeon, who promised me assistance. Crosbie told me that he had lately had a long conversation on the subject with Dr. Cullen, who thought it practicable. It was lucky that I spoke of it to Crosbie, for he was clear for trying it, and threw out many good hints as to what should be done. I resolved to wait on Dr. Cullen and get his instructions. I was this forenoon at the burial of a daughter of the late Mr. Sands, bookseller here. There is something usefully solemn in such a scene, and I make it a rule to attend every burial to which I am invited unless I have a sufficient excuse; as I expect that those who are invited to mine will pay that piece of decent attention.

I afterwards called at the prison, where I found Mr. Todd, Lady Maxwell's chaplain, with John Reid. He seemed to be a weak, well-meaning young man. I again told John in his presence that there was hardly the least chance of a pardon and therefore that he ought to consider himself as a dying man. Yet I did now entertain a small additional glimpse of hope, because I saw in the newspapers that, a few

days before, one Madan got a reprieve after he was at Tyburn, ready to
be turned off, the man who really committed the robbery for which he
was condemned having voluntarily appeared and owned it. I thought
this incident might make the Ministry more ready to listen to John Reid's
story that Gardner was the real thief. John was looking gloomy today.
He told me he had some bad dreams which made him believe he was
now to die.

I then called for McGraugh, who was put into the cage, he was so
violent a prisoner. He was a true Teague. I asked him why he was
confined. He could give but a very confused account; but he assured me
that he had neither stolen victuals and drink nor taken them by force,
but only called for them. I asked him if he had stolen anything. "Only a
paice (piece) of wood," said he; "but then, an't *plaise* your Honour, it was
in the dark." "That will not make it better," said I. Afterwards, however,
I saw that this odd saying of his, like all the Irish sayings at which we
laugh as bulls or absurdities, had a meaning. For he meant that as he had
taken the wood in the dark, it could not be known he had done it; so that
it could be no part of the charge against him and consequently was no
justification of the sentence of the magistrates. I promised to do what I
could for him. I also saw one Macpherson, a young goldsmith confined
for debt, from whom I had a letter telling me that a young woman had
come into prison and lent him her clothes, in which he made his escape
but was taken again; and that the *innocent* girl was imprisoned. I told him
that breaking prison was a crime; that the girl had been aiding in the
escape of a prisoner and therefore was not innocent; but that she would
not be long confined.

My wife and I drank tea at Dr. Grant's. He was clear that a man who
was hung ten minutes cannot be recovered; and he had dissected two. I
was however resolved that the experiment should be tried. Dr. Grant
carried me up to a very good library which he has and showed me a
number of anatomical preparations. The survey of skulls and other
parts of the human body, and the reflection upon all of us being so frail
and liable to so many painful diseases, made me dreary.

SATURDAY 27 AUGUST. And there we were joined by Ilay Campbell,
who walked on with us. He insisted that we should go and dine with him
at a little country-house which he had near Leith. We did so, and shared
his family dinner with Mrs. Campbell and his children. It was a scene
worth taking: a family country dinner with the first writing lawyer at our
bar. He told us that when Macqueen married, which was only about
eighteen years ago, his practice did not exceed ＿＿ a year, though
he had since realized many thousands. Macqueen told him that one year

he had made £1900. Ilay told us that he himself had made £1600 in a year in the ordinary course of business; and that a lawyer's labour is not increased in proportion with his gains, for that he now wrote less than he had done. This kind of conversation excited the solid coarse ambition of making money in the Court of Session. We drank a bottle of claret apiece and a fourth among us. We then drank tea, and Mr. Campbell walked with us a good [way] up as a convoy. I was not a bit intoxicated with what I had drank.

A curious thought struck me of having the Sheep-stealer's Progress in the manner of Hogarth's historical prints. We drank very little.

MONDAY 29 AUGUST. A very curious whim had come into my head: that I would have a portrait of John Reid as my first client in criminal business and as a very remarkable person in the annals of the Court of Justiciary. Keith Ralph, a young painter who had studied under Runciman, had drawn Mr. Lawrie's picture very like. I had him with me this forenoon, and he agreed to paint John. He desired to see him today, to have an idea of his face, to see what kind of light was in the room where he lay, and to judge what should be the size of the picture. Accordingly I went with him. I had before this given a hint of my design to Richard Lock, the inner turnkey, a very sensible, good kind of man; and he had no objection. Accordingly we went up. Mr. Ritchie, a kind of lay teacher who humanely attends all the people under sentence of death, was with John. I was acquainted with Mr. Ritchie, as he had called on me about my client Agnes Adam. After standing a little and speaking a few words in a serious strain, I addressed myself to Ritchie in a kind of soft voice and mentioned my desire to have a remembrance of John Reid, by having a picture of him; that Mr. Ritchie and I could sit by and talk to him, and that I imagined John would have no objection, as it would not disturb him. Ritchie said he supposed John would have none; that he was so much obliged to me, he would do much more at my request; and he would come and be present. Next morning between nine and ten was fixed. Mr. Charles Hay, who waited in the street, went with me to Ralph's and saw some of his performances.

At four this afternoon Adam Bell was with me, along with Nimmo his landlord, consulting me to draw answers to a petition. I found myself much as in session time. Steuart Hall and Mr. Wood the surgeon drank tea. Wood dispelled the dreary country ideas which Steuart Hall would have raised. I took a walk with him to Drumsheugh and round by the New Town, and talked of the scheme of recovering John Reid. He said he did not think it practicable. But that he should give all the assistance in his power to have the experiment fairly tried.

TUESDAY 30 AUGUST. At ten o'clock I was with John Reid. Before I got there, Ralph was begun with his chalk and honest Ritchie was exhorting him quietly. I was happy to see that this whim of mine gave no trouble to John. One of his legs was fixed to a large iron goad, but he could rise very easily; and he at any rate used to sit upon a form, so that he just kept his ordinary posture, and Ritchie and I conversed with him. He seemed to be quite composed, and said he had no hopes of life on account of the dreams which he had. That he dreamt he was riding on one white horse and leading another. "That," said he, "was too good a dream, and dreams are contrary." He said he also dreamt a great deal of being on the seashore and of passing deep waters. "However," said he, "I allwaye (always) get through them." "Well," said I, "John, I hope that shall not be contrary; but that you shall get through the great deep of death." I called for a dram of whisky. I had not thought how I should drink to John till I had the glass in my hand, and I felt some embarrassment. I could not say, "Your good health"; and "Here's to you" was too much in the style of hearty fellowship. I said, "John, I wish you well," or words pretty much the same, as "Wishing you well"—or some such phrase. The painter and Mr. Ritchie tasted the spirits. Richard the jailer makes it a rule never to taste them within the walls of the prison.

John seemed to be the better of a dram. He told me that the Reids of Muiravonside had been there, he believed, for three hundred years; that they had been butchers for many generations. He could trace himself, his father, and grandfather in that business; that he never was worth £10 and never in much debt, so that he was always evens with the world. That in the year 1753 he enlisted in Sir Peter Halkett's regiment. But was taken up on an accusation of stealing two cows, for which he was tried at Glasgow and acquitted; after which, as his pay had run up to a considerable sum, the regiment let him alone, though he was several times taken up as a deserter at the instigation of ill-natured people; that he went up to London on foot and wrought there as a gardener for _____ till there was a hot press, and then he came to Leith in a brig commanded by John Beatson. That after this he enlisted in Colonel Perry's regiment, but that a writer or agent whom he knew in Glasgow got him off by taking a bill from him for £11, for which he granted John a discharge which they concealed, so that the apparent debt above £10 kept him from being forced away; that he was employed for several years as a driver of cattle to England, particularly under Mr. Birtwhistle, the great English drover. That he was art and part in the theft of the sheep from the parish of Douglas, one of the articles in his trial in 1766.

Graham, the man's herd, stole them and delivered them to him half a mile from the farm. That he did not steal the six score; that he married in 1759; that since his trial in 1766 he had led an honest, industrious life; that he received the sheep for which he was condemned from Gardner, and did not suspect them to be stolen. That his wife and children would be present at his death. I dissuaded him from this. He said his wife and he had lived comfortably fifteen years, and she said she would see him to the last and would *kep* him (i.e., receive his body when cut down); that his son, who was a boy of ten years of age, might forget it (meaning his execution) if he only heard of it, but that he would not readily forget it if he saw it. To hear a man talk of his own execution gave me a strange kind of feeling. He said he would be carried to his own burial-place at Muiravonside; that it was the second best in the kirkyard. There were symptoms of vanity in the long line of the Reids and the good burial-place; a proof that ideas of these kinds are natural and universal.

Ritchie and I sat awhile with him after the painter was gone, the first sitting being over. John said, "Death is no terror to me at present. I know not what it may be." Said Ritchie, "You must either be infatuated, or you have, by grace, a reliance on the merits of Jesus Christ." John said he trusted to the mercy of GOD in Christ; that he had been an unfortunate man, and insinuated that his fate was foreordained. Ritchie quoted the passage in James which I had quoted; but he seemed to be much hampered with Calvinistical notions about decrees, while he struggled to controvert John's wickedness being foreordained. Indeed the system of predestination includes all actions, bad as well as good. Ritchie pressed John much to make an authentic last speech. I told him that if he was guilty of the crime for which he was condemned, it was his duty to his country and the only reparation he could make, to acknowledge it, that his example might have a proper effect. He persisted in his denial, and did not seem willing to have any speech published. Ritchie said to me in his hearing that it was a perquisite for Richard, who had a great deal of trouble. I said we should get John to make a speech.

John complained much of Peter Reid for deceiving him by promising to swear as to the bargain between him and Gardner, and then drawing back. "For," said he, "if I had not trusted to him, I would not have told you that I could bring such proof, and then you could have done what you thought proper." He told me that he said to Peter in this very room: "Peter, mony (many) a lee (lie) I have telt (told) for you for which I repent"; and Peter said he would help him to the utmost on this occasion; and he did not think there was much harm in it, as it was to save a man's life; "though it was very wraung (wrong) to swear awa (away) a man's life." This was a kind of casuistical explanation of the ninth commandment: Thou shalt not bear false witness *against* thy neighbour. But—thou mayst do so *for* him. John cried a good deal when he told me this story of Peter Reid. He did not seem to be affected on any other occasion. I argued with him that it was happy that Peter Reid's conscience had checked him and prevented him from being guilty of perjury; that to be sure it was wrong in him to say that he would swear in John's support, but that it was better that he stopped than if he had gone on. John's system upon this subject was so crooked that he did not appear at all convinced.

It was a very wet day. I grew dreary and wanted either Charles Hay or Grange to dine with me, but neither of them could come. I took a little bowl of warm punch by myself, except a glass which Veronica drank. Her sweet little society was a gentle relief, but I was too dismal to enjoy it much. I had a letter from my brother David which was a cordial. I drank tea with Grange, but was gloomy. I had by sympathy sucked the dismal ideas of John Reid's situation, and as spirits or strong substance of any kind, when transferred to another body of a more delicate nature, will have much more influence than on the body from which it is trans-ferred, so I suffered much more than John did. Grange very sensibly observed that we should keep at a distance from dreary objects; that we should shun what hurts the mind as we shun what disagrees with the stomach and hurts the body—a very good maxim for preserving a *mens sana*. At night Mr. Nairne called in and supped with us. He did me some good by his conversation.

WEDNESDAY 31 AUGUST. This was the second day of John Reid's sitting for his picture. Ralph the painter went through his part with perfect composure, hardly ever opening his mouth. He mentioned a Mr. Cochrane of Barbachlaw. John said he was a strange man. He used to drink hard, till he *squeeled* like a *nowt*. He would just play *bu*. Strange that a creature under sentence of death should tell such an anecdote and seem entertained. I spoke to him of his execution, thinking it humane to familiarize his mind to it. I asked him if he was here when Murdison died. He said no, and on my saying, "So you did not see him die," told me that he had never seen an execution. "No?" said I. "I wonder you never had the curiosity." He said he never had. That once, as he and some other drivers of cattle were coming from Yorkshire, they stopped at Penrith in Cumberland, where there was a man to be executed for murder next day; that some of his companions stayed to see it, but he and the rest did not. I then spoke of the way in England of having a cart and ours of having a ladder, and that it was said ours was the easiest way.

"I take it, John," said I, "I shall die a severer death than you." "I dinna (do not) think," said he, "they can feel much; or that it can last ony (any) time; but there's nane (none) of them to tell how it is." I mentioned Maggy Dickson, who had been hanged less than the usual time and was recovered, and said she felt no pain. He told me he saw a Highlandman at Glasgow, a big strong man, who had escaped twice; first, the rope broke. "And," said John, "at that time it was thought they coudna (could not) hang them up again; and the second time, the gallows fell." He said his wife was resolved that he should die in white; that it was the custom in his part of the country to dress the dead body in linen, and she thought it would cost no more to do it when he was alive. He this day again averred the truth of his story that he got the sheep from Gardner. He said to me that there was something he had done a great many years ago, before any of his trials, that had followed him all this time. That it was not a great thing either, nor yet a small thing, and he would let me know it. This was somehow curious and awful. Honest Ritchie, from time to time, threw out serious reflections, as thus: "If any man sin, we have an advocate with the Father, even Christ the righteous. Christ is an advocate, indeed. Other advocates only plead for panels. But he takes upon him the offences of the panels and suffers in their stead." Ritchie also gave a particular account of the behaviour of Pickworth, and promised to give me a copy of a printed narrative of it which he wrote. I did not know before that Ritchie was an author.

I mentioned that it was remarkable that there was always fine weather on execution days, and I asked Ritchie what was the meaning of pigeons flying when people were executed. He said that he thought the notions which some people entertained of that signifying good to the persons executed were *fablish*. John then told of a woman who was executed, who told that morning to a minister after awaking from a sound sleep, "If ye see some clear draps o' (drops of) rain faw (fall) on me after I'm custen owr (thrown over), I'm happy." And John said the clear drops did fall. All this was most suitable conversation for John. I asked him if he had ever seen the hangman. He said no. I said I had seen him this forenoon going into the office of the prison. "Ay," said John, "he'll be going about thinking there's something for him." He seemed to think of him with much aversion and declared he would have no intercourse with him, one way or other; but he seemed somewhat reconciled when I told him that the hangman was a humane creature, and shed tears for unhappy people when they were to be executed. I inculcated upon John that he was now to have no hopes, since no answer had come to his application. He asked if there would not come an answer of some kind. I said not unless they were to grant something favourable, and that must have come before now had it been to come. He said he was thrown into a panic by hearing a horn blow in the street. I was desirous to have his picture done *while under sentence of death* and was therefore rather desirous that, in case a respite was to come, it should not arrive till he had sat his full time. It was finished today and was a striking likeness, a gloomy head. He asked if it would not be better to have had on his bonnet, and said he should have had on a better waistcoat. He asked too if his name would be upon it. I said it would be on the back of it. Said he: "I thought it would have been on the fore (front) side of it." There was vanity again. As the painter advanced in doing it, I felt as if he had been raising a spectre. It was a strange thought. Here is a man sitting for his picture who is to be hanged this day eight days. John himself seemed to wonder somewhat at the operation, and said, "I'm sure you maun hae an unco (must have a strange) concern about this," or words to that purpose. When it was finished and hung upon a nail to dry, it swung, which looked ominous, and made an impression on my fancy. I gave John a dram of whisky today again. When I got home I found several vermin upon me which I had attracted while in the jail. It was shocking. I changed all my clothes.

Lady Colville and Lady Anne Erskine drank tea with us, very agreeably. Mr. Hay and I read no law today. When I came from the prison, we had gone to Heriot's Garden and played at bowls. Maclaurin was in town today, and played with us.

[Received c. 31 August, Lord Erroll to Boswell]

Slains Castle, 27 August 1774

SIR,—I have now lying before me yours of the tenth. I should be very willing to show any favour in my power to a client of yours, but in the present case I am certain no application from me would be of any avail. I never had a good opinion of Mr. Clarke, although he was my tenant. And from your own account of Reid, I cannot find any reason for an indifferent person to apply in his favour. At the same [time] I cannot help applauding your doing so, as you are of opinion the jury condemned him on scrimp evidence, though I think a man being habit and repute of a bad character must always weigh with any jury. Lady Erroll joins me in best respects to you, and I am with very much esteem, Sir, your most obedient servant,

ERROLL.

THURSDAY 1 SEPTEMBER. I breakfasted at Mr. David Steuart's, Writer to the Signet, where was his father, Steuart Hall. At ten I called on Dr. Cullen to talk with him of recovering John Reid. He was gone abroad. I found his son, my brother lawyer, and trusted him with the secret, and he engaged to get me a meeting with his father. It came on a heavy rain; so I sat a good while with Cullen in his study, and had very good ideas presented to my mind about books and criminal law, etc. Every man has some peculiar views which seem new to another. After taking a tolerable dose of law, Mr. Hay and I went for a walk to Heriot's Garden, and then I dined with him. He had Dr. Monro and several more company with him, and it was concerted that we should get information from the Anatomical Professor as to recovering a hanged person, which would be useful to Reid. Harry Erskine was there, and talked so much that it was long before we could get Dr. Monro set upon the subject. He said in his opinion a man who is hanged suffers a great deal; that he is not at once stupefied by the shock, suffocation being a thing which must be gradual and cannot be forced on instantaneously; so that a man is suffocated by hanging in a rope just as by having his respiration stopped by having a pillow pressed on the face, in Othello's way, or by stopping the mouth and nostrils, which one may try; and he said that for some time after a man is thrown over, he is sensible and is conscious that he is *hanging;* but that in three minutes or so he is stupefied. He said that it was more difficult to recover a hanged person than a drowned, because hanging forces the blood up to the brain with more violence, there being a local compression at the neck; but that he thought the thing might be done by heat and rubbing to put the blood in motion, and by blowing air into the lungs; and he said the best way was to cut a hole in the throat, in the trachea, and introduce a pipe. I laid up all this for service in case it should be necessary. He told me that ten or twelve of his students had, unknown to him, tried to recover my clients Brown and Wilson, but had only blown with their own breaths into the mouths of the *subjects,* which was not sufficient. He said some people had applied to him for leave to put on fires and make preparations for recovering Lieutenant Ogilvy in his class. That he thought it would be very wrong in him to allow it, and told them he should have no objection if Lord Justice-Clerk gave his consent. That he spoke to Lord Justice-Clerk, who said that if such a thing was allowed, the College of Edinburgh should never again get a body from the Court of Justiciary. Indeed it would have been counteracting their sentence. He said he dissected Ogilvy publicly, and that there was no hurt on his head by the fall from the gibbet.

I sat long here today, thinking myself well employed in listening to Dr. Monro, whom I seldom met. He asked me to sup with him next day with the Laird of MacLeod. I drank rather more than a bottle of Madeira. It was about ten when we parted. I made a good deal of impression on the company in favour of John Reid's innocence. As I considered him as now a gone man, I resolved to know the truth by being with him to the very last moment of his life, even to walk a step or two up the ladder and ask him *then,* just before his going off, what was the real matter of fact; for if he should deny *then,* I could not resist the conviction.

FRIDAY 2 SEPTEMBER. I lay till near ten. A little after I rose and was at breakfast and Mr. Hay was come, while the tea-things were standing, I was called out to a man—and who was this but Richard Lock, who informed me that John Reid had got a respite for fourteen days; that Captain Fraser had been up with him and read it to him, and that he teared more now than he had ever seen him. I was put into great agitation. All my nerves started. I instantly dressed, and Mr. Hay and I walked out, met Michael Nasmith, who had seen the respite in the Council Chamber, and he went thither with us, when Bailie Brown showed us it. Wright, the stationer, who was at the time _____ , cried out with a kind of unfeeling sneer, "It will be lang (long) life and ill health;" and all the people in the Chamber seemed against poor John. We then went up to John, whom we found in a dreadful state. He was quite unhinged. His knees knocked against each other, he trembled so; and he cried bitterly. I spoke to him in a most earnest manner and told him, since the respite was only for fourteen days, the judges would be consulted and they would report against him. He must therefore consider that he had just fourteen days more allowed him to prepare for his awful change. He moaned and spoke of his being "cut off after all, with a hale (whole) heart." I said he must compose himself. He said he hoped he should, if it pleased GOD to continue him in his senses, as he had hitherto done. I said, "You *would* make this application, though I told you I thought it would have no effect. If you suffer from it, it is owing to yourself." It was striking to see a man who had been quite composed when he thought his execution certain become so weak and so much agitated by a respite. My wife put a construction on his conduct which seemed probable. She said it was plain he had all along been expecting a pardon and therefore was composed, but that now when he found that only a respite for fourteen days had come and that inquiry was to be made at the judges, he for the first time had the view of death. But if I can judge of human nature by close observation, I think he was before this time reconciled to his fate, and that the respite affected him by throwing him into a wretched state of uncertainty. I gave him a shilling to get some spirits as a cordial. Messrs. Hay and Nasmith went with me to the Justiciary Office, but we could learn nothing there but that John Davidson, the Crown Agent, had applied for an extract of the trial on Monday. The respite therefore must have been kept up some days.

I was quite agitated, partly by feeling for Reid, whom I had seen in so miserable a condition, partly by keenness for my own consequence, that I should not fail in what I had undertaken, but get a transportation pardon for my client, since a respite had come. I resolved to walk a little in the fresh air in the Meadow. Hay and Nasmith accompanied me and helped me to calm myself. I thought of applying to Lord Advocate. They were for my taking a chaise and going directly to his country-house at the Whim, which was but fourteen miles off. I thought it would be better to send an express to him with a letter, as I could write in stronger terms than I could speak; and I would ask a transportation pardon from him as a favour which I should consider as a serious obligation for life. I determined that we should call on worthy Nairne and take his advice. He humanely said that since I had obtained a respite, he wished I might save Reid from execution; and he gave it as his opinion that I had better go to Lord Advocate in person. Honest Charles Hay would not leave me in my distress, but accompanied me, as honest Kent did Lear.

We got a chaise at Peter Ramsay's directly, and set off. Charles agreed to wait at an inn not far from the Advocate's, as he was ill-dressed, and it would be better I should wait on the Advocate alone. We talked or rather raved of all the possibilities as to John Reid's affair as we drove along, and Mr. Hay was by this time grown almost as eager to save him as I was. He stopped at an inn at Howgate three miles from the Whim. I was uneasy when by myself, restless and impatient. When I arrived at the house, I was told my Lord was gone to Sir James Clerk's at Penicuik. I drove back to Howgate, where Hay had dined. I took a glass of port and a bit of bread, and then we got into the chaise again and drove to Penicuik. We put up our horses at the inn. He walked with me half way to Sir James's and promised to wait at the village. It was now between five and six. As I approached the house, I saw Sir James and Lord Advocate and some other gentlemen taking a walk after dinner. I had dined here before with Sir James. After making my bow to him, I said, "My Lord Advocate, I am in quest of your Lordship. I have been at the Whim. May I beg to speak with you?" We went aside. He immediately started the subject, answering, "About your friend John Reid." I spoke to him very earnestly. He told me he had seen the respite and my letter to Lord Suffolk and the petition for John. He expressed his unwillingness to have an execution after a respite, but said that the respite here had been compelled by the application coming so late. That the King's business required that an example should be made of this man, and if it were to be asked at him, he could not say that Reid was a proper object of mercy. But that he was to give no opinion one way or other. He made for a little a kind of secret of what was doing. But upon my urging him, he said it lay with the judges, and I must apply to them. I said I did not like to apply to them, and I told him with great sincerity that he was the only man employed by the Crown in the Justiciary Court who had not a strong bias against the panels. I said the Justice-Clerk stood in a very delicate situation here, as he had attacked Reid after being acquitted by his country, and would be supposed to be much prejudiced against him. If I were in his place, I would not wish to make a severe report in such circumstances. The Advocate smiled. He gave me full time and never seemed inclined to go in, but walked on the lawn with a complacent easy behaviour. I showed him that I was really very much concerned here and begged he would assist me; that I should never forget the obligation. He said it would be improper for him to interfere.

Sir James sent and invited me to tea. I went in with Lord Advocate and drank some coffee and eat a crumb of biscuit. I went and looked at Runciman's paintings in Ossian's Hall, and was much pleased. Sir James was extremely polite to me. Lord Advocate carried me in his coach to the village, but as he had a gentleman and lady with him I could get but little said. I however resumed my solicitation and said, "Well, my Lord, you'll think of it." He with a pleasing tone said something to this purpose: "Then as King William said, 'You must not think no more of it.'" Though I did not distinctly hear what he said, it appeared to me that he had an intention to do something for me. He pressed me much to go home with him, but I told him I was engaged in town. Mr. Hay and I drank a pint of white wine and eat a bit of biscuit and then took our chaise again. I observed how curious it was that two beings who were not sure of their own lives a day should be driving about in this manner to preserve the life of a wretch a little longer. Said Charles: "Can we be better employed?" On my coming home, and Mr. Hay with me, my wife, who never favoured John Reid and who was sorry to see me so much interested about him, told me that she had heard some decent-looking men talking tonight on the street against him. One of them said, "I think no laws will get leave to stand now. I wish the law of Moses may get leave to stand." She delivered me a letter from Lord Pembroke in most polite terms, mentioning that he had written to Lord Rochford and urged the affair strongly. This revived my hopes, I went to Dr. Monro's. Colonel Campbell of Finab and his family and the Laird of MacLeod and some other company were there. I played awhile at loo and lost only 18d. We supped very genteelly. I was in a very good frame, had taken a liking to claret and drank a bottle of it. I was pleased at this acquisition to the number of my convivial acquaintances.

[Michael Nasmith to Boswell]

John's wife was with me this afternoon. I gave her a letter to the messenger who apprehended, with three or four queries, but begged him to come to town immediately to give you every information.

She tells me that after John heard the report against him, he had frequent conferences with Gardner, who lived (but was under hiding for the housebreaking) within thirty yards of John, anent the sheep. That the very moment John was taken he told the messenger that he had received the sheep from Gardner, and asked him whether he could not also apprehend him. The messenger, giving his hip a clap, said, "I can, I have a warrant in my pocket against him," and Gardner, within ten minutes after John, was also taken into custody, and they were in company as prisoners for some time. Gardner was sent to Stirling. These are facts you were totally ignorant of. I have begged the messenger's information what passed betwixt John and Gardner while in company. From this something good or bad may be learned. The messenger, if he has any bias, it will be in John's favour. Old acquaintances. I expect the messenger here on Sunday or a letter on Monday. What hopes now have you? Ever yours most sincerely,

M. NASMITH.

SUNDAY 4 SEPTEMBER. Before supper I walked in the garden with the Colonel, who was warm for John Reid, while his father was strenuous against him. It occurred to me that the Colonel's interest with Lord Cornwallis, who is intimate with the King and whose uncle is Archbishop of Canterbury, might be effectual. I asked the Colonel, "Does he know the narrowness of this damned country?" COLONEL. "Yes; was a year in it; despises it, hates it." "Then," said I, "'twill do." The Colonel agreed to write to him, and I was to write at the same time.

MONDAY 5 SEPTEMBER. The Law College went on pretty well. It helped to quiet me. At two I went to Colonel Webster. I suggested to him to mention the prejudice of the judges in this narrow country on some occasions, which he did excellently well. For a moment I considered that it was not right that the supreme judges of a country should be censured by a young colonel whose letter might have influence. But then I thought, since they really have a bias to severity, it should be checked.

And now there is much at stake: the life of a man whom I think innocent, and my own fame.

[Boswell to Lord Pembroke]

Edinburgh, 5 September 1774

MY LORD,—Your Lordship's most obliging letter has confirmed me in the opinion which I formed of your humanity. A respite for fourteen days has come for John Reid. But I understand that some of the judges are desired to make a report concerning him, and as I already hinted to your Lordship that there are prejudices against him in this narrow country which it would take some time to explain, I dread that the report may be unfavourable. If that shall be the case and he shall be yet ordered for execution, his situation will be deplorable, and the application made in his behalf will only serve to augment his misery. I must therefore again intrude upon your Lordship and beg in the most earnest manner that you may make a point of having his sentence changed to transportation. As I have mentioned my obligations to your Lordship for interposing in this affair, I should be sorry to have it thought in this country that Lord Pembroke *strongly urged* a petition for mercy in the case of a simple theft, supposing the charge true, and failed in obtaining it. The cruelty of an execution after respite is equal to many deaths, and therefore there is rarely an instance of it. This poor wretch, even if guilty, does not merit such severity. I am so much distressed with this wretched case that your Lordship will relieve me as well as my client by getting the sentence mitigated, and believe me, my Lord, I shall be most sincerely grateful for the obligation.

WEDNESDAY 7 SEPTEMBER. Mr. Nasmith called with a letter from Brown, the messenger who had taken up John Reid, addressed to John, and mentioning that, as they were upon the road, John asked him if he could apprehend any one else and mentioned Gardner, who was accordingly apprehended. From this letter it appeared to me and Messrs. Hay and Nasmith that John had been lying; for if he had got the sheep from Gardner without suspicion, would not he, when accused of stealing them, have instantly accused Gardner, loudly and keenly? No law was read today, we talked so long of John Reid. I determined to try again to know the truth.

I went up to John a little before two, with the messenger's letter in my hand. Seeing me have a paper, he gave an earnest look, I suppose in expectation that it was his pardon. But I at once accosted him as a dying man, upbraided him with having imposed on me, and said to him what I and Mr. Nasmith had concluded from perusal of the letter. He calmly explained his conduct. "Sir," said he, "Gardner had before this time come to my house and owned to me that he had stolen the sheep, and promised me great rewards if I would not discover him. Therefore, when I was taken up, I would not speak out against him, but wanted him to be apprehended, that he and I might concert what was to be done to keep ourselves safe. But he was but a very little time with me, and then was carried to Stirling." I was not much convinced by this account of the matter. I had wrought myself into a passion against John for deceiving me, and spoke violently to him, not feeling for him at the time. I had chosen my time so as to be with him when two o'clock struck. "John," said I, "you hear that clock strike. You hear that bell. If this does not move you, nothing will. That you are to consider as your last bell. You remember your sentence. On Wednesday the 7 of September. This is the day. Between the hours of two and four in the afternoon; this is that very time. After this day you are to look upon yourself as a dead man; as a man in a middle state between the two worlds. You are not eternity, because you are still in the body; but you are not properly alive, because this is the day appointed for your death. You are to look on this fortnight as so much time allowed to you to repent of all your wickedness, and particularly of yhour lying to me in such a way as you have done. Think that this day fortnight by four o'clock you will be rendering an account to your Maker. I am afraid that you are encouraged by your wife to persist in obstinacy, not to disgrace her and your children. But that is a small consideration to a man going into eternity. I think it your duty to own your being guilty on this occasion if you be really so, which I cannot but think is the case. By doing so you will make all the atonement in your power to society. But at any rate I beseech you not to deny your guilt contrary to truth." This was as vehement and solemn a harangue as could be made upon any occasion. The circumstance of the clock striking and the two o'clock bell ringing were finely adapted to touch the imagination. But John seemed to be very unfeeling today. He persisted in his tale. There was something approaching to the ludicrous when, in the middle of my speech to him about his not being properly alive, he said very gravely, "Ay; I'm dead in law." I was too violent with him. I said, "With what face can you go into the other world?" And: "If your ghost should come and tell me this, I would not believe it." This last sentence made me frightened, as I have faith in apparitions, and had a kind of idea that perhaps his ghost might come to me and tell me that I had been unjust to him. I concluded with saying, "You have paper, pen, and ink there. Let me have a real account of everything." He said he would. Richard Lock had come into the room before I was done speaking. I desired him to advise John to be candid.

Mr. Nasmith met me when I came out of prison and was very impatient to hear about John. In telling him John's explanation of his behaviour when taken up, I became impressed that it might be true, and enlarged on the uncertainty of circumstantial evidence. Nasmith was convinced too, and said, "We are as much in the dark as ever."

And now let me mention some circumstances omitted in my Journal. John's vanity appeared while his picture was drawing, by his asking me if his name would be put upon it. I said it would be put on the back of it. Said he: "I thought it would have been on the fore (front) side." His predestinarian belief appeared from his observing, when I spoke of the wonderful escape of Andrews, etc., from Paisley, "Their time was not come." His wife had been with me since the respite came. I gave her no hopes, but bid her have a cart to carry away his body. "Ay," said she, "there shall be a cart if there's occasion for it"; so I saw that all I could say did not prevent her from imagining that he had a pretty good chance for life.

[John Wilson, Jr. to Michael Nasmith]

Glasgow, 6 September 1774

DEAR SIR,—This day I received yours of yesterday about the case of John Reid, who hath received His Majesty's respite of his capital punishment for fourteen days. I see Mr. Boswell and you are still employed in the cause of humanity, nay, could our politicians see it, of good policy also—rescuing the lives of the lieges from destruction appointed too frequently by the barbarous laws of a civilized nation. Can any sober thinking person believe it that in a country which boasts so much of its knowledge and refinement, there should exist a law assigning death as the punishment of the crime of stealing eighteen sheep? *Ninety and nine* sheep, which once were less valued than one lost and recovered; are less valuable than the life of any of His Majesty's subjects. What pity it is that the sentiments of the excellent philosopher and politician the Marquis Beccaria have not hitherto been capable of opening the eyes of our legislators, who can suffer the laws on so slight occasions to murder the citizens with a formal pageantry.—I am truly sorry that I can add no information from Gardner, from whom you say Reid maintains he bought the sheep, he having above three weeks ago stayed a night only here in his passage to transportation. I am, dear Sir, your most obedient servant,

JOHN WILSON, JR.

FRIDAY 9 SEPTEMBER. After our law Mr. Hay and I had a game at bowls. He dined with me and drank tea. I was now become a man of high estimation in the prison, in so much that prisoners applied to me by petition: "Unto the Honourable James Boswell, Esq., Advocate, The Petition of _____ Humbly Showeth." I did them what service I could. Henry McGraugh's case was now become an object of great attention, the newspapers having many letters about it. Some of them I wrote myself.

["Tyburn" to Boswell]

Sir,—I understand your design. John Reid will steal for you, and the Irishman shall then have plenty from your table. You know that good mutton is pleasant to the Faculty of Advocates: yea, although you know it to be stolen; and if the Irishman had done to you as he has done to others, you and Andrew would be _____ indeed. The case is truly this: the Irishman and Crosbie, Boswell and John Reid, is all alike guilty.

SATURDAY 10 SEPTEMBER. After breakfast Mr. Nasmith called, which interrupted the Law College. Mr. Hay and he agreed with me that as I was to transmit a memorial on the evidence against John Reid, showing its insufficiency, it would be proper to send along with it a declaration by his wife that he was in his own house the night when the theft was committed, and for several nights before. This the woman all along affirmed, and her testimony was the only proof that in the circumstances of the case could be had. I drew a short petition to the Magistrates which Mr. Nasmith got John to sign, and then presented it. Bailie Torry, who then officiated, was timorous, and some clerk advised that it should be intimated to the King's Advocate, Solicitor, or Crown Agent. The Bailie gave judgement accordingly. They were all out of town; and at any rate would have opposed it, though in reality they had no concern with it. The trial was over. The declaration was only a piece of evidence, perhaps not strictly legal, but which might have weight with His Majesty, after a respite had been granted. Bailie Macqueen, to whom Mr. Nasmith spoke first, very gravely said that taking the declaration would be to destroy a trial by jury. We were now in a dilemma. We thought of trying a Justice of Peace, but we could not bear being refused again. Mr. _____ suggested that the declaration might be taken before two notaries public. We sallied forth into the street to look for another notary to join Mr. Nasmith. We met Andrew Dick, Writer to the Signet. He would not be concerned in the matter; and said with a dull sort of sneer, "He may prepare himself for Wednesday come eight days." I was angry at the animal, and told him before Messieurs Hay and Nasmith that John told me that Mr. Andrew Dick and he were fourth cousins. This the creature could not deny; and to have it known mortified him not a little.

We came in to town, sauntered at the Cross, anxious for another notary to join Mr. Nasmith. One Tyrie appeared but declined to give his assistance. We were in a great dilemma. At last I found Matthew Dickie. We went into Hutchinson's and had a bottle of claret for ourselves and a bottle of porter for Mrs. Reid and Richard Lock, who brought her. I then exhorted her to tell nothing but truth; said I was not a judge, so could not administer an oath to her; but that solemnly to declare what was not true would be a great sin. She said, "I am in the presence of GOD." Her declaration then was taken, and she really seemed to speak what was genuine truth.

[Declaration of Janet Reid]

Appeared Janet the wife of John Reid, now lying under sentence of death in the prison of Edinburgh, and solemnly declared and affirmed that her said husband sleeped at home in his own house upon the nights of the sixth and seventh of October last, the last of which is the night on which it is alleged that he committed the theft for which he is condemned, and that he sleeped both those nights in the bed with the declarant, which he also did during every other night of that week, and during the three last nights of the week preceding. That they went regularly to bed each of these nights at or before eleven of the clock, being their usual time of going to bed, and they lay till sun-rising, except upon Thursday's morning, when her husband was called up about an hour before sun-rising to receive a parcel of sheep from William Gardner. And all that she has now solemnly declared and affirmed she is ready and willing to attest upon oath before any of His Majesty's judges. In testimony whereof she hereto adhibits her subscription in our presence and in presence of Charles Hay, Esq., advocate, and Matthew Montgomery, writer in Edinburgh.

(Signed) JANET REID, *praemissa attestor*
MATTHEW DICKIE, No. Pub.
Veritas M. NASMITH, N.P.
CHA. HAY, Witness
M. MONTGOMERIE, Witness

WEDNESDAY 14 SEPTEMBER. After dinner Ritchie called on me and said he was very desirous that John Reid should declare what he had committed long ago, which he thought had followed him. I promised to come to the prison, and accordingly went.

John was very sedate. He told Mr. Ritchie and me that before his first trial, one night he drank hard and lay all night at the side of a sheep-fold; that when he awaked the devil put it into his head (or some such expression), and he drove off all the sheep in the fold (the "*hail hirsle*"); that before he was off the farm to which they belonged, he came to a water, and there he separated four of them, which he took home, killed, and sold; and he said it was alleged that he had taken five, but it never came to any trial. This was but a small matter. John said he would have it published. His owning this theft made me give more credit to his denial of that for which he was condemned, for why should he deny the one and confess the other? I told him that now I believed him, and I acknowledged that I had been too violent with him this day eight days. He seemed to be grateful to me; and said that few would have done so much for a brother, though a twin, as I had done for him. He said that he had always had something heavy about his mind since his last trial and never could be merry as formerly. He said that last night he had strange dreams. He saw a wonderful moon with many streamers. And he and a man who died some time ago, he imagined were walking together, and the man had a gun in his hand; that two eagles—two pretty speckled birds—lighted on a tree. (*I* had very near said that these signified Lord Cornwallis and Lord Pembroke, who were his friends; but I checked myself.) He called to the man to shoot, but he did not; and one of the eagles flew into the man's arms, who gave it to John, and he carried it. Ritchie very foolishly smiled, and said, "Maybe, John, it may be a messenger of good news to you." "Ay," said John earnestly, "a ravenous bird." "But," said Ritchie, "it did not fly on John, but on the other man, who gave it to John." "Well," said I, "that is to say, the bad news will come to Captain Fraser, and he'll deliver it to John."

I asked John if he ever saw anything in the iron room where he lay. He said no; but that he heard yesterday at nine in the morning a noise upon the form, as if something had fallen upon it with a *clash*. Ritchie and he seemed to consider this as some sort of warning. He said he had heard such a noise in the corner of the room a little before his respite came. And he said that the night before James Brown's pardon came, Brown was asleep, and he was awake, and heard like swine running from the door, round a part of the room, and *grumphling*. He seemed to be in a very composed frame. I said it was an awful thought that this day sennight at this time he would be in eternity. I said I hoped his repentance was sincere and his faith in Christ sincere, and that he would be saved through the merits of the Saviour, and perhaps he might this day eight days be looking down with pity on Mr. Ritchie and me. I found that he had hardly written anything.

FRIDAY 16 SEPTEMBER. Charles Hay and I this day completed our course of Erskine's *Institutes*. I dined with him, with Maclaurin, who was in good spirits but offended me by a kind of profaneness in quoting

Scripture. He was of opinion that it was wrong to apply for John Reid; and when I asserted that he was innocent, Maclaurin had a pretty good smile. He said I had worked up my mind upon the subject. That the mind of man might be worked up from little or nothing like soap suds, till the basin is overflowed. We drank moderately, and then played at whist. I went home at night, and was in a strange wearied humour; so went directly to bed.

SATURDAY 17 SEPTEMBER. Mr. Robert Boswell and I breakfasted at my uncle the Doctor's. Richard Lock came in the morning, after my return from the Doctor's, and told me, "It is all over with John Reid. He dies on Wednesday. There's a letter come that no farther respite is to be granted." I was struck with concern. Mr. Hay came, and he and I walked a little on the Castle Hill and then called on Mr. Nasmith. We agreed to dine together at Leith to relieve our vexation at the bad news. I first went up a little to John Reid. His wife was with him. He was not much affected with the bad news, as he had not been indulging hopes. I again exhorted him to tell nothing but truth.

Messieurs Hay, Nasmith, and I walked down to Leith, and dined at Trumpeter Yeats's. We were fain to fly to wine to get rid of the uneasiness which we felt that, after all that had been done, poor John Reid should fall a victim. I thought myself like Duncan Forbes. We drank two bottles of port each. I was not satisfied with this, but stopped at a shop in Leith and insisted that we should drink some gin. Mr. Nasmith and one Ronald, the master of the shop, and I drank each a gill. Nasmith was very drunk, Mr. Hay and I quite in our senses. We all walked up some way or other. Mr. Hay came home with me. I found a letter from Lord Pembroke which gave me still hopes, for he said he would go to town and see the King himself; and I flattered myself that his Lordship might procure an alteration of the doom. Mr. Hay left me. I grew monstrously drunk, and was in a state of mingled frenzy and stupefaction. I do not recollect what passed.

SUNDAY 18 SEPTEMBER. It gave me much concern to be informed by my dear wife that I had been quite outrageous in my drunkenness the night before; that I had cursed her in a shocking manner and even thrown a candlestick with a lighted candle at her. It made me shudder to hear such an account of my behaviour to one whom I have so much reason to love and regard; and I considered that, since drinking has so violent an effect on me, there is no knowing what dreadful crimes I may commit. I therefore most firmly resolved to be sober.

MONDAY 19 SEPTEMBER. It was a wet day, but we had a stout bowling match.

When I got home I found letters for me from Lord Rochford, Lord

Pembroke, Mr. Eden, under-secretary in Lord Suffolk's office, and the Duke of Queensberry, and was finally assured that John Reid would be executed. I was hurt, and also felt an indignation at the Justice-Clerk, whose violent report had prevented my obtaining for John Reid the royal mercy; but I resolved not to write against him till time had cooled me. Mr. Hay called, and was much concerned. He and I went to Mr. Nasmith, who was very impatient. We all agreed that it was a shocking affair. The last resort now was the scheme of recovering John. Mr. Hay promised to call at my house next morning to talk of it. Mr. Nasmith and I went to see Mr. Wood. He was not at home. We found him at Mrs. Alison's in New Street, Canongate, at supper, got him into a room, and spoke with him. He said that a house must be found as near the place of execution as possible, for that the rumbling of a cart would destroy John altogether. He said a stable or any place would do. He would attend and have the proper apparatus, and get Mr. Innes, Dr. Monro's dissector, to attend. I was much agitated tonight. It rained very heavily. I wished it might do so on Wednesday, that the execution might perhaps be hastened.

[Received 19 September, Lord Pembroke to Boswell]

St. James's, Thursday 15 September 1774

I came up this morning on purpose to speak to His Majesty, my dear Sir, as you wished, and I am very sorry not to have been more successful. Lord Cornwallis also has applied in favour of Reid, but the judge's report, which I saw, is so very strong against him that the man's guilt is looked upon here in the most atrocious light possible. Lord Rochford would have urged for mercy had he been able to do it, but he and the King too indeed think the judge must resign if, after his report, any mitigation of the sentence should take place. I am very much concerned at my ill success, and shall be more so if it debars me from receiving your orders on any future occasion where you can make me useful.

I am, Sir, with the greatest truth and regard, your most obedient, humble servant,

PEMBROKE.

[Michael Nasmith to Boswell]

Edinburgh, 20 September 1774

MY DEAR SIR,—This is a matter of secrecy. We have properly speaking no person to advise with. The proposed attempt appears to be attended with so much humanity that the moment any of our friends may have it in confidence they may find themselves in the same situation we ourselves are. I have been therefore deliberating with myself how far the world may think we have acted a worthy part in having attempted to preserve his life.

The jury have returned an unanimous verdict finding him guilty. The Court of Justiciary have been unanimous in finding him worthy of death. Our Sovereign has given it as his opinion that the interests of society are at stake if he is suffered to escape. The voice of the whole people approves. In short, everything sacred in society seems to forbid the attempt.

Humanity and a strong belief of John's innocence have already impelled you to do much for him, but let us cast our eyes forward and see what effects the attempt may have upon the poor wretches who may hereafter be condemned to lose their lives. Death is already sufficiently terrible. I fear much that the proposed attempt, be the event what it will, may be attended with the worst consequences, consequences that neither of us would wish to be the authors of. In the awful approach of eternity the mind is disposed to grasp at every shadow. Few will hereafter come to suffer in this country to whose ears John's story may not have reached. If he is brought to life, they will hold it up as full evidence that they too may—and that there may be a Boswell at hand the moment they are cut down. If the experiment proves ineffectual, they will solace themselves with such thoughts as these: that he was old—that he had been desperately wicked—that though the experiment did not succeed upon him, the world is every day getting more knowledge, it may upon them—that heaven may have foreseen that they could not be otherways reclaimed than by suspending them in a rope and allowing them thereafter to return to life. To step out of this world in such a situation, without repentance, confession, and resignation is a dismal thought.

To me the affair at present appears in these points of view and is not unworthy of the most cool deliberation. What do you think of talking to Mrs. Boswell, who, if I am a right judge, possesses both judgement and humanity in abundance? I am, dear Sir, yours sincerely.

M. NASMITH.

TUESDAY 20 SEPTEMBER. Before breakfast I received a very good letter from Mr. Nasmith dissuading me from the scheme of recovering John Reid, but he did not persuade me. Mr. Hay came and he and I called on Mr. Nasmith and took him with us to look for a place where the corpse might be deposited. We walked about the Grassmarket and Portsburgh, and saw some small houses to let. Mr. Nasmith proposed that we might take one till Martinmas; but then it occurred that the landlord would make a noise if a hanged man was put into it. In short, we were in a dilemma. I thought of the Canongate Kilwinning Lodge, of which I was Master and could excuse myself to the brethren for taking liberty with it; but it was too far off. I did not think it right to trust a caddie, or any low man, with the secret. I asked John Robertson the chairman if he could find a house that would take in the corpse till the mob dispersed. He thought none would do it. Mr. Nasmith went out of town. Mr. Hay, after a short party at bowls, went with me and called for Mr. Innes, Dr. Monro's dissector. Mr. Wood had not yet spoken to him; but he very readily agreed to give his help. He however could not help us to get a house. I called on Wood. Neither could he help us as to that article; and he began to doubt of the propriety of the scheme. I however remained firm to it, and Mr. Hay stood by me. Mr. Innes suggested one George Macfarlane, a stabler, where a puppet-show had been kept. Mr. Hay and I went to the Grassmarket, where he lived. But first it occurred to me that there was one Andrew Bennet, a stabler, whom I had lately got out of prison. We went to him. He had no family but his wife, and they were both fools. They were prodigiously grateful to me, called me *his Grace*, Andrew having reproved his wife for calling me only *his Honour*. I told them that the friends of the poor man who was to be executed next day were anxious to lodge his body in some place till the mob should disperse, and, as he was a client of mine, I was desirous to assist them; so I hoped Andrew would let them have his stable for that purpose. He agreed to it, though his wife made some objection, and though he said he would rather let his *craig* (throat) be cut than allow it, unless to oblige me. I sounded them as to letting the body into their house; but Mrs. Bennet screamed, and Andrew said very justly that nobody would come to it any more if that was done. It is amazing what difficulty I found in such a place as Edinburgh to get a place for my purpose. The stable here entered by a close next entry to the door of the house, and had no communication with the house; so that the operators must be obliged to take their stations in the stable some time before the execution was over. It was a small stable, and there was a smith's shop just at the door of it; so that we could not be private enough. However, I was glad to have secured any place.

Mr. Hay and I then went to George Macfarlane's. He was not in. We had not dined, as we did not choose to see my wife while we were about such a project, which I had communicated to her and which shocked her. We called for punch and bread and cheese, all of which proved wretched. We sat about an hour, waiting for the landlord's coming in, that we might have tried if he would let us have a better place, but he did not come. I observed that we were reduced to do the meanest and most disagreeable things for this strange scheme, as much so as candidates in a borough election.

I called at home at five, Hay having gone to a coffee-house and engaged to meet me at the Cross at six. I found my wife so shocked that I left her immediately and went down to the prison. I was now more firmly impressed with a belief of John Reid's innocence, the Reverend Dr. Dick having come to the bowling-green in the forenoon and told me that, as he was to attend him to his execution, he had talked with him very seriously, and (the Doctor used a very good expression) had got behind all the subterfuges of such a mind as his, such as his thinking it right to deny, to leave a better character for the sake of his wife and children, and had found him firm and consistent in his declaration that he was not guilty. The Doctor said this affair gave him great uneasiness; and he told me that the Reverend Dr. Macqueen was to go along with him to attend at the execution; that he also had been with John, and was of the same opinion. I begged that he and Dr. Macqueen would be particularly attentive to investigate the truth as much as possible, as I really believed he was condemned on insufficient evidence, and, from his solemn averments of his innocence, thought him not guilty of the crime for which he was condemned; such averments being in my opinion an overbalance not for positive, or even strong circumstantial, evidence, but for such evidence as was brought against him, which I thought could produce no more than suspicion.

When I came to the prison I found that John Reid's wife and children were with him. The door of the iron room was now left open and they were allowed to go and come as they pleased. He was very composed. His daughter Janet was a girl about fifteen, his eldest son Benjamin about ten, his youngest son Daniel between two and three. It was a striking scene to see John on the last night of his life surrounded by his family. His wife and two eldest children behaved very quietly. It was really curious to see the young child Daniel, who knew nothing of the melancholy situation of his father, jumping upon him with great fondness, laughing and calling to him with vivacity. The contrast was remarkable between the father in chains and in gloom and the child quite free and frolicsome. John took him on his knee with affection. He said to me that his daughter Jenny was the only one of his children whom he had named after any relation; and he went over all the names of the rest. They had almost all Old Testament names. They were seven in all. I again exhorted him to truth. One Miln in Leith Wynd, a kind of lay teacher, and Mr. Ritchie were with him; and he was to have some good Christians to sit up with him all night.

Mr. Hay went with me again to Mr. Innes, who was satisfied with Bennet's stable and desired that there should be a blanket and a good quantity of warm salt prepared. He went again to Bennet's, and took a dram of whisky of his own distilling; and he and his wife promised to have the blanket and the salt in readiness, I having said that some surgeon had advised his friends to rub the body with warm salt to preserve it, as it was to be carried to the country. Bennet, though a fool, had smoked what was intended; for he said, "Could they not cut him down living?" I said that would be wrong. I should have observed when I was with John this evening, it gave me some uneasiness to think that he was solemnly preparing for an awful eternity while at the same time I was to try to keep him back. He spoke himself very calmly of *the corpse,* by which he meant his own dead body; for I spoke to his wife before him about it: that I had secured a place for it, but I wished she could get a better place for it to be laid in till the mob dispersed. She said she would try Mrs. Walker at the sign of the Bishop in the Grassmarket, who was very friendly to her. It was a comfort to me that neither John nor his wife had the least idea of any attempt to recover him.

Mr. Hay and I met my worthy friend Grange in the Grassmarket tonight. He was much against the attempt. After supper Mr. Wood called and told me that he had the proper apparatus ready; that he had also engaged Mr. Aitkin, another surgeon, to attend, and that, if I insisted on it, he was willing to make the experiment, but that as a friend he could not but advise me against it; that it would be impossible to conceal it; the mob would press upon us, and continue looking in at the door. A great clamour would be made against me as defying the laws and as doing a ridiculous thing, and that a man in business must pay attention in prudence to the voice of mankind; that the chance of success was hardly anything, and this was to be put in the scale against a certainty of so many disagreeable consequences. But he suggested another thought which had great weight with me. "This man," said he, "has got over the bitterness of death; he is resigned to his fate. He will have got over the pain of death. He may curse you for bringing him back. He may tell you that you kept him from heaven." I determined to give up the scheme.

WEDNESDAY 21 SEPTEMBER. John Reid's wife called on me before breakfast and told me that Mrs. Walker said she was welcome to the best room in her house for the corpse; but that afterwards her landlord had sent to her that she must quit his house if she allowed such a thing. I said that there would be no occasion for any place. The mob would not trouble the corpse; and it might be put directly on the cart that she expected was to come for it. After breakfast Mr. Nasmith came, and was pleased to find that the scheme of recovery was given up. He and I went to Bennet's and told him there was no use for his stable. We walked backwards and forwards in the Grassmarket, looking at the gallows and talking of John Reid. Mr. Nasmith said he imagined he would yet confess; for his wife had said this morning that he had something to tell me which he had as yet told to no mortal. We went to the prison about half an hour after twelve. He was now released from the iron about his leg. The Reverend Dr. Webster and Mr. Ritchie were with him. We waited in the hall along with his wife, who had white linen clothes with black ribbons in a bundle, ready to put on him before he should go out to execution. There was a deep settled grief in her countenance. She was resolved to attend him to the last; but Richard whispered to me that the Magistrates had given orders that she should be detained in the prison till the execution was over. I dissuaded her from going and she agreed to take my advice; and then Richard told her the orders of the Magistrates. I said aloud I was glad to hear of it. The Reverend Dr. Macqueen, who afterwards came in, told her it would be a tempting of Providence to go; that it might affect her so as to render her incapable to take care of her fatherless children; and Mr. Ritchie said that the best thing she could do was to remain in the prison and pray for her husband. Dr. Macqueen said to me he was so much impressed with the poor man's innocence that he had some difficulty whether he ought to attend the execution and authorize it by his presence. I said he certainly should attend, for it was *legal;* and, besides, supposing it ever so unjust, it was humane to attend an unhappy man in his last moments. "But," said Dr. Macqueen, "I will not pray for him as a guilty man." "You would be very much in the wrong to do so," said I, "if you think him not guilty." Dr. Webster and I had no conversation as he passed through the hall except inquiring at each other how we did.

John's wife then went up to him for a little, having been told both by me and Mr. Nasmith that she could not hope for the blessing of Providence on her and her children if by her advice John went out of the world with a lie in his mouth. I followed in a little, and found him in his usual dress, standing at the window. I told him I understood he had something to mention to me. He said he *would* mention it. He had since his trial in 1766 stolen a few sheep (I think five), of which he never was suspected. "John," said I, "it gives me concern to find that even such a warning as you got then did not prevent you from stealing. I really imagine that if you had now got off you might again have been guilty, such influence has Satan over you." He said he did not know but he might. Then I observed that his untimely death might be a mercy to him, as he had time for repentance. He seemed to admit that it might be so. He said that what he had now told me he had not mentioned even to his wife; and I might let it rest. I called up Mr. Nasmith, with whom came Mr. Ritchie. I said he might acknowledge this fact to them, which he did. I asked him, if I saw it proper to mention it as making his denial of the theft for which he was condemned more probable, I might be at liberty to do so? He said I might dispose of it as I thought proper. But he persisted in denying the theft for which he was condemned. He now began to put on his white dress, and we left him. Some time after, his wife came down and begged that we would go up to him, that he might not be alone. Dress has a wonderful impression on the fancy. I was not much affected when I saw him this morning in his usual dress. But now he was all in white, with a high nightcap on, and he appeared much taller, and upon the whole struck me with a kind of tremor. He was praying; but stopped when we came in. I bid him not be disturbed, but go on with his devotions. He did so, and prayed with decent fervency, while his wife, Mr. Nasmith, and I stood close around him. He prayed in particular, "Grant, O Lord, through the merits of my Saviour, that this day of my death may be the day of my birth unto life eternal." Poor man, I felt now a kind of regard for him. He said calmly, "I think I'll be in eternity in about an hour." His wife said something from which he saw that she was not to attend him to his execution; and he said, "So you're no (not) to be wi' me." I satisfied him that it was right she should not go. I said, "I suppose, John, you know that the executioner is down in the hall." He said no. I told him that he was there and would tie his arms before he went out. "Ay," said his wife. "to keep him from catching at the *tow* (rope)." "Yes," said I, "that it may be easier for him." John said he would submit to everything.

I once more conjured him to tell the truth. "John," said I, "you must excuse me for still entertaining some doubts, as you know you have formerly deceived me in some particulars. I have done more for you in this world than ever was done for any man in your circumstances. I beseech you let me be of some use to you for the next world. Consider what a shocking thing it is to go out of the world with a lie in your mouth. How can you expect mercy, if you are in rebellion against the GOD of truth?" I thus pressed him; and while he stood in his dead clothes, on the very brink of the grave, with his knees knocking together, partly from the cold occasioned by his linen clothes, partly from an awful apprehension of death, he most solemnly averred that what he had told concerning the present alleged crime was the truth. Before this, I had at Mr. Ritchie's desire read over his last speech to him, which was rather an irksome task as it was very long; and he said it was all right except some immaterial circumstance about his meeting Wilson with the six score of sheep. Vulgar minds, and indeed all minds, will be more struck with some unusual thought than with the most awful consideration which they have often heard. I tried John thus: "We are all mortal. Our life is uncertain. I may perhaps die in a week hence. Now, John, consider how terrible it would be if I should come into the other world and find" (looking him steadfastly in the face) "that you have been imposing on me." He was roused by this, but still persisted. "Then," said I, "John, I shall trouble you no more upon this head. I believe you. GOD forbid that I should not believe the word of a fellow man in your awful situation, when there is no strong evidence against it, as I should hope to be believed myself in the same situation. But remember, John, it is trusting to you that I believe. It is between GOD and your own conscience if you have told the truth; and you should not allow me to believe if it is not true." He adhered. I asked him if he had anything more to tell. He said he had been guilty of one other act of sheep-stealing. I think he said of seven sheep; but I think he did not mention precisely when. As he shivered, his wife took off her green cloth cloak and threw it about his shoulders. It was curious to see such care taken to keep from a little cold one who was so soon to be violently put to death. He desired she might think no more of him, and let his children push their way in the world. "The eldest boy," said he, "is reading very well. Take care that he reads the word of GOD." He desired her to keep a New Testament and a psalm-book which he had got in a present from Mr. Ritchie and which he was to take with him to the scaffold. He was quite sensible and judicious. He had written a kind of circular letter to all his friends on whom he could depend, begging them to be kind to his family.

Two o'clock struck. I said, with a solemn tone, "There's two o'clock." In a little Richard came up. The sound of his feet on the stair struck me. He said calmly, "Will you come awa now?" This was a striking period. John said yes, and readily prepared to go down. Mr. Nasmith and I went down a little before him. A pretty, well-dressed young woman and her maid were in a small closet off the hall; and a number of prisoners formed a kind of audience, being placed as spectators in a sort of loft looking down to the hall. There was a dead silence, all waiting to see the dying man appear. The sound of his steps coming down the stair affected me like what one fancies to be the impression of a supernatural grave noise before any solemn event. When he stepped into the hall, it was quite the appearance of a ghost. The hangman, who was in a small room off the hall, then came forth. He took off his hat and made a low bow to the prisoner. John bowed his head towards him. They stood looking at each other with an awkward uneasy attention. I interfered, and said, "John, you are to have no resentment against this poor man. He only does his duty." "I only do my duty," repeated the hangman. "I have no resentment against him," said John. "I desire to forgive all mankind." "Well, John," said I, "you are leaving the world with a very proper disposition: forgiving as you hope to be forgiven." I forgot to mention that before he left the iron room Mr. Ritchie said to him, "Our merciful King was hindered from pardoning you by a representation against you; but you are going before the King of Heaven, who knows all things and whose mercy cannot be prevented by any representation." The hangman advanced and *pinioned* him, as the phrase is; that is, tied his arms with a small cord. John stood quiet and undisturbed. I said, "Richard, give him another glass of wine." Captain Fraser, the gaoler, had sent him the night before a bottle of claret, part of which Richard had given him, warmed with sugar, early in the morning, two glasses of it in the forenoon, and now he gave him another. John drank to us. He then paused a little, then kissed his wife with a sad adieu, then Mr. Ritchie kissed him. I then took him by the hand with both mine, saying, "John, it is not yet too late. If you have anything to acknowledge, do it at the last to the reverend gentlemen, Dr. Macqueen and Dr. Dick, to whom you are much obliged. Farewell, and I pray GOD may be merciful to you." He seemed faint and deep in thought. The prison door then opened and he stepped away with the hangman behind him, and the door was instantly shut. His wife then cried, "O Richard, let me up," and got to the window and looked earnestly out till he was out of sight. Mr. Nasmith and I went to a window more to the west, and saw him stalking forward in the gloomy procession. I then desired his wife to retire and pray that he might be supported in this his hour of trial. Captain Fraser gave her four shillings. It was very agreeable to see such humanity in the gaoler, and indeed the tenderness with which the last hours of a convict were soothed pleased me much.

The mob were gone from the prison door in a moment. Mr. Nasmith and I walked through the Parliament Close, down the Back Stairs and up the Cowgate, both of us satisfied of John Reid's innocence, and Mr. Nasmith observing the littleness of human justice, that could not reach a man for the crimes which he committed but punished him for what he did not commit.

We got to the place of execution about the time that the procession did. We could not go upon the scaffold nor be seen by John, lest it should be thought that we prevented him from confessing. It was a fine day. The sun shone bright. We stood close to the scaffold on the south side between two of the Town Guard. There were fewer people present than upon any such occasion that I ever saw. He behaved with great calmness and piety. Just as he was going to mount the ladder, he desired to see his wife and children; but was told they were taken care of. There was his sister and his daughter near to the gibbet, but they were removed. Dr. Dick asked him if what he had said was the truth. He said it was. Just as he was going off, he made an attempt to speak. Somebody on the scaffold called, "Pull up his cap." The executioner did so. He then said, "Take warning. Mine is an unjust sentence." Then his cap was pulled down and he went off. He catched the ladder; but soon quitted his hold. To me it sounded as if he said, "just sentence"; and the people were divided, some crying, "He says his sentence is *just.*" Some: "No. He says *unjust.*" Mr. Laing, clerk to Mr. Tait, one of the town clerks, put me out of my doubt, by telling me he had asked the executioner, who said it was *unjust.* I was not at all shocked with this execution at the time. John died seemingly without much pain. He was effectually hanged, the rope having fixed upon his neck very firmly, and he was allowed to hang near three quarters of an hour; so that any attempt to recover him would have been in vain. I comforted myself in thinking that by giving up the scheme I had avoided much anxiety and uneasiness.

We waited till he was cut down; and then walked to the Greyfriars Churchyard, in the office of which his corpse was deposited by porters whom Mr. Nasmith and I paid, no cart having come for his body. A considerable mob gathered about the office. Mr. Nasmith went to Hutchinson's to bespeak some dinner and write a note to *The Courant* that there would be a paragraph tonight giving an account of the execution; for we agreed that a recent account would make a strong impression. I walked seriously backwards and forwards a considerable time in the churchyard waiting for John Reid's wife coming, that I might resign the corpse to her charge. I at last wearied, and then went to the office of the prison. There I asked the executioner myself what had passed. He told me that John first spoke to him on the ladder and said he suffered wrongfully; and then called to the people that his sentence was unjust. John's sister came here, and returned me many thanks for what I had done for her brother. She was for burying him in the Greyfriars Churchyard, since no cart had come. "No," said I, "the will of the dead shall be fulfilled. He was anxious to be laid in his own burying-place, and it shall be done." I then desired Richard to see if he could get a cart to hire, and bid him bring John's wife to Hutchinson's. Mr. Nasmith and I eat some cold beef and cold fowl and drank some port, and then I wrote a paragraph to be inserted in the newspapers. Mr. Nasmith threw in a few words. I made two copies of it, and, both to the printer of *The Courant* and *Mercury,* subjoined my name to be kept as the authority. Richard brought John's wife and daughter. "Well," said I, "Mrs. Reid, I have the satisfaction to tell you that your husband behaved as well as we could wish." "And that is a great satisfaction," said she. We made her eat a little and take a glass, but she was, though not violently or very tenderly affected, in a kind of dull grief. The girl did not seem moved. She eat heartily. I told Mrs. Reid that I insisted that John should be buried at home; and as I found that as yet no carter would undertake to go but at an extravagant price, the corpse might lie till tomorrow night, and then perhaps a reasonable carter might be had. Mr. Nasmith went to *The Courant* with the paragraph, and I to *The Mercury.* I sat till it was printed. It was liberal in Robertson, who was himself one of the jury, to admit it; and he corrected the press.

It was not about eight in the evening, and gloom came upon me. I went home and found my wife no comforter, as she thought I had carried my zeal for John too far, might hurt my own character and interest by it, and as she thought him guilty. I was so affrighted that I started every now and then and durst hardly rise from my chair at the fireside. I sent for Grange, but he was not at home. I however got Dr. Webster, who came and supped, and he and I drank a bottle of claret. But still I was quite dismal.

THURSDAY 22 SEPTEMBER. I had passed the night much better than I expected and was easier in the morning. Charles Hay called and after I had given him a detail of all my conduct towards poor John, he said emphatically, "Well, GOD has blessed you with one of the best hearts that ever man had."

INDEX

Adam, Père (French Jesuit), 167–168
Advocates, Faculty of, 95
Album amicorum (autograph book), 129
Alemoor, Lord, 341
Alexander the Great, 197
Alford, Lord (Sir John Graham), 211
Alva, Lady, 274
America, plans to visit, 276, 279
Anhalt, Count of, 113
Ardmillan, Ayrshire, 259
Auchinleck (Elizabeth Boswell), Lady, 2nd
    wife of Lord Auchinleck, 268–270,
    306
Auchinleck (Euphemia Erskine), Lady,
    (mother of JB), 77, 78, 110, 175, 199,
    201, 202, 269
  death of, 4, 65, 211
  marriage contract, 318
Auchinleck (Alexander Boswell), Lord
    (JB's father), 3–4, 220
  advice given JB, 78, 235
  affection for JB, 268–269
  allowance for JB, 4, 77, 199–200
  on JB's depression, 107–110
  on JB's trip to Italy, 153, 163
  character, 152–153, 230
  confidence in JB, 225–226
  desired JB to study law, 4, 16, 69, 78
  disapproved of JB's journals, 3–4, 69,
    76, 78
  Douglas memorials, 236
  father-son relationship, 69–70, 75–78,
    85–86, 239, 281, 296, 318–319
  friendships, 135, 230
  Hamilton memorial, 229
  illness, 201, 235
  Irish expedition opposed by, 258
  jurist, 3–4, 220, 306
  law studies in Holland, 101
  letters to JB, 4, 75–78, 96, 107, 110,
    202, 211–212
  meeting with SJ, 312
  opposition to JB's desire for commis-
    sion in the Guards, 25–26, 31, 78

opposition to marriage to Margaret
    Montgomerie, 219, 262, 275, 277,
    285, 357
  opposition to JB's plans for travel, 16,
    119, 199–200
  relations with JB and wife, 279, 281,
    283–286, 339, 357
  second marriage, 265–273, 278–279,
    285, 300, 306, 318–319, 339
  trial of John Reid, 342, 346–347
  wanted JB to marry Catherine Blair,
    230–232, 235
Auchinleck (estate and family), 15, 47, 93,
    230–231, 235, 267, 281–282
  JB heir to, 4, 15, 153–154
  female succession, 281–283, 319
  Lord Auchinleck threatens to sell, 318
Auld, Andrew, 350–351

Baden-Durlach, Prince of, 140–141
  JB's desire for Knights of the Order of
    Fidelity, 140–141
Baillie, Jamie, 239, 266
Baldwin, Henry (printer), 329
Bâle clock, Switzerland, 141–143
Baretti, Giuseppe Marc Antonio, 184,
    254, 302
Beggar's Opera, The, 242
Bell, Adam, 342, 364
Bennet, Andrew, 384–386
Berlin, 123, 128
Berne, Switzerland, 143
Billon, Capt. Antonio, 176–178
Black, William, 346–347, 350, 352–353
Blackmore, Sir Richard, 303
Blair, Dr. (Edinburgh minister), 59, 65,
    232, 346
Blair, Catherine (the "heiress"), 226, 230,
    240, 256–257
  courtship of, 233–238
  dialogue on love, 234–235
  engagement to Sir Alexander Gilmour,
    237–238
  ward of Lord Auchinleck, 230–232, 235

Blair, Hugh, 249
  A Dissertation on Ossian, 249
Bosville, Elizabeth Diana, 230–231
Bosville, Godfrey, 246, 317
Boswell, Charles (natural son of JB and
  Peggy Doig), 104
Boswell, David (brother of JB), 6, 26, 201,
  202, 234, 317, 331, 367
Boswell, Doctor, 224, 286, 290
Boswell, Elizabeth (*see* Auchinleck [Eliza-
  beth Boswell], Lady, 2nd wife of
  Lord Auchinleck)
Boswell, James (glass-merchant), 111
Boswell, James (grandfather), 298
Boswell, James (Entries are arranged
  under the following headings: Bio-
  graphical details; Journals and jour-
  nal-writing; Opinions; Traits; and
  Writings)

  BIOGRAPHICAL DETAILS:
  born in Scotland, 3
  early life, 3–4, 14–15
  father-son relationship, 3–5, 16,
    48–49, 69–70, 75–78, 85–86,
    239, 281, 296, 318–319
  biographer of SJ, 3–5
  commission in Guards sought by, 4,
    11–16, 25–26, 31, 78
  father wants him to study law, 4, 16,
    69, 78
  to be Laird of Auchinleck, 4, 15, 95,
    153–154
  executions, fascination with, 4, 63,
    179, 245, 302, 368–369
  prostitutes and disease, 4, 8, 16–17,
    21, 38–40, 43, 55, 57–59, 61,
    64, 71, 74–75, 79–80, 85–86,
    92–93, 110–111, 130, 135–
    136, 141, 165, 174, 207, 211,
    227–228, 231, 233, 237–238,
    246, 252, 270, 277, 289–292,
    321
  first meeting with SJ, 5
  family background, 6, 80, 140
  allowance, 8, 11, 31, 48, 111, 129
  lodgings, 8, 10, 15, 55, 83–84, 244,
    299
  church attendance, 9, 15, 22, 24,
    72–73, 97, 104, 136, 169, 243,
    275–276, 359
  silver-hilted sword purchased by,
    10–11

melancholy and depression, 14, 27,
    54, 58, 62–65, 108, 151–152
law studies, 14, 16, 40, 48–49, 51, 69,
    78, 92, 236
venereal disease, 16, 36, 38–44, 53,
    95, 174, 227–228, 231, 233,
    270, 277, 289–290
religious beliefs, 15, 22, 72, 93–94, 97,
    130, 149, 151, 154, 243, 254–
    255, 282, 328, 359–360
father-son relationships, 16, 51, 81,
    85–86
affair with Louisa, 32–36
first nights attendance, 45–46
desire for fame and money, 47–48,
    55, 91, 267
daily routine, 47, 126
meeting with SJ, 65–66
in Holland, 70–115
"Inviolable Plan" of studies, 70,
    94–96
Greek, study of, 93, 97, 98
interest in career in Parliament, 95,
    129, 297
law studies at Utrecht, 96–115
letters from SJ, 97–98, 198
servants, 99, 105, 122–124
letters from Lord Auchinleck, 96,
    107–108, 109–110, 202, 211–
    212
health in Holland, 104–106
return to Edinburgh, 108, 255, 335
European travels, 108, 119–160
at German Courts, 119–141
disapproval of hunting stags, 119
daily letters to SJ, 126
legal career, 129, 219, 223, 237–239,
    247, 250, 278, 313, 335–336,
    358–359
ambitions, 139, 364
Order of Fidelity, JB's desire for,
    140–141
Scots pride, 146
in London, 154
Corsican travels, 163–215
death of mother in Edinburgh, 165,
    211–212
in Geneva, 166–170
meetings with Voltaire, 166–170
Italian travels, 171, 173, 175, 181–
    212
meetings with Rousseau, 174,
    185

Boswell, James (*cont.*)
  letter from mother, 175
  Turin adventures, 175–179
  Rome visit, 179–181
  Latin studies, 180
  Venice, 183–184
  tour of Corsica, 187–211
  travels through France, 206–211
  foot problems, 208–210, 231
  amorous episode with Thérèse Le
      Vasseur, 213–215
  search for a wife, 217–307
  admitted to the bar, 219
  affair with gardener's daughter, 221–
      223, 230
  courtship of Margaret Montgomerie,
      221, 255–307
  affair with Mrs. Dodds, 223–226
  courtship of Catherine Blair, 233–238
  honors given to, 235
  journey to London, 242–244
  mistaken for Wilkes, 248–249
  marriage agreement, 255–256
  Irish expedition, 258–262
  resented father's plan to remarry,
      268–273, 285, 300, 318–319
  thoughts on going to America, 276
  at Shakespeare Jubilee at Stratford,
      289–296
  portraits in Corsican dress, 295, 299
  marriage to Margaret Montgomerie,
      305–307
  as literary man, 311–312
  tour of the Hebrides with SJ, 312
  trial of John Reid, 341–356

JOURNALS AND JOURNAL-WRITING, 3, 6,
    44, 69–70, 164, 277–278, 337
  anecdotes and stories, 6
  books based on journals, 69–70
  discussed with SJ, 86–87
  European journals in French, 94
  ideas concerning, 75
  legal encounters, 313
  London Journal, 1–66
  London to Holland, 67–115
  memorandum written daily, 138
  missing entries, 120, 213, 313
  purpose of, 6, 120–121, 125
  recollecting SJ's conversation, 70
  revision considered, 120–121
  search for a wife, 217–307
  self-identification, 120–121

  should it be burnt or kept in archives,
      87
  style and writing practice, 44, 47–48,
      96–97, 138
  tour of Corsica, 187–211
  trial of John Reid, 341–356

OPINIONS:
  on benefit of philosophy, 60
  on Britain's right to tax colonies, 265
  on capital punishment, 355–356, 377
  on cockfights, 17
  on conversations, 6, 11, 17, 83, 323
  on crime and punishment, 188–189,
      220
  on death and dying, 56, 164, 241–
      242, 245, 298, 311, 330, 359
  on evil of illicit love, 86, 93
  on executions, 189
  on fame and famous men, 177
  on French and English manners, 13,
      17–18, 127
  on galley-slaves, 207–208
  on ghosts and superstitions, 182, 198,
      376
  on human happiness, 53, 56, 58, 197
  on human nature, 205
  on immortality, 56
  on independence, 77
  on infidelity, 301, 323
  on Italian women and manners, 176–
      177
  on marriage, 86, 124, 193, 197, 221,
      271–273, 301, 323
  on masters and servants, 204–206
  on poetry, 24
  on predestination, 360, 366–367
  on publishing, 46–47
  on religion and religious sentiments,
      4, 22, 111, 170–172, 190, 342
  on soldiers, experienced or inexperi-
      enced, 359
  on succession, male or female, 281–
      283, 319
  on swearing, 324
  on systems of government, 57, 89–90
  on truth, 196
  on war and poverty, 21, 62

TRAITS, 4, 19, 22–23, 29, 36, 47, 64,
    74, 90, 105, 254, 297
  ambitiousness, 47, 51, 54–55, 129
  appearance and attire, 98, 111, 135–
      136, 148, 171–172, 199

Boswell, James (*cont.*)
 attainment of superior character, 80,
  243–244
 claims "second sight," 75
 as described by servant (François
  Mazerac), 114–115
 desire to acquire sensible habits,
  80
 dignity and constancy, 64, 94, 255–
  256
 disposition to make people happy,
  259–260, 302
 dissipation and vice, 72, 78, 85, 111,
  219, 257
 drinking and drunkenness, 183, 220,
  228, 232–233, 258–259, 280–
  281, 328–329, 337–341, 358–
  359, 381
 eternal disputer, 208
 executions, attendance at, 4, 189, 241
 fondness for children, 30
 fondness for tea, 49
 foot problems, 165
 friendships, 135, 184
 genius, 47–49, 327
 good opinion of self, 64
 health, 8, 36, 124, 181, 237
 independence, 56
 indolence and carelessness, 56–57
 life-style, 78
 likes extra pillows at night, 102–103
 lively and entertaining, 4, 34, 64,
  194–195
 melancholy moods, 27, 43, 49, 54, 58,
  62–65, 90, 93, 104–107, 123,
  151, 165, 179, 313
 mimicry, 76, 78, 139
 Mountstuart on, 183
 nightmares, 63
 persistence, 121
 religious beliefs, 9, 15, 80–81, 151,
  236, 257
 repeating gossip, 14
 sought company of illustrious men,
  4–5
 talents as courtier, 139–140
 vanity, 293
 violent temper, 271, 340
 wishes to be man of consequence, 42

 WRITINGS:
  Account of Corsica, 69, 120, 164–165,
   220, 230–232, 243–244, 254,
   256, 267, 289
  French translation, 295
  publication of, 240–241
  reaction of SJ, 247, 253, 295
  reviews and criticism, 243, 246–247,
   254
  anecdotes about great men, 144
  Boswell family, account of, 231
  Curious Productions, 85
  Epic Poem (with Dempster and Erskine), 38
  essay on marriage, 271–273
  in French language, 94
  "Inviolable Plan," 70, 94–96
  Italian Journal, 181
  "Journal of a Tour to Corsica," 187–
   199, 263
  Journal of a Tour to the Hebrides, 69,
   312
  journals, letters and essays, 52
   See also James Boswell, Journals
   and journal-writing
  law papers, 236
  *Letters Between the Hon. Andrew Erskine
   and James Boswell,* 60–61,
   72–74, 76
  Life of Samuel Johnson, 3, 69–70, 311,
   324–325
  London Journal, 1–66
  "A Matrimonial Thought" (poem),
   306
  memorandum written daily, 138
  Ode on Ambition, 56, 169
  Parliament (poem), 169
  poems and poetry, 14, 24, 36–37
  prologue to *The Discovery* (Sheridan),
   36–37, 46
  Scottish dictionary, 98, 103–104, 302
  "On Second Marriages: A True Story
   In Queen Anne's Reign,"
   271–273
  "Sketch of My Life," 152–153
  Verses, 294
 Boswell, John (brother), 4, 78, 110, 201,
  330–331
 Boswell, Margaret Montgomerie (wife of
  JB),
  accompanies JB to Ireland, 258–264,
   284–285
  Lord Auchinleck and, 262, 280, 283–
   286
  JB's courtship, 255–307
  JB's proposal, 274–277
  disapproval of SJ, 312
  letters from JB, 221, 283, 292–293, 300

Boswell, Margaret Montgomerie (*cont.*)
  letters to JB, 163, 233–234, 263–264,
    268, 280–281, 305
  on death of Lord Eglinton, 304–305
  marriage contract, 220–221, 255–256,
    306–307
  objects to JB's drunkenness, 281, 338, 381
  and John Reid affair, 385, 392
  separation from JB, 315, 330
Boswell, Robert, 229, 380
Boswell, Sally (JB's illegitimate daughter),
  235–237, 240
Boswell, Thomas, 296
Boswell, Veronica (daughter of JB), 311,
  342, 357, 359, 367
Boufflers, Chevalier de, 168
Boyd, Jane (aunt), 258, 261
Boyd, Mary Anne (Irish heiress), 256–257
  JB in love with, 256–257, 259, 261, 264
Brookes, Kitty (prostitute), 246
Brown, Mrs. (friend of Lord Eglinton),
  65, 305
Brown, George (Lord Coalston), 238, 239,
  342, 347
Brown, James (criminal), 380
Brown, Rev. Robert, (at Utrecht) 96–98,
  100, 106, 110, 274
Browne, Isaac Hawkins, 327
Bruce, James, 232
Bruce, John, 229
Bruce, Robert, 230
Brunswick, Court of, 122–128
Brunswick, Duke and Duchess of, 125–
  128, 130–131
Burgaretta, Countess, 176–178
Burke, Edmund, 312, 333, 354
Bute, John Stuart, Lord, 9, 55–56
  master of King's wardrobe, 96
  unable to secure commission for JB,
    55–56

Cadwaldin, Mrs. (painter), 60
Cairnie, Dr., 277
Cambridge University, 64
Campbell, Bruce, 232
Campbell, Colonel, 373
Campbell, Ilay, 320, 359, 363–364
  Campbeltown schoolmaster case, 319–
    320
  Lord President of the Court of Ses-
    sions, 335–336, 344
Campbell, Mr. and Mrs. Walter, 274
Campbeltown schoolmaster cause, 318–
  320

SJ on, 319–320
Capraja (Genoese Island), 231
Cathcart, Sir Johns, 239
Catholic Church, 139
Chaillet, Colonel, 176
Chalmer, John, 236, 278
Chalmers, Robert, 336
Chambers, Robert, 247, 250–251, 291
Chandler, Mr. (printer), 60
Chesterfield, Lord, 323
Churchill, Charles, 82
Claxton, John, 327
Cleland, John, author of *Woman of Pleas-
  ure*, 324
Clerk, General, 246
Clerk, Sir James, 372–373
Coalston, Lord, *see* George Brown
Cochrane, Basil (Commissioner of Cus-
  toms), 270, 339
Cochrane, James, 286
Cochrane, Mr. (banker), 8, 72, 199
Cochrane, Willy, 207
Cockburn, Archibald, 344, 352
Coke, Lady Mary, 127
Colebrooke, Sir George, 333
Colquitt, Dr., 127
Colville, Lady, 339, 369
Congreve, William, 39–40
Connoisseur, The, 72
Constant, Colonel, 166
Cornwallis, Lord, 374
Corsica, 119, 163–215, 259
  argument over infallibility of the Pope,
    116
  JB believed to be English envoy, 190,
    192, 194
  costume for Shakespeare Jubilee, 290–
    292, 295, 299
  criminals, 194
  defeat and destruction of, 263
  English support of, 190, 195
  hangman of, 189
  "The Journal of a Tour to Corsica,"
    187–199
  ordnance sent by JB, 257
  peasants and soldiers, 192, 194
  purpose in visiting, 187
  Sollacarò, 190
  voyage to, 186, 188
Corte (capital of Corsica), 188–189
Corte, University of, 235
Courant, The, John Reid's death notice,
  391–392
Court of Justiciary, 370, 383

Coutts & Company, 24, 75, 199
Craufurd of Auchenames, 30–31, 259, 321
Crawford, Lady, 236, 241–242, 271
Critical Review, criticism of *Letters,* 74
Crookshanks (Lord Eglinton's steward), 50, 304–305
Crosbie, Andrew, Advocate, 341–342, 362
Cullen, Dr., 362, 369
Cust, Sir John, 315

Dalhousie, Lord, 236
Dalrymple, Lady, 339
Dalrymple, Sir David, 51, 98, 153–154, 224, 232
Dalrymple, Sir John, 329, 356–357
Davidson, John (Crown Agent), 372
Davies, Thomas (publisher and bookseller), 5, 20, 24, 65, 83, 290, 297
Deleyre, M., 179
Dempster, George, M.P., 11–12, 37–38, 63, 85, 89–90, 268, 278, 317, 332
   advice on love and marriage, 38, 264, 268
   advocates seat in Parliament for JB, 297
   ambitions, 44
   country lodgings at Kensington, 63, 65, 80
   pleasant companion, 52
   took JB to House of Commons, 54, 332
Denbigh, Lord, 321
Denis, Madame (Voltaire's niece), 167–170
Dick, Rev. Dr., 385, 390–391
Dick, Sir Alexander, 226, 263, 270
Dick, Andrew, 278–279
Dick, Sir John B. (British consul at Leghorn), 244, 254, 267
Dickie, Matthew, 229, 236, 265, 379
Dictionaries: to ascertain pronunciation, 322–323
   English, 104
   Johnson's *Dictionary of the English Language,* 82, 93, 319
   Scottish, JB's plans for, 98, 103–104, 302
   Sheridan's dictionary, 322–323
Diego, Hannah (convict), 62
Digges, Mr. and Mrs. 32–33
Dilly, Charles (publisher and bookseller), 325
Dilly, Edward (publisher and bookseller), 240, 245–246, 289, 316, 329, 334
   Account of Corsica published by, 240

Discovery, The (comedy by Mrs. Sheridan), 45–46, 52
Dodds, Mr. (woolen draper in Newcastle), 287–289
Dodds, Mrs. ("Circe"), JB's mistress, 223–233, 236–240
   with child, 232–233, 240
   mother of Sally, 236–237, 240
Doig, Peggy, 104
Douglas, General, 12
Douglas, Dr. Andrew, 7, 9, 25, 29, 38–40, 53
   friend and doctor, 7, 40
   treats JB, 39–40
Douglas, Archibald James Edward, 273, 317
   birthday celebration, 266–267
Douglas, James Prebendary, 239
Douglas, Margaret, Duchess of, 226
Douglas, Capt. William of Kelhead, 266, 276
Douglas Cause, 231, 235–236, 266–267
Douglas memorials, 230
Dresden, 135
Drummond, Duncan, 207
Dryden, John, 47
Dublin, Ireland, 261, 285
Dumfries, Lord, 76
Dundas, Henry (His Majesty's Solicitor), 344
Dundonald, Lord, 339

Eccles, Mr. (Irish gentleman), 80, 83
Edinburgh, 8, 44, 83–84, 237
   Arthur's Seat, 84, 297
   Castle Hill, 270
   Clerihue's (coffee-house), 224, 238, 239
   Goldsmiths Hall, 265
   Grassmarket, 386–387
   Greyfriars Churchyard, 391
   Heriot's Gardens, 342, 359
   High Street, 311–312, 330
   Holyrood House, 357
   London versus, 12
   Parliament House, 273
   society, 238
   Tolbooth (prison), 356
   visit of SJ, 312
Edmonstone, Colonel, 181–182, 202
   on Italian tour, 182
Eglinton, Alexander Montgomerie Lord, 7–8, 28–29, 35, 43, 60, 63–64, 71, 79, 82, 85, 236, 323

Englinton, Alexander (*cont.*)
  advice on marrying, 237, 281
  JB receives card from, 23
  commission discussed with, 55–56
  death of, 304–305
Eglinton, Archibald Montgomerie, 325
Election law, 236
Elibank, Lord, 211
Elizabeth, German Princess, 125–127
Elvira's, tragedy by Mallet, 38
English Dictionary, The (Johnson), 88, 93,
  104, 319
Entertainment, English, 79
Erroll, Earl of, 357, 369
Erskine, Captain Andrew, 11–15, 25,
  28–29, 35, 50, 55, 62, 226, 229
  advice and sympathy, 38
  Institutes, 380
  publication of *Letters,* 60–61
  visit with, 44
  warns JB about repeating gossip, 14
Erskine, Lady Anne, 11, 29, 55, 369
Erskine, Lady Frances, 9, 25
Erskine, James, 51, 80
European travels, 94, 108–109, 119–160
  France, 200, 206–211
  Lord Auchinleck's low opinion of, 108,
  119
Executions, 368–369
  attendance at, 4, 63, 179, 245, 302
  Raybould's, 241–242
  John Reid, 356–392
    scheme to recover, 362-363, 364,
    367–370, 382–387

Faculty of Advocates, Scotland, 95
Fergusson, Sir Adam, 259
Ferrara, Italy, 183
Fife family, 11
Fitzherbert, William, 327
Flanders, 108
Flexney (bookseller), 60
Foot Guards, JB's desire to join, 4, 11–16
Forbes, Mr. (surgeon), 289
Forbes, Duncan, 51, 236, 381
Forbes, Sir William, 213, 245, 340–341
Forfar politics, 237
Forrester, Sally, 79
Foulis, Robert (printer), 231
France, travels in, 200, 206–211
  language, 32, 36, 94
  manners, 17, 127
Francois, Abraham, 144

Franklin, Dr., 254
Fraser, Captain, 371, 380, 390
Frazer, George, 236, 239, 335
Frazer, James, 266
Frederick II, King of Prussia, 131
Froment, Madame and Monsieur de, 113,
  122–123
Fullarton, William of Rosemount ("the
  Nabob"), 239–240, 257

Galley-slaves, 207–209
Galloway, Earl of, 102, 270
Gardenstone, Lord, 341
Gardner, William, 348, 350–353, 374, 375
  accused of stealing sheep, 363, 375-377
Garrick, David, 37, 42, 64, 73, 292–294,
  296, 306, 312, 324, 327
  misunderstanding between SJ and, 5,
  327–328
  *The Prologue spoken at Mr. Garrick's Open-
  ing Drury-Lane Theatre* (Johnson), 82
  Sheridan's opinion of, 9–10
Geelvinck, Catherina Elizabeth (Hassel-
  aer), 98–102
  JB in love with, 99–102
  fortune, 109
Gellert (German author), 134
Geneva, 109, 172–173
Genoa, 199, 204
Gentili, Count, 298, 316
George II, King of Great Britain, 7–8
George III, King of Great Britain, 25, 47,
  81, 126
German campaign, 21
German Courts, 108, 119–141
  abuse of German soldiers, 128
  accommodations, 128, 134, 137–138
  Brunswick, 122–127
  dances and music, 125–126
  injury to eye, 124
  Wittenberg in Saxony, 133–134
German language, 134
Ghosts and superstitions, 55, 182, 376
Gibson, James (forger), 245
Gilmour, Sir Alexander, 11, 237–239
Glasgow, 279–280
Glover, Richard, 143
Glyn, Sir Richard, 245
Godolphin, Lord and Lady, 39–40
Goldsmith, Oliver, 24, 46, 81, 83, 297,
  311–312, 326, 332
  on effect of luxury, 334–335
  on SJ, 24

Goldsmith, Oliver (*cont.*)
  She Stoops to Conquer, 311, 334
Gordon, Lord Adam, 8
Gordon, Alexander, 238
Gordon, Duke and Duchess of, 234
Gordon, Sir William, 211
Gottsched, Professor, 134
Gould family, 11, 25, 29–30, 59
Government, systems of, 57
Graham, Capt. Mungo, 122
Granby, Marquis of, 26, 30–31, 50
Grange, *see* Johnston, John, of Grange
Grant, Baron, 51
Gray, Alexander, 343–344, 347
Greenwich, boat trip to, 92–93
Gregory, Dr., 232
Gronovius, Abraham, 112
Guards, attempt to get commission in,
    11–16, 30–31, 43, 52, 59, 94
  aid of Lady Northumberland, 25–26,
    30–31, 50
  father disapproves of, 78
  purchase of, 31, 56
  Royal Horse Guards Blue, 25–26
  turned down by Duke of Queensbury,
    11–16, 24–25, 40
Guelfucci, Abbé, 196, 298
Guthrie, William (historian and critic),
  246–247, 249

Hague, The, 112
Hahn, Johannes David, 98, 110, 112
Hailes (Sir David Dalrymple), Lord, 51,
  98, 224, 232
  advises JB, 153–154
Hall, Steuart, 364, 369
Hamilton, James George Duke of, 266
Hänni, Jacob (servant), 112, 123–124,
  143–144, 175, 186, 203–206, 210
Harwich, JB sails from, 93
Hasselaer, Monsieur and Madame, 112
Hastie cause (Scottish schoolmaster), 311,
  318–320
Hay, Charles, 358–361, 362, 367, 373,
  377–381, 392
  scheme for recovering John Reid, 383
Hay, James, 240
Hay, Robert (trial of), 224, 231, 241
Hay, William, 239
Hayward's apartment, 31–33
Hearts of Oak (English song), 195
Heaton, Mr. (of Lincoln's Inn), 334
Hebrides, 3

SJ's desire to visit, 91
tour through, 163, 312
Helvétius (philosopher), 64, 110
Henderson, Matthew, 237, 340
Henley, machine to level hill, 251–252
Henries & Cochrane, 8, 72, 199
Herusalem, Ap, 126, 128
Hoggan, Captain, 317, 319
Holborn, 60
  St. Andrew's Church, 72
Holland:
  Journal, 70–115
  law studies at Utrecht, 96–115
Home, George, 27, 53, 60, 62
Home, Henry, *see* Lord Kames
House of Commons, 44, 54, 332
House of Lords, 325
  attendance at, 7–8
  JB's appearance before, 311
  Bruce-Carstairs against Miss Bruce, 325
  Scotch appeals in, 317
Hume, David, 47, 64, 90, 154, 184, 214,
  220, 224, 254, 286
  SJ and, 249
Hume's *History,* 44, 62
Hyndford, Lord and Lady, 236

Idler (Johnson), 24, 87
Inglis, James, 348, 350
Innes, Alexander, 360–361, 382, 384–385
Ireland, 60
  JB's visit to, 258–262
Irene (Johnson), 12, 87
Isham, Col. Ralph Heyward, 213
Italian tour, 109, 153, 187, 254–255
  amount spent on, 199–200
  with Lord Mountstuart, 182
  love-adventures, 176–178
  robberies and assassinations, 204–205

Jachone, dog given to JB by Gen. Paoli,
  165, 198, 206–210
James, Sir, 58, 65, 71
Jardine, Dr., 85
Jefferys, Mr. (sword-cutter to his Majesty),
  10–11
Jerusalem, Abbé, 126, 128
Jesuits, 139, 167–168
Jewish synagogue, visit to, 324
Johnson, Samuel, 247–254, 286, 317, 341
  affection for JB, 91–93, 125, 133, 164
  agrees to provide JB with study plan,
    81

Johnson, Samuel (*cont.*)
  anecdotes about, 19, 86
  attempts to keep a journal, 333
  JB's first meeting with, 5, 65
  JB leaves for law studies in Holland, 70
  on JB's marriage, 295
  JB's plan to write life of, 311, 324–325, 333–334
  on JB's relationship with his father, 62, 81, 85–86, 300, 311
  on JB's trip to Corsica, 164–165, 198–199, 253, 295
  Campbeltown schoolmaster cause, 319–320, 326–327
  chambers in the Inner Temple, 73
  desire to visit Western Isles of Scotland, 91, 163
  dining with, 333
  displeased with JB quoting his letter, 253
  entertaining companion, 24, 65
  friendship with JB, 70, 85–87, 317–318
  horseback riding, 78–79
  knowledge of the world, 288
  letters from JB, 125–126, 253
    written at tomb of Melanchthon, 132–133, 198
  letters to JB, 97–98, 104, 198, 253
    on Corsica, 198–199, 295
  meetings with Sir Alexander Macdonald, 321–322
  Margaret Montgomerie and, 219, 312
  at New Inn Hall, Oxford, 247
  Opinions:
    on adultery, 251
    on advantages of subordination, 89
    on authors, 82, 249
    on beauty independent of utility, 324
    on being a country gentleman, 330
    on Churchill, 82
    on colonists, 300
    on conversation, 66, 79–83, 97–98, 327–329, 332–333
    JB's recording of, 83
    on Corsica, 198–199, 253, 295
    on death and dying, 301–302
    on discipline and punishment by schoolmasters, 311
    on distinction of rank, 89–90
    on education of children, 86, 91
    on father-son relationships, 85–86, 318–319
    on Garrick, 5, 73, 327–328

    on Goldsmith's apology, 332
    on inequality, 335
    on infidels and innovators, 196
    on knowledge of human nature, 196, 288
    on language, study of, 301
    on leisure and intellectual improvement, 335
    on liberty, 66, 54
    on luxury, 334–335
    on moral good, 73
    on morality of the law, 248
    on political and moral principles, 335
    on political systems, 83, 90–91
    on scorpions, 250
    on Scotland, 65, 83, 249, 322–323
    on subordination of rank, 89–91, 335
    on superiority and mediocrity, 65–66
    on religious services, 73
    on truth, 89
    on why part of mankind is black, 80
    on John Wilkes, 66
    on women, 251
    on women preachers, 93
    on young acquaintances, 90
  at Oxford, 24, 247, 291
  General Paoli and, 196–197, 301, 324
  pension, 9
  reproaches JB for quoting him without permission, 164
  reunion with, 215
  Rousseau and, 158
  Sheridans and, 9, 19, 36
  tour of Hebrides, 91, 163, 312
  Traits, 326
    appearance, 9, 65, 80
    bearish manners, 9, 65, 290
    good humor, 84, 303
    impatience, 303
    indolence, 93
  visit to Auchinleck estate, 312
  visit to Edinburgh, 312
  witness to JB's marriage contract, 307
  Writings, 82
    The English Dictionary, 82, 93, 104, 319
    The Idler, 24, 87
    Irene (tragedy), 12, 87
    The Life of Savage, 82
    London: a Poem, 93
    Prologue spoken at Mr. Garrick's Opening Drury Lane Theatre, 82
    The Rambler, 24, 81, 82, 87

Johnson, Samuel (*cont.*)
  Rasselas, 82
  The Translations of the Third and Tenth
    Satires of Juvenal, 82, 87
Johnston, John, of Grange, 6, 226, 228–
  229, 268–269, 367, 392
  advice on love and marriage, 268
  against attempt to recover John Reid,
    386
  friend of JB, 235, 242
Johnstone, Naval Captain, 28
Journal Amoureux, 36
Journals and journal-keeping, *see under*
  James Boswell
Judges, prejudice of, 374
  bias to severity, 336, 374–375
Juvenal, SJ's writings on, 82, 87

Kames, (Henry Home) Lord, 254
  Elements of Criticism, 166, 254
  John Reid's trial, 342, 355–356
Kellie family, 12, 37, 169
Kennedy, David, 254, 270, 332
Kennedy, Dr. Gilbert, 289, 295
  Lisbon Diet Drink, 295
Kennet, Lord, 346, 355
Kinlock, Mr. (London merchant), 287–
  289
Kinlock, Mademoiselle, 113
Kinnaird, Jeanie (prostitute), 238
Kinnoul, Lord, 240
Kinross, Bruce, 325
Kneet, Lord, 239

La Belle Irlandaise, see Mary Ann Boyd
Lade, Lady, 333
Lainshaw (home of Margaret Montgomer-
  ie), 258–259, 279–280
Langton, Bennet, 341
Law, moral principles, 248
Law College, 362, 378
Lawrie, John (clerk to JB), 330, 342
Leeds, Duchess of, 40
Legge, Mr. and Mrs. (The Baron), 87–88
Leghorn, 186, 188
Leith, races at, 274, 275
Lennox family, 140
Le Vasseur, Thérèse (Rousseau's compan-
  ion), 4, 147–148, 151, 157–160, 212–
  215
  accompanies JB to London, 165, 213–
    215
  correspondence with JB, 173–174

gift of garnet necklace, 160, 165, 173
Leven, Lord, 236
Lewis, Paul, 62–63
  execution of, 63
Leyden, 111–112
Ligonier, Lord, 12, 15, 40
Lindsay, Lady Anne, 339
Lisburn, Ireland, 262
Lives of the Admirals (Campbell), 82
Livingston, Doctor, 224, 229
Lochée's Military Academy at Chelsea,
  treatment of boys, 362
Lock, Richard (inner turnkey), 364–365,
  371, 376–377, 379–380, 387, 389
Lockhart, Alexander, 337, 341
London: arrival in, 214–215
  authors and writers, 4, 46, 81
  JB's desire for annual journey to, 154,
    220–221, 280–281
  JB's enthusiasm for, 14, 31, 94
  Bow Church, 85
  Buckingham House, 21–22
  Clifton's, 80
  compared with Edinburgh, 12
  Covent Garden, 13, 16–18, 20, 31, 55,
    59, 246, 334
    Piazza Coffee-house, 59
  Covent Garden Church, 27–28, 55
  Covent Garden Theatre, 16–18, 20, 31,
    59
  Cox's Museum, 319
  crime and robberies, 29
  Drury Lane Theatre, 37, 42, 45–46, 59,
    82
  father disapproved of JB's going to, 16
  Guildhall, 245
  Holborn, 54–55, 59
  Hyde Park Corner, 38
  journeys to, 6–7, 95, 242–244, 292, 311,
    315–317, 330–331
  Kensington Gardens, 63–65, 80
  Lincoln's Inn Fields, 53
  lodgings, 8, 10, 15
    Crown Street, Westminster, 10
    Downing Street, Westminster, 8, 10,
      84
    Half Moon Street, Piccadilly, 244
    near Burlington Gardens, 299
  London Bridge, 38, 59
  Mitre Inn, 80, 81, 83–86, 320
  population growth, 319
  Red Lion Inn at Charing Cross, 11
  Roman Club, 244

London: arrival in (*cont.*)
  Rose Tavern, 45
  St. Clement's Chop-house, 59
  St. James's Church, 9
  St. James's Park, 11, 53–54, 57, 59
  St. Martin's Church, 30
  St. Paul's Church, 24, 88, 93
  Mrs. Salmon's famous wax-works, 82
  scenes, 46, 88–89, 316
  Shakespeare's Head, 71–72
  Southampton Street in the Strand, 55,
    59
  Spring Garden Chapel, 54
  Star and Garter, 79, 244
  Thames River, 59, 88–89, 92–93
  Tower of London, 62
  Turk's Head Coffee-house, 92–94
  Vauxhall, 79
  Westminster Abbey, 74
  Westminster Bridge, 64
  Whitehall Chapel, 24
London: A Poem (Johnson), 93
London Chronicle, The, 328, 332
London Journal, 1–66, 226
London Magazine, 295, 325, 329
Longueville, Rev. David, 111
Louisa (actress), affair with, 16–38
  end of affair, 40–42, 45
  returns money to JB, 20–21, 45, 49
Love, Mr. and Mrs. James, 65, 297
Love in a Village (new comic opera), 13
Lumisden, Andrew, 181
Luther, Martin, grave of, 132–133
Lyons, France, 209–210

Macaulay, Mrs. Catharine, 90–91, 252–
  253, 334–335
Macdonald, Mr. (surgeon), 268, 270, 277
Macdonald, Sir Alexander, 317, 321–323
Macdonald, Sir James (Lord Advocate),
  28, 45, 56, 91–92, 291, 372–373
  appeal in behalf of John Reid, 382–383
Macdonald, William, 266
Macfarlane, George, 384
Macfarlane, Lady Betty, 3, 11–12, 24, 55
McGraugh, Henry, case, 362–363, 378
Mackenzie, Alexander, 339
Mackenzie, Sir George, *Criminals*, 342, 346
Mackye, John Ross, 321
Maclaine, Archibald, 106–107
Maclaurin, John, 357, 369, 380–381
MacLeod, Norman (Laird of MacLeod),
  334, 370, 373

Maconochie, Alexander, 246–247, 266–
  267, 270
Macqueen, Rev. Dr. Daniel, 360, 385, 390
  execution of John Reid, 387
Macqueen, George, 363
Maison des Modeles (models of build-
  ings), Saxe-Gotha, 137–138
Mallet, David, 38
Mallet, Paul Henry, 181–185, 202
Malloch, David, 38
Mansfield, Lord William Murray, 255,
  325, 333–334
March, Lord, 85
Marggraf (chemical professor), 130
Marischal, George Keith Lord, 108, 111,
  113, 128–129, 187
  accompanied JB through Germany, 122
  partisan of Corsica, 185
  Rousseau and, 131, 145, 148–151
  travels with, 111–112, 122, 129, 131
Marseilles, 206
Maule, Baron, 51
Maxwell, Captain, 29
Maxwell, Lady (Miss Stewart), 109
Mazerac, François (servant), 98–99, 105,
  114–115
Medows, Captain, 254
Melanchthon, Philipp, wrote letter to SJ
  on tomb of, 131–133, 198
Memoirs of Miss Sidney Bidulph (Sheridan), 9
Mercury, The, 392
Methodists, 92
Micheli, Mme., 183–184
Miller, Thomas (Lord Justice-Clerk), 240,
  342, 356
  report on John Reid, 382
Milton, John, 143
Mirabel, Lady, 34–36, 39, 43
Mitchell, Andrew (British Envoy to Ber-
  lin), 123
Mitchelson, Samuel, 226
Monboddo, James Burnett Lord, 229,
  239, 265–266, 268, 273–274, 275, 336
  intervenes with Lord Auchinleck, 273–
  274
Moncrieffe, Stewart, 236, 239, 270, 280,
  340–341
Monier, Père (French Jesuit), 139
Monro, Dr., 370, 382
Montgomerie, Margaret, *see* Boswell, Mar-
  garet Montgomerie (wife of JB)
Montgomerie-Cuninghame, Captain Alex-
  ander, 258–259

Montgomerie-Cuninghame, Elizabeth, 239, 258–259, 336, 339–340
Montgomery, James William (Lord Advocate), 343–344, 352–353
Montgomery, Matthew, 379
Morgagni, Giovanni Battista (anatomist), 250
Morison, Mr. (Scottish antiquary), 179–180
Mount Alexander, Countess Dowager, 261
Mountstuart, John Stuart Lord, 163, 181, 183, 202, 263, 317, 320–321, 336
JB travels through Italy with, 199, 202
Mudford, Anthony (servant), 244
Mure, Baron, 336–337
Murray, Colonel, 340
Murray, Alexander, 210, 237
Murray, Lord John, 13
Museums and libraries, 135, 143
British republican writings in, 143
Dresden, 135

"Nabob" (*see* Fullarton, William)
Nairne, William, 59, 339–340, 344, 361, 372
Nasmith, Michael, 341–342, 354, 359, 360, 371, 374–377, 380, 386–387
against scheme of recovering John Reid, 382–383
execution of John Reid, 388–392
Needham, Mr. (of the Royal Society), 177
Neill, James, 278
Newgate prison, 62
Newhall, Lord, 359
Newspapers, English, 138
Nicholls, Mr., 64
Northumberland, Lady Elizabeth (Seymour), 13–14, 34–35, 43
attempts to obtain commission for JB, 4, 14, 25–26, 30–31, 40, 50, 53–54, 61–62
Northumberland, Lord, 23
appointed Lord Lieutenant to Ireland, 60–61
Nouvelle Héloïse (Rousseau), 136, 147

O'Brien, William, 327
Ode on Ambition (Boswell), 56, 169
Ogilvie, Rev. John, 83
Oglethorpe, Gen. James Edward, 324, 326
Orme, Alexander, 239
Osborne, Sir Francis, 329

Oxford, Lord, 255
Oxford University, 29, 58
expulsion of methodist students, 328
literary retreat, 291
George Selwyn at, 29

Palmer, Rev. Richard, 288, 315–316
Pandects (rational system of law), 96
Paoli, Gen. Pasquale de, 120, 163, 164–165, 185, 198, 235, 263
appearance, 190–191
on JB's marriage, 300, 305, 307
on bravery of Corsicans, 193–194
character, 192
classical scholar, 191
English lessons, 300
gives dog to JB, 165, 198, 206–210
interest in physiognomy, 189, 191
interviews with, 191, 297–298
invited JB to lodge with him, 316
and SJ, 196–197, 301, 324
at Leghorn, 267
London meeting with JB, 297–298
on marriage, 192–193, 197
meets Duke of Queensberry, 298
provides JB with guards, 197–198
recommendations from Rousseau, 186–187, 191
on relations with Great Britain, 195
vivacity of mind, 195–196
Paris, 108–109, 165, 200, 210
Parker, Elizabeth (prostitute), 57
Parkhill *v.* Chalmers, 334
Parliament, ambitions for, 95, 129, 297
Paterson, Robert (sheep herder), 343–344, 348
witness at John Reid's trial, 345–346
Payne, Benjamin (highway robber), 245
Pembroke, Lord Henry Herbert, 359, 361, 373, 380–382
letter from JB on prejudice of judges, 375
promises to see King about John Reid, 381–382
Penn, William, 197
Percy, family of, 13–14, 25
Perjury, crime of, 361–362, 367
Persian Letters, 182
Peyton, V. J., 319–320
Pictet, M. Constant, 167
Pitfour, Lord James Ferguson, 92, 346–347, 355
Potsdam, 124–125

Pottle, Frederick A., 94
Preston, Sir George, 236, 263–264, 337,
    339, 342, 357
Price, Chase, 138
Pringle, Sir John, 45, 66, 210, 225–226,
    246, 254, 289
  advises JB to marry, 225
Prisons and prisoners, 62–63
Pronunciation and accents, 322
  Scottish, 315, 322
Public Advertiser, The, 72

Quakers' meeting, 93
Queensberry, Duke of, 244, 266–267, 273,
    317, 382
  on JB's commission in the Guards,
    11–16, 24–25, 40
  Gen. Paoli and, 298

Rae, David, 237, 336
Ralph, Keith, 365
  portrait of John Reid, 364–365, 367,
    369
Rambler (Johnson), 24, 81–82, 87, 95
Rampager, 362
Raybould, John (forger), 237, 241–242
Reformation, 131–132
Reid, Janet (wife of John Reid), 378–379
Reid, John, trial for sheep-stealing, 219,
    339, 341–392
  JB's belief in innocence of, 385–387,
    390–391
  JB's visits in prison, 362–363
  declaration by wife, 378–379
  denial of theft, 388
  discusses own execution, 366–369
  dreams, 365, 380
  evidence against, 376–377, 379, 385
  execution and burial, 387–392
  family background, 365–366
  Gardner accused by, 363, 374–377
  indictment, 343–344
  judges, 342
  jury, 345
  petition to King, 359–361, 382–383
  portrait by Keith Ralph, 364–365, 367,
    369
  predestination belief, 377
  refusal of Lord Erroll to intervene, 369
  Reid's "declaration," 350
  respite of 14 days, 371–373
  scheme to recover, 362–364, 367–370,
    382–387

  second trial, 313–314
  sentence to death, 355–356
  summations, 352–354
  theft and reset of theft, 343–344, 352–
    353
  transportation pardon sought by JB,
    358, 361, 372, 375
  vanity of John Reid, 366, 369, 377
  verdict of guilty, 354–356
  wife and children, 385, 388–389, 390,
    391
  witnesses, 343, 345–351
Reid, Peter, 366–367
Reynolds, Miss (prostitute), 291–292
Reynolds, Sir Joshua, 312
Reynst, Peter Hendrik, 109, 112
Richardson, Rev. Robert, 112–113
Rieu, Monsieur, 168
Rilliet, Madame, 168, 172
Ritchie, Alexander (lay preacher), 364–
    368
  execution of John Reid, 379–380, 387–
    388
Rivarola, Count, 187, 191
Robertson, Mr. (London contractor), 242–
    243
Robertson, William (historian), 249
Rochford, Lord, 373, 381–382
Roe, Stephen, 245
Roguin, Mlle., 210
Roman antiquities, 180–181
Roman Catholicism, 22, 120, 151, 180,
    190, 209
Rome and Vatican, 179–181
Roosmalen, Madame, 101
Rose, James (at Utrecht), 99, 104–106
Ross, David, 236–237, 239, 263
Ross of Auchnacloich *vs.* Mackenzie of
    Ardross, 336
Rostini, Abbé, 192
Rothes, Lord, 31
Rousseau, Jean Jacques, 64, 89, 174
  anecdotes about, 151, 176, 179
  JB's request for advice, 152
  on JB's "Sketch of My Life," 152–153,
    155
  on JB's trip to Corsica, 163–164, 185,
    215
  on child's duties toward parents, 157–
    158
  conversations with, 147–152, 155–160
  on education, 142
  Emile, 145

Rousseau, Jean Jacques (*cont.*)
  in England, 165
  on SJ, 158
  letters from JB, 146–147, 152–153, 172–173, 186–187
  Letters from the Mountain, 167, 173
  letters of introduction given to JB, 187
  Thérèse Le Vasseur (lifetime companion), 4, 150–151, 157–160
  Lord Marischal and, 131, 148–151
  meetings with, 109, 120–121, 145, 147–152, 155–160
  Nouvelle Héloïse, 136, 147
  in Paris, 210
  Plan for Perpetual Peace . . . , 150
  recommendations to, 145–146
  rejected dogma and authority in culture and religion, 120
  "The Savoyard's Creed," 142, 156
  trip to Môtiers, 144–145
  on Voltaire, 159
  on women and morals, 156
Royalty, 137
  reverence for, 125–126

St. Gilles, Comtesse de, 176–178
St. James's Chronicle, 211
Saint-Pierre, Abbé de, 150–151
San Remo, 204
  grotto to Madonna Annunziata, 204–205
Saxe-Gotha, Princesse Fréderique, 136–137
Saxe-Gotha, Court of, 136–137
  Maison des Modeles, 137–138
Saxony, Court of, 133–135
Schaffgotsch, Count, 130
Schoolmaster case, 318–320
  See also Hastie cause
Scotch appeals, 334
Scotland and Scottish people:
  anecdotes, 44
  antiquities, 302
  company of Scotch people, 46
  difference between English and, 13, 103–104
  familiarity of Scots, 158–159
  history of, 103
  SJ's prejudice against, 5, 83, 249
  justice, 220
  pronunciation and accents, 103–104, 315, 322
  Rousseau and, 149, 151

Voltaire views, 166
Scots law, 105–107
Scots Magazine, The, 56
Scott, Walter, 242
Scottish Dictionary, 98, 103–104
  SJ urges JB to continue with, 302
Selkirk, Lord, 266
Selwyn, George, 28–29
Sessions, Court of, 233, 358, 359
  College of Justice, 358
  judges, 336
  review of, 318
  Winter Session 1773–4, 313
  Summer Session 1774, 313, 335–336
Seton, Colonel, 340
Shakespeare Jubilee at Stratford, 289–295, 296
Shaw, Robert, 349
Sheldon, Captain and Mrs., 293
Sheridan, Frances (Chamberlaine), 9, 19
  asks JB to write prologue to *The Discovery*, 36–37, 45–46
Sheridan, Thomas, 16, 19, 66, 290, 296
  on JB's prologue, 37
  on Garrick, 9–10
  opinion of SJ, 9, 19
  on poets and poems, 37
  on systems of government, 57
Sheridan's dictionary, 322–323
Sidney, Algernon, 143
Sinclair, General, 78
Sinclair, Robert, 344, 346
Small, John, 242–243
Smeaton, Rev. David, 232
Sommelsdyck, M. de, 230
Spaen, Monsieur and Madame, 122
Spain, proposed travels in, 81, 109
Spectator, The, 12, 38, 158, 299
Spleen, The, 24
Steele, Sir Richard, 46
Steuart, David, 369
Steuart, Sir James, 267, 279
Stewart, Andrew, 339
Stewart, Castle, 340–341
Stewart, Frank, 291
Stewart, Houstoun, 62, 228, 242
Stewart, Margaret, 109
Stobie, John, 226, 229, 263
Strange, Robert, *Catalogue of Pictures*, 264
Strangeways, Lady Susan, 327
Stuart, James Archibald, 323
Stuart, Margaret (Cunynghame), 323

Stuart, royal family, 140, 182
Suffolk, Lord, 358, 361, 382
  petition for John Reid sent to, 361, 382
Sumner, Mr. (Master of Harrow School),
  30
Suspicious Husband, The, 236
Sutherland, Countess of, 274
Switzerland, tour of, 109, 119, 141–160

Taylor, William, 226
Temple, Capt. Robert, 59, 63–65, 74, 79,
  84–85, 95
  Lord Mountstuart and, 181
Temple, Rev. William Johnson, 59, 72, 74,
  84–85, 95, 107, 185, 214
  advice on study habits for JB, 74, 82,
    84–85, 266
  JB asks advice on marriage, 233–235,
    256–257, 266
  correspondence from JB, 108–109,
    221–223, 233–235, 256–257, 261–
    262
    about Catherine Blair, 233–235
    about gardener's daughter, 221–223
    about Irish heiress, 256–257
    about Voltaire, 170–172
  friendship of JB, 135
  Hume and, 286
Terrie, Mr. (landlord in London), 8, 10,
  15, 43
Thames River, 59, 88–89, 92–93
Thanksgiving day for the Peace, 63
Thornton, Bonnell (critic), 72–73
Thrale, Henry, 327, 333
Tissot, Dr. Simon Andre, 264
  On the Health of Literary Persons, 264
Topham, Mrs. 287
Torraz, M. (banker), 175
Toulon, 206
Traill, Dr. (Bishop of Down and Connor),
  262–263
*Translations of the Third and Tenth Satires of
  Juvenal, The* (Johnson), 82
Treesbank, Lady, 258–259
Tronchin, Théodore, 174, 175
Trotz, Christian Heinrich (at Utrecht), 96,
  98–99, 101, 106–107
  new scheme for Scots law, 105–106
Turin, 175–179
Tyburn prison, 63, 378

Utrecht, law studies, 94, 96–115, 119

Vernet, Monsieur, 149
Vintner Tricked, The, 242
Voltaire, François Marie Arouet de, 64,
  99, 109, 159, 163, 166–170, 174–175
  anecdotes, 144, 176
  Château de Ferney, 166–170
  conversation with, 168, 170–172
  criticism of Lord Kames's *Elements,* 166
  on fear of death, 174–175
  Mahomet, 169
  Philosophical Dictionary, 159
  in Switzerland, 141–142

Wallace, Professor, 275–276
Wallace, Sir Thomas, 260
Walpole, Horace, 211
Walton, Izaak, 359
Wayman, Dr. 220
Webster, Alexander, D.D., 263–264, 337,
  339–340, 361, 387
Webster, George, 335, 357, 361
Webster, James, 21, 23, 58, 359, 374
Wedderburn, Alexander, 56
Wemyss, Lord, 140
Wentworth, Lady, 183
Wilkes, John, 62, 66, 165, 211, 245, 255,
  295
  JB mistaken for, 248–249
Williams, Anna (blind old lady lives with
  SJ), 93, 215, 289, 332
Willison, George, painted portrait of JB,
  181
Wilmot, Dr., 250
Wilson, John, Jr., 377
Wilson, William, 224, 242, 329, 341
Winckelmann, Abbé, 181
Wood, Alexander (surgeon), 364, 382
Wright, John, 321
Wright against Ure, 321

Xavier, Prince (Elector of Saxony), 135

Yonge, Sir William, 323

Zerbst, Prince of, 131–132
Zuylen, Belle de ("Zelide"), 96, 98–102,
  112–113, 237, 254
  JB in love with, 112–113
  character of, 109
  fortune, 109
  vivacity and wit, 97, 123
Zuylen, Monsieur de, 99, 112–113